Personality

and Power

ALSO BY IAN KERSHAW

Hitler, 1889–1936: Hubris

Hitler, 1936–1945: Nemesis

*Fateful Choices: Ten Decisions that
Changed the World, 1940–1941*

To Hell and Back: Europe 1914–1949

The Global Age: Europe 1950–2017

PERSONALITY AND POWER

Builders and Destroyers of Modern Europe

IAN KERSHAW

PENGUIN PRESS   NEW YORK   2022

PENGUIN PRESS
An imprint of Penguin Random House LLC
penguinrandomhouse.com

First published in Great Britain by Allen Lane,
an imprint of Penguin Random House UK, 2022.

Illustration credits appear on page 455.

LIBRARY OF CONGRESS CATALOGING-IN-PUBLICATION DATA
Names: Kershaw, Ian, author.
Title: Personality and power: builders and
destroyers of modern Europe / Ian Kershaw.
Description: New York: Penguin Press, 2022. |
Includes bibliographical references and index.
Identifiers: LCCN 2022038162 (print) | LCCN 2022038163 (ebook) |
ISBN 9781594203459 (hardcover) | ISBN 9780593492567 (ebook)
Subjects: LCSH: Heads of state—Europe—History—20th century—Case studies. |
Europe—Politics and government—20th century—Case studies. |
Political leadership—Europe—History—20th century—Case studies.
Classification: LCC D412.7 .K47 2022 (print) | LCC D412.7 (ebook) |
DDC 940.53/1—dc23/eng/20220816
LC record available at https://lccn.loc.gov/2022038162
LC ebook record available at https://lccn.loc.gov/2022038163

Printed in the United States of America
1st Printing

In Memory of Stephen

Contents

Lenin addresses a huge crowd in Petrograd at the opening of the Second Comintern World Congress in July 1920.

Preface

Some political leaders, democrats as well as dictators, each of them a striking personality, obviously leave a big mark on history. But what brings strong personalities to power? And what promotes, or limits, their use of that power? What social and political conditions determine the type of power they embody and whether authoritarian or democratic leaders can flourish? How important is personality itself, both in gaining power and then in exercising it? Television, social media and journalism all elevate the role of personality into something approaching an elemental, unconstrained political force that imposes change through individual will. But are leaders, however powerful they might seem, actually restricted by forces far outside their control?

These are fundamental questions of historical analysis. But recent experience of the leadership of Donald Trump, Vladimir Putin, Xi Jinping, Recep Tayyip Erdoğan and other 'strong leaders' has perhaps given them new relevance.

Exceptional times, it could be said, produce exceptional leaders who do exceptional things – often terrible things. Systemic crisis is the common factor. The case-studies of twentieth-century European leaders in this book, some dictators, others democrats, are – all but one – of such exceptional leaders, products of exceptional preconditions for their specific exercise of power. The one leader explored here who does not fit this pattern, Helmut Kohl, had exceptionality thrust upon him when the collapse of the Soviet bloc unexpectedly offered the opportunity to unify Germany. Until then, Kohl had been an entirely unexceptional democratic leader. His case perhaps makes the point that, under settled conditions when there is no systemic crisis, political leaders merely nudge the lever of historical change a little, driven as they are by considerations of electoral appeal and wider forces of economic, social or cultural change that they are at best only able partially to control and which they are happy to go along with. The case-studies I have chosen focus squarely on the exceptional and do not examine the unspectacular, though sometimes valuable and beneficial, actions of those European political leaders during the twentieth century who introduced partial and incremental change. Looking to more 'normal', less exceptional, leaders would have produced a different book. But I had to make a selection. And it is hard to deny that those I *have* included did in important – often extremely negative – ways significantly change European history.

What follows is a series of interpretative essays on the attainment and exercise of power by a number of striking political personalities. These are emphatically *not* mini-biographies. Each of the leaders selected has, given their importance and huge impact, naturally been the subject of many biographical studies, which have built upon a vast amount of historical research. I have leaned on these biographies and other important works related to the individuals in question. I make no claim to have undertaken primary research myself on any of these individuals, apart from Hitler, for whom I could draw on detailed work that I undertook some years ago.

Each chapter follows a similar pattern. I look first at the personality traits and the preconditions that favoured a particular type of personality, providing the potential for the leader to acquire power. I then selectively explore aspects of the exercise of that power and the structures that made it possible. Each chapter concludes with an assessment of the leader's legacy. The Introduction outlines the framework of enquiry and poses a number of general propositions about the conditions and exercise of power which are then addressed comparatively in the Conclusion. I have kept notes and references to a minimum.

This is a book about history – if recent and often still painful history. Europe has moved on from the times depicted here – and, with every regard for some daunting present-day problems, overwhelmingly for the better, especially if we contemplate the horrors of the first half of the twentieth century. Recent events have highlighted social and political themes – racism, imperialism, slavery, gender and identity issues – which have taken on new or at any rate different forms of expression than was the case in the previous century. And politics is no longer a man's world, as it once was, something much to be welcomed. Only one of the case-studies in this book is of a woman – a reflection that politics in the twentieth century was very much a male preserve. No person of colour is included – a reminder that European politics in the twentieth century was not just a man's world, but a white man's world. The changes in our own times are themselves an indication that forces far beyond even the most powerful political leader induce long-term social transformation.

History offers few if any persuasive prescriptions for the future. It does, however, suggest that politics in the hands of powerful personalities who claim to have a panacea for current ills and offer sweeping change to bring about radical improvement is rarely desirable. 'Be careful what you wish for' is a useful notion to keep in my when considering the claims of potential political leaders. For my own part, I would be happy to avoid 'charismatic' personalities altogether in favour of leaders who, if less colourful, can offer competent, effective governance based on collective deliberation and well-founded, rational decisions aimed at improving the lives of *all* citizens. But that is probably another definition of utopia.

Ian Kershaw
Manchester, October 2021

Helmut Kohl during his visit to Dresden on 19 December 1989. The tumultuous reception from the huge crowd left him convinced that the 'historic hour' of German unification was close.

Introduction: The Individual and Historical Change

How far was Europe's turbulent twentieth century determined by the actions of political leaders? Did these leaders 'make' Europe's twentieth century? Or were they made by it? These questions are part of a wider question: how important are individuals in the shaping of history? Do they fundamentally alter its course? Or do they at best divert the tide into new, temporary channels? We often instinctively and unquestioningly presume that political leaders were more or less personally – implicitly, it sometimes seems, even solely – responsible for determining the historical path that was taken. But how and why were they in a position to act as they did? What constraints did they face? What pressures were they under? What backing or opposition conditioned their actions? In what settings did the leaders of quite different types of political system thrive? And how important was the role of personality? How far did this colour, even determine, crucial policy decisions? To what extent did political leaders personally, through freely taken decisions, effect the change they came to represent? These questions apply to democratic as well as to authoritarian leaders.[1]

The question of the individual's impact on historical change has often, and repeatedly, preoccupied historians.[2] Indeed, not just historians: Leo Tolstoy devoted numerous pages of his epic *War and Peace* (published in 1869) to philosophical reflection on the role of the individual will in shaping historical events and, by emphasizing 'fate', attempting to refute the notion that these are determined by 'great men'.[3] Indirectly, the question has lain close to the centre of historical enquiry ever since the study of history became a professional discipline in the nineteenth century. But while it has often been raised as a theoretical or philosophical issue, it is seldom confronted directly and empirically.

The German historian Imanuel Geiss did reflect in the 1970s in general terms upon the role of personality against the background in Germany of what had become a strong aversion to personalized history. The aversion was in part a reaction to an earlier tradition in German historical writing which had elevated the role of powerful, often visionary individuals in shaping Germany's fate. Mainly, however, it was a reaction against the catastrophe of very recent German history, often implicitly if not explicitly taken to be the work of one man, Adolf Hitler. The leadership cult in the Third Reich which attributed all 'achievements' to the 'greatness' of the Leader, then the reversal of this after 1945 in the readiness to blame Hitler personally for the entire disaster that had befallen Germany, had by the 1960s resulted in an almost complete denigration of the role of personality in history. This was the case both in West Germany, where forms of structural history came to dominate, and, in extreme fashion (given Marxist-Leninist emphasis on the outright primacy of economics) in East Germany. Geiss sought a middle path between exaggeration and rejection of the individual's role. But he did not step far beyond – not notably lucid – abstractions. 'The significant personality', he adjudged, 'does not make history, but rather allows it to be better recognized through the medium of individuality ... A great personality at best impresses his own personal stamp on his age.' The question of the role of the (great) personality in history leads, then, he added, 'unavoidably to the question of the social, that is, collective possibilities and limitations, to the question of freedom and compulsion in our human existence'.[4]

Strong emphasis on structural determinants of historical change and the diminution of the role of the individual meant that biography, a conventional component of Anglo-American historical writing, for long played no significant part in Germany in interpreting the past. After the fall of the Iron Curtain, however, in Germany and elsewhere this started to change. The decline of Marxist intellectual influence that followed the collapse of the Soviet bloc, and the spread of the new 'cultural history' which ruled out any 'master narrative' or grand theory behind historical change, brought with them a fragmentation without underlying pattern or discoverable meaning, encouraging a renewed focus on the will, actions and impact of individuals. A 'general turn away from the abstract and toward the concrete', it has been noted, prompted a move 'from system and structure to the subject, to the unique and the individual'.[5]

As the millennium approached, one of Germany's leading historians, Hans-Peter Schwarz, produced a lengthy, stylishly written 'portrait gallery' of the twentieth century, a work which would have been unthinkable in Germany a generation earlier. Through the 'art form of the biographical essay', Schwarz compared his book with a 'walk through a museum of history ... in which the portraits of the most varied great figures of the twentieth century are to be seen: the face of the century as a succession of faces'. He acknowledged that 'the factor of personality is only one among many'. 'Still, who would seriously contest its significance?' he added.[6]

Images of political leadership have, of course, been far from static. Even among their supporters today's 'strong leaders' are seldom imbued with the 'heroic' characteristics of 'men of destiny' whose deeds forged the fate of their nations as were political leaders in the nineteenth century, when belief in the 'Great Man' arose from the spirit of romanticism of that era.[7] Thomas Carlyle's celebrated series of six lectures, delivered in 1840, were extremely influential in spreading such beliefs. His lectures, entitled *On Heroes, Hero-Worship, and the Heroic in History*, helped to establish the 'great man' (women did not figure) approach to history. History, in Carlyle's view, 'is at bottom the History of the Great Men who have worked there ... All things that we see standing accomplished in the world are properly the outer material result, the practical realisation and embodiment, of Thoughts that dwelt in the Great Men sent into the world.' 'Great Men' were, in Carlyle's assessment, wholly positive figures. A 'Great Man' was no less than 'the living light-fountain, which it is good and pleasant to be near ... of native original insight, of manhood and heroic nobleness'.[8]

Most of Carlyle's 'heroes' were drawn from religion (such as Mohammed and Luther), or from literature (Dante, Shakespeare). In his final lecture, though, he turned to politics, singling out Cromwell and Napoleon, both of whom had restored order from revolutionary chaos. 'In rebellious ages, when Kingship itself seems dead and abolished,

Cromwell, Napoleon step forth again as Kings', was how he put it.[9] The 'hero' – or 'Great Man' – had shaped history through strength of will: this was the underlying message. It was little wonder that, a century on, Hitler was an avid admirer of Carlyle – or that Carlyle is now so little read.[10]

Jacob Burckhardt, the eminent nineteenth-century Swiss cultural historian, also pursued the question of 'historical greatness' in an essay, based on lectures he had delivered in 1870 but published only in 1905, after his death. Though he admitted that 'true greatness is a mystery', he argued that we are 'irresistibly driven to see those in the past and present as great through whose actions our special existence is governed'.[11] 'The great man', he stated, was marked out by being unique and irreplaceable.[12] Burckhardt's main concern was with 'greatness' in culture (especially in artists, poets and philosophers), and among major religious figures (he also singled out Mohammed and Luther). In the political sphere, he sought to distinguish 'greatness' from 'mere power', and could find no 'greatness' in those he described as 'merely mighty destroyers' ('die bloßen kräftigen Ruinierer').[13] Those who destroyed but created nothing forfeited any claim to greatness. 'Great men' for Burckhardt were those who were able to change history by freeing society from 'dead forms of life'.[14] The determinant of 'greatness' in his eyes lay in more than the execution of individual will. Rather, it was how the will of the individual reflected (according to standpoint) the will of God, the will of a nation or the will of an era.[15] How this might be defined remained unclear.

Both Carlyle and Burckhardt sought 'greatness' in personality. But their attempts at definitions of 'greatness' were nebulous. Perhaps it is indeed possible to arrive at objective definitions of genius, amounting to greatness, in art and culture. Maybe it makes objective sense to say Michelangelo or Mozart or Shakespeare were 'great' artists because expert aesthetic evaluation of their genius and their artistic qualities shows how far these soar above the work of their contemporaries. Burckhardt suggested that greatness among artists, poets and philosophers lay in their ability both to capture the spirit of their age, but also to convey an undying interpretative framework for understanding to future generations.[16] On a lesser plane, but one where achievements can be precisely measured, it is possible to speak of great sportsmen and women, those whose performances tower far above all others. But this is far removed from political 'greatness'.

Lucy Riall, an expert on modern Italian history, recently re-examined the concept of historical greatness by seeing it as a political and cultural construction, an approach which she deployed in her biography of Garibaldi.[17] 'For Italians and non-Italians alike', she suggested, 'Garibaldi was, and remains, the Great Man *par excellence*.'[18] But she makes clear that this was a construct – an 'invention' of Italian society, with a major input by Garibaldi himself. 'By interrogating the concept of greatness', she concludes, 'a political biographer can uncover the process by which greatness is acquired, manipulated, and employed and perhaps offer some explanation of our need for heroes'.[19] Few would deny the value of exploring the reasons why at certain times societies – sections of them, anyway – were ready to see greatness in their political leaders (who were only too happy to see it in themselves). And it is self-evidently important to understand how regimes were able to manipulate and exploit such views. But looking to the conditions in which leadership cults are created and flourish still leaves open the issue of whether and by what criteria specific political leaders can indeed be adjudged 'great'.

In the realm of politics, trying to define 'greatness' objectively seems to me to be ultimately a futile exercise. What are the criteria? Burckhardt was ready to adjudge Genghis Khan to have been 'great' in leading his followers from a nomadic existence to 'world conquest'. However, he rejected that appellation for Timur (Tamerlane), Genghis's self-styled heir, regarding him as a 'mighty destroyer' who left the Mongols in a worse state than he found them. Can the distinction be seen as anything other than a subjective judgement? Both rulers were rightly feared as their armies rampaged across huge swathes of conquered territory, leaving countless thousands of victims in their wake. On moral grounds, each was a repellent example of boundless cruelty. Moral judgement played no part in Burckhardt's assessment of 'greatness' in these cases. This seems to be based on the effectiveness of their conquest (for the conquerors, not the conquered). 'Greatness' appears to be purely in the eye of fairly specific beholders. And does it, anyway, help an understanding of their acquisition and exercise of power any better to deem Genghis 'great' or Timur, on the contrary, to be lacking in 'greatness'?

Perhaps in evaluating the distant past it is possible to leave morality out of the equation. Morality as a criterion of judgement fades over time until it disappears altogether. Perhaps this should not be the case; but it is. Few pay much heed to the scale of slaughter in judging the achievements of a conqueror centuries ago. But is that so in modern times? Modern political power invariably demands moral choices and ideological positions. These are bound to alienate as well as attract admiration. What level of moral opprobrium stands in the way of acknowledging 'greatness'? Arguably the most reviled political leader in modern history is Hitler. Few today would use the word 'great' to describe the chief author of a world war, the Holocaust and the destruction of his own country. Yet it has been suggested that he might be thought of in terms of 'negative greatness'.[20] Moral revulsion, in this view, is outweighed by recognition of his immense (if catastrophic) impact and undoubted historical significance. Leaving aside what might be seen as an implicit, if unintended, apologia, this points again to the emptiness of the notion of historical 'greatness'. Even if it could be adequately defined, it reduces historical change in extreme fashion to the actions of individuals. It amounts to a personalization of history that, unless embedded in a deeper causal framework, has very limited explanatory power.

Defining political 'greatness' faces a further objection. The term is not only a loose one, but is also susceptible to shifting values. In the western world hardly any modern political leader has been described as 'great' more than Sir Winston Churchill.[21] His leadership during the Second World War has rightly been seen as a vital part of the victory of the western Allies, of liberty over tyranny in the western world. But claims to his 'greatness' have had to contend with the fact that his views on race and colonial empire have come over time to be seen as obnoxious – to the extent that his statue in Westminster had to be protected against demonstrators in the 'Black Lives Matter' protests, who saw Churchill as a racist imperialist. His assumption of white superiority over the indigenous population of British colonies was characteristic of the ruling elite at the time (and of many other people besides). He made numerous remarks that would come to be regarded as abhorrent, though they were commonplace in his era. (Allegations that he was responsible for the terrible Bengal famine of 1943–4 are, however, wide of the mark. Whether he could have done more to alleviate the appalling suffering is still a contentious issue, but military shipping priorities in the middle of a world war clearly posed obvious limitations on what was possible.)[22] To a later age, his attitudes towards race are repugnant, as is the approval Churchill showed towards eugenics. (He was, however, unlike many contemporaries, invariably supportive of Jews, backed the Balfour Declaration to give Jews a homeland and was entirely lacking in antisemitism.) None of this detracts from Churchill's outstanding achievements. But it poses moral judgements that have uneasily to be balanced and subjectively assessed in reaching a verdict on 'greatness'.

It is to my mind best to leave behind the search for 'greatness' in political leaders. The issue is not whether or not by some nebulous definition a leader was 'great'. The focus instead should be squarely on that leader's historical impact and legacy. Moral judgement – whether a 'great' leader has to be a force for good, or whether 'negative greatness' is possible – then falls away (although the historian's use of language itself inevitably has moral overtones). This still, of course, leaves open the question of the role of the individual in history.

Why particular individuals stand out, come to prominence, attain power and are able to exercise that power to effect political change plainly *is* closely related to specific traits of personality, perceived strengths of character and ability. It is commonplace to say that such an individual is 'charismatic'. In itself, all that usually says is that an individual is appealing, or attractive, in some – usually undefined – way. But what is attractive or appealing to some is often repellent to others. And why might the personality traits of a particular individual be politically unattractive at one time, highly appealing at another? This points, evidently, to the specific context, or conditions, in which an individual is seen to be 'charismatic', contributing often significantly to that individual's political effectiveness.

The way in which the German sociologist Max Weber (1864–1920) deployed the notion of 'charisma' is useful in linking the role of an individual to the social and political framework in which that individual's personality is highly effective. Weber did not use 'charisma' to mean that an individual necessarily possesses extraordinary qualities that objectively amount to 'charisma', even if some political leaders obviously do exhibit particular talents for, say, public speaking, or have potentially engaging and attractive personal traits. Rather, he placed the emphasis upon the perception by a 'following' of believers (the 'charismatic community') in the outstanding qualities of a proclaimed leader. In this sense, the 'following' *create* the 'charisma' that they find in the 'chosen one' – seeing in that individual heroism, or greatness; a 'calling' (or ideological message), which they find appealing.[23] In modern political conditions, 'charisma' can be and invariably is manufactured and sustained by government-controlled media and mass parties, so that what is viewed as 'charisma' is to a great extent the artificial product of the 'marketing' of an individual through a political movement, media profiling or plain propaganda. Dictators spend much time and energy in creating a personality cult which, alongside a strong repressive apparatus, serves to consolidate and maintain their grip on power.[24] The mass adulation of the Leader in dictatorial regimes is artificially generated, not a reflection of the genuine personal qualities of that Leader.

'Charismatic' figures can, of course, lose as well as gain their special aura, usually through failure – sometimes catastrophic – and their inability to live up to expectations. There are obvious exceptions to the claim of the British right-wing Conservative politician Enoch Powell that 'all political careers end in failure'. Yet the scale of failure of political leaders once thought of as outstanding but later to be rejected is again witness to the transient role of individuals, and the forces beyond their control that determine their own scope for action and the wider nature of historical change. Any assessment of the role of the individual in 'making history' should start, therefore, by looking in the first instance, not just at personality, but also at the conditions that shape that individual's contribution.

A potentially fruitful approach to this – one which was the antithesis of the 'great man' theory – is presented by Karl Marx, in the first lines of his short tract, written in the first months of 1852, *The Eighteenth Brumaire of Louis Bonaparte*. Marx's well-known dictum ran: 'Men make their own history, but not as they please, in conditions of their own choosing, but rather under those directly encountered, given and inherited.'[25] There is no need to be a Marxist (and I have never been one) to see the implications for understanding historical change. Far from looking at historical 'greatness', Marx sought to explain how a personal nonentity, even a buffoon (which is how he viewed Louis Bonaparte, Napoleon III), had been able to assume dictatorial powers in the coup of December 1851. He found the answer in the inability of any social class to impose its rule over French society at the time – an unusual and inevitably transitory condition in his view. The workers had been defeated in the 1848 revolution, while the bourgeoisie was divided and politically weakened. The weakness both of the proletariat and of the bourgeoisie permitted Louis Bonaparte, witheringly described by Marx as a 'serious clown' who had arisen out of an 'adventurous vagabond career',[26] to take over executive authority in the state, and to bribe, cajole and otherwise manipulate the slum proletariat and peasant small-holders into providing popular support for his dictatorship.

His subsequent scope for the personal exercise of power was conditioned by the balance of the social and political forces that had provided the structural framework for his takeover of power. This gave Louis Napoleon a 'relative autonomy' from class forces; for a time he could act without their constraint. It is not necessary to retain this interpretation of class equilibrium. But the emphasis upon the structural pre-existing conditions highlights the potential for individual leaders to exploit crisis, and the turbulence of exceptional circumstances, to acquire extraordinary scope for the exercise of personal – often tyrannical – power. More generally, it offers a corrective to conventional over-emphasis upon the untrammelled role of the individual in effecting historical change. By starting, as it were, at the 'wrong' end, in emphasising context and conditions rather than personality and individual achievement, it encourages analysis that does not deny the role of the individual, but looks in the first instance to the framework in which that role was possible. This was the basis of the political scientist Archie Brown's stimulating and penetrating analysis of modern political leadership, whose starting-point is that 'leaders everywhere operate within historically conditioned political cultures', noting that there are, especially in democracies, 'many constraints on the top leader, even though an excessive focus on the person occupying the highest rung of the ladder has become all too common'.[27]

Everyone, of course, has a personality – a reflection of inbuilt traits of character, moulded from infancy and influenced by upbringing, education, life opportunities and social environment. But not every personality points towards characteristics geared to leadership, whether in politics, in business or in other walks of life. Psychological studies of personality types and leadership qualities much deployed in business circles are perhaps of reduced value when it comes to political leadership. Dependability, a sense of responsibility, open-mindedness, emotional stability, sociability, industriousness, agreeable temperament, coolness under pressure and readiness to collaborate are no doubt in principle desirable qualities in a business leader.[28] But it is easy to think of political leaders who do not fit these credentials and even reject their desirability but were (and in the contemporary world sometimes still are) nevertheless – at least for a time – highly effective.

The conditions in which a particular type of personality might be effective as a political leader vary so much that generalizations are difficult. What works in a settled democracy might be wholly ineffective in the political turbulence of a major crisis. A dictator may well have personality traits that are repulsive to most people in a prosperous, pluralistic society, but are acclaimed in the crises that bring many dictators to power in the first place. It is impossible to understand Hitler, for example, without grasping the searing, unendurable impact on German society of the First World War and the Great Depression. 'Effectiveness' can be short-lived, leading eventually to disaster, but for a time at least it can exist, and have immense consequences. The conditions largely determine the impact of a specific personality-type.

Conditions also shape the type of power that is likely to be exercised. Following Michael Mann's framework, we might think of four separate, though interrelated, sources of power: ideological, economic, military and political.[29] Circumstances dictate which is likely to predominate at any particular time. A specific personality-type is likely to come to prominence, find popular appeal, and gain institutional support, depending on circumstances and the particular constellation of power. Greatly differing qualities of leadership were historically demanded, for example, where an institutionalized ideology existed largely unchallenged, than from a situation where instability, political crisis or war prevailed.

Where there is peace, where prosperity is growing and spreading, and where core values in human rights, liberal freedoms, pluralist democracy, the rule of law, division of powers and a capitalist economy relatively free of crisis are generally accepted as the basis of stable and civilized society, a leader is likely for the most part to accept institutional constraints on action and not to seek to transform the political system itself. Such conditions generally prevailed after the Second World War until recently in western Europe and the USA. As new geopolitical tensions and economic crises have highlighted the precarious foundations of intensified globalization, however, a different style of populist leadership (epitomized by Donald Trump in the USA, and in a much more minor key by Boris Johnson in Britain) has flourished, at least for a time, in fertile terrain.

In deeply contested and crisis-ridden political systems, such as existed in many parts of Europe between the wars, a quite different type of personality, ready and willing to advocate and pursue radical change through extensive use of violence, was more likely to gain acclaim, and power. During the two world wars themselves, military objectives and prerogatives were self-evident primary determinants. Military power, for a short but hugely destructive time, overrode all else. In such conditions, even dictators like Hitler, Mussolini and Stalin were in good measure subordinated to its demands and constraints. Military commanders, whose qualities differed from those of the political leaders, necessarily exercised in practice a good deal of power, even if they were only relatively autonomous of the political leadership.

Individual power can be seen, following Max Weber, as the ability of a leader to carry out his own will despite resistance.[30] In pluralistic, liberal democracies that will is usually expressed as the consensual decision of a Cabinet or other governmental apparatus, and power is diffused throughout society by a network of institutions and organizations. Opposition generally takes place in the context of a parliament or assembly, through the mass media, sometimes through popular protest, and within the governing apparatus itself. But opposition, while it can be vociferous, even heated, takes place within a system that rests on consensus, and a government leader is more often than not still able to carry out his or her will through an institutional framework that penetrates society. Power, in Michael Mann's terms, can thus be defined as 'infrastructural'. It is power *through* states.

The opposite expression of power, that deployed in dictatorships, is what he calls 'despotic power', or power *over* states. Here, power is exercised directly by an authoritarian leadership that demands and expects complete obedience to commands from above (backed by high levels of coercion).[31] Opposition is repressed, opinion heavily manipulated, and the will of the leader is more evidently and directly crucial to the exercise of power. Even here, however, despotic power is not wholly independent of infrastructural power. A leader needs strong institutional support through the military, the security, police and judicial apparatus, and a panoply of party organizations. Even when the leader's personal power is waning, as for instance Hitler's was in the last months of the war, the support mechanisms can ensure that a dictatorship remains extremely strong. The question of personality and power stretches, therefore, beyond biography and the psychological predisposition and personal attributes of a leader to the conditions that circumscribe leadership.

What follows views the history of the twentieth century in Europe through the prism of some of the century's outstanding – for better, or, often, for worse – political figures, each either a head of state or a head of government. I confine the assessment to case-studies of a selection of European political leaders whose impact was of major significance and, importantly, ranged more widely than just their own country. Others can easily be imagined. I have after much reflection omitted some European leaders – Willy Brandt and François Mitterrand, for example – who might be adjudged to have a good case for inclusion. They might have formed part of a different cast of political leaders, mostly social democrats or liberals of one or other persuasion, who made important contributions, mainly in the second half of the twentieth century, to advances in social justice and human rights. My emphasis on crisis conditions, the type of leader these produce and the role of individuals at crucial junctures of change inevitably – perhaps mistakenly – directs the focus away from such types of leadership. On the other hand, there are scant grounds for leaving out of consideration those leaders whom I *have* included. Their importance seems self-evident.

The range could obviously be extended without difficulty to include non-European leaders – US presidents from Woodrow Wilson to Bill Clinton prominent among them, but also including other global figures such as Mao or Ayatollah Khomeini – whose actions have contributed significantly if indirectly to shaping Europe's twentieth century. Franklin Delano Roosevelt, an intriguing personality and undeniably important US President, gave me greatest pause for thought. The part he played in European, not just American, history during the Second World War does not need emphasizing. But inclusion of even one non-European leader would give rise to the obvious objection: why stop there? That would, however, involve widening the enquiry to political arenas, and the role of individuals within them, that stretch far beyond the continent of Europe. It would be impossible in such cases to avoid consideration of the domestic politics of other countries, which shaped the individual leader but often had only a tangential influence at best on Europe. That would simply explode the limits of what is possible here.

Nor do I deal with individuals, however influential, who made a significant mark in politics – in opposition, protest or resistance movements – but did not become state leaders. On the same grounds I have excluded Jean Monnet and Robert Schuman, neither of them head of government or state yet the architects of what eventually turned into the European Union, unquestionably one of the most significant developments of the twentieth century – though a project in the main of collective endeavour, not individual creativity. Beyond politics, it is of course equally easy to think of outstanding figures who have made indispensable contributions to the arts, science, medicine, business and the economy, and many other spheres. But this book is not about such figures.

Together, however, the twelve European leaders under review here undeniably influenced in significant ways the unfolding of Europe's history during the twentieth century. Most of them did so at a time of crisis for their country. Lenin emerged from the crisis of the Tsarist autocracy during the First World War. The crisis of the devastating civil war that followed the Bolshevik Revolution and the power-vacuum following Lenin's death laid the platform for Stalin to take power. Mussolini was a beneficiary of the post-war political crisis in Italy. Even well over a decade after it ended, the lasting trauma of the First World War provided the foundations for Hitler's rise to power amid the comprehensive crisis of state and society that brought the destruction of German democracy during the great depression of the early 1930s. Franco gained power as the victor in the brutal civil war of a crisis-ridden country. Churchill was appointed Prime Minister in Britain's grave political crisis as the German army was overrunning much of western Europe. De Gaulle's power emanated from two separate crises – of defeated, occupied France, and later the crisis of the Algerian War. Tito cemented his claim to power through his leadership of military resistance in the multi-faceted crisis of war-torn, occupied Yugoslavia. Gorbachev was elected General Secretary of the Soviet Communist Party as the Soviet Union was forced to grapple with the deep-seated crisis of its failing economic and political system.

Crisis also produced extraordinary leaders in post-war democracies. Adenauer's leadership was framed in good measure by the critical condition of Germany as it emerged, destroyed and occupied after 1945, and by the acute tensions and dangers of the Cold War. Thatcher's leadership was forged out of the economic and, in some senses, cultural crisis that gripped Britain in the 1970s.

The twelfth case-study included in my selection is the only one that did not emerge from one or other form of national crisis. Helmut Kohl came to office in West Germany in the wake of the economic difficulties that followed the oil shock of 1979 – a second after the first oil shock of 1973 – but in conditions of underlying political stability and prosperity. He had already been West German Chancellor – and arguably a less distinguished Chancellor than either of his immediate predecessors, Helmut Schmidt and Willy Brandt – for seven years before he faced what might be seen as a 'benign' crisis as the Cold War came to an end and German Unification became a realizable goal. But in that context, Kohl too became a significant figure in Europe's twentieth century. That is the line-up.

The case-studies seek to test a number of general propositions:

The scope for individual impact is greatest during or immediately following huge political upheaval when existing structures of rule break down or are destroyed.

Single-minded pursuit of easily definable goals and ideological inflexibility combined with tactical acumen enable a specific individual to stand out and gain a following.

The exercise and scale of personal power are heavily conditioned by circumstances of the takeover of power and the earliest phase of its consolidation.

Concentration of power enhances the potential impact of the individual – often with negative, sometimes catastrophic, consequences.[32]

War subjects even powerful political leaders to the overwhelming constraints of military power.

The individual leader's power and room for manoeuvre are in good measure dependent upon the institutional basis and relative strength of support, primarily among the secondary conduits of power, but also among the wider public.

Democratic government imposes the greatest limitation on the individual's freedom of action and scope to determine historical change.

There is no mathematical formula that can assign relative weighting to personal and impersonal factors in the assessment of historical change. A focus on specific instances – formative or fateful decisions, for example – when personal intervention made a significant impact may, however, help in reaching wider conclusions.

This is a book about historical leadership in the twentieth century, not today's leaders in the first part of the twenty-first century. Nevertheless, the questions it raises about the conditions that influence the types of individuals who come to power, the structures of government that frame the exercise of power and the circumstances in which individual personality comes to play a decisive role in historical change have relevance for our own times as they did for those of our earlier generations.[33]

Lenin, returning after a lengthy illness, presides over a particularly well-attended meeting of Sovnarkom (Council of People's Commissars) on 3 October 1922. Standing behind Lenin are Alexei Rykov (left) and Lev Kamenev, both later executed in Stalin's purges. This may have been Lenin's last Sovnarkom meeting, since he was seriously ill again from December 1922.

VLADIMIR ILYICH LENIN

Revolutionary Leader,
Founder of the Bolshevik State

The immense upheaval created by the First World War had, among its many far-reaching consequences, one which was to reverberate throughout Europe, and in the world beyond, for over seven decades: the Bolshevik Revolution of 1917. And at the centre of that earth-shaking event stood Vladimir Ilyich Ulyanov, known to history by the pseudonym he had adopted around 1902: Lenin.[1]

Lenin has a strong claim to be at the forefront, or very close to it, of any parade of makers of Europe's twentieth century. Yet to state the claim raises obvious questions. How far did an event (and its lasting impact) of such magnitude as the Russian Revolution depend upon a single individual? What *was* Lenin's personal contribution to the establishment, consolidation and lasting impact of Bolshevik rule? After all, he was not even the most dynamic revolutionary driving force in Russia at the time. That was Leon Trotsky, who has been described as 'a revolutionary genius'.[2] And Lenin was dead by the end of January 1924, after just over six years in power, in the last fifteen months or so of which he was largely incapacitated by a series of strokes. What did he do personally to direct the revolutionary reshaping of Russia, and how could he ensure that his policies were carried out in such a vast country – larger than the rest of Europe put together?

Why did Lenin, in any case, turn out to be the leader of the revolution that changed Russian and European history? It was not as if he stood alone in his determination to transform Russia. The disaffection with Tsarist rule and spread of Marxism in the Russian empire from the 1880s onwards had spawned many would-be revolutionaries, some of them significant figures in the numerous subversive political factions and groupings that sprang up. What was special about Lenin? How and why did he emerge to gain acceptance as the dominant revolutionary leader? What personality traits took him to supreme power in the new state and sustained him throughout the savage civil war that followed immediately on the revolution? And in a state whose philosophy elevated the importance of impersonal determinants of history and played down, accordingly, the role of the individual, why did Lenin have such a profound and lasting legacy, inside and outside the Soviet Union? These questions amply indicate that Lenin offers an intriguing case-study in the impact of the individual on history.

PRECONDITIONS OF POWER

Russia in 1917 was ripe for revolution. Massive loss of life in the First World War, mounting demoralization of soldiers at the front, unbearable hardship of the civilian population, and the Tsar's obstinate refusal to contemplate reform equated to a climate of imminent insurrection. Strikes, demonstrations and bread riots accompanied strident demands for peace and growing denunciation of the Tsar. Revolution indeed broke out in February that year. It had nothing to do with Lenin: he was still living in Swiss exile at the time.

In fact, there had already been a short-lived attempted revolution in autumn 1905 as internal disaffection was magnified by the humiliating defeat that year in the Russo-Japanese War. A combination of state oppression and largely cosmetic constitutional concessions towards representative government headed off the worst danger that had faced the regime. The power of the Tsarist autocracy remained intact. The ferment of unrest was, however, only contained, not dispelled.

The reality was that the political system could not be fundamentally changed through gradual reform. Civil society was weak, an independent basis of law non-existent. Violence was commonplace. The property-owning middle class was small, the intelligentsia tiny though disproportionately radicalized under the impact of state oppression and the spread of revolutionary ideas. Beyond a small elite, few people felt that they had any stake in the socio-economic system or the regime that upheld it. Over 80 per cent of the population of the vast and over-whelmingly poor country were peasants, many of them deeply hostile to the state and its officials. Most of them lived in primitive conditions in village communes and were economically dependent on those who owned the land. In the industrial big cities, which had swollen dra-matically in size over the preceding two decades, an impoverished, downtrodden proletariat had no legal means of redress for their griev-ances. Unlike the far larger German industrial working class, which Marxists had seen as the likely fount of revolution, and which by the eve of the First World War was represented by the biggest workers' party in Europe, the urban Russian proletariat had neither a stake in Russian society nor any political means of altering it, short of revolu-tion. This made them available for revolutionary mobilization given the right circumstances.[3]

The First World War provided those circumstances. The disastrous losses – over 2 million dead, around twice as many wounded – and immense hardships of the war created conditions that had not existed in 1905. However deep the disaffection had been then, striking work-ers and rebellious sectors of the peasantry had not overcome their different interests to produce a coherent and unified revolutionary force. In 1917 the revolutionary potential of the industrial working class at least temporarily joined that of the peasantry. Another differ-ence was of vital importance. In 1905 the military, an essential pivot of the regime, despite some unrest and naval mutiny following the defeat to the Japanese, had remained overwhelmingly loyal to the Tsar. In 1917 the gathering crisis in the Russian army proved unstop-pable. Defeatism, desertion and demoralization led to ever more shrill demands for peace, coupled with growing rage against the Tsar and the regime he led, naturally held responsible for the calamity. The extreme disaffection of the front soldiers now allied itself with the revolutionary mood among workers and peasants. This gravely imperilled the Tsarist regime. Another attempt at revolution, as in 1905, was probable at some stage in any event. But without the war as the unifying factor in the drive to destroy the Tsarist regime, it might, as in 1905, once more have proved unsuccessful.[4]

There was another fundamental difference. A successful revolution needs leadership and organization. The 1905 revolution had lacked the leadership that could give it focus and galvanize its disparate rebellious sectors into a single, unstoppable force. And it lacked organization. In 1917 there was Lenin and his small, but ruthlessly committed, tightly knit Bolshevik Party. The confluence between revolutionary uprising and revolutionary leader was far from inevitable. In fact, it depended on an unlikely contingency – beyond Lenin's control – without which the course (and most likely the outcome) of the Russian Revolution would have unquestionably been different. This was the most direct precondition of all.

Only a remarkable stroke of good fortune enabled him to take advantage of the enormous upheaval that followed the uprising in Petrograd in the last week of February 1917, which took him by surprise. Though he expected revolution at some point, as late as January 1917 Lenin thought that he might not live to see it.[5] But when the Tsar was forced to abdicate on 2 March, he knew that the longed-for revolution was a fact. This time, unlike 1905, he had to get back to Russia as soon as possible. In the middle of a European war that was more easily said than done. This is where fortune came to his aid – and, it is not going too far to claim, altered European history.

Had not the German government agreed, via intermediaries, to permit him and around thirty associates to travel from Switzerland to Russia by train, it is hard to see how Lenin would have been in a position to return to revolutionary Petrograd. It was, of course, far from pure chance, and not even an incomprehensible miscalculation, that the Germans agreed to help Lenin. Increasingly under pressure in the war, they saw the advantages in promoting revolution in Russia to pave the way for a ceasefire on the eastern front that would allow them to concentrate their efforts in the west. But had they not done so, and had Lenin not returned to Russia that spring, it is doubtful that he would have had the legitimacy among the revolutionaries to take the leadership of the more radical revolution in October. Trotsky, no less, thought the success of that revolution depended on Lenin.[6] But to be on the spot to lead it depended, by a bizarre irony, on the German imperialists he so much detested.

When he returned to Russia in April 1917, Lenin was unknown to the vast majority of Russians. Few Russian workers even knew his name.[7] He had lived for a decade in exile, mainly in western Europe.

The Bolshevik Party that he led was fanatical and ruthless, to be sure, but was still little more than a small revolutionary faction without any substantial mass base and a tiny membership of only 23,000 activists at most.[8] In the extraordinary transformation of this hard core into a rapidly expanding party which within months was wielding power in the state, Lenin's single-minded political acuity played a decisive role. Neither the Social Revolutionaries nor the Mensheviks, the two main rival parties to the Bolsheviks in 1917, had a leader to match his organizational brilliance.

Lenin's chances of gaining power did not at first seem high. The February Revolution had toppled the Tsar and led to the formation of a provisional government, whose aim was to lay the foundations for the introduction of widespread social liberties and establish constitutional rule. This rapidly proved illusory. The scale of the political upheaval and revolutionary fervour erased any hope of moving to a stable form of social democracy resting on a legal framework of constitutional government. But this did not mean that the provisional government was from the outset bound to give way to a second – Bolshevik-led – revolution. Moves to end the war would have been popular and could have bought it time. This might have staved off a Bolshevik revolution.[9] Instead, at a time when its authority was visibly waning, the provisional government launched a new, disastrous military offensive, whose failure had the predictable effect of both discrediting itself and pouring oil on the revolutionary fires.

A revolution led by Lenin's Bolshevik Party had, in fact, at first seemed unlikely. Lenin only arrived back in St Petersburg – Petrograd as it was now called – on the night of 3 April. It was the first time he had set foot in his own country for a decade. And within weeks he had left again. In order to avoid arrest he was forced to go into hiding on 6 July and three days later fled in disguise across the border into Finland. It looked as if he might be finished. In fact, he was only just starting.

PERSONALITY: EMERGENCE OF
A REVOLUTIONARY LEADER

Lenin was unprepossessing in outward appearance. An American jour-
nalist, John Reed, who saw him at close quarters during the revolution
in 1917, described him as short and stocky, bald, with 'bulging little
eyes, a snubbish nose, wide generous mouth, and heavy chin'. He was
dressed in shabby clothes – altogether 'unimpressive', wrote Reed, as
'the idol of a mob', but 'a leader purely by virtue of intellect ... with
the power of explaining profound ideas in simple terms'.[10] However
'unimpressive' he was in physical appearance, no one who encountered him could overlook him. Nor was there any doubt about his
acute intelligence (which he came to ally in his political career with
superb political, manipulative and organizational skills). He had astonishing energy and exuded dynamism. He was an electrifying speaker
(for those attuned to his wavelength), a gifted polemicist whose sharp
mind and aggressive debating style enabled him to triumph in most
verbal as well as written disputes, a masterly expositor of Marxist
dialectics in his prolific writings. It was not just the quality of his mind.
He was immensely strong-willed and sure of himself. His choleric,
volatile temperament, intolerance and certainty that he was always
right made it difficult for anyone with a more open mind, less dogmatic view, or less assertive manner to fend off his dominance.

He lived for politics. Nothing else mattered much. He was hard to
befriend. In fact, he had hardly any genuine friends. Even his later
close entourage of associates in the Bolshevik leadership were comrades in a political cause, not personal friends. His small circle of
intimates did not stretch much beyond his wife, his sisters and younger
brother, and his one-time lover Inessa Armand, who, even after their
two-year affair had ended in 1912, stayed close to him until she died
in 1920. He was an obsessive individual, punctiliously insistent on
pedantic forms of order; even disturbing his neatly arrayed pencils
could provoke an outburst of temper. He was ambitious, utterly and
determinedly single-minded in pursuit of the intended revolutionary
transformation of Russian society. He was intolerant and completely
unbending towards Marxist ideologues with rival views, even those

whom he had at one time seen as close allies. It could, in fact, practically be guaranteed that at some point or other he would turn against one-time associates and fall out with other Marxist theorists. And towards class enemies – a widely elastic category – he was merciless, openly advocating and welcoming terror to destroy them.

Throughout his life he suffered from ill health. Crippling headaches, insomnia, nervous tension that sometimes took him close to a breakdown, stomach complaints and excessive tiredness (unsurprising, given his punishing work schedule) were recurrent problems that sometimes found release in volcanic explosions of rage. Almost certainly he also developed hypertension and arteriosclerosis, the cause of the severe strokes that would kill him in 1924. Until he took power in Russia in 1917 he was able to recuperate from the pressure that often brought on or exacerbated his bouts of illness through lengthy holidays, during which he enjoyed long walks, swimming and other physical exercise.[11] Relaxation invariably revitalized him. But it was scarcely possible after 1917. It has been plausibly suggested that he sensed he would die early, as his father had done. He had long seen himself as a man of destiny. Perhaps anticipating an early death made him all the more anxious to fulfil his life's work by completing the revolution with all haste.[12]

His background did not at first sight mark him out as a future revolutionary leader. He had been born in 1870 in Simbirsk, a town on the Volga nearly 450 miles to the east of Moscow, to a solidly bourgeois family. The Ulyanovs were a cultured family, interested in literature, art and music. Their household was built on the common middle-class values at the time such as order, hierarchy, obedience.[13] They were not overtly political. They saw themselves as loyal subjects of the Emperor, though favoured liberal, modernizing reforms that would make Russia more like the more enlightened societies of western Europe – a stance which, respected though the Ulyanovs were, was looked on askance by the conservative sectors of the town's upper crust.

Vladimir was the third of the six surviving children (two died as babies) and remained attached to his family, particularly to his mother until her death in 1916, his elder sister, Anna, and his younger sister, Maria, who was to stay devotedly with him to the end. His parents were ambitious for their offspring and strongly committed to their education. He was a clever, bookish boy who left his grammar school in 1887 as the top pupil in his year, attaining exceptionally high marks in all subjects. In August that year he entered Kazan university, farther up the Volga from Simbirsk, to study jurisprudence. But within four months, along with a number of fellow students, he was expelled from the university following their involvement in a disturbance aimed at ending restrictions on student societies. By then, he had already come into contact with revolutionary activists and begun to explore ideas about the politics of revolution.

In 1886 his brother, Alexander, who had become politically radicalized while studying natural sciences at St Petersburg university, attached himself to a group of friends who dreamed of transforming society and conspired to instigate a revolution in Russia by blowing up Tsar Alexander III. Their amateurish assassination attempt on 1 March 1887 led to the arrest and interrogation of the group by the Okhrana, the Tsarist secret police. Alexander admitted his crime, was sentenced to death and on 8 May 1887 was hanged. The execution of his brother left in Vladimir a searing hatred of the Romanov dynasty. He became convinced that Tsarism had to be overthrown. Perhaps Alexander's death triggered latent sentiments in Vladimir, but this would be no more than guesswork. In any case, any temptation to look for a psychological explanation of all that was to follow should be resisted. Whatever the initial impulse, Vladimir soon started reading subversive literature. His commitment to future revolution would consume him for the next thirty years – the great part of his life – before the short but dramatic experience as the practitioner of actual revolution after 1917.

He began to explore Marxist thought and to move in the small circles of committed revolutionaries. During the 1890s this led to arrest by the Okhrana and (comfortable) exile in a pleasant part of eastern Siberia, where he was joined by his wife-to-be – they married in 1898 – Nadya Krupskaya, herself already dedicated to the revolutionary cause. Fear of future arrest and imprisonment took him from 1900 onwards into self-imposed exile abroad and an odyssey through abodes in Zurich, Munich, London, Paris, Geneva and Cracow, together with visits to various west European cities.[14] The future workers' leader never had to earn his living through conventional regular work. He was financially supported – even into his forties – by his mother, then increasingly by wealthy benefactors to the party. He was eventually able pay himself a salary from Bolshevik funds. It was enough to maintain a relatively modest lifestyle and enable him to concentrate fully, far away from Russia, on thinking about and planning for revolution.[15]

Lenin's personality, dimly visible in his early years, took definitive shape during the long years spent writing, attending meetings and congresses, engaging in disputations, organizing and preparing for the revolutionary moment he was certain would come, though had no way of bringing about. However fruitless this existence often seemed, it shaped his leadership credentials in the eyes of those who came into contact with him, and, not least, in his own eyes. As they evolved, his ideas gave him a certain aura within the revolutionary opposition of the visionary leader-in-waiting. But he also learned many of the tricks of the trade in the ruthless competition for primacy in the milieu of would-be revolutionaries.

He first came to wider attention as a leading Russian theorist of Marxist revolution with the publication in 1902 of his tract *What Is to Be Done?* (the title plagiarized that of an anti-Tsarist novel by Nikolai Chernyshevsky that he had admired in his youth). Before then he had been mainly seen as an adept of Georgi Plekhanov, a Marxist theorist living in exile in Zurich. Plekhanov had emphasized that revolution in Russia would come not from the peasantry (as the Russian Populists, idealizing the peasant commune, had claimed), but from the mobilized industrial working class. Lenin had, in fact, left Russia in 1900 to join Plekhanov in Switzerland. But relations soon soured. With *What Is to Be Done?* Lenin (who had meanwhile adopted that pseudonym) stepped completely out of Plekhanov's shadow. His book laid the basis for turning Marx's theories of revolution into political action by asserting the need for an organized, centralized conspiratorial party of committed revolutionaries as a vanguard to lead the proletariat in the class struggle. The revolutionary vanguard party needed a leader. Lenin was staking a claim to that leadership.[16]

He was also gaining invaluable experience in factional infighting. The Second Party Congress of the Russian Social Democratic Labour Party (a revolutionary party formed in 1898 on a Marxist programme), held in London in 1903, was a bruising affair. An arcane dispute about the terms of party membership brought a split between factions led by Lenin and Julius Martov, once a friend but from now on an implacable political opponent. A miscalculation by Martov, who was not equal to Lenin in political manoeuvring, saw him defeated in a vote on the side-issue of membership of the editorial board of the Marxist newspaper, *Iskra* (The Spark) – first published with a small print-run in December 1900. Lenin won the vote and dubbed his faction 'Those of the Major-ity' (the *Bol'sheviki*), a description he was happy to retain even when, later, his faction was for the most part actually a minority grouping. Martov clumsily fell into the linguistic trap, which would haunt his faction in later years, by accepting that they were 'Those of the Minor-ity' (the *Men'sheviki*), implying their lack of popularity.[17]

Lenin's response to the 1905 revolution in Russia, which he had merely viewed from afar, had been to radicalize his rhetoric still further, demanding the creation of a 'provisional revolutionary dem-ocratic dictatorship of the proletariat and the peasantry', backed by terror, following the overthrow of the Romanovs.[18] This widened the split with the Mensheviks. They emphasized the need for middle-class leadership of a 'bourgeois-democratic' revolution as the first stage on the way to socialism, whereas Lenin was by now insisting on bypassing this stage.[19] The factional split was temporarily and super-ficially overcome, for tactical reasons, in 1906, though soon reasserted itself and became ever more embittered, with further splintering of both the Mensheviks and the Bolsheviks, until a formal and complete split in 1912.

During most of the decade preceding the 1917 Revolution, the Mensheviks had more support within Russia than the Bolsheviks. But on the Bolshevik side of the factional divide Lenin's extreme and unbending radicalism was appealing. His intransigence and belliger-ence in bitter theoretical and organizational disputes were positive attributes for his followers. And his stream of journalistic articles both kept him in their eye and embellished his status as a leader. He was, nevertheless, no more than the leader in exile of a small revolutionary party. Most of the Russian industrial workers whom he saw as the spearhead of revolution were uninterested in impenetrable factional disputes or theoretical writings and had barely heard of him. And for all his haranguing from abroad, what Lenin could not do was to engineer the circumstances in which the revolution he was ceaselessly preaching about would become reality.

When at the age of forty-six Lenin returned to Russia in 1917 after the February Revolution and deposition of the Tsar, it was to a country that he had scarcely lived in for almost two decades. Though virtually unknown to most Russians, among those committed to the most radical form of revolution, members of the Bolshevik Party, he was viewed as little less than a prophet – a guru of revolutionary thinking and also the inspirational organizer of a revolutionary movement whose time had come.

LEADING THE REVOLUTION

Lenin was by 27 March 1917 on his way to Russia, via Germany, Sweden and Finland, arriving in Petrograd on the night of 3 April. On the journey he jotted down the blueprint of a radical strategy for the takeover of power by the proletariat and poorer peasants: his 'April Theses'. He lost no time on arrival in expressing his uncompromising radicalism to the crowd of supporters who were waiting to welcome him. He advocated 'world socialist revolution', declaring, as he stood on an armoured car brought by local Bolsheviks, that his followers should provide no support to the provisional government.[20] Arriving from long years of living abroad, Lenin was fired up with revolutionary zeal, which he conveyed in a series of speeches over the following days. His unwaveringly clear aim and self-certainty singled him out. But at this moment few, even among his closest followers, were prepared for such a radical approach.

When he explained his 'April Theses' at a meeting of Bolsheviks on 4 April, attacking those who wanted to work alongside the Mensheviks, the response was mainly critical. Lev Kamenev, one of the most prominent figures in the Bolshevik Party and later to become a leading light in the government after the October Revolution, thought Lenin's approach madness and in *Pravda* on 8 April rejected his 'general line' as 'unacceptable'. Under Stalin, two decades later, this would have been suicidal. And, indeed, Kamenev was to be one of Stalin's victims among the 'Old Bolsheviks'. But 1917 was not 1937, and Lenin was not Stalin. Any attempt to rule out opposition from within the Bolshevik ranks on his return to Petrograd would have been unthinkable and, in any case, simply not feasible. His entire career in revolutionary politics had been built on tenacious and determined fighting for his views and countering strong criticism. He was in no position in 1917 other than to continue in this vein. And although his own authority was soon far stronger, the internal pluralism of competing interpretations lasted throughout his years in power and only came to an end under Stalin.

Many revolutionaries who had lived through the recent events in Russia were wary of going too fast and favoured some accommodation with the provisional government. A big part of Lenin's brilliance as a revolutionary leader was his combination of unalterable ideological radicalism with tactical flexibility. He adjusted his message while sticking relentlessly to his underlying strategy. Diluting the rhetoric of 'revolutionary war' and 'dictatorship', he called for policies which he knew to be widely popular: nationalization of banks and industry; expropriation of agricultural land; peace; and rule not by parliament, but by the soviets (councils controlled by workers and soldiers).[21] He astutely encapsulated the core of his revolutionary programme in a pithy and striking slogan which he appears to have first seen on a banner during a street demonstration in April: 'All Power to the Soviets'.[22]

During the weeks that followed, Lenin relentlessly hammered home his message in a whirl of activity in Petrograd – forty-eight articles in *Pravda* in May, twenty-one speeches in May and June.[23] His militancy was undimmed. He incessantly stressed that the Bolshevik Party had to become the leading force in the soviets, which were still dominated by the representatives of rival revolutionary parties, the Mensheviks and the Social Revolutionaries (a party, founded in 1901, which chiefly represented peasant interests). He had able lieutenants, who worked tirelessly within the party and were later to play important roles in the Bolshevik regime – among them Lev Kamenev, Grigory Zinoviev, Nikolai Bukharin, Joseph Stalin and an important recruit from the Mensheviks, Leon Trotsky.[24] Each of them had talents useful to a revolutionary party. Trotsky in particular stood out as a brilliant speaker, superb agitator and outstanding organizer. But he was distrusted on account of his Menshevik past and late conversion to Bolshevism (only in 1917). He was also abrasive, arrogant and egotistical, effortlessly making enemies. None of the paladins thought of usurping Lenin's place. They all acknowledged his outright primacy.

Ceaseless propaganda started to pay dividends in increasing support for the Bolsheviks, who were able to exploit the prevailing immense turmoil and dreadful living conditions as inflation rocketed, food provisions dwindled and numbers of deserting soldiers increased.[25] When violent demonstrations against the government took place in early July, Bolshevik hotheads thought the moment had come for an armed insurrection. Lenin was absent, briefly recuperating from stress and fatigue during a short holiday on the Finnish coast. He returned to Petrograd in a rage, forced to restrain the Bolsheviks from what he saw as an ill-judged and premature attempt to seize power at a time when they still lacked both sufficient organization and extensive popular backing.

The Bolsheviks temporarily lost face, and the government went on the counter-offensive. Lenin was denounced as a German spy and faced imminent arrest (undoubtedly to be followed by punishment that would have eliminated his ability to direct the Bolshevik tactics). He fled from Petrograd on 9 July, eventually travelling to Finland, where he remained undercover until the end of September. From his refuge he was in no position to control or shape events. They nevertheless moved in his direction. Had they not done so, Lenin might have been no more than a footnote in history.

The biggest disaster for the embattled provisional government was self-inflicted. This was the decision by Kerensky, Minister of Defence, to launch an offensive on the south-western front, beginning on 1 July. It was meant to help the Allies on the western front (troubled by mutinies in the French army), but undertaken mainly in the hope that popularity arising from a victory would restore morale in the army and shore up the beleaguered provisional government.[26] But for a country whose war-weariness was extreme, and where agitation for peace – not just from the Bolsheviks – fell on ready ears, it was a high-risk move that swiftly backfired. By the middle of the month the offensive had collapsed, and Russian forces were in headlong retreat. Kerensky himself took over as Prime Minister of a government whose popularity was visibly draining away. His problems increased when his commander-in-chief, General Lavr Kornilov, a former Tsarist officer, marched troops on Petrograd on 28 August. Whether this was an attempted coup or whether Kornilov was trying to force Kerensky to take a tougher line against the Bolsheviks is unclear. In either case, it quickly failed. Kerensky was compelled to seek the help of the Bolsheviks in dissuading the troops from backing Kornilov, playing into their propaganda that they had been indispensable to halting a counter-revolution.

The affair further undermined the provisional government and strengthened the Bolsheviks. Their support had greatly increased since the spring. The popular backing for the government, and for the parties that had entered the government, in contrast, was in freefall. Workers, many of whom had been locked out by their employers, were taking over the running of factories, peasants were seizing land, soldiers were deserting. Lenin took the view that the time had come. 'If we wait and let the present moment pass,' he stressed (writing from his Finnish 'exile'), 'we shall *ruin* the Revolution.' His comrades in the leadership were far less sure. But Lenin showed great political skill as well as remarkable strength of conviction in persuading them that he was right. He outlined the strategic points that had to be seized in an uprising. He insisted: 'History will never forgive us if we do not take power now.'[27]

It was in this highly febrile atmosphere, which by now had become conducive to a much more radical revolution, that Lenin, heavily disguised, with a false passport, made his return to Petrograd, arriving there on 7 October. Though all Bolsheviks acknowledged him as their leader, he met with opposition – also by two of the party's leading lights, Kamenev and Zinoviev – when he put the case over the following days for immediate armed insurrection. But his strong arguments, force of conviction and recognized status as leader carried the day. Rumours on 23–4 October that Kerensky was bringing loyalist troops to the city to reimpose control prompted his move.[28] In a state of nervous tension, Lenin decided the time had come to act.

In previous days Trotsky, the chairman of the Petrograd Soviet and effective head of the mainly Bolshevik Military Revolutionary Committee, had played the key role in preparing for an armed insurrection. He was also to instigate the – largely improvised – seizure of power on 24–5 October. He was undoubtedly the most important person in the entire revolutionary movement – apart, that is, from Lenin. For

Trotsky himself recognized Lenin's supremacy. His leadership as the party's founder was not in question. Trotsky has been described as the operational commander, while Lenin was the commander-in-chief.[29]

The seizure of power was basically completed with hardly any bloodshed during a single day, 25 October. The provisional government surrendered. Few imagined that whatever government replaced it would last long. Lenin's role, in the days and weeks that followed, was crucial in determining that it did. His years of thinking about revolution could now give way to revolutionary practice. The first step was for the Congress of Soviets to agree the composition of a revolutionary government. This was attended by Mensheviks and Social Revolutionaries as well as Bolsheviks, so it was far from inevitable that Lenin would get his way. But the ground for Bolshevik dominance had been laid. By the time the Congress met the revolution was a fait accompli. And the Central Committee of the Bolshevik Party, its members browbeaten by Lenin, had already decided on the government it wanted.[30] Lenin actually proposed to Trotsky, who had led the insurrection, that he should head the government. Lenin, it seemed, wanted to concentrate on leading the party and did not want to preside over the government, or even join it. But Trotsky, deferring to Lenin's primacy, refused the offer.[31] History could have taken a different course had Trotsky complied with Lenin's request.

As it was, the Congress decided that Lenin would be chairman – in effect, Prime Minister – of a Council of People's Commissars (a government Cabinet, known by its Russian acronym as Sovnarkom). The Bolsheviks, though the largest representation among the 670 delegates, did not have a majority. But they successfully provoked the Mensheviks, Social Revolutionaries and others to walk out of the Congress, leaving them in command. So a government comprising only Bolsheviks, though provisional until the convening of a constituent assembly, was established.

Its first decrees, composed at speed by Lenin, were of huge significance.[32] A Decree on Peace immediately halted the war on the eastern front as the basis for completion of a peace treaty. The Decree on Land – popularly known as Lenin's decree[33] – abolished landownership without compensation and ended a market in land. They were accompanied by the imposition of press censorship and the dispatch of Bolshevik commissars to establish military control. Further decrees followed within the next two weeks: on the eight-hour day for workers, on free education and on the rights of the peoples of Russia (abolishing national and religious privileges, protecting ethnic minorities and offering national self-determination). The decrees helped to win support for the Bolsheviks among front soldiers, national minorities and, crucially, much of the peasantry (whom Lenin needed to attract to his cause from their overwhelming backing for the Social Revolutionaries). Lenin also had to defeat opposition from those within his own ranks, headed by Kamenev and Zinoviev, who wanted a broader coalition government. Once again his intransigence paid dividends. The rest of the Central Committee, the hard core of the leadership, backed him. He consolidated his control over the Bolshevik Party in Petrograd, and his leadership of Sovnarkom was unchallenged. Across the huge country in the early weeks after the revolution, the Bolsheviks established power through the local soviets, which they penetrated and took control of. Where there was opposition, the Red Guards forced compliance.[34]

How limited support for the Bolsheviks was in the country, however, was revealed by the results of elections on 12 November to the Constituent Assembly – the last openly pluralist elections for over seven decades. Lenin had not wanted the election, foreseeing the negative outcome for the Bolsheviks. But in this case he yielded to opposition from practically his entire entourage. The provisional government had promised democratic elections to a Constituent Assembly. 'It would look very bad', one of his most trusted allies, Yakov Sverdlov, argued, to block elections at the very outset.[35] But Lenin's forebodings were realized. Of 41 million votes cast, the Bolsheviks polled under a quarter. The Constituent Assembly met on 5 January 1918. It lasted one day. Red Guards opened fire on workers demonstrating in favour of the assembly, killing nine and wounding twenty-two. Next morning they prevented delegates from attending.[36] Any hope of pluralist democracy was extinguished. The Bolsheviks held power and were determined to extend and monopolize it, not surrender it to other parties. But they were far from winning over the country. Political persuasion, machination and manipulation were not enough.

The move to increased coercion, violence against opponents and outright terroristic repression was inexorable. While in his Finnish refuge in the summer of 1917, Lenin had continued work on his book which would appear the following year, *State and Revolution*. In this he argued that violence was necessary *after* the successful acquisition of power to destroy the capitalist class and erect a 'dictatorship of the proletariat'. Only over an indefinite period of time would this state 'wither away' and usher in a genuinely communist society. In the meantime, the war against the enemies of the proletariat had to be waged with the most ruthless weapons available. Lenin had extolled the use of terror as an expedient weapon from the beginning of his career as a revolutionary theorist. On 7 December 1917 he had Sovnarkom set up the 'Extraordinary Commission', better known as the Cheka, the dreaded secret state police. Under its head, Felix Dzerzhinsky, and with a small staff at first, it swiftly expanded and by the following summer was well on the way to becoming a state within a state. Its task was to eliminate opposition to the revolution, though who the counter-revolutionary 'enemies' were was left undefined – an obvious invitation to an arbitrary widening of the terror.[37] 'We must encourage the energy and the popular nature of the terror,' Lenin was to write in June 1918.[38] By that time he was the head of a state in the midst of a ferocious struggle for survival in an unimaginably brutal civil war as the revolutionary government faced organized counter-revolution backed by foreign powers. In these extreme conditions, the level of state-sponsored terror would explode.

STATE LEADER

Lenin's full exercise of power over the entirety of the enormous country was confined to an extremely short period between the end of the civil war in autumn 1920 and his partial incapacitation following his serious stroke in May 1922. And from then until his death, months in which he was largely an invalid, amounted to little more than a year and a half.

There was no question in the months of huge turmoil that followed the October Revolution of Lenin acting as a despot, even if he had sought to do so. Government in the early post-revolutionary phase was very different to the supine rubber-stamp for tyranny that it later became under Stalin. Much had to be improvised. And Lenin had to adjust to at least embryonic structures of revolutionary government that were already in place by the time the Bolsheviks seized power. He had to manage the enormous, and tempestuous, gatherings of the initially multi-party All-Russian Congress of Soviets, theoretically the supreme governing body already under the provisional government. This had first met in June 1917, before the Bolshevik Revolution, and a further five meetings took place between November 1917 and November 1918. Complete Bolshevik domination was only established during the course of 1918. The huge Congress essentially ratified – though at first this was no mere formality – policy that had been agreed at the Bolshevik Party's Central Committee, an institution dating back to 1898, where decisions were arrived at through majority voting. Here, too, there were heated debates, and Lenin often had to contend with fierce opposition, which he had to counter through persuasion and political skill, not diktat. Factions were permitted until officially banned in the interests of party discipline at the Tenth Party Congress of March 1921.

Increasingly, nevertheless, there was centralization and an established 'party line' laid down from above. The Central Committee, tiny when first created but comprising nineteen members in March 1919, had become too unwieldy for quick and efficient policy decisions. It was agreed, therefore, that there should be a 'political bureau' (and also an organizational bureau and secretariat). This was to formalize what had actually existed in embryo since the October Revolution. From April 1919 onwards, regular weekly meetings of the five-man leadership group in the 'Politburo' took place. It comprised Lenin, Trotsky, Stalin, Kamenev and Nikolai Krestinsky, a stalwart Bolshevik, who lost his position in 1921 after siding too closely with Trotsky. This was the core body that determined policy – a 'super-government' as it has been called.[39] Its remit was unrestricted. Lenin seldom produced reports for the Politburo, and during its meetings would for much of the time seemingly content himself by sending little written notes to other members. But at any moment he could spring into life with a ferocious attack on a proposal. In the small body, his standing, his decisiveness and his strength of will were

invariably sufficient to ensure that he prevailed. And once the Politburo had agreed its line, managing the Central Committee, and
thereafter the large Congress, became much easier.

Though his supreme authority was acknowledged by all in the
party, Lenin's decisions were challenged and hotly debated. The aura
that he carried with him as the party's long-standing theorist, but even
more so as the revolutionary leader who had been proven right in his
calculations time after time, helped him to prevail in the inner-party
disputes. The beginnings of a personality cult around the 'great leader',
deliberately started after the attempt on his life in 1918 to dispel
rumours that he had been killed, portrayed him as the 'people's Tsar'
and embellished his personal standing.[40] He also remained until the
effects of the bad stroke took their toll an indomitable, powerful
and agile thinker and debater. He usually got his way. The leading
Bolsheviks – Trotsky, Stalin, Zinoviev, Kamenev and Bukharin – were
power-hungry. But, divided among themselves, they all bowed to
Lenin, and their in-fighting bolstered his own power and prestige.[41]
Their own ruthlessness, and that of their subordinates in the Bolshevik hierarchy, were instrumental in stamping out opposition at lower
levels throughout the country. This, however, took time. The opposition was at first extensive. The threat from the enemies of revolution
during the civil war, and the fear of the severest recriminations for
lack of compliance from within the Bolshevik movement, gradually
forced opponents into line.

Before Russia plunged into the full depths of civil war, the question
of extricating it from the world war presented Lenin with his first major
challenge as head of state. He had promised peace through his first
government's first decree on 26 October 1917. The vast majority of
the population, including most of the soldiers in an army still comprising more than 7 million men, fervently wanted the end of the
war.[42] But Lenin found himself at odds with his party over the issue of
converting the temporary armistice agreed with the Central Powers in
mid-December into a peace settlement. He did not want peace for its
own sake. He saw it as a breathing-space, a step to what he thought
would be international civil war and the triumph of revolution
throughout Europe. Stalin, Kamenev and Zinoviev were among those
doubtful about the revolutionary potential in western Europe. Trotsky,

the External Affairs Commissar, however also expected revolution to spread across Europe and thought an extended truce would give it time to ferment. He failed, though, to persuade the Central Powers of Germany and Austria-Hungary to prolong the armistice. Instead, in January 1918 he conveyed to the Bolshevik leadership their ultimatum to come to terms or face invasion.

Lenin favoured acceding to the demands. But his peace proposals were turned down by party opponents – Bukharin to the fore – who would not countenance the proposed treaty with the hated imperialist powers. That left them with an insuperable problem. Some put their trust in a 'revolutionary war' to defend themselves against the 'imperialists'. Most nonetheless saw this as an impossibility: a small and inexperienced revolutionary force would have no chance against the might of the German army. Trotsky's position of 'neither war nor peace', a policy aimed at buying time to foment European revolution, won their support. That, too, proved impossible to sustain once the increasingly impatient Central Powers repeated their ultimatum in mid-February. If Russia did not agree to peace, they insisted, they would invade.

Lenin finally gained a slim majority in the Central Committee on 18 February with the threatened invasion already underway. Even now the split over how to proceed hindered action, and it was five days later, when Sovnarkom was given only hours to accept the dictated terms, that Lenin's arguments were reluctantly accepted by the majority (Trotsky abstained). Lenin told the decisive meeting of the Central Committee: 'These terms must be signed. If you don't sign them, you are signing the death warrant of Soviet power within three weeks.' This was most likely no exaggeration. A German occupation of the core of Russia would probably have destroyed the Bolshevik Revolution.[43] A further revolutionary earthquake may well have followed before long – though it would most likely have taken a different course.

Neither Lenin nor Trotsky would put his name to the brutal Treaty of Brest-Litovsk, signed on 3 March 1918. Russia lost huge tracts of territory, a third of its population, and half of its industrial and agricultural resources. It was little wonder that Lenin described it as 'an obscene peace'.[44] But he saw it as only a temporary, necessary concession to superior might before the imperialist powers were shaken by social revolution. And his internal opponents had been able to offer no serious alternative. Trotsky and Bukharin had both had to concede to Lenin's unwavering arguments. Trotsky was at this time second only to Lenin at the pinnacle of the regime. He could, and did, disagree openly on occasion with Lenin. But he accepted Lenin's superiority. He never attempted to supplant him.

During the horrific civil war which broke out in full force in summer 1918 and ravaged Russia for more than two years, as counter-revolutionary forces backed by the western Allies tried to destroy the new regime, Trotsky, as People's Commissar for Military Affairs, played an indispensable role. His organization and direction of the Red Army, which he had founded in February 1918, saw it expand by 1920 to become a formidable fighting force of over 5 million men. His ceaseless energy as he travelled the length and breadth of Russia, his dynamism in sustaining morale, his unbending determination, not least, his utter ruthlessness, and his growing experience and skill in military tactics proved crucial to the eventual victory of the Red Army. The survival of Bolshevism, which had seemed in dire jeopardy at the start of the civil war, was ensured by its end. That owed more to Trotsky than to any other individual – with the exception of Lenin himself, who controlled the political direction of the war from his position as chairman of Sovnarkom and its inner decision-making bodies, the Politburo and the Central Committee.[45]

Others in the party leadership – among them Stalin, whose insistence on running the defence of Tsaritsyn on the Volga in his own way brought a direct clash with Trotsky – also played important parts. Beyond the antipathy between Trotsky (whose high-handed manner made himself generally unpopular in the higher echelons of the party and beyond) and Stalin, there was near constant conflict among leading Bolsheviks. Unlike Trotsky, who was invariably on the move, Lenin hardly ventured out of Moscow (where the government had been based since March 1918). He was no autocrat, and he did not always get his own way in the heated debates of the Central Committee. He had to work through his subordinates. But his authority, sometimes backed by threatened resignation, generally prevailed.

A priority was securing the food supply, shortages made far worse by the Central Powers now controlling large food-producing areas of the country. As food ran short, leading to a flight of workers from hungry cities, and to hoarding, a black market and hiked prices in the countryside, Lenin successfully pressed in May 1918 for the introduction of a 'Food Dictatorship'. Armed brigades were dispatched into villages to requisition grain by force. All the surplus of peasant farming was deemed state property. Where they found none they blamed the 'kulaks' – the richer peasants – for concealing the grain. It was a harbinger of Stalin's later onslaught on the kulaks. Lenin himself set the tone for a violent campaign with horrifying rhetoric. He attacked kulaks as 'blood-suckers' who had 'grown rich on the hunger of the people'. He declared: 'Ruthless war on the kulaks! Death to all of them.'[46] On 11 August 1918 he ordered the Bolshevik leadership of Penza on the Volga to undertake exemplary executions of kulaks, and to seize all their grain: 'Hang (and make sure that the hanging takes place *in full view of the people*) no fewer than one hundred known kulaks, rich men, bloodsuckers,' he demanded.[47]

Rationing, rigid control of labour and nationalization of large-scale industry, accompanied by a rapid growth in bureaucracy, all followed as part of 'War Communism'. And as compulsion became an everyday part of life, terror inexorably began to spiral. Wild escalation followed an almost successful assassination attempt on 30 August that left Lenin with two bullets lodged in his shoulder. On 5 September 1918, prompted by a report by the Cheka chief, Felix Dzerzhinsky, Sovnarkom promulgated a decree 'On Red Terror', stipulating 'that in the present situation the security of the rear by means of terror is an absolute necessity' and 'that it is essential to protect the Soviet Republic from class enemies by isolating them in concentration camps'. Lenin, recuperating from the attempt on his life, was not present at the Sovnarkom meeting. But there is not the slightest doubt that he approved.[48] As the civil war raged, so did his apoplectic fury against the enemies of the revolution and his pressure to meet them with merciless terror. He demanded 'widescale terror against the counter-revolutionaries', he expounded the need for 'unrestrained power based on force and not on law', he made recommendations for the way the Cheka dealt with prisoners, and he ensured that the Cheka had his personal protection.[49]

The Cheka carried out tens of thousands of summary executions (among them the royal family, shot during the night of 16–17 July).

Arbitrary arrests and shootings were commonplace. The total number killed by the Cheka during the civil war is not known, but is estimated to have been several hundred thousand. Terror had been implicit in Bolshevik thinking from the beginning. In the civil war it became central to the system.[50] Lenin saw it as integral to state policy.[51] No leading Bolshevik demurred. Approval of the use of terror in the interests of the Bolshevik state was in their DNA. Trotsky wrote in 1920 that anyone recognizing the historic importance of the Soviet system 'must also sanction the Red Terror'.[52] Stalin entirely agreed with his arch-enemy Trotsky on this point. He would later take the use of state terror to further, unplumbed depths and, in contrast to Lenin, turn it against the Bolsheviks and their leaders themselves. But the centrality of terror to Bolshevik rule had already been firmly established by Lenin.

In two areas Lenin encountered significant reversals. The first proved to be lasting, and to carry important consequences for future Soviet development. It followed directly from Lenin's decision in 1920 to expand the revolution. The trigger was the attempt by the Poles, under their commander-in-chief Marshal Józef Piłsudski, to invade Ukraine with the aim of creating a federal union of Poland and Ukraine. By 7 May Polish troops were in Kiev. In little over a month the Red Army managed to force Piłsudski back. But Lenin wanted to go further. He saw an opportunity for a 'revolutionary war' against Poland, which, he believed, would stir wider revolution in Europe. Others – most importantly, Germany – would follow, domino-style. Trotsky, though he favoured world revolution, was doubtful that the Red Army had the capacity to undertake a successful invasion of Poland. Stalin was concerned that the last major army of the Whites could pose a threat to southern Russia through exploiting the Red Army's deployment in a war with Poland. There was also scepticism that patriotic Polish workers would back an attack on their own country in the name of international revolution. But Lenin was unmoved. He was certain he was right. There were no formal meetings on the issue in Sovnarkom, the Central Committee and the Politburo. Some of the important party leaders were, for good reasons, not in Moscow. And there was agreement on the desirability of at least bloodying Piłsudski's nose. Without concerted opposition,

Lenin's insistence on the invasion of Poland was enough. And once Lenin had taken the decision, other Bolshevik leaders backed it.[53]

However, the forces of the Red Army that marched on Warsaw suffered a crushing defeat at the hands of the Polish army on the Vistula in mid-August 1920.[54] Lenin sought to evade the responsibility that was plainly his for the disaster, profiting from the internal distraction caused by the open animosity between Trotsky and Stalin. The upshot was plain. With the resounding defeat of the Red Army the dream of a 'European socialist revolution' was dead.[55] The path opened up for the eventual move to the policy of 'socialism in one country', the prime advocate of which would be Joseph Stalin.[56]

The second reversal proved over time, though only in the years following Lenin's death, to be temporary. The severe economic distress caused by the draconian impositions of War Communism had led to serious unrest – strikes in the cities, peasant revolts in the countryside and, in March 1921, an uprising of the garrison in Kronstadt, near Petrograd, where the sailors had in 1917 been ardent Bolshevik supporters. Trotsky had the rising put down with great savagery. Even so, it was obvious: without altering economic policy the regime was in danger. In fact, even as the Kronstadt rising was taking place, Lenin was addressing the Party Congress on the need for an economic U-turn, which he had successfully put to the Politburo the previous month.

This was the introduction of what became known as the New Economic Policy (NEP), which ended the highly unpopular requisition of foodstuffs. Instead, after paying a tax in kind of 20 per cent, peasants were to be allowed to sell their surplus produce on the free market.[57] Trotsky, as he reminded Lenin, had actually proposed this the previous year, but Lenin had at the time rejected the suggestion. Lenin never apologized or showed contrition. The result, nevertheless, was a policy that only not upturned the harsh measures of War Communism but ran counter to a long-existent part of Lenin's thinking, which had never been favourable to the peasantry. He of course denied that there was any ideological deviation from the precepts of Bolshevism, and his authority proved sufficient to overcome the considerable opposition within the party. Opponents bowed to pragmatic necessity and could offer no alternative. The NEP was approved.[58]

Peasant unrest gradually melted away as the NEP took effect, and it stimulated economic growth. It soon, however, led to problems of food supply as peasants held back produce to exploit market demand. Inevitably, then, the NEP remained contentious within the party, and divisive within the Bolshevik leadership. Lenin saw the NEP as a tactical retreat, but also as a programme that would consolidate the revolution over a period of ten years or more. The aim remained collectivization of agriculture, by which production would be concentrated in large farming cooperatives (*kolkhozes*) with state contracts to ensure adequate food provision. In theory, the long-term process of collectivization would be a gradual, voluntary process.[59]

Within weeks of the adoption of the NEP, Lenin's health, never robust, was in sharp decline. By mid-summer 1921 he was seriously ill and forced, with extreme reluctance, to reduce his activity. The revolutionary workers' leader was moved to an imposing mansion on an estate at Gorki, a few miles from Moscow, and, while he was still capable of working, ferried to the Kremlin in a grey Silver Ghost Rolls-Royce, with tank-tracks and skis fitted to allow it to navigate snow-bound roads. On 25 May 1922 he suffered a bad stroke. He had further physical collapses during the second half of the year, leaving him incapacitated at times, paralysed down his right side, hardly able to speak and unable to write legibly.

Towards the end of the year he dictated what became known as his Political Testament, warning the Central Committee about Stalin. He had been well disposed towards Stalin earlier in the year and had made him the party's General Secretary. But his illness was making him intensely choleric. He and Stalin had subsequently disagreed about the status of the non-Russian Soviet republics. (The outcome, the creation of the Union of Soviet Socialist Republics, the USSR, a name suggested by Stalin, would take effect from 1924.) The friction with Stalin intensified.[60] Aware that his days were numbered and evidently concerned about the succession, Lenin criticized all the main contenders who might take over from him. But he reserved his most withering criticism for Stalin. He warned that Stalin would abuse the power concentrated in his hands – though there was no suggestion that the deployment of terror was what Lenin was fearing. Probably an abusive phone-call by Stalin to Lenin's wife, Krupskaya, finally triggered the warning. Possibly, as has been suggested, the Testament was actually Krupskaya's own work, not the dictation of an incapacitated leader.[61] There is little doubt, nevertheless, that as his life approached its end Lenin was deliberately undermining any claim Stalin might have to succeed him. His attempt to have Stalin removed as the party's General Secretary failed – with baleful consequences. Stalin's subtle manipulation of the Twelfth Party Congress in 1923, which Lenin was too ill to attend, ensured that he avoided his removal from office. Lenin's Testament was, nevertheless, perhaps recognition by Lenin not just that his own power was at an end, but that power more generally was shifting from the state, through Sovnarkom, the Council of People's Commissars, to the party – whose organization was controlled by Stalin.[62]

A power-struggle was inevitable given Lenin's hopeless medical condition, even had he lingered longer. As it was, he was by mid-1923 no longer actively capable of ruling Russia. A final stroke on 21 January 1924 brought his death early that evening.[63]

LEGACY

Though in power for only a short time, Lenin left a profound legacy to Russia, the rest of Europe and the world beyond. Communism – Lenin had in 1918 suggested the Bolsheviks rename themselves the Russian Communist Party (Bolshevik) – became a central force in many parts of the globe. In the Soviet Union, the essentials of the system of rule that Lenin established remained intact until the collapse of the Soviet Union more than seven decades later.

The ideology that underpinned that system – its very name, Marxism-Leninism, linking Lenin to Karl Marx as its defining creators – interpreted history as determined by impersonal economic forces and class relations. Yet at the same time it glorified its founder. There was no contradiction. Marx (and later Lenin) had always stressed that political struggle was necessary to transform class relations. Lenin's role as the leader of that struggle in Russia obviously gained him a special place in the Soviet pantheon. The construction of a personality cult of quasi-religious veneration of Lenin went, however, much further. It began immediately after his death with a big upsurge in public interest in his body. Decomposition was halted and a 'Commission for the Immortalization of Lenin's Memory' established. A faction that saw the political value of embalming his body triumphed over opponents (who included his widow, Krupskaya).[64] Preservation of the corpse served the need of providing a symbol of unification: the individual as the representative of eternal truth, 'the sole authentic interpreter of the laws of history'.[65] And it had the potential for widespread appeal in a largely peasant society whose cultural world – though nominally atheist – was built on intertwined religious and superstitious beliefs.[66]

Lenin remained the totemic figure of Soviet communism to the end. The personality cult that was being built around him in his last years displayed its full efflorescence after his death and came to serve as a model for the Stalin cult.[67] His embalmed body was put on permanent display in a specially built mausoleum for the worship of believers. Portraits, monuments, the renaming of Petrograd as Leningrad and numerous other signs of near deification of a prophet constructed the myth of the untouchable leader. 'Lenin is dead, Leninism lives,' intoned Zinoviev at the funeral.[68] Stalin, too, to confirm his own place in the apostolic succession, publicly burnished a doctored version of the Lenin myth, though his own, even more grotesquely overblown personality cult eventually put that of the founder of Bolshevism in the shade. Khrushchev's denunciation of Stalin in 1956 then re-established the sainthood of Lenin. Actually, Lenin's most direct legacy had been Stalin's accession to power. Stalin had been a protégé of Lenin (despite the warning in the Testament), had profited from Lenin's reluctance to name his successor, and, while deviating significantly from the way Lenin had ruled, had built his tyranny on the framework of Leninism. But Khrushchev now depicted Stalin as breaking fundamentally with Lenin's legacy. Stalin's dictatorship was viewed as an evil heresy – a malign turn away from the path of the true gospel. The effect was to restore Lenin's unrivalled stature. He represented the infallibility of the Communist Party. His ideological precepts remained its guiding light. Even in the 1980s Gorbachev began by wanting not to destroy but to uphold Leninism.

According to surveys of Russian opinion around the centenary of the 1917 Bolshevik Revolution, more than half of those questioned thought Lenin had played a positive role in their country's history – though few possessed detailed knowledge of what he had actually done.[69] He is now a figure from the distant past, with little relevance for today's Russia. For President Putin the continued macabre spectacle of the unburied corpse of Lenin is awkward. Lenin symbolized revolution. Putin emphasizes the stability he has established after the chaotic Yeltsin era. On the other hand, many Russians still admire the strength and prestige of the Soviet era. Removing Lenin from his mausoleum risks unleashing a new debate about the Russian past. Putin would presumably prefer to avoid that. So for now at least Lenin stays where he is.[70] His corpse in Red Square has lasted far longer than the Soviet system itself.

Outside Russia, insurrectionist movements in many countries throughout the twentieth century, and a number of communist regimes, adopted at least parts of Lenin's ideology. The conflict between capitalism and communism, central to the history of the twentieth century, was delineated by the alternative state system and its underlying ideology that Lenin was indispensable to creating. The murderous struggle between fascism and communism, culminating in the most catastrophic war in history, was the decisive phase in a conflict that lasted until the end of the Cold War. Indirectly at the least, Lenin can be said to have influenced the course of history to the end of the twentieth century, and beyond.

The Russian Revolution was an epochal episode in twentieth-century history. And in that pivotal juncture in history Lenin's personal role was crucial. He was borne along by the revolutionary currents of his time. He was their beneficiary, not their creator. But a revolution in Russia was not preordained to follow the path that it actually took. The way the revolution changed Russia and Europe is unimaginable without Lenin's leadership. He seized the opportunity that arose, though he never lost sight of clear ideological goals. Without him the twentieth century would have been different, if in ways we can only dimly imagine. Lenin made a greater impact on history than any other individual of his era. He was a prime maker of Europe's twentieth century.

Mussolini, still exuding optimism, is greeted by admirers in October 1942. His popularity was actually in steep decline by this time. The drastic collapse in Italy's military situation led to his toppling in July 1943.

2

BENITO MUSSOLINI

Icon of Fascism

For nearly a quarter of a century Benito Mussolini had a profound impact on the history of Italy and, increasingly, on the whole of Europe – indeed through imperialist conquest and as the ally of Germany and Japan during the Second World War on the world beyond Europe. In Italy he presided over a dictatorship that lasted for more than two decades. Before wartime fortunes rebounded in devastating fashion on the country, he enjoyed the backing of millions of Italians, and was idolized by many of them. In other countries in interwar Europe, not only those drawn to fascism but also many conservatives saw him as an icon.[1]

He wanted war. Under Mussolini, Italy was involved in war in one form or another in the 1920s and 1930s in Corfu, Libya, Ethiopia and Spain. But when general European, then world, war came to Italy after 1940, it inflicted misery, suffering and devastation on the country and on the territory in Italian hands. It led to Mussolini's own deposition in 1943, a short but extremely bloody restoration to power under German aegis, and his violent death at the hands of partisans in April 1945. The leader who had earlier held millions in thrall left behind a country in ruins.

'One man and one man alone', Winston Churchill – who had at one time admired Mussolini – declared in a broadcast to the Italian people on 23 December 1940, was responsible for Italy's fate.[2] This was a gross oversimplification aimed at inserting a wedge between Mussolini and the Italian people. The question remains even so: was Mussolini's personal role indispensable to the path from the rise of fascism to the calamity of the wartime years? If indeed it was, then other questions immediately pose themselves. What conditions made

Mussolini's takeover of power in Italy possible, then enabled the exercise of that power in such fateful fashion? What did Mussolini himself do to engineer his accession to power? And to what extent did he personally determine policy once in power? How powerful was Mussolini, actually, during the catastrophic war years? Was he increasingly acting under German pressure, buffeted by forces beyond his control? Or would such a view simply overlook and excuse his personal, and brutal, direction of policy down to the very *finale furioso* itself? Mussolini, who posed as the very epitome of macho, 'manly' omnipotence, offers an intriguing case-study of the extent to which the individual controls his own destiny, and – far more importantly – that of his country.

PERSONALITY AND POLITICAL EMERGENCE

Short (only 5 feet 6 inches tall), squat, bald, with outlandishly histrionic gestures, exaggerated 'manliness', strutting arrogance, pugnacious face, rolling eyes, jaw aggressively jutting out, legs astride, chest puffed out, Mussolini was a caricaturist's dream. His image as dictator easily fostered the assumption that, beneath the pompous bluster, he was little more than an absurd, clownish figure, 'a vain, blundering boaster without ideas or aims', at most a 'gifted actor' and propagandist.[3] But that would be seriously to underrate what a malign, cruel individual he was, the baseness of his character, the brutality of his politics and the assault on humanity that he directed as Italy's leader.[4]

His domineering personality had been visible at an early age. He was strongly opinionated, intolerant of opposing views, authoritarian in attitude, short-tempered, vindictive and an advocate of violence as a political method. He was unquestionably intelligent, with a quick mind and an excellent memory. He was intensely serious-minded, with little sense of humour. He admitted to having few genuine friends. To a later age few features of his character seem attractive. But to many of his contemporaries, alienated by decades of ineffective, corrupt factional government exercised by a seemingly unchanging dull oligarchy of liberal notables, Mussolini exuded vitality and energy. He offered restless dynamism, uncompromising action, indomitable willpower, an irresistible spirit of revolutionary change. His appearance, his clothes, his mannerisms, the poses he struck, his political rhetoric – all offered something radically new, dramatically different from the tired and dreary politics of the bourgeois elite, a necessary and decisive break with the past. He seemed to represent a modern era, an age of the masses. To a clientele committed to violent revolution, especially when his personality traits were later embedded in a 'heroic' image of a 'man of destiny' (which Mussolini saw himself to be), his traits of character could have great appeal. His well-cultivated manly, virile, martial demeanour fitted a widespread accepted ideal of strong leadership.[5] He certainly never lacked women admirers. He seems himself to have been practically addicted to sex.[6] His countless, mainly fleeting relationships stretched from his early years to his last – in this case strong – attachment to the woman who would share his fate in 1945, Clara Petacci. His wife, Rachele Guidi, whom he had married in 1915 and bore him five children, put up with what she could not alter in his character and behaviour.

He had come from a poor background. He was born in 1883, the eldest of three children, in the hamlet of Dovia in the Predappio district of Emilia Romagna in northern Italy, a provincial backwater in no easy reach of the nearest cities of Bologna and Ravenna. Though poor, his parents had some standing in the community. His father, Alessandro, a blacksmith and smallholder, was an early enthusiast for socialism (tinged with anarchism), critical of the Church, landowners and the political establishment, and served for a while as a councillor in Predappio. Both his socialist leanings and his choleric temperament rubbed off on his son. Benito's mother, Rosa, was more gentle, the local schoolteacher and, unlike her husband, a pious Catholic. Benito was a bright boy who read a good deal, and had some talent for music. But his involvement in two minor stabbing incidents during his school years already showed a violent streak.

By 1902 he was beginning a career in journalism, writing for a socialist weekly and displaying an aptitude for provocation and agitation which brought in subsequent years clashes with the police, arrest and short periods of imprisonment. His fiery journalism, with its blistering attacks on the political establishment, made him known in socialist circles before the First World War. He backed the revolutionary wing of the Socialist Party and – remarkably in the light of what was to come – vehemently opposed Italy's colonial war in Libya in 1911. A year later, aged twenty-eight, he was made editor of the big socialist daily *Avanti!*, based in Milan.

At the outbreak of war in 1914 Mussolini was still a committed socialist. But that was very soon to change. His socialism was, in fact, eclectic. He knew his Marx. But he was ready to draw, where it suited him, on other ideas, including Vilfredo Pareto's theory of elitism, Friedrich Nietzsche's 'will to power' and Georges Sorel's 'struggle against decadence'. Ideas in themselves were not important to him unless they could mobilize, unless they were vehicles to power. It was not a matter of power for its own sake. Italy, united as a country for little more than half a century with a national monarchy only since 1861, was politically and socially highly polarized. Its ruling class was a narrow and corrupt oligarchy. In the eyes of the socialists, power was needed to destroy bourgeois society and to force through a social revolution.

When world war began Mussolini was still advocating Italy's neutrality. But workers across Europe were joining their national armies. Socialist parties were supporting the war. Marxist internationalism, he recognized, had failed; socialism would be incapable of destroying the old order. The emotional appeal of nationalist fervour across Europe, on the other hand, was enormous. War itself, he started to reason, would be the agent of revolutionary change. Marx himself had argued as much. Influential voices, some on the Left, were arguing that Italy had to join the conflict in order to break with the past and build a better future. Mussolini's growing doubts about socialism and about Italy's neutrality were the ingredients that blended together in his dramatic conversion to the cause of intervention.

His private opinion was by now conflicting directly with his public stance. In October 1914 he suddenly told *Avanti!* readers that his earlier views were wrong. He took the decision alone, and in opposition to the party leadership (though far from all party members). He had to resign as editor and was soon afterwards expelled from the Socialist Party. He quickly became one of the foremost advocates of intervention (which took place with Italy's entry into the war on the side of the Entente – Britain, France and Russia – on 23 May 1915). Within a fortnight he had launched a new paper to support the cause,

Il Popolo d'Italia, initially still left-wing in tone, but financially backed by industrialists who stood to gain from Italy's intervention in the war. By 1922 it was the official paper of the Fascist Party.

By December 1914 the editorship of *Il Popolo d'Italia* gave him the publicity he needed to become the chief spokesman of the small groups – some of whose members were ex-socialists who favoured intervention – calling themselves 'Fascists of Revolutionary Action', though their influence at the time was negligible.[7] (*Fasci* was a term that loosely meant 'groups', after the bundles of rods that were the symbol of order in ancient Rome.) In Mussolini's thinking, national revolution had meanwhile replaced a Marxist understanding of class struggle. He saw a struggle not between classes, but between 'proletarian' and 'plutocratic' nations. Establishing Italy's stature as a great power, not fighting for the triumph of the proletariat within Italy, was his new gospel. Expansion and armed conquest would be the proof of the country's greatness. Power meant the destruction of 'decadent' society and its replacement by a resurgent nation built on the values of the 'new man' – strength, vitality, will, dominance. Socialism, in contrast, with its emphasis on the working class, not the nation, equality, not rule by the strongest, international peace, not preparation for war, was now the ideological enemy. Mussolini sensed the potential for a new movement that could exploit the extreme disorientation and discontent left by the war. By February 1919 small numbers of seriously disaffected but politically rootless individuals, mainly intensely aggrieved veterans, were starting to come together, calling themselves 'Fasci di Combattimento'. On 23 March 1919 Mussolini summoned a meeting of around fifty of them to form such a grouping in Milan. It was one of thirty-seven similar groupings in Italy at the time.[8] But this one would under Mussolini's direction prove the basis of what became the Fascist Party.

From there to the 'seizure of power' in 1922 was a long and winding path. Little of this route was under Mussolini's personal control. There was nothing inevitable about Mussolini's takeover of power.[9] Without the prevailing social, economic and political preconditions his dictatorship would not have been possible. Without the intensely damaging, deeply polarizing effects of the First World War on Italy, without the widely perceived threat of socialist revolution that prompted a breakdown of order, and – even then – without the readiness of the conservative power-elites to make him Prime Minister, Mussolini would never have become Italy's dictator.

PRECONDITIONS OF POWER

Before the First World War the liberal oligarchy that ran the country was able without undue difficulty to exploit but contain the growth of extreme nationalism and imperialism without being threatened by it. The social and political power of the political elites rested on no strong popular base, given an extremely limited suffrage, though faced as yet no revolutionary danger from Right or Left. The Italian Socialist Party, founded in the early 1890s, was growing but still small, largely confined to the developing industrial belt in the north, and divided between reformists and a revolutionary wing (to which Mussolini at the time belonged). The Left was in no position to challenge the political order. The populist Right as yet barely existed.

The war changed all this. It left behind a demoralized population, angry at the country's leaders, humiliated by military weakness. The ruling class of liberal notables had forfeited any claim to popular legitimacy. They felt forced to widen the extremely restricted electorate, granting the vote to all adult males in December 1918. The voting system was altered to introduce proportional representation the following year. This resulted, however, in big gains in elections in November 1919 for the socialists, now easily the largest party in parliament and declaring that they wanted to destroy the bourgeoisie. The other big electoral winner was the newly founded Italian People's Party (the Popolari, representing Catholic interests). The upshot was that the liberal-conservative elite was no longer able to control and manipulate parliamentary politics. As disorder mounted, the unstable governmental system could not cope. The social order, and the power that went with it, seemed under threat. The prospect of socialist revolution – a fearful spectre in many people's eyes – loomed large.

At the same time the fury on the Right at the territorial redistribution that had been agreed by Allied leaders at the Treaty of Versailles in June 1919 knew no bounds. Italy, nationalists and fascists loudly claimed, had been cheated out of its rightful gains from victory – a 'mutilated victory' they called it. In reality, the gains actually made were not inconsiderable and effectively rounded off Italy's national borders with the acquisition from Austria of (the mainly German-speaking) South Tyrol and the north-eastern coastal region centred on Trieste. But extreme nationalist feeling was not placated. Imperialist gains had been demanded, commensurate with the presumed status of a victorious 'great power'. Resentment was directed at the lack of gains *outside* Italy. Expectations had been aroused of acquiring Dalmatia, a protectorate over Albania, a 'zone of influence' on Turkey's Adriatic coast and extended colonial territory in Africa. The small port of Fiume (now Rijeka, in Croatia), only partially populated by Italians (who hoped through belonging to the Italian nation-state to restore the prosperity once enjoyed under the Austro-Hungarian empire), became the particular flashpoint of fascist agitation after it had been occupied by an Italian force led by the proto-fascist poet Gabriele D'Annunzio in September 1919.[10]

The social, political and ideological turmoil spawned by the war intensely sharpened class conflict. Strikes, factory occupations, looting of shops and seizure of land in 1919 and 1920 – the so-called 'two Red years' (*biennio rosso*) – seemed to denote a political system out of control. The middle classes, seeing their savings eroded through inflation and their property threatened, wanted order. Reports, embroidered by the right-wing press, of Bolshevik terror in Russia left them terrified about the threat of socialist revolution in Italy. The foundation in January 1921 of a Communist Party looking to Lenin's Russia did nothing to soothe the nerves.

This is where the various small paramilitary organizations calling themselves Fasci came in useful. Demobilized ex-servicemen formed the initial core of the fascist movements that now sprang up in towns and cities of northern and central Italy. As the movement expanded, it recruited across the social spectrum, though not strongly among the urban proletariat, and its leaders were predominantly middle class. Students (mainly from middle-class backgrounds) were significantly over-represented among the members of the paramilitary squads. Most obviously early fascism was an overwhelmingly male, youthful movement.[11] There was no coherent ideology. But there was intense rage at the corrupt liberal establishment and demand for violent action to destroy what they saw as a rotten state whose leadership had betrayed the nation. This is what fascism boiled down to: complete destruction of the old political and social order and utopian promises of a new society driven by belief in national rebirth and glory.[12] Violence was central. Thousands of acts of political violence, leading to hundreds of deaths, were perpetrated by fascist paramilitary squads.[13] Mussolini's Milan fascist group advertised a Left-sounding programme which was, however, aimed at anti-elitist populist agitation rather than an agenda for practical implementation. The programme was discarded by 1921.[14]

The numerous fascist groupings, not just Mussolini's, quickly became a vehicle to repress socialism and destroy any stirrings of social disorder instigated by the Left. Though initially an urban phenomenon, by 1920 fascism was spreading rapidly into the countryside of northern Italy. Young, thrusting provincial leaders, like Italo Balbo in Ferrara, formed links with local landowners and industrialists.[15] Landowners recognized the value of financing paramilitary bands of fascist thugs (*squadristi*) to evict troublesome tenants, break strikes, beat up opponents and terrorize socialists or anyone else who stood in their way. Landlords started only to hire workers who were members of fascist organizations, which were incorporating earlier anti-socialist 'citizen defence' militias.[16] By 1921 the fascists were being aided by government money and arms; the police stood by as they inflicted horrific beatings on hapless opponents.

Mussolini's supremacy over the rapidly spreading fascist movement could not be taken for granted. Powerful provincial fascist chieftains acknowledged his standing, but his authority did not go unchallenged. Balbo in Ferrara, Dino Grandi in Bologna and Roberto Farinacci in Cremona were the most forceful of the leaders who were not prepared to give unquestioned obedience to Mussolini's orders. They, and the squads they controlled, were more important than Mussolini to the spread of fascism.[17] Mussolini feared by 1921 that he was losing his grip on agrarian fascism. He was concerned, too, that the violence of the squads, backed by their local chieftains, was becoming counterproductive and posing an obstacle to hopes of gaining state power. The fascists had won thirty-five seats (out of 535) in the parliamentary elections of May 1921, so formed only a small minority in the lower house of parliament, the Chamber of Deputies. To counter the weakness, Mussolini proposed in July that year, with little or no consultation, a remarkable and diametric shift in policy: a parliamentary coalition with the Socialist Party and People's Party (both still electorally strong). This led in August to a 'pact of pacification' – and a crisis in relations with the provincial grandees.

The pact appalled the fascist provincial chiefs. Grandi openly challenged Mussolini's claim to be *padrone* (boss) of 'our movement'.[18] Mussolini, demanding obedience, resigned as leader. The chieftains met without him and offered the leadership to the 'hero' of Fiume, the fascist poet D'Annunzio, who, however, did not envisage himself in the position and declined. The crisis called for compromise. Mussolini climbed down. He acknowledged his tactical mistake. For their part, the provincial bosses, whatever their power in their own fiefdoms, recognized that Mussolini alone had the national standing to hold together the entire fascist movement. That was his strength and their weakness. They publicly acknowledged his authority, while he accepted the continuation of violence, insisting only that it now be organized and the squads turned into a national militia. The Fasci themselves were to be politically coordinated. In a theatrical display in November 1921, the Fascist Party was officially established. In his newspaper two weeks later, Mussolini suggested that 'people may perhaps desire a dictator'.[19]

The central government meanwhile continued to display its weakness and lack of popular support. Between October 1917 and October 1922 there were no fewer than seven changes of government, under five prime ministers.[20] The fragmentation of the liberal-conservative Right opened up the political space for the growing force of fascism.[21] By mid-1922 Mussolini's movement had more than 300,000 members. This was the point at which the conservative elites became ready to entrust government to Mussolini. The weakness of the elites, not Mussolini's personality or political skill, was the decisive prerequisite to his power.

Without the support of the fascists, the members of the Cabinet reasoned, there was no hope of bringing stability to the country's governance. They were far more worried by the socialist Left than the fascist Right, and when Mussolini's forces crushed a feeble socialist-inspired attempt at a general strike in August 1922, they could perversely interpret fascism as the defender of the law – even though they knew he was preparing an armed insurrection. The conservatives felt they could not rule without the fascists. But without government support, the fascists were not strong enough to take power. The basis of the political deal that would give power to Mussolini took shape. Government ministers believed that they would be able to control him. It was the mistake that, little over a decade later, the German political elite was to make about Hitler.

Mussolini played a double game. His political duplicity was a big part of his success. He encouraged, on the one hand, the violence of the fascist squads and fired up his militants to seize power by force. On the other hand, he portrayed himself to leading members of the government as the only man who could restore order in the state and rebuild the economy. In office, he indicated, he would disband his paramilitary army. He kept his options open and acted with little or no deliberation with radical fascist leaders, whose agreement with anything other than an armed insurrection he could not take for granted. None of the provincial fascist leaders could have operated as Mussolini did. They were effective organizers of street-fighter thuggery but lacked Mussolini's opportunistic tactical skill.

The Prime Minister, Luigi Facta, a liberal in office only since February 1922, dithered until the night of 27–8 October. The violence of fascist squads (in which twenty-two people died) had by then escalated menacingly. They occupied prefectures (which controlled the police), post offices and railway stations in the big cities and important main transport links to the capital.[22] Facta finally bowed to the request of Rome's army commander to impose martial law and declare a state of emergency. The army had shown that, when it wanted to, it was well able to suppress fascist mobs; overnight the occupied buildings were retaken with ease. Crucially, King Victor Emmanuel III agreed to sign the declaration of the state of emergency. Then he changed his mind. He was wrongly informed that the army would be unable to defend Rome against the fascist militia.[23] In fact, it would have had no difficulty in crushing the weakly armed fascist militia, numbering no more than about 30,000, poised outside Rome.

Myth, in a dictatorship, is often more powerful than fact. The image of the heroic leader on horseback at the head of his legions in a triumphant 'march on Rome' became the foundation legend of Mussolini's rule and a staple of the Duce cult. In reality, after agreeing his appointment as head of government with the King, and that tens of thousands of *squadristi* would march past and salute the sovereign before returning home,[24] Mussolini travelled to Rome by train from Milan, wearing a suit and a bowler hat. He had not 'seized' power; he had been invited to take it. On 29 October, the King appointed Benito Mussolini as Italy's Prime Minister.

DUCE

Until Mussolini became dictator, no special significance was attached to the word 'Duce', which had simply been used to indicate a leader, without the mystical connotations it later acquired. Mussolini himself had been referred to by early fascist supporters as 'Duce', but other local chiefs were addressed in the same way.[25] The full-blown Mussolini cult emerged only after 1925.

Before then, Mussolini was feeling his way – though he was already offering a new style of government, and acting with dynamism, increasing confidence and boldness. This was possible because of the almost complete compliance in his rule shown by the conservative-liberal elites, by the army and by the King. Even at this early state their stance ranged from passive acquiescence to outright complicity. The objectives Mussolini outlined on assuming the premiership – end the disorder, balance the budget and instil discipline – might have been the aims of any conservative administration. The methods to attain those ends were not. However, the violence used to 'restore order' was acceptable – as long as it was directed at suppressing political 'troublemakers' on the Left. The socialists – intimidated, savagely maltreated, terrorized into quiescence – in fact posed no genuine political danger. And the second-largest party in parliament, the People's Party, was bought off by increased financial support for priests and bishops and backing for Catholic social policy.

Mussolini trod more carefully in dealing with the political elite. He spoke in moderate terms at times when he felt it necessary while with barely veiled menace at others. He needed parliamentary backing, and the fascists were still a small minority in the Chamber of Deputies. Beyond the office of Prime Minister he himself took responsibility for foreign affairs and for the Ministry of the Interior (giving him control of the police). Otherwise, his government was made up of non-fascists (drawn from nationalists, liberals and the Popolari). His fascist comrades were aggrieved that they had not gained the fruits of power, but Mussolini had shrewdly calculated that at least for the time being he could not dispense with non-fascist support. He was rewarded on 16 November 1922 with huge votes of confidence (only the socialists and communists opposing) in both the Chamber and the Senate and given emergency powers for a year, enabling him to act without parliamentary approval. Senior fascists, left out of government, were placated by a significant innovation introduced by Mussolini in December 1922: the creation of a Fascist Grand Council. This was solely dependent on Mussolini, who appointed its members and decided its agenda. It formed an outlet for the party to influence the shaping of government policy.

Meanwhile, the fascists controlled the streets. The squads were turned into part of a national militia and served in effect as a vicious political police. Mussolini issued a general amnesty to pardon thousands who had perpetrated the most brutal attacks on socialists and others. He declared that the violence would be stopped; in practice he licensed it to continue. In truth, he had far from complete control over the squads, which were still run by local fascist bosses unwilling to surrender their power. The basis for extensive centralized state control over its citizens was nevertheless laid in the initial phase of the regime. The police, now under Mussolini's direction, and the judicial authorities were complicit in the extremes of coercion, and in the mass arrests of political opponents. Elected local government officials from opposition parties were peremptorily deposed and replaced by fascists. Press censorship was introduced; there was as yet no ban on opposition newspapers, though much intimidation of oppositional journalists. And the Fascist Party itself, which more than doubled its membership within a year, spread its tentacles of social control and at the same time served as a vehicle to bolster Mussolini's power and public standing.[26]

Mussolini exploited the confidence he had won in parliament to push through in 1923, by a combination of manipulative skill and threats, the major change that would replace parliamentary government by dictatorship. In July the large non-fascist parliamentary majority approved a piece of political chicanery that in the autumn became a new electoral law. This awarded two-thirds of the seats in the Chamber of Deputies to any party that won a quarter of the votes. In fact, in the elections the following April after a campaign in which political opponents were subjected to violence, the fascist-dominated national bloc gained more than two-thirds of the votes anyway. Opposition parties were reduced to a beleaguered rump in the Chamber of Deputies. Parliament from now on was no more than a rubber-stamp for policy determined by the fascist government. And there, Mussolini's domineering personality and assertive direction of policy were what counted.

Two months after the election, however, he faced a major crisis that lasted until early 1925 and for a time threatened his own position of power and the existence of his government. It was seen at the time as the crisis of fascism.[27] When the leader of the Socialist Party, Giacomo Matteotti, was kidnapped by fascists on 10 June 1924 and subsequently murdered, it was widely believed that the assassination was on Mussolini's order. Almost certainly he was at least indirectly implicated. The political crisis that followed lasted for six months. The socialists completely misplayed their hand. Boycotting parliament in protest, along with the Popolari, simply benefited the fascists. Mussolini helped to placate the political elite by handing the vital Ministry of the Interior to the 'respectable' former nationalist Luigi Federzoni and having the fascist militia swear an oath of loyalty to the King.[28] The liberal and conservative political class, the King, army and business leaders, the Pope too, saw Mussolini as a lesser evil than any prospect of a revival of the Left and did not withdraw their support. It was less easy for Mussolini to keep his own party in check. The murder of a fascist deputy in September intensified the fury of the radicals, intent on completing the fascist revolution. In a tense autumn, Mussolini could not ignore the divisions within the party and the renewed outbreaks of violence in the provinces. It became a test of strength. He had to control the local fascist bosses. It could only be done by establishing the ultimate supremacy of the state over the party.[29] On 3 January 1925 he acted to resolve the situation, publicly accepting in parliament responsibility for all that had happened, appeasing the radicals by acknowledging that 'the only solution is force'.[30] Remarkably, Mussolini had emerged from the crisis strengthened, not weakened. In what amounted to a second 'seizure of power', the steps to full dictatorship followed.

Non-fascists were removed from the Cabinet. Mussolini himself took over no fewer than eight ministries by 1929 (including again the Ministry of the Interior). Opposition parties were banned by 1926. Rigorous press censorship was introduced, strikes and lockouts prohibited, dissidents arrested as the police state expanded. The last barrier to the completion of the fascist state fell in 1929 with the signing of the Lateran Pacts with the papacy. Mussolini had personally driven through the negotiations which led to recognition of the sovereignty of the Vatican, regulated relations with the papacy and confirmed Catholicism as Italy's state religion. The eulogies that poured in – Pope Pius XI himself described Mussolini as a man sent by 'Providence' to free the country of the false doctrine of liberalism – took the Italian leader's prestige to new heights.[31]

The Fascist Party itself, the source of continued internal unrest and external disorder, had been brought to heel in 1925 by making Roberto Farinacci, arguably the most unruly, arch-extremist, thoroughly thuggish of all the provincial bosses, National Secretary of the party. The poacher became gamekeeper. Farinacci attempted to impose iron discipline but failed to contain persistent outbreaks of violence and within little more than a year was dismissed by Mussolini to be replaced by more administratively competent but politically subservient party secretaries, the ultra-loyal Augusto Turati and then Achille Starace. Institutionally, the party was by 1927–8 no longer challenging the state, but was reduced to serving as its central body of political organization and mobilization.[32] It offered upward mobility to local elites. But it had lost its adrenalin. The 'wild men' and unruly elements of the early party were purged or contained. The violence became controlled by the state.[33] The movement's elan dissipated. The party turned largely into a vehicle for acclamation of the Duce, the chief propaganda agency and a means of social control. It was the prime basis of Mussolini's power.

The party and its subordinate organizations penetrated practically all areas of public life during the 1930s – welfare, youth clubs, leisure activities, sports clubs and much besides. Nearly half of the population belonged to one or other fascist affiliation by 1939. Where the boundaries of party and state were drawn was increasingly difficult to define precisely. The entire amorphous, interwoven complex of organizations and institutions in party and state revolved around Mussolini. By the 1930s he operated without institutional constraints. The Council of Ministers and Fascist Grand Council met only when Mussolini wanted them to and were effectively no more than receptacles for his directives. In 1939 the Chamber of Deputies was renamed the Chamber of Fasces and Corporations. Mussolini was now constitutionally 'the Supreme Leader'.[34]

He alone decided – though (nominally, at least) he had to report to the King. His right to take decisions was recognized on all sides, including the King and the army chiefs (who had no collective voice and, whatever their reservations, were never rebellious). Of course, many decisions were in effect preformed before being presented to him in brief audiences (on average no longer than a quarter of an hour) by his underlings. Decisions, dozens a day, were taken, often impulsively, without reflection and deliberation. But without his authorization, the machinery of government could not function. He spent long hours a day on government business. But it was, of course, a sheer impossibility for him to keep a close eye on the work of all the ministries he was in theory at least running. He was unwilling to delegate. So he was grossly overstretched, drowning in a morass of often minor matters requiring his concern.[35] Bureaucracy inevitably became bloated in consequence. So did the scope for functionaries of both party and state to anticipate, pre-empt or second-guess Mussolini's intentions.[36]

What impressed foreign observers most about the regime was its extraordinary energy. Mussolini, whatever the manifold failings of his character, exuded restless vitality. The utopian goals of moulding 'the new man', building a great nation, preparing for imperial glory could always be exploited by propaganda to convey the image of unquenchable drive and dynamism, which Mussolini himself embodied. He recognized earlier than practically anyone the mobilizing potential of the mass media, the growing power to influence the population through the spread of newspapers, radio and film. His portrait on postcards or placards was ubiquitous. The beginnings of radio allowed his broadcast speeches to be relayed to the public through loudspeakers set up in the central squares of towns and cities. He was the first populist politician of the mass-media age.

Monopoly control of propaganda manufactured the single most important unifying element in the fascist state: the cult of the Duce. This was the cement that, more than anything else, held the fabric of the fascist state together. The cult had a strong pseudo-religious dimension. Mussolini was practically deified in the eyes of many Italians.[37] His bombast and theatrical gestures when addressing huge rallies – ridiculous to a later age – were used to convey an image of strength, determination and defiance. He was shown in school-books as the constant labourer for his people. Pictures of him bare-chested, on horse-back, swimming, running, in racing-cars or playing with lion cubs, emphasized his 'manly' qualities. Letters poured in every day from ordinary Italians, lauding him to the skies, praising his wondrous abilities, thanking him for his glorious achievements. He plainly revelled in the absurd excesses of the Duce cult, depicting him as an almost super-human new Caesar, an omnipotent and all-knowing god-like genius.[38]

How many people believed this nonsense it is impossible to tell. But Mussolini did. And so did millions of others. He was certainly popular where the Fascist Party, its functionaries and the regime in general were not. His popularity probably reached a peak after the declaration of victory in Ethiopia in 1936, though popular discontent seems to have been only temporarily transcended by the military success.[39] Planning for the war had begun already in 1932. Ethiopia would, it was imagined, together with the existing colonies of Eritrea and Somalia, provide 'living space' for millions of Italian settlers and enable exploitation of the rich mineral deposits of east Africa.[40] By October 1935 he felt ready to launch the imperialist war he had long wanted. The war in Ethiopia, waged by a large army against far inferior forces, was brutal in the extreme, including indiscriminate bombing and extensive use of poison gas. Yet it took until the following May until victory could be proclaimed. Propaganda trumpeted the Duce's military genius. Mussolini was at the height of his powers.

He had, however, an Achilles heel. It only became visible much later, but was actually there from the beginning of the regime, embedded in the very structural conditions of his takeover of power. It was reflected in 1936 by the fact that it was the King of Italy, not Mussolini, who was proclaimed Emperor of Abyssinia (Ethiopia). It was a sign that, although Mussolini did indeed dictate policy, his power was not absolute: there was a higher authority, an alternative source of legitimacy. The monarchy stood, unobtrusively, in the way of his total power. And the armed forces, though under Mussolini's direction, owed their loyalty to the head of state – to the King.[41]

King Victor Emmanuel III was indeed weak, supine, a nonentity who, furthermore, welcomed the suppression of socialism, the crushing of democracy and the establishment of an authoritarian state. Mussolini despised the King and had only for opportunistic reasons restrained his innate republicanism. The reservations about policy that the King sometimes expressed in audiences with Mussolini, and which occasionally leaked out, irked him enormously. He fumed privately on several occasions that he wanted to be rid of the monarchy at the first opportunity.[42] But he had never felt strong enough to do that. And as war approached, he could not risk any major dissension that might pose a threat to national unity and undermine the legitimacy of the regime. So the opportunity never came.

While the regime was strong, as it was in the mid-1930s, the existence of the monarchy and the alternative source of loyalty it represented was an irritation, no more. Moreover, the victory in Ethiopia seemed to prove that Mussolini had been right, and the doubters – especially in the military – wrong. His own power was enhanced as a consequence. But, not that Mussolini or anyone else noticed it at the time, the high point of his power was about to pass. By 1936 he was entering the German orbit, attracted both strategically and ideologically, and was soon to become a satellite circling round a far greater power, drawn in ever closer to the point of destruction. Without sensing it, he was becoming a weak dictator. And when he turned out to be an obstacle to Italy's national survival, the alternative source of power emerged from near invisibility and the King almost effortlessly deposed the once mighty dictator.

WEAK DICTATOR

This sounds like a contradiction. Applied to Hitler – its initial usage – the concept is inappropriate and misleading.[43] But it fits Mussolini from the mid-1930s far better. It does not, of course, mean that he ceased to decide policy, nor that his power to do so was contested. Nevertheless, the existence of an alternative source of loyalty in the monarchy would prove a fatal weakness. And once Italy, from 1936 at the latest, became increasingly, and by the middle of the war totally, dependent upon Germany, Mussolini's power was gravely weakened. It was impossible for him to extricate himself from the growing subordination to Hitler. Ultimately it would destroy him. In that sense, too, he was increasingly a weak dictator.

Could he have trodden another path? Most of Europe's authoritarian leaders in the 1930s did not, after all, voluntarily engage in military conflict with the well-armed western powers. On the Iberian peninsula the Spanish dictator Francisco Franco and the Portuguese leader António de Oliveira Salazar kept out of the Second World War and survived until the 1970s. Might Mussolini have done something similar to avoid the destructive clutches of Hitler's Germany? That was never an option. The counterfactual musing misses the point that Mussolini genuinely *wanted* the alliance with Germany. He actively courted the Rome–Berlin Axis. It was an ideological choice, not one compelled by impersonal determinants.[44] And arrogant pretentiousness played its part. He saw himself, as the founder of fascism who had ruled Italy for nearly a decade and a half, as the superior partner in the relationship with Hitler – the 'senior dictator'. Avoiding what he saw as the opportunity offered to him by the alignment with Germany would have run completely counter to his personality and to his ideological impetus. From the first he wanted war, military conquest and empire. His rule in Italy had been built on such aims. The drastically changed international situation by the mid-1930s meant that his ideological ambitions were offered what seemed a favourable geopolitical option. Aligning with Germany gave Mussolini the chance to challenge the western powers and the prospect of the imperialist expansion in the Mediterranean and in north Africa that fascism had sought from the outset.

Close alignment did not seem likely at first after Hitler had come to power in Germany in 1933. Behind a richly embellished propaganda façade, the initial meeting of the two dictators, in Venice in June 1934, was less than cordial, mainly because of tension over the status of

Austria.[45] The prospect of German domination of central Europe, in particular its control over Austria, was threatening to Mussolini, and, when Austrian Nazis assassinated the Chancellor, Engelbert Dollfuss, in July 1934, Italian troops were mobilized to guard the Alpine Brenner Pass. In April 1935 Mussolini joined France and Britain in the 'Stresa Front', partially aimed at blocking any German moves to control Austria. Western opposition to the Ethiopian war and German neutrality then led to a major shift. Mussolini signalled that he would not now oppose Austria coming under Germany's aegis, and he gave the green light to the German reoccupation of the Rhineland in March 1936. By the autumn Italian and German forces were testing their weaponry in support of the nationalists in the Spanish Civil War. Mussolini had turned his back on the West and committed himself to what, by November 1936, was proclaimed as the new Axis Pact of Italy and Germany.

His state visit to Germany in 1937 marked a psychological shift in Mussolini's relationship with Hitler. He was so effusively impressed by the German dictator and by what he had seen in Germany and had learned of German rearmament that his earlier sense of superiority turned into the beginnings of an inferiority complex.[46] He was soon dancing to Hitler's tune. He could do nothing but acquiesce in the annexation of Austria and the carve-up of Czechoslovakia in 1938. When German forces occupied what was left of Czechoslovakia the following March, Mussolini could only lament that 'every time Hitler occupies a country he sends me a message'.[47] Italy's annexation of Albania in April 1939 did little to diminish Mussolini's bruised pride.

Mussolini was the driving force in the fateful subjugation of Italian to German interests. Of that there is no doubt. He had taken the steps, usually with little or no consultation, that had irreversibly tied Italy to the fortunes of Germany. His personality – his sense of pride, self-belief, ebullient, exaggerated optimism and certainty that history was favouring the interests of the Axis – formed an important part of the process. His impatience with sceptical, let alone critical, views, his impulsiveness and his tendency to let emotion override rationality did not make for sound judgement. The course of foreign policy was, however, not his work alone, nor the dictatorial imposition of decisions on unwilling sectors of the regime.

The ruling class – including the officer corps, the party, business leaders, big landowners, the state bureaucracy, the Church and the King – had supported (if with varying degrees of enthusiasm) the war in Ethiopia and, though with greater foreboding, the moves towards closer alignment with Germany.[48] It was one thing, however, to win a colonial war, another to fight a major European war. Generals who had advocated and carried out the bombing of civilians in Ethiopia and later in Spain had cold feet about taking on the western powers in what could turn out to be a long war for which Italy was ill-equipped.[49] They were only too well aware of Italy's slow progress in rearmament. Industrial inefficiencies and lack of financial strength posed big obstacles to a rapid build-up of armed strength. Economic demands at home did not permit a major armaments drive. Military spending even fell by 20 per cent in 1937–8, and a big armaments programme authorized by Mussolini in summer 1938 could not make up for the weaknesses overnight. The dictator, while itching for war, was compelled to recognize that 'Italy needs ten years of peace'.[50]

It was plain, as Hitler's aggression took Europe to the brink of war, that Italy would not be granted such time. The anxiety among military leaders about involvement in a war for which they were so ill-prepared grew. But they went along with Mussolini's policy anyway. There was no semblance of any collective opposition. Mussolini was aware that popular opinion was opposed to involvement in a new war. Police reports indicated, too, that belief in fascism was waning. And the attachment to Germany was deeply unpopular.[51] Mussolini was no racial fanatic like Hitler. But antisemitism formed nonetheless part of his racist mentality. His racism was of long standing, and he played a big personal role in stepping up an antisemitic campaign to help revitalize the sagging dynamic of the regime. It culminated in vicious anti-Jewish legislation in 1938.[52] This tapped into existing anti-Jewish feeling in Italy, which, though scarcely comparable with that in Germany, had grown significantly since fascism's rise to power.[53] Trying to whip up antisemitism could not, however, hide the widespread antipathy towards a new war.

Italy became even more closely entangled with Germany in May 1939 with the signing of the Pact of Steel, a military alliance that pledged mutual support in the event of either country becoming involved in war. With this, Mussolini gave unconditional backing to a German war over which he had no control whatsoever. By mid-August, with war imminent, the King himself was scathing about the 'pitiful' state of the army and adamant that Italy had to stay out of the war. He wanted to be involved in any 'supreme decisions'.[54] Mussolini could not take the risk of a war that the armed forces were in no state to fight. Even as German troops were being mobilized, he was compelled to admit, to his great embarrassment, that Italy was not yet ready to fight. It was a blow to Mussolini's prestige. He had to content himself with the novel status of 'non-belligerence' – scarcely an advertisement for fascist martial values.

Mussolini struggled to contain his chagrin at being unable to join the war. His bellicosity did not diminish in the slightest. But he had to accept that military preparations would not be completed for some years. The astonishing speed of the German victory over France in May and June 1940 dramatically altered the situation. The King and the chiefs of the armed forces, and also Mussolini's son-in-law, the Foreign Minister (since 1936) Count Ciano, all until this point arguing against intervention, now saw the chance of quick gains from a war that, it seemed, Germany was certain to win. Mussolini informed his military chiefs on 29 May of his decision – taken without consultation – to enter the war. There was no opposition. Italy joined the war on 10 June, hoping for substantial territorial gains and to avoid being dragged into a protracted conflict. But victory had to come soon.

Italy's lack of readiness for a long war was not confined to the inadequate modernization of its weaponry, the shortfalls in armaments production, low supplies of raw materials and the weak industrial base of its economy. The leadership of the armed forces was an additional impediment. Mussolini had pressed the King into giving him, on 29 May 1940, command of the political and military conduct of the war. The King had, however, insisted on retaining the supreme command in his own hands. This was purely nominal at the time. But in 1943 it would prove crucial.[55] As it was, Mussolini's execution of his military command role was amateurish. The war occupied him for about six or seven hours a day. He still found plenty of time to play tennis, go riding, improve his German, have a summer holiday on the Adriatic coast in 1940 and, above all, his voracious sexual appetite undiminished, invite a variety of women partners to share his bed during the afternoons.[56] He did little to establish coordinated strategic planning, and the service chiefs of the army, air force and navy were not in practice subject to any incisive intervention by the Chief of the General Staff, Marshal Badoglio.[57] The armed forces had not adequately attuned to the demands of new, more mobile warfare. The ingrained conservatism and foot-dragging of Badoglio and the service chiefs did not fit easily with Mussolini's impulsiveness, impatience for action, dilettante knowledge of operational matters and insistence on such nebulous entities as willpower and 'extreme energy'.[58] Mussolini bore the chief responsibility for the disastrous conduct of the war. But the military were willing accomplices. The predictable catastrophe was that of an entire system, not solely of one man.

The route to the abyss is well known. The decision to attack Greece, taken solely and impulsively by Mussolini in mid-October 1940 in the face of warnings from the military, turned into a humiliation. (At least, Mussolini's order to raze to the ground all Greek towns with more than 10,000 inhabitants could mercifully not be carried out.) Italy's war at sea was lost after weak air defences allowed British bombers to destroy Italian warships at Taranto in mid-November 1940. Far worse was to follow. Half of the army of 230,000 men sent to fight in the icy wastes of the Soviet Union did not return. Military procrastination in north Africa enabled British forces eventually to gain the upper hand, leading to a devastating Italian defeat and around 400,000 soldiers entering Allied captivity.[59] The Italian occupying force in Croatia, despite great barbarity,[60] proved unable to defeat the Partisan movement. Air raids on Italian cities intensified in the first half of 1943 as defences proved woefully inadequate. Heavy bombing of the major industrial centres of northern Italy – Genoa, Turin and Milan – undermined morale and increased unrest, which became overtly political, among workers in big armaments factories. Anti-war feeling and hostility towards Mussolini's regime, already mounting the previous autumn, accompanied by a drastic deterioration in living standards, led to damaging strikes, most notably in the huge FIAT works in Turin in March and April 1943.[61] On 10 July the Allies landed in Sicily. The bombing of Rome on 19 July was both a shock and a clear signal that Mussolini's leadership was taking Italy to complete ruin. The military leaders and the King himself now looked to distance themselves from the impending catastrophe and to deny their own culpability by attributing the entire blame to Mussolini.

Another structural weakness in Mussolini's dictatorship, beyond the monarchy's presence as an alternative source of legitimacy, now manifested itself. The Fascist Grand Council had so far been little more than a powerless acclamatory body. Incorporated as an institution of the state since 1928, it merely rubber-stamped his decisions. He summoned it infrequently and did most of the talking when it did meet. It remained, nevertheless, a potential focus of collective opposition if ever it roused itself to independent action. Precisely this is what happened in 1943.

Behind his back, fascist bosses were looking for a way out of the coming ruin and had no wish to go down in flames with the party radicals. Mussolini did not object to a gathering of the Grand Council. He knew he faced criticism but feared nothing more. And the meeting would force his critics out into the open. Astonishingly, he did not sense what was coming. Possibly the bouts of severe stomach trouble that he had suffered for some months reduced his alertness and energy. At any rate he was unusually passive. At a ten-hour meeting during the night of 24–5 July, after ritual affirmations of loyalty, there was strong criticism of Mussolini's leadership. The dictator professed himself ready to have the King reinstated as effective commander-in-chief. Dino Grandi, the former boss of Bologna, briefly Foreign Minister, and for a time ambassador to London, succeeded in putting a motion to restore some powers to the monarchy. Remarkably, Mussolini allowed a vote – and lost; no fewer than nineteen of twenty-eight leading fascists supported Grandi's resolution.

Even at this point Mussolini appeared unaware of the gravity of his situation. He went to see the King on the afternoon of the 25th to report on the outcome of the Grand Council meeting with no sense of foreboding. At the brief audience, however, the King told him that he had become the most hated man in Italy, the war was lost, army morale was collapsing, and he was replacing him as Prime Minister with Marshal Badoglio. As he left, Mussolini was arrested by the guards waiting outside and taken into custody. Plans to do so had been secretly afoot for some time. There was no fascist uprising to save the

Duce. His power simply evaporated. The King, no more than a willing appendage for over twenty years, perhaps surprised himself by the ease with which he was able to remove the once mighty dictator.

Mussolini's political obituary had, however, been prematurely written. On 12 September – four days after Italy had surrendered to the Allies – he was spectacularly rescued by the Germans from his internment at an Apennine ski-resort. Soon he was restored to power, with his headquarters near Salò on the shore of Lake Garda in northern Italy – but it was as head of government in a German puppet-state in the half of the country not yet conquered by the Allies. He had lost a good deal of weight, had nearly constant stomach pain and was a diminished figure in every way. He had, though, recovered much of his sagging energy. He saw his task as to reinvigorate fascism, destroy traitors and remove the stain of Italy's humiliation.[62] His illusory vision was national rebirth under his leadership.

He returned in these final months to the radical roots he had never fully left behind. Under his rule, the Salò Republic (officially the Italian Social Republic) was fascism at its bloodiest, most brutal, most ruthless. The Germans backed his regime, to be sure. But they did not impose or order his actions. He fired up – not that they needed encouragement – the militia, police formations and fascist fanatics to execute anti-fascist partisans without mercy. Anyone seen as a threat or potential opponent was exposed to the terror of the death-squads. The regime was viciously antisemitic. In November 1943 Jews were declared to be 'members of a hostile nationality'. The previous month the Germans had instigated and carried out the deportation of Rome's Jews. Mussolini, aware since 1942 of the Nazi extermination programme, remained silent. His security police helped to round up the Jews and hand them over to the Germans.[63] The last phase of Mussolini's dictatorship amounted to an Italian civil war in which tens of thousands, fascists and anti-fascists, were killed.[64] Without German military and financial support, the Salò Republic could not have held out throughout 1944 and into 1945. Looming German defeat signalled its inevitable collapse. As the end approached, living conditions worsened immeasurably, the partisans gained the upper hand and support for Mussolini disintegrated, apart from the still dangerous remnants of desperadoes and fanatics. The once powerful dictator blamed the Italian people for not being worthy of him. His fate was sealed once the Germans, behind his back, arranged a ceasefire for Italy with the Allies.

Dressed in a German uniform, Mussolini fled northwards but, together with his lover, Clara Petacci, was captured by partisans near Lake Como and executed on 28 April 1945. The corpses were driven to Milan and, in the Piazzale Loreto, mocked, vilified and violated by the large crowd that had gathered, then hung upside down in an adjacent petrol station.

LEGACY

Mussolini's legacy was a country in ruins. He had plunged his country into a war which brought national catastrophe to Italy and inflicted death and destruction on parts of Africa and the Balkans. The entire Italian political establishment, despite misgivings at times, had backed him for over twenty years. A large, if unquantifiable, number of Italians beyond committed members of the Fascist Party had supported him at the height of his powers. Mussolini had hardly been the sole cause of Italy's catastrophe. He had, however, been its central driving force. He plainly held chief responsibility. Without him the course of Italian history would have been less calamitous – certainly different.

Part of that history, which had helped make Mussolini possible, had been Italy's great-power pretensions. He had benefited from such aspirations, had magnified them through imperialist conquest, but had ended by obliterating them once and for all. Italy's future after the war lay in the negation of practically all that Mussolini had stood for. Post-war reconstruction, largely under American aegis, abolished the monarchy, established a democracy, the rule of law, a pluralist party system and a market economy (if one still with extensive state involvement) that opened up Italy to foreign trade. Where Mussolini had sought conquest and domination, post-war Italy turned to international cooperation and in 1951 was a founding member of the supranational entity that became the European Economic Community (and much later the European Union). Within Italy, however, the corruption in politics and public life that had existed before Mussolini then flourished during his rule remained. So did the anti-communism that had been part of Mussolini's rhetorical armoury, sustained in good measure as a by-product of the Cold War. This saw the expulsion of the communists from government in 1948 and the continued dominance of conservative Christian Democracy – underpinned, as fascism had been, by the support of the Catholic Church.

Mussolini's immediate legacy had been the chaos that followed the end of the war. There was initial savage retribution carried out by partisans.[65] Before the end of 1945, however, the 'wild' purges had been channelled, partly under American pressure, into judicial channels. Too many people had too great a vested interest in avoiding continued raking of the coals of their complicity in fascism. A general amnesty in June 1946 pardoned most wartime crimes and ensured a high level of continuity in public life of civil servants, police and judges who had served under Mussolini.[66] The highest in the land who had been most complicit in fascist rule survived largely unscathed. King Victor Emmanuel abdicated and went into exile in Egypt. Marshal Badoglio, protected by the Allies, retired to his country home and lived long enough to write his self-serving memoirs. Marshal Graziani, the 'butcher of Ethiopia', sentenced in 1950 to nineteen years in prison, was released after three months. Other military leaders and captains of industry also escaped serious recrimination.[67] Rebuilding the country – politically, economically, socially – took precedence over any serious attempt to perpetuate the reckoning with the past. This fitted the national mood. After traumas and turmoil, most people wanted to return to a semblance of 'normality'. Drawing a veil over the fascist past suited the majority of Italians.

The desire for national rehabilitation in a curious way linked historical interpretation from Right and Left. Figures who had played prominent roles in the party, government or the military rushed to publish memoirs aimed at putting the blame on Mussolini and exonerating themselves. On the Left, the emphasis was on the 'true' Italy of the anti-fascist resistance which had redeemed the honour of the country that Mussolini had so grievously sullied. The former dictator, and the support for the regime he led, in these ways escaped serious analysis until the publication, beginning in the 1960s, of Renzo De Felice's mammoth, multi-volume biography of Mussolini.[68] The work conveyed a sympathetic picture of Mussolini: a dictator who had united a bitterly divided society, who was forced by the Germans to abandon his sensible strategy of concentration on the Mediterranean, who did not share Hitler's anti-Jewish mania, but who was eventually driven to destruction by his subordination to the Axis alliance.[69]

Few Italians waded through the thousands of pages of the biography. But the enormous publicity spawned by De Felice's volumes left an impression that in some ways stuck.[70] It was convenient to see Mussolini as an essentially mild dictator who, whatever his mistakes, had meant the best for his country. Endemic governmental crises no doubt contributed to *one* underlying thread within the pluralist Italian political culture that welcomed – at least in theory – a strong hand to root out the corrupt political establishment and impose order.[71] A sizeable body of public opinion was prepared to this end to overlook the personality flaws and calamitous decisions of a populist leader who promised fundamental reform and national revival. This thread found expression, following a massive corruption scandal in the 1990s, in the burlesque figure of Silvio Berlusconi, whose colourful personal life, control of the mass media, populist style and creation of a new party (Forza Italia) to challenge the establishment, bring neo-fascists into government and revitalize the country evoked echoes of the past. The readiness of nearly half of those questioned in 2019 to welcome a strongman in power who is not accountable to parliament or elections suggests that Mussolini's ghost is even now not completely exorcized.[72]

Mussolini's political legacy was directly sustained by a neo-fascist party, founded in 1946, the Movimento Sociale Italiano. In elections it seldom won more than around 6 per cent of the vote, but it fed into wider currents in Italian politics. Factional infighting and political adjustments have brought changes of name in recent decades and some distancing from Mussolini. Residual support for neo-fascism has remained at broadly similar levels.

A small hard core of unreconstructed fascist sympathizers have continued their devotion to Mussolini. Each year thousands of them still make the pilgrimage to his birthplace in Predappio. After his death, fervent neo-fascists had discovered and exhumed his remains from the initial unmarked grave in a Milan cemetery. After being kept in utmost secrecy for eleven years in a Capuchin friary near Milan, they were eventually reinterred in 1957 in the family crypt in his home town. On what would have been his hundredth birthday in 1983, more than 30,000 neo-fascists turned up to pay homage. If not in such numbers, they keep on coming. For Predappio, Mussolini in death has been good for business.[73]

Visits to the Mussolini shrine in Predappio by a minuscule proportion of the Italian population are merely trips down nostalgia lane for unteachables or part of Mussolini-related tourism. Mussolini still casts a shadow over today's Italy, though it is a hazy, fading one. Few Italians actively remember him, and he has little or no relevance to their daily lives. According to an opinion survey in 2018 nearly two-thirds of them view Mussolini negatively.[74] They recognize, as does the world outside, the personal role he played in bringing war, suffering and disaster to their country – and beyond it to parts of Africa and to Europe.

Hitler, in discussion during a reception at the Berghof, his Alpine residence on the Obersalzberg near Berchtesgaden, on his fifty-fifth birthday, 20 April 1944. Celebrations were muted in view of the rapidly worsening military situation. Hermann Göring is on the left of the picture.

ADOLF HITLER

Instigator of War and Genocide

'I must in all modesty name my own person: irreplaceable . . . The fate of the Reich depends on me alone.'[1] Hitler was exhorting military officers on 23 November 1939 to prepare to attack France and Britain without delay. He saw himself treading in the footsteps of 'the great men of German history'. Many Germans would have agreed that Hitler was irreplaceable. And more than ever following the astonishing victory over France the following June, they would have endorsed his claim to 'greatness'.

Five years later many who had once lauded him now condemned him. While about 10 per cent of those questioned in opinion surveys still praised him as late as 1950, most Germans had turned against him by the time of the Nuremberg Trials of the major war criminals (November 1945–October 1946).[2] Other prominent Nazis, some of whom had, like Hitler, killed themselves at the end of the war, were, of course, also held responsible for 'the German catastrophe'. But the 'leadership principle' that had underpinned Nazi rule allowed surviving subordinate Nazi leaders to claim that they had just been obeying orders. Military leaders proffered the same excuse: that, despite their objections, having sworn an oath of allegiance to Hitler, they had been obliged to implement 'Führer orders'. War crimes and genocide, they protested, had not involved the Wehrmacht; they were the work of Hitler, his arch-loyalist police chief, Heinrich Himmler, and the SS. Top civil servants claimed that they were simply doing their duty in carrying out orders and had done what they could to dilute the effect of any that were inhumane. Ordinary people declared that they had been helpless in the totalitarian police state that Hitler had built. One way or another, Hitler served as the alibi of a nation.

A backlash to the extreme personalization of historical interpretation emerged during the 1960s. In the process the role of Hitler was diluted. He was in a way reduced to little more than the representative figure and exponent of powerful interests – political, economic, social and military. Far from being a dictator who exercised sole, untrammelled rule, he now tended to be viewed as acting in response to structural internal and external pressure. No one doubted that he had a gift for demagogic propaganda. That apart, however, he seemed to be the archetypal 'man without qualities'. He was set upon upholding his prestige and authority, but otherwise indecisive and uncertain, influenced by those around him, in fundamental questions 'a weak dictator'.[3]

Hitler, it seemed, had been either omnipotent, or not much more than a cypher. Interpretations were polarized. It was a zero-sum game. Did this have to be the case? Surely Hitler could be the decisive factor in policy-making while accepting that he was subject to other forces, internal and external, and that the dictatorship was far from a one-man show? The key question is to ask how Hitler's power operated; where his own role endorsed, intersected with, was subordinated to or overrode other important interests in the structure of the dictatorship. Hitler's personality has to be included as part of any attempted answer. But it cannot be the sole answer. How important was it to his rise to power, and then to the way the dictatorship functioned? Did he personally take the crucial decisions? If so, was he giving voice to a pre-existing consensus or did he override opposition? Was he able to control the forces around him? Could he have acted differently, adopted alternative policies? Was it the case, and if so how was it possible, that he personally could be in a position, as he claimed in 1939, to determine Germany's fate?

PERSONALITY AND POLITICAL BEGINNINGS

Hitler had perhaps the most recognizable face of any twentieth-century politician. It has come to represent the face of political evil. The toothbrush moustache and lank strand of hair falling from right to left over his forehead, the staring eyes and a hard, unsmiling countenance are unmistakable. For his opponents, the face always lent itself to caricature, scorn and ridicule. For his millions of followers in the Third Reich it was, however, the face of political greatness. To them it signified authority, strength of will, 'manly' qualities, undaunted courage, stern paternalism. It was the personalized representation of triumph out of adversity, national grandeur and German military might. Whatever the portrayals and however they were viewed, the visual image was a product of the suggestive techniques of modern propaganda. In photos from his early years Hitler's face does not stand out in any obvious way – neither handsome nor repulsive, just unremarkable.[4]

He was of middling height (at about 5 foot 8 inches, a little taller than Mussolini or Stalin). He had no athletic physique and, unlike Mussolini, avoided any sporting poses that might invite mockery. He looked bizarre when he had turned up to Munich salons in the early 1920s in a long trench-coat and leggings and carrying a riding-whip. Relaxing in Bavaria around that time, he liked to wear the traditional Lederhosen. For martial effect he frequently wore party uniform and later, during the Second World War, military uniform. Otherwise, he appeared slightly awkward in suit and tie, more so when formal occasions demanded evening dress.

His family background had been troubled. His father, Alois, a minor Austrian customs official based at the time of Adolf's birth in 1889 at Braunau am Inn, just over the border from Bavaria, was a harsh, irascible, domineering presence. His gentle, submissive mother, Klara, mollycoddled the boy in compensation, all the more so after her husband's death in 1903. Her own death from cancer in 1907 was followed by unhappy years for Adolf in Vienna. After spending what money he had inherited, he was forced to enter a Men's Home for vagrants and scrape a living through hawking paintings of city landmarks before leaving for Munich in 1913. The outbreak of war the next year gave him, already a passionate German nationalist, a cause to believe in.

It was for him a cause with a racist aim. The immense suffering and sacrifices would be worthwhile, he railed in 1915, if the homeland were to be 'purer and cleansed of foreignness' and the 'inner international-ism' broken.[5] Conceivably, the death and destruction that he witnessed on a daily basis from the first days of the war intensified his indifference to human suffering and deepened the pitiless brutality that he later showed in abundance. He was not a 'front soldier' as he later claimed, but spent the war behind the lines as a dispatch-runner. Since they had what front-line troops scorned as an easy time of it, the dispatch-runners were not popular within the regiment. Delivering dispatches to the front was at times, however, dangerous work. There is no reason to doubt that Hitler was a conscientious and committed soldier. He was wounded in 1916, awarded the Iron Cross First Class in 1918 and ended the war in hospital, temporarily blinded by mustard gas. While there, he was traumatized by the news of Germany's defeat.[6]

The following months, back in the army in Munich amid revolu-tionary turmoil, marked his political awakening. The short-lived, Soviet-style 'Councils Republic' in Munich in April 1919 was a turning-point. From then on his army superiors saw him as a useful talent for countering socialism and indoctrinating troops with nation-alist sentiment. His prejudices and resentments, at their core an extreme hatred of Jews, congealed into an ideology, or 'world-view' (as he called it), that drove his political existence. The question of where Hitler's pathological antisemitism came from cannot be defini-tively answered. Its origins are hidden, psychological explanations guesswork. It is best seen as a process: exposure to the anti-Jewish phobias while in Vienna (one of the most antisemitic cities in Europe at the time), a deepening of hatred as he shared the views of many that Jews were responsible for Germany's defeat and the 1918 revolution, and its cementing as the cornerstone of his political 'world-view' in Munich in the first year or so after the war. Kurt Eisner, the head of the revolutionary government in Bavaria who was assassinated in February 1919, was Jewish, as were several leaders (east Europeans with Bolshevik connections) of the even more radical 'Councils

Republic' in April. The link between Jews and socialist revolution was decisively sealed in Hitler's mind.

Far more important than guesswork about its origins is the significance of antisemitism to Hitler's later party and state leadership. Without doubt the obsessive drive to destroy the power of the Jews (as he saw it), and ultimately to destroy the Jews physically, came to form the centre-point of his personal political motivation. Only through destroying their power and influence within Germany could, in his view, the nation's lost greatness be restored. The Jews, in his warped thinking, had caused the national humiliation at the end of the First World War. They had fomented unrest at home. And rapacious 'Jewish finance capital' had profited hugely from the war at the expense of the German people. In his thinking, the power of the Jews was ubiquitous. It followed that Jews had to be destroyed everywhere. Another war would be necessary to destroy the destroyers, to undo the past, rewrite history and establish German domination throughout Europe. That all lay in the future. But the core of this thinking went back to the years immediately following the First World War.

Already by September 1919, evidently regarded in his army circles by then as an 'expert' on 'the Jewish Question', he was arguing that the 'final aim' of a national government had to be 'the removal of the Jews altogether'.[7] It was not a blueprint for the Holocaust. But he had become convinced that the Jews were the root of all evil. The idea gained ubiquitous explanatory power in his mind. Their power had brought defeat and socialist revolution to Germany. He was soon seeing them both as the power behind Anglo-American capitalism, which had financed the Allied war effort, and as the dominant force in the growing threat of Bolshevism. By the time he wrote his two-volume tract *Mein Kampf* between 1924 and 1926 he had added a second keystone to his ideological edifice.[8] He had become convinced that Germany, to secure its economic future, had to acquire by conquest 'living space' in the east. Jewish settlement was widespread in eastern Europe and Russia. A war for 'living space', not that Hitler would spell it out for many years, implicitly meant a war to destroy the Jews.[9] The twin ideas, destruction of the Jews and acquiring 'living space', formed the kernel of an ideology that was to remain essentially unchanged down to his death in 1945 in the Berlin bunker.

How this personal 'world-view' over time became transmuted into state policy once Hitler had taken power in Germany was a far from straightforward process. Hitler's personality was only one component in that process. His personality is in any case not always easy to separate from the imagery that enveloped him once he became famous and, particularly, once he had acquired power in the state. Some lasting and defining traits of character, perhaps resembling his father's, are nevertheless discernible in his early years. He was already domineering, choleric, intolerant and egocentric. There were signs that he was bitter, harboured resentment and had strong dislikes that could easily turn into hatred. Did they arise from personal experience, deep humiliation that left an indelible mark – perhaps sinking into vagrancy in Vienna? It is impossible through the mists of time to establish what could have been so damaging to his self-esteem that it left such profound, all-consuming hatred in him.

Other characteristics were not necessarily endearing, but scarcely pointed to an individual who might change the world. He wholly lacked light-hearted humour. He was prudish about sex. He was preoccupied with cleanliness. He had grandiose – and highly dogmatic – ideas about architecture, art and music, topics on which he was genuinely knowledgeable, if far from open-minded. He was certainly intelligent and had an excellent memory. But he had lacked diligence and application at school and subsequently made no systematic attempt to pursue qualifications in art or architecture after failing the stiff entry requirements for the Viennese Academy of Fine Arts in 1907. Like some other autodidacts, he was a highly opinionated know-all with strong views on more or less everything and more than ready to voice them.

He was in these early years very much an acquired taste. His personality was off-putting more than winning. Perhaps unsurprisingly, he had few close friends. His only boyhood friend appears to have been August Kubizek, who listened admiringly while Hitler endlessly pontificated about architecture and Wagner's operas. A few years later he had another close friend, Ernst Schmidt, who served alongside him as a regimental dispatch-runner throughout the war and seems to have been impressed by Hitler's 'artistic nature'.[10] He got on well enough with the others in the group of dispatch-runners, though they saw him as slightly odd. After he entered politics following the war, his entourage continued to be almost entirely male-dominated. Until Eva Braun entered the scene in 1931 (and remained with him until their joint deaths in the bunker) he had no lasting intimate friendships with women. What relationships there were (for instance, with Maria Reiter in the mid-1920s and his niece, Geli Raubal, who killed herself in 1931 in his Munich flat) were of brief duration and with women far younger than he was (which was also the case with Eva Braun). How much truth there was in the lurid allegations about sexual perversions put about by his political enemies is impossible to know. Hitler's sexuality has always prompted speculation. No definitive answers can be provided.[11] In any case, they would play no notable part in explaining the impact of his personality on the political course that took Germany and Europe to world war and genocide.

Once he made his way in politics, Hitler's personality traits could be turned into assets: strong views, intolerance and an extraordinary talent for demagogic rhetoric that was invisible in the first half of his life, were essential features of the rising political star. But until 1919 no one was much impressed by Hitler, or attached importance to anything he said.

That soon changed. In summer 1919, deployed by the army on instruction courses for men about to be demobilized, he first showed how he could whip up an audience through fiery rhetoric. This ability was again on display when, with a remit to report back on its activity to his army superiors, he attended a meeting of the German Workers' Party in Munich in September 1919. After joining the small party that month – at the time one of seventy-three similar parties in Germany – he soon became its star speaker in Munich's beerhalls. On 24 February 1920 in a pungent address to an audience of 2,000 in one of them, he announced the party's twenty-five-point programme of what, from now on, would be called the National Socialist German Workers' Party – the Nazi Party for short. A political 'career' was launched.

It was unimaginable to the audience that thirteen years later the man they were listening to would be appointed as Reich Chancellor of Germany. For that to happen, the country had to be transformed in a fundamental fashion. Hitler's personality, to be sure, played its part in that transformation. But without the changes sweeping over Germany he would have been in no position to influence the country's destiny.

Without the searing impact of the First World War on Germany, Hitler would have remained a political nobody. Without the devastating impact of the Great Depression of the early 1930s on Germany, Hitler would not have been thought of as a possible head of government. And without the readiness of the small but influential sector of the political elite with the ear of the Reich President, Hitler would not have been appointed Reich Chancellor. These were the crucial preconditions within which Hitler's personality became of prime significance.

PRECONDITIONS OF POWER

Germany was traumatized by the legacy of war, defeat and revolution – at times, it seemed, on the verge of civil war. Fears of communism mounted as the right-wing press spread news of the horrors in Russia. Politics became polarized. The newly founded democracy was endangered. A general strike prevented a right-wing coup in March 1920. The army brutally crushed a workers' 'Red Army' in the Ruhr shortly afterwards. An attempted communist rising in Saxony was put down by the Prussian police in 1921. Paramilitary violence was commonplace. Hundreds of politically motivated murders, most of them by the extreme Right, took place. Hatred of the Versailles Treaty (concluded in June 1919), which had imposed significant loss of territory and swingeing reparations on the defeated country, kept the political temperature high. In 1923 it boiled over when a default on reparations payments led to French occupation of the Ruhr and hyperinflation.

Hitler's personality started to make an impact in the political hothouse of Bavaria, which had become a haven for the anti-republican extreme Right. His rhetorical pyrotechnics fitted the atmosphere perfectly. His speaking style drew the crowds to the Munich beerhalls and made him indispensable to the small but rapidly expanding Nazi movement. His raucous condemnation of the new democracy and his extreme racist nationalism were what his audience wanted to hear. Stoking up violence against political enemies and vitriolic attacks on Jews as the cause of Germany's ills matched the pre-existing views of his listeners. Hitler could speak their language. The power of his rhetoric derived from his ability to convey in simple, direct and highly emotive terms the anger, resentment and hatred that seared his own psyche.

In an early display of prima donna tantrums – a feature of his personality – Hitler exploited his indispensability to take absolute control of the party's leadership in 1921. By 1923 he had manoeuvred himself into a leading role in the sizeable paramilitary scene in Bavaria. This was the platform for the ill-fated putsch attempt on 9 November. Hitler's subsequent arrest, trial and imprisonment ought to have meant his political end. Convicted of high treason, he should have faced at best a lengthy jail sentence, possibly even the death penalty.[12] As it was, the leniency of the Bavarian authorities allowed Hitler to turn his trial into a propaganda platform for the nationalist cause and to use his unduly short prison sentence – a mere five years, from which he was released on parole after eight months – as an opportunity to bolster his standing on the radical Right. While in comfortable internment, Hitler wrote the first volume of *Mein Kampf* and received effusive messages from followers, which enhanced his already growing feeling that he was the Leader for whom Germany was waiting. Few actually *were* waiting. The banned Nazi Party had collapsed into warring factions. Economic stability was restored and democracy emerged shaken but intact. Democracy seemed to have a future after all. The prospects of Hitler coming close to the portals of power appeared remote.

If the Great Depression had not set in from 1930 onwards, Germany would have been spared Hitler's dictatorship and all that followed from it. As long as economic improvement continued, as it did until 1929, the gate to power was locked to Hitler. Crisis was his oxygen. Without crisis he could only appeal to a radical political fringe. And unless he could attain power in the foreseeable future his magnetism would evaporate; he would most likely fade back into insignificance. Had democracy become consolidated, the Nazi movement – refounded in 1925 and always prone to factionalism – might well have disintegrated. The general election of 1928 seemed to indicate that Germany was heading on a positive path. The strongly democratic parties had done well, the nationalists badly, and the Nazi Party looked to be on the way to political oblivion, or at least redundancy. It was rescued by the onset of devastating economic depression.

Hitler had been able to do little to influence events until the onset of the Depression. What he did do, however, was to forge the re-established Nazi Party as a 'Leader party'. Unquestioning obedience to his will and quasi-feudal loyalty were the bonds that held together the potentially centrifugal elements within the movement.[13] The 'idea' of National Socialism – which Hitler deliberately left as a vision of national resurgence rather than a defined programme – became insep-arable from his person. The foundations were laid for the full emergence of the cult of the Leader, still at this point confined to the small num-bers of the party faithful. It was, of course, a manufactured product, carefully cultivated by the party leadership and advertised through relentless propaganda. But it built upon expectations of 'heroic leader-ship' that had been present in populist-nationalist circles in Germany even before the First World War and had become more widespread on the Right during democracy's travails in the 1920s. An almost messi-anic tone could be heard in the expression of a nationalist Protestant publicist in 1932: 'The true statesman unites in himself fatherliness, martial spirit and charisma ... Thus, the true statesman is at one and the same time ruler, warrior and priest.'[14]

The way to power was, however, completely unclear. All that was possible was ceaseless agitation – and the conviction that something would turn up, that events would at some point move in a favourable direction. The party's organization was also in a better state than it had been before the Putsch, the work not of Hitler but of his chief lieutenant at the time, Gregor Strasser (who had first come to prom-inence while Hitler had been interned in 1924). The numbers of party members were growing, and as the Depression started to grip Ger-many around 100,000 activists were ready to exploit the emerging crisis.

What unfolded between 1930 and 1933 was more than a cata-strophic economic slump: it amounted to a comprehensive crisis of economy, society, culture and the state.[15] The acute divisions plainly visible in the post-war crisis, but seemingly overcome as conditions had improved, returned with a vengeance. The ideological chasm of Left and Right opened up the political space for nationalist populism at its rawest, hammered home daily by the rapidly growing Nazi movement and accompanied by escalating violence from its paramili-tary wing. It was highly effective.

The Nazi Party's electoral rise was meteoric: 2.6 per cent of the vote in 1928, 18.3 per cent in 1930, 37.4 per cent in 1932 – making it easily the largest party in the German parliament (the Reichstag). Hitler failed only narrowly in 1932 to prevent Paul von Hindenburg, the revered war hero, from being re-elected as Reich President. By the time he took power in January 1933 the Nazi Party had around 850,000 members, and its paramilitary wing, the SA (Sturmabteilung – 'Storm Department'), comprised some 400,000 Stormtroopers, not all of whom were party members. The Nazi movement was, then, more than three times bigger than the Fascist Party had been at the time of Mussolini's accession to power in 1922.

Once the Depression set in, Hitler came into his own as a populist agitator, railing against internal enemies and the iniquities of the 'system', working on the assumption that 'the only stable emotion is hate'.[16] His style of campaigning was modern. In 1932 he was the first politician to use the aeroplane to get him from city to city to address rallies by now of tens of thousands drawn to his message. The message itself was kept deliberately open: destroy those who were ruining Germany, and the democracy they represented, and build a new society – a 'people's community' – under his leadership. He spoke less directly about the Jews than he had done a decade earlier. But his views were not hidden, and were implicit in his unbounded denunciation of Germany's political system. The masses cheered as he openly advertised his intolerance and determination to sweep away democracy. But to do that he had to have control of the government. And winning elections could not on its own give him that control.

Constitutionally, the Reich President (the head of state) appointed the Reich Chancellor (the head of government). It was a real power, not a formal nicety. In August 1932, after the Nazi Party had been the resounding winners of the previous month's election, Reich President von Hindenburg refused Hitler the Chancellorship. Five months later, following a further election, in November 1932, at which the Nazi Party *lost* 2 million votes and subsequently found itself in deep crisis, Hindenburg changed his mind and appointed Hitler Reich Chancellor on 30 January 1933. Circumstances, not Hitler, had changed. Hitler had in the preceding weeks gambled everything on the Chancellorship and would settle for nothing less. Without the readiness of the inner core of the political establishment to hand him what he wanted, it would probably have been nothing at all.

Germany's national-conservative ruling class helped to dig their own grave between 1930 and 1933.[17] The severe economic cuts made by Reich Chancellor Heinrich Brüning deepened the crisis rather than ameliorating it. Democracy became unworkable, and government increasingly ran on the basis of emergency decrees promulgated by the Reich President. As the crisis deepened, Hindenburg replaced Brüning with openly anti-democratic Chancellors – first Franz von Papen and then General Kurt von Schleicher. Neither was able to offer any solution to the multi-faceted crisis without bringing the Nazis into government. They were willing to do this, but not to offer Hitler the Chancellorship. They were, however, in a quandary. They could and did undermine democracy. But they could not replace it with the authoritarian government they wanted, run by the traditional narrow political caste. Hitler had the mass support that they lacked. He played on the inability of the conservative elite to sustain their own power without his help. But his price remained high. He stubbornly insisted on his appointment as head of government able to make use of the Reich President's powers to bypass parliament by issuing emergency decrees. This was the major stumbling block in the depths of the state crisis.

Offered a route into government, though without the Chancellorship, the Nazi Party almost broke apart in December 1932, when Gregor Strasser proved ready to join Schleicher's cabinet as Vice-Chancellor. Hitler remained adamant that only the Chancellorship would suffice. In a showdown with Strasser, Hitler prevailed. The loyalty of the party to him was reasserted. It was a key moment at which history might have taken a different turn. A defeated Strasser resigned his party offices. He was yesterday's man. Characteristically, Hitler dismantled the organizational structure Strasser had built.[18] The purpose of the party, he stipulated, was propaganda, mobilization and loyalty to the idea embodied in the Leader. In contrast to the Italian dictatorship, where the Fascist Grand Council provided an organization that ultimately brought down Mussolini, the Nazi Party was never allowed to develop an institutional framework that could in any way challenge Hitler's total supremacy.

In the political impasse of January 1933 the deal was eventually reached which gave Hitler what he wanted. Business leaders, large landowners and not least the military – anxious to avoid being dragged into what they saw as potential civil war – all sought an authoritarian solution, though not necessarily a Nazi government. Von Papen finally brokered the deal that gave Hitler the Chancellorship, but hedged him in – or so it was thought – by conservatives who would 'tame' him once he had governmental office. At midday on 30 January 1933, a fateful day not just for Germany but for the whole of Europe, President von Hindenburg appointed Hitler as Reich Chancellor.

DICTATOR

The speed with which Hitler consolidated his hold on power was little short of astonishing. What took Mussolini years was accomplished in months. A wave of terror in the first weeks after Hitler's takeover saw the police, aided by Nazi paramilitaries and unconstrained by legal niceties, imprison tens of thousands of communists and socialists in makeshift prisons and camps, where they were subjected to heinous maltreatment. Anyone standing in the Nazis' way was endangered. Political enemies were the main target at this time. But Jews were already exposed to attacks by Nazi thugs and soon faced boycotts of their businesses and discriminatory legislation.

On the night of 27 February 1933 the Reichstag (the German parliament building) was burned down in an arson attack. Who was responsible has never been fully clarified.[19] More important than the authorship of the fire were its consequences: next day an Emergency Decree suspended civil liberties indefinitely. On 23 March an Enabling Act gave Hitler dictatorial powers, initially for four years. Two days earlier Hitler had appeared the image of humility and modesty as he bowed to Reich President von Hindenburg at the theatrical 'Day of Potsdam' – the ceremonial opening of parliament staged by the propaganda maestro, Joseph Goebbels. Many non-Nazis, initially hesitant, were won over. They welcomed the 'national renewal' (including the brutal assault on the Left) and were ready to give Hitler a chance to prove that he was no longer a rabble-rousing party fanatic, but a statesman of stature. A whirlwind of activity over the next few months saw opposing parties dissolved, trade unions banned, and by mid-July the establishment of the Nazi Party as the only political party permitted. Through a combination of intimidation, blandishments and enthusiasm for the new regime, the organizations and institutions that had formed the basis of a richly pluralistic social life were forcibly nazified – or rushed to nazify themselves. Hitler had needed to do remarkably little beyond lay down the framework for action to bring about this dramatic transformation in Germany.

In June 1934, however, he was compelled to act, and did so ruthlessly to stamp out the one remaining threat to his regime. The leader of the Stormtroopers, Ernst Röhm, had become vocal in demanding the completion of the Nazi revolution. He aimed at making the Stormtroopers the dominant force in the state. His ambition to turn the huge paramilitary organization into a people's militia posed an obvious and direct threat to a crucial pillar of the regime, the army (the Reichswehr). When Hitler was falsely led to believe by the army leadership that a Stormtroopers' putsch was imminent, he struck with utter ferocity. Röhm, a long-standing close comrade, was among the 200 or so killed in the purge. So were Gregor Strasser, former Chancellor Kurt von Schleicher and a number of others who had crossed Hitler in the past. Hitler took public responsibility for the murderous 'cleansing action'. Remarkably, this inordinately strengthened him. The display of ruthlessness demonstrated a regime that would obviously stop at nothing. More than that: the army leadership was now beholden to Hitler and keen to demonstrate its loyal support; the judiciary supported non-judicial killing in the interests of the state; not least, the SS (Schutzstaffel – 'Protection Squad'), which had carried out the 'action', emerged as the outright winner in extending its own power-base within the regime. Its fanatical head, Heinrich Himmler, took over the running of the political police from Hermann Göring, and the SS expanded into a unique organization, blending legally unconstrained powers over the police and concentration camps with the status of an elite organization whose ideological dynamism was directed at eradicating internal enemies and building a racially pure society.

When Reich President Hindenburg died in early August 1934, Hitler seized the opportunity to make himself head of state. Hitler's power in the state was now absolute. He could not be removed other than by a highly unlikely coup by the army or SS, or by assassination from an unknown individual (such as the attempt that narrowly failed in November 1939). State power meant the power of the Leader. No law superseded the expression of his will.[20] Hitler's authority as Leader rested, according to Hans Frank, the leading Nazi lawyer, not on his institutional position but on his 'outstanding achievements'.[21] It amounted, in Max Weber's terms, to 'charismatic authority' – perceived 'heroic leadership' invested in a leader by his following. That this 'charisma' was a fabricated product needs no emphasis. But its effect was real enough.[22] In practice, it put Hitler's power beyond all legal constraints.

In internal affairs Hitler needed to do little to drive on the dynamic of the regime. The principle of 'working towards the Führer' along the lines he would wish, suggested by a Nazi official,[23] meant that there was no need for a stream of directives from on high. Radical initiatives at all levels of the regime were in effect invited in anticipation of Hitler's presumed intentions. Hitler was temperamentally unbureaucratic. His style of government was to keep aloof from often divisive political decisions as far as possible. He disliked any collective forum of debate, where his own views might be questioned, and meetings of the Cabinet – the central body of Reich government – became infrequent and from 1938 onwards stopped altogether. Coordination of government business was carried out by the head of the Reich Chancellery, Hans Heinrich Lammers. But often Lammers struggled to obtain an audience to meet Hitler. Decision-making was accordingly inefficient and haphazard in many spheres of government. Party administration was immensely bureaucratic but diffuse, at least before Rudolf Hess's flight to Scotland in 1941 paved the way for Martin Bormann to instil greater ideological drive and coordination.

Hitler was most relaxed during his lengthy sojourns at the Berghof, his alpine residence above Berchtesgaden, where in his 'court' circle of admirers his lengthy monologues brooked no opposition.[24] The opulence of the Berghof belied the image of a simple 'man of the people'. The enormous royalties from sales of *Mein Kampf* permitted his populist claim that he took no government salary. And to maintain the fiction that his entire life was devoted solely to the German people, his relationship with his partner, Eva Braun, was kept under wraps, other than among his 'court' at the Berghof.

As long as things moved in accordance with the broad ideological imperatives that he represented – rebuilding the nation, destroying its internal enemies and preparing it for war – there was no need to interfere. He had his satraps – key subordinates, dependent upon him for their own spheres of power and therefore loyal lieutenants – in place. His long-standing faithful acolyte Rudolf Hess was in charge of the party. Joseph Goebbels completely controlled the crucial propaganda apparatus. Heinrich Himmler ran the burgeoning SS empire. Hermann Göring took over the preparation of the economy for war after the former Economics Minister and financial wizard Hjalmar Schacht had masterminded the early economic recovery. Robert Ley presided over the immense Labour Front, the Nazi replacement of former free trade unions. The coming man was Albert Speer, the young architect whose talent, organizational drive and aesthetic taste soon took him into Hitler's high favour.

Powerful instruments of rule stood at Hitler's disposal. An elaborate and sophisticated state bureaucracy strived to carry out what civil servants understood to be Hitler's intended policies. The party, meanwhile, grew vastly in size, with sub-organizations penetrating every aspect of society. It served as an immense mobilizing force, ceaselessly promoting adulation of the Leader and ensuring conformity and political control. The SS saw itself as a racial elite, an organization wholly committed to the pursuit of racial purity and internal security. The army leadership, though not nazified, stood behind a Leader who ensured that unlimited funds were poured into rearmament. Big business enjoyed the profits that were rolling in from a reinvigorated economy and benefited from the crushing of left-wing militancy. The Christian Churches opposed inroads into their domain but posed no political danger to the regime. Whatever popular discontent existed – for example, over social conditions, labour policy or attacks on the Churches – could find no organizational expression and could be defused by the series of spectacular successes in foreign policy that punctuated Hitler's early years in power. The elaborate, overblown Führer cult was enhanced by loudly trumpeted triumphs such as the reoccupation of the Rhineland in March 1936. Approval of Hitler's leadership co-existed with disdain for the lower representatives of Nazi rule. Many sensed, and feared, another war. But there was an exhilaration, too, especially among the young, at the opportunities offered to them by such a vibrant, strong and dynamic Germany.

Hitler was far from a passive dictator. Nazi rule created tensions and pressures. But when they reached a critical point, Hitler intervened decisively. The anti-Jewish ideological drive led to a spiral of persecution. In 1935, when anti-Jewish violence carried out by party hotheads was threatening to damage the economy and the hooliganism prompted popular criticism, Hitler acted to channel the aggression into incisive discriminatory legislation – the notorious Nuremberg Laws. The following year, when a Nazi official in Switzerland was killed by a young Jew, Hitler ordered the lid to be kept on anti-Jewish violence. In the year of the Berlin Olympics, meant as a showpiece of the new Germany, party radicals were kept in check. Two years later, however, it was a different story. Hitler had set the tone for a new assault on Jews with an incendiary speech to the Nuremberg Party Rally in September 1937. As foreign-policy tensions mounted the following summer, attacks on Jews intensified. Goebbels was the instigator of the infamous 'Crystal Night' nationwide pogroms on 9–10 November 1938. But Hitler had given the authorization. He assiduously detached himself from the widely unpopular wanton destruction of property – synagogues and many Jewish homes and businesses – that night, and from the violence in which hundreds of Jews were murdered or injured. But he approved the extreme measures that immediately followed, which saw 30,000 Jews sent to concentration camps, deprived Jews of any means of a livelihood, made them social pariahs, drove tens of thousands to flee abroad and handed responsibility for anti-Jewish policy to the Security Service, run by Himmler's right-hand man, Reinhard Heydrich.

Hitler's personal decision-making was most evident in the domain of foreign policy. Of course, he had to respond to pressures both external and at home which were articulated by the Foreign Office, the military leadership and representatives of big business. There were many influences on foreign policy. But Hitler's personality was not the least of them. That he himself took the key decisions is not in question. In early 1936, for instance, he saw that disarray of the western democracies over Italy's war in Ethiopia provided the opportunity for a spectacular reoccupation of the Rhineland. Despite cold feet among diplomats and in the military leadership, he took the decision to go ahead. The weakness of the western powers was fully laid bare as they did nothing beyond protest at the blatant breach of international treaties. The euphoric response to his triumph within Germany bolstered still further his standing at home and abroad.

His actions in foreign policy were opportunistic – though within unchanging ideological parameters. He seized the moment to act. But his decisions all pushed in one way: towards war sooner rather than later. Between 1933 and 1935 he had publicly professed peace. He was nonetheless already preparing for war. In summer 1936 a key choice had to be made between a rearmament drive and consumer spending: guns or butter. In his memorandum for the Four-Year Plan that August, Hitler decided that guns had priority. Göring was given responsibility for ensuring that Germany's army and economy were made ready at all speed for a coming showdown with Bolshevism. In February 1938 Hitler took advantage of sexual scandals in the armed forces leadership to make important changes in structure and personnel. (It turned out that the War Minister, Field Marshal Werner von Blomberg, had married a former prostitute, and the head of the army, Colonel-General Werner von Fritsch, was – falsely – accused of homosexuality.) He markedly strengthened his control over the army, and with the appointment of Joachim von Ribbentrop as Foreign Minister placed a totally subservient but outrightly hawkish figure in a key position of government as war loomed ever closer. During the spring and summer, Hitler took the vital decisions to annex Austria and then, as war seemed almost certain, to force the western democracies – enfeebled by their long-standing appeasement policy – to hand over the Sudetenland to Germany and dismantle the state of Czechoslovakia (completed by German occupation in March 1939).

In spring 1939 he decided to attack and destroy Poland that autumn. His foreign-policy triumphs together with the adulation of the masses and the constant fawning of his entourage – by-products of the outlandish Führer cult – had long since made him a believer in his own myth. His grandiose building plans were signs of his megalomania. He thought himself infallible – a genius to rank alongside the great figures of history. Poland would only be a beginning.

As another summer of tension drew on, Hitler's will for war faced no significant internal obstacles. Those in the military leadership who had the previous summer been worried about war with the western powers showed fewer qualms in 1939 (and none about destroying Poland). The inevitability of war, no longer in any doubt after the signing of the Non-Aggression Pact with the Soviet Union in August, was the consequence of the policies that Hitler had pursued over the previous years. He frequently used the argument that time was not on Germany's side: war could not wait. Economic, military and diplomatic pressures had indeed mounted to a point where the momentum for war was unstoppable. But Hitler's personality was part of the equation. He avidly thirsted for war. Wherever deep in his psyche the feelings came from, the untrammelled aggression, the desire for revenge, the fear of loss of prestige, the unwillingness to contemplate any compromise, the belittling of any critic of his own judgement all contributed to the drive to war. In the frantic last days before the attack on Poland, no less a figure than Hermann Göring, number two in the Nazi hierarchy, suggested it was not necessary 'to go for broke'. Hitler replied: 'All my life I've always gone for broke.'[25]

WAR LEADER

It was scarcely by chance that by autumn 1939 Hitler's twin personal obsessions – war and removal of Jews – had become central aims of the regime. It was, of course, hardly Hitler's work alone. Every sector of the regime had meanwhile committed itself to the pursuit of those aims. But the ideological impetus that emanated from Hitler himself, at the pinnacle of the regime, had been essential. Hitler had integrated the Nazi movement, mobilized the activists and legitimized initiatives taken by others. His personal ideological obsessions had become the driving force of government policy. Relentless propaganda had ensured that extreme national assertiveness and hatred of Jews had permeated much of society. And now the war he wanted had arrived. Racial objectives could be pursued in ways that international constraints made impossible in peacetime.

Hitler was impatient to act. The war had to be won while the western democracies were weak and before the USA, neutral but increasingly opposed to Germany, might be in any position to intervene. As soon as Poland was defeated in autumn 1939, he wanted to turn on the West. His generals were still at this stage able to deter him, making plain that the armed forces were in no state of readiness to attack France. He had kept out of interference in military operations in Poland. He intervened more actively in the invasion of Denmark and Norway in April 1940 (when despite the rapid victory the leaders of the armed forces had an early foretaste of what they saw as his deficiencies in military judgement). From now on his personal intervention in the direction of strategy and even tactics would prove decisive in the German war effort.

His frustration with strategic planning for the crucial western offensive made him open in spring 1940 to a daring alternative, devised by General Erich von Manstein, for an attack on France through the Ardennes Forest, where the enemy least expected it. The strategy worked. The world watched with astonishment as victory over France was won by mid-June, after a devastating campaign of under five weeks. It was a triumph like no other. A vital consequence was that Hitler's generals had to accept that his strategic instincts in preparing the attack had been vindicated. They were accordingly weakened in voicing any criticism of his future military directives. Hitler's own contempt for his generals had meanwhile grown as the counterpoint to his ineffable sense of his own greatness. When he told them on 31 July, less than a month after he had returned to Berlin following the momentous triumph over France, of his decision to prepare for war against the Soviet Union by the following spring, some had private misgivings. But there was broad agreement with the strategic goals that Hitler outlined. None voiced opposition.

Ideological imperatives were uppermost for Hitler. But his economic advisers were telling him that Germany's resources were not sufficient to fight a long war. Britain (backed by its empire) could not be persuaded to come to terms, bombed into submission or militarily conquered, and it was clear that before too long Germany would have to contend with the might of the USA. To establish dominance over the whole of Europe, acquiring the resources of the Soviet Union was vital. The unprovoked attack that began on 22 June 1941 inflicted such swift and damaging blows on the Red Army that for a short time complete victory seemed imminent. But by early December it was plain that Germany faced a long war in the east while, in the west, the USA, with its incomparable economic and military resources, now joined the war. Hitler's declaration of war on the USA on 11 December 1941 was in essence a desperate move – though it was not devoid of strategic purpose. His hope was that the USA would be tied down by the war with Japan (opened with the Japanese attack on Pearl Harbor on 7 December), and that German U-boats would sever the supply lines of war equipment to Britain. When, by the end of 1942, these hopes had evaporated, the desert war in North Africa was lost and the Soviet victory at Stalingrad had marked the crucial turning-point on the eastern front, Germany was left to engage in a ferocious rearguard struggle to try to stave off defeat. During the remainder of the war, Hitler's leadership became a liability to his military commanders, who, however, were divided among themselves and had no collective mechanism for challenging, let alone refusing to implement, his orders. More than that, his unbreakable power was the insuperable obstacle to any attempt to find a negotiated end to the war. When the despairing attempt to assassinate him failed in July 1944, total military defeat loomed as the outcome of Hitler's all-or-nothing war gamble.

Genocide was no incidental by-product of the war. It was central to it. The erosion of legality, the growth of arbitrary police power and the ambitions of the SS leadership, which focused on its plans for racial cleansing throughout Europe, had all evolved over the previous six years of Nazi power and developed their own dynamic.

The crucial steps into genocide still needed Hitler, however, not just to set the tone, but to provide the necessary authorization. Hitler personally licensed the extreme barbarism that took place following the invasion of Poland that, for the most part, the SS initiated, instigated and implemented. The 'hard ethnic struggle' in Poland, Hitler had told a small group of Nazi leaders on 17 October 1939, should be unconstrained by legal restrictions.[26] Around the same time, within Germany itself, he gave written authorization for the 'euthanasia action' which led to the killing of tens of thousands of the mentally and physically handicapped.

The immense ethnic resettlement plans, hurriedly improvised in

Poland and carried out with unspeakable barbarity, created insuperable organizational problems for the Nazi overlords. Genocidal possibilities were mooted. To remove the Jews, ideas of shipping them to rot in Madagascar briefly surfaced in 1940 but were soon abandoned. When Hitler confirmed in December, however, that the attack on the Soviet Union would go ahead the following May, new vistas appeared. The preparations for the invasion of the Soviet Union envisaged a massive extension of racial 'cleansing'. The SS leadership, authorized by Hitler, started planning for the deportation of millions of Jews into the icy wastes of the Soviet Union, where further millions already lived, with a view to a 'final solution' of 'the Jewish question' once the war – presumed to be a short one – was won. Plainly, they were intended to die there. By 1942 the SS's genocidal plans for racial empire in the east envisaged future deportations of 31 million mainly Slavs to rot and die out in Siberia. Jews were not included: they would already have been 'liquidated'.[27]

There was a dramatic escalation in the mass shooting of Jews in the Soviet Union during summer 1941, after Hitler had given Himmler wide-ranging police and security powers in the east. Hitler asked to be kept informed of the work of the agencies that carried out the killing.[28] But the method of mass shooting was unsatisfactory for the Nazi killers. Experiments were accordingly undertaken with the use of poison gas, developing techniques already deployed in the 'euthanasia action'. And what would happen to Jews outside the Soviet Union was still unresolved. When the war in the east could not be swiftly won, but the relentless pressure from Nazi bosses to deport Jews in their domains continued unabated, the drive to find a 'solution' became totally and urgently genocidal. The decision to deport Reich Jews to the east, taken in September 1941 – a decision that Nazi leaders acknowledged had to come from Hitler – pushed on the genocidal momentum to a new stage. Preparations to kill Jews at small extermination installations within Poland soon followed. The first gassing of Jews took place at Chelmno in the annexed region of western Poland at the beginning of December 1941. The genocidal momentum gained new force immediately following the declaration of war on the USA on 11 December. 'The world war is here,' Hitler told party leaders the next day. 'The annihilation of the Jews must be the necessary consequence.'[29]

Hitler was alluding to the 'prophecy' he had made in the Reichstag on 30 January 1939, when he threatened the 'annihilation of the Jewish race in Europe' in the event of another world war.[30] He repeated his 'prophecy' in four broadcast addresses to the nation in 1942, as the death-camps in Poland went into full operation, and altogether on more than a dozen occasions. The conviction that the war would bring about the final destruction of European Jewry served for subordinate Nazi leaders as a spur to turn Hitler's presumed wishes into reality. The repetition of the 'prophecy' was also a way of making public in programmatic fashion the extermination of the Jews, while not divulging any detail of what (probably from uncertainty about the response of the German population to open knowledge of the mass murder of Jews) was an intensely secretive project. Even in his close circle Hitler avoided speaking of the fate of the Jews, other than in elliptical terms. But all the key steps needed his authorization.[31] And he did discuss extermination policy directly in private with Himmler, who repeatedly claimed that he was acting under Hitler's authority.[32]

Hitler carries overall responsibility for what later generations came to call the Holocaust.[33] But he was also directly involved. He personally licensed, authorized, approved and legitimated what his underlings were doing. A complex process of radicalization from 1933 onwards had culminated in the lurch into outright genocide in 1941. Hitler's approval – but, more than that, his ideological justification which he imparted to every agency in the regime – had been essential at every crucial step. The equation is straightforward: no Hitler, no Holocaust.

Himmler ensured through speeches to SS and party leaders in October 1943 that they were made fully aware of their complicity in the extermination programme. Bridges had been burned. There was no way out. The complicity helped to bind the subordinate leadership close to Hitler as the military situation deteriorated inexorably and defeat became ever more certain. The military knew, too, that they could not escape their involvement in terrible barbarity on the eastern front. Fear of what defeat at the hands of the Red Army held in store was an extremely strong motivating force to keep fighting, even when it was increasingly clear that all was lost.

Hitler's relations with his military leaders were disastrous during the last two war years. His interference in tactical as well as strategic matters actually increased as the war progressed. Volcanic explosions of rage became more common as impossible orders could not be carried out. Dismissal of capable generals could bring no objective improvement in the military situation or halt the decline in Germany's war fortunes, but allowed Hitler to find scapegoats for his own shortcomings as a military leader. As defeat became more inevitable, he had nothing to offer other than fading resort to the strength of willpower and the determination – made known to all around him – that whatever happened there would be no capitulation as there had been in 1918. 'We'll never capitulate, never,' his Luftwaffe adjutant, Nicolaus von Below, recalled him saying. 'We can go down. But we'll take a world down with us.'[34]

The mounting military calamity in summer 1944, as the Allied landings in France were secured and the Red Army swept through central Europe from the east, prompted on 20 July the attempted assassination of Hitler and coup d'état led by a group of army officers spearheaded by Colonel Claus Schenk Graf von Stauffenberg. Its failure and the terrible reprisals that followed ensured that there would be no further attempt from within to topple Hitler. The catastrophic last phase of the war had to be endured by all Germans. Hitler's rule could only be ended from outside – by total military defeat.

The power elite that had backed and profited from Hitler's policies in earlier times, and had implicated themselves in war crimes and genocide, were left with nowhere to go. Fear of Allied and especially Soviet revenge sustained their bonds with Hitler, even as the enemy advanced remorselessly and the Reich fell apart. There was no institutional framework, no mechanisms of power, no collective will to stop Hitler driving Germany to perdition. And a rising from below was unthinkable, given the extent of terroristic repression So there was nothing for it but to suffer the worst in the last months of the war and to await with apprehension the repercussions of complete defeat.

In the last phase of impending catastrophe, Hitler's constant bipolar insistence on either total victory or total defeat met its logical denouement. It could only be total defeat. In that case, for Hitler there was nothing left worth saving. The monstrosity of his ego was completely unhinged. Propped up by medicines and pep-pills, he was by this point a physical wreck and mentally unbalanced. He turned his vengeful destructiveness on the German people themselves. They had proved themselves unworthy of him, he concluded; they deserved their own destruction. Albert Speer, the Armaments Minister, who had close connections with major industrialists, helped to ensure out of self-interest that Hitler's 'scorched earth' orders were not implemented. Other Nazi leaders either fled to save their skins as the end approached or recognized, like Hitler, that only self-destruction remained. Most of them were already thinking of their alibi: it had all been Hitler's fault; they had only been carrying out orders. In the Berlin bunker, Hitler clung to illusions before coming to terms with reality and taking the easy, and obvious, way out. A self-destructive, suicidal trait had long been deeply embedded in his character. Now, with the Soviet enemy almost literally at the door, he took the only exit remaining and killed himself.

LEGACY

The Second World War and the Holocaust defined the twentieth century as nothing else did. Hitler was the chief author of both. It would be absurd to reduce such epoch-defining momentous events to the actions of one man. It would be equally absurd to deny Hitler's centrality to them. The motive force of his personality had been to prepare Germany to fight a second world war to expunge the national humiliation of the first, and to eradicate the ethnic minority, the Jews, whom he nonsensically saw as the cause of that disaster and of every other ill to befall his people. He had made no secret of his intentions long before he ever became a contender for political power. In the midst of a complete crisis of state and society, the German political elite had nonetheless allowed this man to take supreme power in the country. In subsequent years every agency of political power had bound itself inextricably to him. And millions of Germans, until the steep fall in his popularity in the last war years, had cheered him and supported in different degrees the policies that led ultimately to the abyss. Germany's descent within such a few short years from a cultured, civilized, democratic society to one ready to engage in unimaginable inhumanity was so steep that its enduring legacy was more than incomprehension: it was a trauma that gripped not just an entire nation, but an entire continent. That lasting trauma is indelibly linked to the name of Hitler.

Hitler left behind nothing constructive, such as Europe's conqueror over a century earlier, Napoleon, had done. What economic modernization had taken place in the 1930s had been subordinated to the needs of war preparation. His own country was so totally destroyed that, under enemy occupation, it was reconstituted four years after his death in two mutually hostile states which were only reunited after the passage of four decades. Bombed towns and cities were the obvious signs of a country's physical devastation, a dislocated population and broken families a reflection of human loss. Hitler's bitter legacy of ruin and suffering was felt across the whole of Europe, in eastern Europe and the Soviet Union quite especially. And nearly every country had to contend with a further legacy: collaboration with Hitler's occupying forces.

The destruction of the Jews, the centrepiece of his ideology and at the heart of the German war that he had unleashed, was his only aim that came close to realization. Jewish communities that had enriched European culture for centuries were wiped out. Israel and the USA were the main beneficiaries of forced Jewish emigration. The foundation of the state of Israel would most likely have come about at some point without the Holocaust. But Hitler's lethal assault on European Jewry both accelerated the development and provided moral legitimation for a development of enormous significance for post-war global history.

War and genocide have made Hitler's legacy worldwide. Other dictators have perpetrated heinous, grotesquely terrible crimes. These have for the most part been inflicted on the population of their own countries. Hitler's were continent-wide and, in their implication, worldwide. Far more non-Germans than Germans suffered from his rule. The drive for racial empire had subjected millions to Nazi terror. Every European country's history, and beyond Europe especially that of the USA, is indelibly scarred by the memory of the Second World War, German occupation and family loss. Hitler is synonymous with the creed of racial hatred, hyper-nationalist aggression, the attempted domination of a master race and indescribable inhumanity.

Hitler completely destroyed the old Germany. The eastern provinces of the Reich, stretching through Poland to Russia's borders, were lost for ever, and with them the large estates of Germany's aristocracy that lay in these regions. Gone too was the once-mighty state of Prussia and with it the military ethos that had been such a strong strain of German political culture. Other long-standing social traditions, loyalties and structures were also broken or damaged beyond repair.[35] Hitler had in the end accomplished a political and social revolution. But it came about through the destruction he had caused. It was the complete opposite of the one he had wanted.

Germany, and Europe more widely, have over subsequent decades recovered physically and politically from Hitler's devastation. As the outright antithesis of the values of the Hitler era, modern Germany is the cornerstone of Europe's constitutional, liberal, democratic value-system. From the 1950s onwards West Germany (from 1990 unified Germany) has lain at the centre of the European 'project' of supranational integration, the most committed driving force of what turned into the European Union. Facing up to the Nazi past has been a long and incomplete process, hampered for many years in West Germany by slow and limited judicial prosecution of Nazi crimes.[36] Intensely troubling and difficult as it has been (and still is), it has been an essential element of the political and social transformation. Most other countries have faced their own dark pasts less courageously and more hesitantly.

The moral stain left by Hitler has, nevertheless, been harder to erase than the physical ruins he bequeathed. For almost two decades after his death it was largely suppressed, consciously or subconsciously, in West Germany by a population anxious to put the horrors of the recent past behind them, while in East Germany it was submerged beneath a Marxist-Leninist interpretation that attributed the collapse of civilization to the imperialist aggression of monopoly capitalism and emphasized the triumph of Soviet communism. It took the grandchildren's generation to turn a glaring spotlight on the extent of complicity in the crimes of the Nazi era and to focus public awareness on the centrality of the Holocaust – the greatest crime of all. The bitter 'historians' dispute' that occupied the West German press for weeks in 1986 revolved around the place of the Holocaust in contemporary political culture. It was a clear indication of Hitler's long shadow over German social and political consciousness.

Neo-Nazism, of course, continues to exist in Germany and in many other countries of the world. Its hardcore support still venerates Hitler. The sense of power and domination of presumed inferiors that he embodied will probably never be totally eradicated among a small minority of society. Belief in Hitler and Nazism has tiny electoral resonance, though as an underground political force is still capable of promoting disturbing racial violence. The wider populist Right which has gained ground in recent years in many European countries, including Germany, while incorporating neo-Nazis in its base of support, has to tread extremely carefully to avoid overt association with Hitler. Any express linkage would be anathema to its political hopes. It is yet a further indication of the moral stigma that the name 'Hitler' still carries, in Germany but far beyond.

Reminders of the moral stain still regularly occur in the twenty-first century, over seventy years after Hitler's death. The return of a valuable painting, stolen from its Jewish owners during the Third Reich, might be such a reminder. So might a chance infelicitous remark by a politician. Any comment that might hint at approval of something that Hitler said or did – in fact anything other than an expression of outright, total condemnation – might spell the abrupt end of a political or media career.

Europe's twentieth century had its positives as well as negatives. But its first half, especially, was terrible. And Hitler, more than any other individual, symbolizes the horror of that epoch. That he personally contributed in such a baleful way to the making of that history stands beyond question. He was the prime mover of the most fundamental collapse of civilization that modern history has witnessed. Other European leaders – Churchill and Stalin more than any – left indelible marks on Europe as a consequence of the victorious war they led against Hitler. But Hitler had done more than anyone else to cause that war. His colossal impact on European history during his era was second to none.

Stalin leads the funeral procession of Mikhail Kalinin, the former Chairman of the Presidium of the Supreme Soviet in Moscow's Red Square on 5 June 1946. Directly behind him (from left to right) are Lavrenti Beria, Georgi Malenkov and Vyacheslav Molotov. They still had cause to fear the dictator even in his last years.

4

JOSEPH STALIN

Terrorizer of his own People, Hero of the
'Great Patriotic War'

Stalin was by any reckoning one of the most significant makers of twentieth-century Europe. His main contribution was in remodelling the society and economy in his own country before leading the Soviet Union to victory over Nazi Germany in the Second World War, then fundamentally reshaping Europe by imposing Soviet rule over almost the whole of the eastern part of the continent in a division that would last until the end of the Cold War. The extraordinary drive to victory by the Red Army, recovering from crushing initial defeats, and the enormous resilience of the Soviet people as it surmounted almost unimaginable suffering and astounding loss of life, were both, however, products of the system of rule that had taken shape in the Soviet Union under Stalin – a system whose inhumanity almost defies belief.

Terror, on a colossal scale and directed primarily against the citizens of his own country, was the hallmark of Stalin's regime. The numbers of those executed, imprisoned, incarcerated in barbarous conditions in labour camps, deported to hostile environments or dying of politically instigated famine ran into the millions. At the height of the terror in 1937–8 no one could feel safe. Fear ran through the land. Extremities of cruelty were part of the Soviet war effort. After the war, massive repression sharply increased once more, receding only after Stalin's death.

In his thunderous denunciation of Stalin as he addressed the twentieth Congress of the Communist Party of the Soviet Union on 25 February 1956, the First Secretary of the Party, Nikita Khrushchev, attributed sole blame for the regime's crimes of inhumanity to the dictator himself. 'Everything', he declared, 'was dependent upon the wilfulness of one man.'[1] The role of the individual in history has seldom been so starkly characterized.

Yet Khrushchev's withering attack on the ruler of the Soviet Union from 1929 until his death in 1953 – a plain attempt to exonerate other party leaders (including himself) and innumerable Soviet citizens for their part in the horror – raises obvious questions about how it had been possible for Stalin's 'wilfulness' alone to cause such extreme inhumanity. What were the mechanisms of rule? Why were so many in far-flung parts of the vast country ready to implement (or anticipate) orders from a dictator who seldom ventured out from Moscow, other than to his vacation retreat in Sochi on the Black Sea? Close to the centre of the debates that have never ceased to reverberate around the Stalin era is the question of whether it was a logical consequence of the Bolshevik Revolution or an aberration attributable to the personality of the dictator. Was the terroristic repression intrinsic to the Soviet system itself? Or was it a horrific outflow from the dictator's warped mind, a dreadful but time-bound break with the structures of Soviet rule as devised by Lenin?

PERSONALITY

Stalin's complex personality mystified contemporaries and has remained impervious to full understanding by later analysts.[2] It is generally accepted that he had a significant personality disorder.[3] But the precise nature and derivation of the disorder remain unclear. Psychological guesswork is not underpinned by medical evidence. Even so, there are innumerable pointers to his inordinately suspicious nature, amounting to outright paranoia. He saw betrayal round every corner and was obsessive about the threat of assassination (though, as far as is known, no attempt on his life was ever made).[4] Towards the end of his life he told Khrushchev that he trusted no one, not even himself.[5]

Yet even here there were contradictions. When in public he did not wear a bullet-proof vest. He shook hands with well-wishers outside his holiday home in Sochi. He even went for a ride on the Moscow metro one evening in 1935, alarming his bodyguards but seemingly enjoying the company of his fellow passengers. Whatever the extremities of his paranoia – and it was not totally irrational: there were plenty who *would* have liked the chance to get at him – he was not simply insane, as was often surmised by outsiders during the Great Terror of 1937–8. He remained in control of his emotions. He seldom raised his voice or displayed anger. He was lucid and calculating.[6] Still, whichever way it is approached, his paranoid distrust of everybody and everything was central to his character and a key determinant of his behaviour as Soviet leader. It fitted into another key characteristic: he was deeply vindictive and coldly pitiless towards his countless victims. If intrinsic to his personality, his paranoia and vengefulness deepened as time went on, intensified no doubt by long exposure to acute insecurity as a young revolutionary, and then as a leading Bolshevik during the Revolution and civil war. The combination of his existing propensities and the specific context in which he rose to power, together with the real as well as imagined dangers that accompanied a life at the pinnacle of a system, took his paranoia to unlimited extremes.

He was only 5 foot 5 inches tall. His sallow, pockmarked face (a result of contracting smallpox at the age of six) was dominated by his full moustache, discoloured teeth and yellowish eyes. His hair was brushed back from his forehead. In meetings he tended to say little, but listened intently and inscrutably – sometimes, for those in his company, with barely concealed menace. He usually wore a worker's tunic (until he donned military uniform as a Marshal of the Soviet Union during the war), and spoke quietly with the accent of his native Georgian tongue. He was enormously hard-working and highly intelligent. He read voraciously – which included enjoying reading about the cruelties of Ivan the Terrible, and appreciating the cynicism of Machiavelli's *The Prince*. In his own way he was an intellectual, well versed in Marxist-Leninist dialectics, on which he wrote a good deal (invariably claiming to be the pupil of Lenin).

His ambition to gain power, and, having attained it, to protect it with utter ruthlessness was unbounded. But it was not power for its own sake. He was a deeply driven ideologue. As a young man he had swallowed the tenets of the Leninist interpretation of Marxism. To the central doctrine of class struggle Lenin had added the vital ingredient of 'the dictatorship of the proletariat' led by a vanguard revolutionary party which would pursue the drive to eradicate the rule of the exploiting class. Stalin's own variant of these principles led to early disagreements (on practical application rather than fundamentals) with Lenin himself and later underpinned the brutal clashes with his rivals as he rose to power and then consolidated it. There was little room in his life for anything beyond the struggle for power and the ideological basis of that power.

His personal life was wholly subordinated to the revolutionary cause and his ambitions for power. An only son, he lost contact as a young man with his father (who died in 1909, allegedly stabbed in a pub brawl). In later life he rarely saw his mother (who lived a further thirty years after her husband's death) and did not attend her funeral. His first wife, Ekaterina Svanidze, died in 1907, probably of tuberculosis, less than two years after their marriage. His second wife, Nadya Alliluyeva, only sixteen when they married in 1919, committed suicide in 1932, beset by ill-health and distraught at her husband's disdainful neglect of her. He had a poor relationship with his two sons, Yakov (who was to die in German captivity) and Vasily (later an air force officer but a dissolute individual and sore disappointment to his father).[7] During her childhood, Stalin was smotheringly affectionate towards his daughter, Svetlana, though he was later domineering, possessive, at times brutish, and the relationship remained troubled. From the late 1930s onwards his housekeeper, Valentina Istomina, a simple, quiet, unthreatening woman, was his regular companion, kept well in the background.[8] But no relationship was indispensable to him. Everyone was expendable who did not suit his purposes.

It is too simple to explain the later gross inhumanity as predetermined by his childhood and upbringing. The primitive conditions and raw poverty of his childhood in Gori, in Georgia, where he had been born in 1878 as Joseph Dzhughashvili (the name 'Stalin' – man of steel – was a later invention), the son of Vissarion, a cobbler, and Ekaterina, a washerwoman, seamstress and cook for the better-off, were miserable, though little different from those of many other families at the time. And most Georgians, however poor their living conditions, did not grow up like Stalin. The dreadful beatings he took from his drunken father did, however, provide a background of brutality. He detested his father, though was said to have acquired his vindictiveness. In contrast, he was strongly attached, at least at that time, to his mother, who idolized him – she had already buried three children by the time he was born – and wanted her son to have the education she herself had lacked. She hoped that he would eventually become a priest.

He was a talented school pupil, and in 1894, aged fifteen, he left for further education in the theological seminary in Tiflis (Tbilisi), where, however, he rebelled against the strict discipline which he endured until 1899. By then he had lost his religious faith and was on the way to finding a new faith in Marxism. He immersed himself in Marxist literature and began his acquaintance with Lenin's writings. He heroized the exiled Marxist leader, though did not swallow all that he wrote uncritically. Before the end of the century he was involved in Marxist propaganda activity in Tbilisi. Between then and the Russian Revolution of 1917 he emerged from obscurity to become one of the leading figures in the revolutionary movement, at first in the Caucasus, and then in the broader Russian empire. Through his chosen nickname, Koba, he identified himself with a romantic Georgian outlaw hero who avenged the oppressed.

Lenin (who had lived since 1900 mainly in western Europe) soon came to admire Stalin's organizational and propaganda abilities, and in 1912 had him co-opted onto the party's Central Committee, where one of his duties was to edit the new daily newspaper *Pravda*. The murky, violent factionalist milieu of the revolutionary movement rounded off the formation of his character. Stalin, as he consistently called himself from 1912 onwards, had numerous brushes with the brutal Tsarist police, was in and out of prison, suffered periods of exile (including long exile in Siberia during most of the First World War) and among other activities organized armed robberies. If brutality was deeply ingrained in a character first shaped in Gori and Tbilisi, his years as a young revolutionary, and then his experience of the harsh realities of revolution and civil war, turned him into the figure known to history.

Lenin's backing assured him of a prominent place in the Bolshevik leadership in 1917, though his role was behind the scenes rather than in prominent public view. Other revolutionaries, most notably the dynamic Leon Trotsky, Grigory Zinoviev, Lev Kamenev, Alexei Rykov and

Nikolai Bukharin, threatened to eclipse his importance. Their rivalries would surface during and after the October Revolution that brought the Bolsheviks to power. Trotsky maliciously put it about that Stalin's role in the revolution had been only a minor one, labelling him 'the outstanding mediocrity of our party'.[9] Stalin's resentment simmered in private. But it did not go away. None of his main rivals would survive Stalin's years in power. The antagonism with Trotsky was already manifest during the revolution and civil war. He became emblematic of the internal enemies seen to menace the Soviet Union. Trotsky would eventually be tracked down and assassinated in 1940 in Mexico.

The terrible civil war that followed the Bolshevik Revolution augmented the already pronounced traits of Stalin's personality and reinforced still further his ideological beliefs. Support of the victorious Allies for the White counter-revolutionary forces reaffirmed his conviction that the world was divided into two camps, imperialism and socialism.[10] Stalin deployed extreme violence to extract grain from recalcitrant peasants and terrorized the population to comply with the demands of the Reds. Terror towards class enemies was shared by all leading Bolsheviks. But Stalin's bloodthirstiness stood out.[11] He saw internal treachery at every turn and was merciless in rooting it out to destroy those he saw as traitors. Human life had no value to him other than in furthering the revolutionary cause. And he plainly enjoyed the power he arrogated to himself, sometimes defying orders from Moscow (and showing particular contempt for Trotsky).

There were early signs of concern in the Bolshevik leadership that Stalin might abuse his power. As already noted in Chapter 1 above, the dying Lenin himself famously offered a warning in a document that was made public in May 1923 and came to be seen as part of his Testament: 'Comrade Stalin, having become General Secretary, has accumulated enormous power in his hands, and I am not quite sure whether he will always be able to use this power carefully enough.' A postscript deepened the foreboding: 'Stalin is too rude, and this defect, which is tolerable in the intercourse between us Communists, is intolerable in the man filling the function of the General Secretary' (the powerful position in command of the party's organization that Stalin had taken over in 1922).[12] The document's authenticity is not beyond question.[13] But whether authentic or not, the upshot was the same: Stalin's claim to succeed Lenin had been undermined by the great leader himself. Lenin's withering character assassination was read out to delegates at the Thirteenth Party Congress in May 1924. Stalin's position as General Secretary was in jeopardy. He owed his retention of the crucial post to Zinoviev and Kamenev – anxious to prevent Trotsky gaining power. For Stalin, who subsequently claimed to have inherited the mantle of the revolutionary hero, Lenin's crushing verdict was a lingering and important component of his insecurity, another lasting incitement to his paranoia.

Had it ended Stalin's hopes of power, history would undoubtedly have taken a different course, and few would have shown much interest in the biography of a relatively minor player in the Bolshevik Revolution and its immediate aftermath.[14] But during the next quarter of a century, Stalin would play a major part in determining the future not just of the Soviet Union but of the European continent. What part, exactly, and how his personal role was possible are, however, not straightforward to explain. The historical impact of Stalin needed no less than the transfer of his personal paranoia to the mechanisms of the state system. This process in turn was dependent upon the type of society that was ready to implement his rule, and upon the ways in which Stalin came to power, and then was able to monopolize it.

PRECONDITIONS

Stalin was able to acquire outright supremacy in the Soviet Union only through triumphing in the five-year power-struggle that followed Lenin's death in 1924. The prerequisite for him winning the battle for succession was his control of the Communist Party's organization once he had become General Secretary in 1922. This gave him a vehicle for maximizing power that none of his rivals could match. But beyond that, he showed great political skill in outmanoeuvring them.

A precondition for the way in which Stalin was able to exercise power after 1929 was the type of society that had emerged from nearly three decades of colossal turmoil and upheaval.[15] These decades had produced: a failed revolution against Tsarist rule in 1905; massive losses in the First World War; the overthrow of the Tsar in an incomplete revolution in February 1917; the Bolshevik Revolution in October 1917, entailing incitement to terror against class enemies – a loose category embracing the bourgeoisie, the clergy and richer peasants (kulaks); the utter savagery of a three-year civil war that cost the lives of nearly four times as many Russians – over 7 million in all – as the First World War had done; brutally coerced requisitioning of grain leading to famine and mass shootings of rebellious peasants in 1921–2; then a backtrack from early policies of extreme coercion to a 'New Economic Policy' (NEP) that lasted until 1928, permitting a degree of market economy in agriculture produce but prompting urban unrest at profiteering and corruption.

This was a society without parallel in Europe. The enormous disruption and dislocation that Stalin inherited provided a platform for the terror that was to explode in the 1930s. Already before the period of his rule, the Soviet Union (created in 1922, coming into effect in 1924) was an extraordinarily violent society in which human life was cheap, and arbitrary terror and repression by police, party and state were endemic. Legality as understood in the West was non-existent. This was not new to Soviet Russia. Exposure to unconstrained police power and punishment by forced labour, sometimes by deportation to the wastes of Siberia, where thousands were left to perish, had been widespread in the Tsarist state. The revolution had then seen several hundred thousand Russians fall victim to the terror of the secret police, the Cheka. And by the late 1920s an army of party officials and bureaucrats (apparatchiks) had swelled in number – controlled from the centre by an organization in the hands of Joseph Stalin.

Lenin's death unleashed the extremes of factional infighting that his presence and standing had been able to contain during his time as undisputed leader. Factions were endemic to Bolshevism, even if officially banned. Debates within Marxism were as bitter and as subject to accusations of heresy as theological disputations in the Middle Ages. There were significant differences of interpretation on the future of the revolution – accelerated industrialization and world revolution (favoured by Trotsky and his followers), continuation of the peasant-based NEP (supported by Bukharin) and 'socialism in one country' (which both Stalin and Bukharin came to endorse). But personal rivalries and ambitions for power, while interwoven with factionalism, were even stronger than ideological differences. Positions were in practice fluid. Lenin had warned that the antagonism between Stalin and Trotsky would divide the party. And this was certainly part of the jockeying for power that followed the leader's death.

Trotsky, a forceful speaker, a good organizer, and popular in the party and in the Red Army, had made powerful enemies. This temporarily united bitter rivals. The wider keenness to block the chances of Trotsky succeeding Lenin brought together the troika (as it became called) of Stalin, Zinoviev and Kamenev. But the negative integration temporarily uniting the troika was fragile. There were other factions. Stalin also cultivated the support of Bukharin, who had a sizeable following. This, too, was purely tactical.

In 1924–5 the troika undermined Trotsky. By the end of 1925, however, Zinoviev and Kamenev had become more worried about Stalin than about Trotsky and the following year swapped their allegiance, now joining forces with Trotsky. They were, though, no match for the powerful combined opposition of Stalin and Bukharin, and all three and their followers were expelled from the party in 1927. Zinoviev and Kamenev were readmitted the following year, humbled and contrite.[16] Trotsky, on the other hand, was banished into distant exile in 1928 and in 1929 expelled from the Soviet Union altogether. Stalin combined his control of the party's organization and astute tactical manoeuvring to turn now against Bukharin and his followers, the chief remaining obstacle to his power. By the end of 1929 Bukharin's supporters had been ousted from any organizational base of support they had enjoyed in the party. Nothing further stood in the way of Stalin's supremacy.[17]

These intrigues and power machinations in high places passed by the vast majority of a largely illiterate peasant society. But their lives were about to be drastically altered by the outcome of the power struggles. The NEP had been successful until 1926, restoring industrial production to the level of 1913. But the question of how quickly the Soviet Union should modernize, and whether this could be better achieved by forced industrialization (necessarily involving a tight squeeze on the peasantry) or by investment in agricultural production, remained a matter of heated debate. And meanwhile the NEP was running into trouble. Bukharin, the chief advocate of continuation of the NEP, was weakened. Peasants held back food rather than

sell it at the depressed official prices. Racketeers exploited food shortages and sold produce at black-market prices. Stalin's response was
characteristic. He returned to the brutal methods used in the civil war.
He went to Siberia in 1928 to oversee the confiscation of hoarded
grain, extorted from the peasantry with great violence.[18] That same
year he put forward the first Five-Year Plan of rapid industrialization,
accepted by the Party Congress in 1929.

Stalin had by this time triumphed over his rivals, had gained the
party's backing for his leadership and had won the battle over the
future direction of the Soviet economy. The basis for the full emergence of his personal rule and the unfolding of unprecedented terror
at all levels of society had been laid.

CUMULATIVE RADICALIZATION

The concept of 'cumulative radicalization', invented to help explain the
internal development of Nazi rule,[19] can be applied equally well, if not
better, to Stalinist rule in the Soviet Union during the 1930s. Years of
revolutionary upheaval had destabilized society. Since its creation the
Soviet Union had in effect been in a permanent state of emergency. Stalin profited from this and extended it. The sense of a society embattled
against powerful internal and external enemies who were seeking to
destroy it encouraged belief in phantoms – foes of such strength that
they could only be combated by extreme terror. Stalin's long-standing
arch-enemy, Trotsky, acquired the status of a bogey man behind all presumed conspiracies whose supporters could be found in every crevice,
ready to collaborate even with the class enemy of international imperialist capitalism to bring down the Soviet Union. This was the climate in
which personal paranoia could become the paranoia of an entire state
system, with unprecedented levels of terror against all presumed opponents as its expression.

Stalin was at the centre of the mounting horror, without question.
He directly instigated, encouraged, authorized or confirmed all the
major decisions that set the radicalization of gross inhumanity in train.
He personally ratcheted up the pressure to extend the terror. He personally approved orders for mass executions. But the implementation

of Stalin's imperatives in such a vast country depended upon an elaborate apparatus of power, which in turn involved the readiness of willing agents of the regime at every level in a hugely expanding party and state bureaucracy to carry out directives, however inhumane.[20]

This was made possible by a top-down, highly centralized command system that demanded unquestioning obedience to orders from superiors at all levels and uncritical belief that 'the party is always right'. And the party, the vehicle of the 'dictatorship of the proletariat', dominated the state. Stalin held no office of state until he became Prime Minister in 1941, succeeding his most faithful devotee, Vyacheslav Molotov, who had held the post since 1930. His position as party General Secretary was what counted. As he consolidated his absolute power, the institutions of the party atrophied. The meetings of the Party Congress, which had been annual under Lenin, became infrequent. Stalin turned the Congress into merely an acclamatory assembly. The Central Committee, the party's sovereign body, was reduced to a rubber-stamp for Stalin's decisions. The Politburo, the equivalent of the Cabinet in western governmental systems, increasingly registered decisions dictated to it by Stalin.[21] Its members were dependent on Stalin's favour and lived in fear of his disfavour. At the centre of the web was Stalin's inner group of acolytes, no more than a handful of long-standing courtiers, chosen for their lapdog subservience, each of them highly conscious of his inferiority to the leader. Among the most important besides Molotov were Lazar Kaganovich (chief organizer of collectivization), Klim Voroshilov (in charge of defence) and Anastas Mikoyan (commissar for foreign trade), grandees of the land with Stalin's backing, nothing without it. This group – ultimately, therefore, Stalin himself – controlled all appointments of significance in party and state. The downward pyramid of power and patronage was enormous.

At the foot of the pyramid, an immense conglomeration of bureaucrats and functionaries, high-handed bosses of production lines and agents of the dreaded People's Commissariat of Internal Affairs, the NKVD owed their existence quite literally to their readiness to carry out, even to anticipate, orders. Of course, they did not act only out of fear, however pervasive insecurity and the accompanying distrust were. Idealism ran alongside careerist opportunism – the sense, especially among the huge influx of young party members, that they were helping to build a new society. Stalin, they believed, was making this possible. Whether they swallowed the excesses of the manufactured cult of the great leader or whether they cynically paid lip-service to Stalin-worship for the sake of conformity, the effect in creating an untouchable idol at the pinnacle of the Soviet system was much the same.[22] The enormous turnover of party members (much of it from purges, executions and incarceration), placing young and ambitious new members into positions of authority and localized power, ensured that there was never any shortage of those whose own mini-despotism relied upon uncritical implementation of directives.

Stalin's deep-seated sense of insecurity made him an obsessive micro-manager who intervened at all levels of government. But he was dependent for this on the streams of reports reaching him from agencies in all parts of the Soviet Union. The most important of these came from the secret police, the NKVD. This was in effect a state within the state – except that even authoritarian states usually (though not always) operate by rules, and the NKVD was subject to no rules (let alone legality) other than the commands of Stalin. Moreover, satisfying Stalin meant taking the initiative in finding victims and fulfilling quotas of 'enemies' and 'traitors' to be eradicated. The NKVD's reports to Stalin were often furnished from denunciations and detailed ever more expansively the seemingly alarming growth in numbers of internal enemies. Stalin avidly and meticulously read the reports, authorized mass arrests, approved execution lists (383 of them, containing the names of 44,000 individuals, in 1937–8 alone)[23] and encouraged the police to widen the net and multiply the numbers designated for execution, jail, or dispatch to long terms in the Gulag labour camps (which formed part of the NKVD's expanding empire).

The size of the secret police grew enormously under Stalin. By 1938 its numbers totalled around a million.[24] Its agents were given big pay rises, and its leaders received awards for their service, as well as other emoluments and perquisites of power. But even for the NKVD, the executors-in-chief of the terroristic regime, there was no safety. As the paranoia spread through the entire system in the course of the 1930s, the NKVD was incited to denounce, arrest and execute many of its own personnel.

Terror had been part of the Soviet system from the beginning. But its grotesque explosion during the 1930s was a direct reflection of Stalin's personal leadership of the Soviet Union in specific conditions that encouraged and facilitated its spread across all parts of Soviet society.

The process of radicalization began with the ruthlessly forced collectivization of agriculture in the early 1930s. Stalin had been far from alone in pressing this policy. It might have taken place under another leader. But the ultra-violent, brutally uncompromising way in which it was implemented bore Stalin's hallmark.[25] The numbers executed, deported or imprisoned have been estimated at 4 to 5 million.[26] Tens of millions more were forced off their land and into collective farms. Many were driven to starvation as grain production plummeted. Stalin personally stipulated in 1932 that anyone caught stealing grain from a collective farm should suffer the death penalty.[27] Famine as a direct consequence not of natural disasters but of policy decisions caused the death of over 5 million people. The incitement to unbounded violence in order to eradicate the – arbitrarily defined – 'kulaks' (wealthier peasants) acclimatized a society already inured to raw brutality to mass murder in the cause of rooting out proclaimed class enemies.

A second major spurt of intensifying terror followed in the wake of the assassination of the popular Leningrad party boss (and close associate of Stalin) Sergei Kirov in 1934 by a disturbed malcontent whose wife was having an affair with Kirov. There is no evidence that Stalin was implicated. But the evident security failings fostered his suspicions about treachery. Stalin instructed the NKVD on what was needed. The NKVD reacted in predictable fashion, swiftly dreaming up the existence of terrorist organizations in Leningrad and Moscow and linking them to Stalin's old rivals Zinoviev and Kamenev. A witch-hunt for their followers led to hundreds of arrests, the exile of thousands more and the expulsion from the party of over 280,000 members.[28] The NKVD forced 'confessions' of plans to kill Stalin, and inevitably came to implicate far-away Trotsky and his supporters, as well as, closer to hand, Bukharin too, in 'terrorist activities'. The paranoia was by now rapidly spreading throughout the entire system. It did not take much to direct it towards the upper reaches of the party, the army and even the secret police itself.

The lurch into the most acute phase of the assault on overwhelmingly fictional 'internal enemies' in what has been aptly described as the 'Great Terror' of 1937–8 came as the increasing likelihood of general war in Europe highlighted the threat facing the Soviet Union from aggressive 'imperialist powers'. Suspicion about Trotsky's influence intensified still further. A 'fifth column' of 'fascist spies and enemies' was envisaged as lurking in every crevice of the Soviet Union.

The purge of the party elite and the Red Army's leadership took place in this fevered atmosphere. The 'old guard' of Bolsheviks from Lenin's time was eliminated, the party elite destroyed. Bukharin's show trial in 1938 and inevitable execution followed the earlier ones of Kamenev and Zinoviev (shot following a show trial in 1936). Around 30,000 Red Army officers were among those purged. Some 20,000, including the leading military strategist Mikhail Tukhachevsky, were executed, leaving the leadership of the Red Army gravely weakened (and encouraging the Soviet Union's enemies to underestimate its fighting capacity). The purge was extended to Soviet foreign intelligence, with the effect both of reducing its capability and of diminishing Stalin's trust in its reports. The NKVD itself came under suspicion. Hundreds of its agents, at home and abroad, were purged. Its former head, the repugnant Henrikh Yagoda, was executed in 1938, two years after his dismissal, under bizarre accusations of harbouring spies and traitors in the NKVD. His successor, the even more abhorrent Nikolai Yezhov, almost as paranoid as Stalin and his chief executioner during the 'Great Terror', was then himself denounced in late 1938 by his own deputy, Lavrenti Beria, on absurd charges of betraying state secrets to foreign spies, tortured under Beria's supervision and ultimately executed in 1940.[29]

By the time Stalin halted the 'Great Terror' in late 1938 around 700,000 had been shot, a million and a half more arrested. Nearly 3 million languished in prison camps. By then there was an obvious need to rebuild not just the party cadres but, far more urgently, the leadership of the Red Army, and to prevent further damage to industrial production when defence preparations were an outright priority.

Stalin's terror in the 1930s was directed at his own people. Indirectly, however, its ramifications extended far beyond Soviet borders. Communist parties throughout Europe and their fellow travellers, prominent among them many western intellectuals, were either wilfully ignorant of Stalin's crimes against humanity or ignored them in their enthusiasm for the radical alternative the Soviet Union offered to crisis-ridden western capitalism and fascism. Even where they recognized the inhumanity, they justified it as a regrettably necessary means towards the worthwhile end in prospect of building a socialist society. There was an even more malign international by-product. The reaction against Stalinism slotted easily into the ideological armoury of the radical Right in numerous European countries, especially in Germany. Fascism profited from Stalinism. Moreover, the potential spread of Bolshevism, underlined by Soviet involvement in the Spanish Civil War, alarmed the conservative as well as fascist Right. But it was on the extreme Right, most of all in the shrill rhetoric emanating from Hitler's Germany, that the ground was being laid for a showdown with Stalin's Soviet Union.

As war in Europe became certain by summer 1939, Stalin knew that the Soviet Union was far from ready to defend itself against the attack from Germany (possibly allied with other 'imperialist powers') that was certain to come. The western democracies had shown their readiness to come to an arrangement with Nazi Germany. No help could be expected from that quarter. The need to buy time was behind Stalin's readiness in August 1939 to sign a pact with the ideological arch-enemy (which suited Germany too, to allow it to focus on destroying Poland, before turning against the West). The crash programme of industrialization, driven through on the back of brutal collectivization, had seen an enormous increase in the production of weaponry. But industry could still not meet the rapidly rising demand for armaments. In addition, the purges had left a shortage of experienced officers. The military weakness of the Red Army was revealed in the Winter War against Finland in 1939–40, and Stalin was made aware by a searing report from his Defence Commissar in December 1940 of the grave deficiencies in the armed forces.[30] Production of armaments was by now swiftly accelerating, and the armed forces had more than trebled in numbers since 1938. Still, Stalin knew that the Soviet Union would not be militarily ready to face invasion before 1942 at the earliest.

When invasion did come, in June 1941, it shocked Stalin to the core, despite the many detailed warnings that he had received that it was imminent. His calamitous miscalculation of German intentions had systemic as well as personal causes. The entire system was built upon toadying to Stalin, not daring to contradict him. So nobody challenged his wilful denial of German plans to invade. And Stalin regarded practically all intelligence reports as 'disinformation'. The distrust that ran through the entire system led therefore to Stalin's disbelief in the solid intelligence he was receiving from several well-placed sources. His extraordinary misjudgement had catastrophic consequences. During the first weeks following the invasion on 22 June, an untold military calamity unfolded. By December, losses of the Red Army numbered 2,663,000 killed and 3,350,000 taken prisoner (most of whom would die in German captivity).[31]

Stalin personally, but also the endemic flaws in the system of rule over which he presided, had been responsible for the catastrophe. Yet in under four years the Soviet Union would go on to win arguably the greatest military victory in history. If Stalin was responsible for the calamity of 1941, does he also deserve the accolades for the victory in 1945?

WAR LEADER

Without the staggering Soviet contribution to the defeat of Nazi Germany, Allied victory in 1945 – the crucial turning-point in the twentieth century – would conceivably only have been feasible through German surrender following the devastation by atomic bombs of Berlin, Munich and other cities. The scale of Soviet losses is scarcely imaginable: at least 25 million dead, some 17 million of them civilians; 84 per cent of the 34.5 million men and women mobilized killed, wounded or captured.[32] No single factor explains the Soviet achievement. Central was certainly the readiness to defend family, home and country against a barbaric invader waging a war of annihilation. A new emphasis on patriotism, accompanied by greater religious tolerance, played its part. Revenge for what a pitiless enemy had done to loved ones was an added strong motivation. Alongside that went the elemental fight for survival, the most basic motivating factor of all soldiers, together with the loyalty towards immediate comrades upon whom self-survival depended. The Soviet victory was the victory of an entire society, attained at phenomenal sacrifice and loss. But it would not have been attained without leadership, involving a collective effort of mobilization, military and civilian.

So what was Stalin's personal contribution to this leadership, and to Soviet victory? He later took the accolades, basking in the glory of the war hero, ensuring that the victory laurels should not be 'usurped' by the fabled military commander Marshal Georgi Zhukov.[33] However absurd the attempt was to claim sole credit for the victory, it is not easy to imagine that it could have been attained under a different leader. Especially after the magnitude of the early losses following the German invasion in 1941, strong personal leadership from the top was needed to turn what seemed like certain defeat into gathering military strength, resounding victories and ultimate triumph. Stalin had a direct impact in several crucial spheres of the Soviet war effort: terror; propaganda; military command; and diplomatic negotiations. In each area, the personality of the leader played a significant part.

The terror of the 1930s had moulded a society, dragooned it into submission out of dread of the most drastic punishment for disobedience or nonconformity. The terror against Soviet citizens was pared down during the war, though by any yardstick other than that of the 1930s it remained at an astounding level. It had Stalin's express imprimatur.

Fear percolated downwards in the army. Commanders feared Stalin. They were right to do so. The supreme commander on the western front, General Dmitri Pavlov, and his three immediate subordinate generals, were arrested, suspected of treachery, tortured and executed following the huge Soviet losses and fall of Minsk (opening the route to Moscow) during the devastating German advance in the first week of the war. Pavlov was the scapegoat for what had actually been Stalin's calamitous error in ignoring the warnings of the German invasion. However, the execution of such a high-ranking commander sent a clear signal. Commanders treated their subordinates brutally. Later in the war the commander of the 62nd Army at the Battle of Stalingrad, Vasily Chuikov, would personally assault subordinate commanders who displeased him.[34] Disobedience among the rank-and-file attracted severe exemplary punishment. Those accused of being 'cowards and traitors' were peremptorily executed. Soldiers had good cause, therefore, to fear their commanders. Hundreds of thousands of Soviet soldiers were arrested for desertion and condemned to death, dispatched to serve in penal battalions or sent to prison camps (both of which last were tantamount to a death sentence). NKVD units were stationed behind the front line poised to shoot deserters. Many soldiers thought it was a lesser risk to advance towards German guns than to retreat to face the weapons of the NKVD. Those recaptured from the enemy were imprisoned and often executed.[35]

Civilians faced homelessness, destitution and famine as the scorched-earth policy ordered by Stalin in June 1941 destroyed their homes, farms and villages.[36] Those deemed 'internal enemies' – a broad category that could include vagrants, prostitutes, gypsies or petty thieves – were executed or deported to Siberia. Hundreds of thousands of workers were imprisoned for often minor infringements of draconian labour laws. Simply being late for work could have the most dire consequences.[37]

Non-Soviet citizens living in border areas and regarded as a threat to security were in severe danger. In March 1940 Stalin personally signed (as did his close entourage) approval for Beria's proposal to shoot 25,700 Polish officers, some of whose remains were later discovered in the forest of Katyn. Hundreds of thousands of Poles had by then, following the division of Poland in 1939 between Germany and the Soviet Union, been deported on Stalin's orders from eastern Poland to Siberia or central Asia. Later in the war, Stalin had over 3 million people from large ethnic minorities within the Soviet Union – among them Volga Germans, Crimean Tatars, Kalmyks and Chechens – suspected of sympathizing with Germany, expelled from their homelands and deported en masse to inhospitable regions in central Asia.[38]

Stalin's wartime terror was a continuation, not a break, with pre-war policy. His approval, and in many cases his express orders, are not in doubt. Terror was, of course, not the only reason why the Soviet people fought so tenaciously. But it was an arguably indispensable part of the Soviet war effort. For liberal minds, it is an uncomfortable thought that defeating Nazi Germany might well have been impossible without Stalin's terror.

Stalin also headed the propaganda drive to stir support and sustain the readiness to fight. He admitted to Averell Harriman, later the American ambassador, 'that the people won't fight for world revolution and they won't fight for Soviet power'. 'Perhaps', he added, 'they will fight for Russia.'[39] A big effort from the beginning went into bolstering the image of a patriotic struggle in an appeal to national sentiment to foster resistance to the foreign invader.[40] In his first speech of the war to the Soviet people, on 3 July 1941, Stalin combined threats of merciless reprisal against 'cowards, deserters and panic-mongers' with patriotic rhetoric, using traditional appeals to the family that spoke of his 'brothers and sisters' as well as 'comrades' and 'citizens'.[41] There was also a return to God. Churches were reopened, priests brought back from the camps and troops sent into battle with God's blessing. Stalin even met the head of the Russian Orthodox Church, who publicly gave his support to the defence of 'the holy borders of our motherland'.[42]

The Stalin cult was embellished still further to bolster the unity of people and leader. It came close to the deification of the 'great leader', appropriating the age-old simplistic peasant-style belief in the stern, authoritarian but beneficent 'father Tsar'. Stalin's own crucial importance to the stability of the regime was plainly demonstrated at the most critical moment of a critical year, amid the growing panic of Moscow citizens in mid-October as the fall of the city to the Germans seemed likely. All was made ready for Stalin to leave the Soviet capital for safety beyond the Urals. Awaited at the station, his train under steam, at the last minute he decided not to go. As news quickly circulated that he was remaining in Moscow, staying at the head of his people and in command, morale was quickly restored. Molotov, perhaps over-dramatically, later surmised that the Soviet Union would have collapsed had Stalin left. Nonetheless, Stalin's decision to stay played no small part in shoring up the patriotic effort at a vital juncture.[43]

Stalin's chief contribution to Soviet victory was in his planning and direction of the Red Army's operations from 1942 onwards. As Supreme Commander (from July 1941) he had overall responsibility for the conduct of the war. His relations with his military commanders were of vital importance. These underwent a significant transformation in 1942–3.

Stalin's terrible blunders and military incompetence during the catastrophic first months of the war were compounded by the lack of a coordinated command structure at the time of the invasion, and the inexperience of both planners and field commanders.[44] In early 1942, after the Red Army had halted the German advance on Moscow, Stalin made a further costly strategic error. It was not purely a matter of Stalin's wilfulness. His military leaders were not of one mind on strategy. The General Staff had concluded, nevertheless, that levels of equipment and available trained reserves demanded a 'strategic defensive' over subsequent months, to be focused on the 'central sector' of the front (the approaches to Moscow). Stalin overrode these recommendations and insisted on offensive strikes 'on a broad front'.[45] A consequence was the disastrous loss of the Ukrainian city of Kharkov in May 1942 (despite the Red Army's superiority of numbers). The situation worsened with the complete loss of Crimea by the beginning of July. Between them, Kharkov and Crimea cost some 370,000 men and untold quantities of weaponry.[46] Further disaster unfolded with the fall of Rostov on 23–4 July, which opened up the route across the River Don to the Caucasus oilfields. The grave military position in the summer even drew an admission from Stalin that his own personal mistake had been at least partly responsible for the debacle.[47] He reacted in characteristic fashion, however, by an order on 28 July declaring it the duty of every soldier to fight to the last drop of blood. There was to be 'not one step back'. 'Panic-mongers', 'cowards' and 'traitors' were to be eradicated.[48]

In late August 1942, Stalin appointed General Zhukov to be Deputy Supreme Commander – overall military leader, that is, beneath Stalin himself – and to take command in the vital Stalingrad area, where the Germans were threatening to break through. The backing Stalin gave to the tactical planning of Zhukov and the Chief of the General Staff, General Alexander Vasilevsky, was crucial to the Soviet victory at Stalingrad. But Stalin's own role should not be underestimated. Zhukov was impressed by Stalin's attentiveness, knowledge of the situation and close concern with detail.[49]

From Stalingrad onwards his readiness to take advice from his generals improved, even if he still could not resist interfering. Moreover, this turning-point in the war on the eastern front was the overture to the stunning series of Soviet victories during the last two years of the war, ending with the taking of Berlin in 1945. The defeats of the first year and a half of the war had heightened tension between Stalin and his generals. The victories of the last two and a half years understandably led to a far better working relationship. Stalin had fully supported his key commanders, making few personnel changes during the victorious phase of the war. Much of the credit for the successful military operations goes, of course, to the Red Army's commanders, foremost among them Zhukov. The Red Army's leadership itself became more experienced, learned from mistakes and made important innovations in technology, weaponry and organization. Stalin backed the changes and ensured through ruthless demands on industry and manpower that the necessary supplies, reserves and firepower were always available. He remained in ultimate charge of strategy and all vital military decisions. But he was prepared to yield to the advice of his top commanders.[50]

As Germany's defeat became more certain, Allied leaders met to determine the shape of Europe after the war. Stalin, Roosevelt and Churchill had the first of these meetings at Tehran in November 1943 – the first time Stalin had left the Soviet Union since taking power. A second momentous meeting, with the war in Europe approaching its end, took place at Yalta, on the Black Sea, in February 1945. The third was at Potsdam in August 1945 following Allied victory in Europe. At each of the meetings the key figure was Stalin. What Europe would look like for the next four and a half decades was largely agreed at these three conferences. By Yalta, the conquests of the Red Army had largely established the harsh realities that underpinned the diplomacy. But what was decided at Yalta had in good measure been prefigured by the conference in Tehran.[51] Although no final decisions were taken at Tehran, the crucial redesignation of Poland's borders was essentially agreed. It was also in principle determined that post-war Germany would be split up. Yalta, with much of eastern Europe by then under Soviet control, confirmed that Poland's future would effectively be shaped in Moscow. Potsdam confirmed the division of Germany.

Stalin held the whip hand in the 'Big Three' deliberations, thanks, of course, to the exploits of the Red Army. But he attained his aims through clever, well-informed, skilful negotiations, mastery of detail, command of geopolitics – and through sheer force of personality. Roosevelt and Churchill left Tehran and Yalta thinking that they had achieved satisfactory outcomes in the talks. They thought they had won Stalin's friendship and could trust him. Both had indeed come to like the Soviet dictator. But, then, Stalin was a good play-actor who could be charming and jovial, with a sharp (if dark) sense of humour. He pulled the wool over the eyes of both Roosevelt and Churchill.

He impressed his interlocutors. Anthony Eden, the British Foreign

Secretary, remarked that Stalin would be his first choice on a negotiating team.[52] Averell Harriman, who had frequent dealings with Stalin between 1941 and 1946, thought he was better informed than Roosevelt and more realistic than Churchill.[53] General Alan Brooke, Chief of the Imperial General Staff, had perceptively summarized his thoughts on Stalin in his diary during the visit to Moscow with Churchill in August 1942:

> He is an outstanding man, that there is no doubt about, but not an attractive one. He has got an unpleasantly cold, crafty, dead face, and whenever I look at him I can imagine his sending off people to their doom without ever turning a hair. On the other hand there is no doubt that he has a quick brain and a real grasp of the essentials of war.[54]

Stalin was a monstrous individual, who led a monstrous regime, one that was moulded in his image. But this very monstrosity steered the Soviet Union to victory over Germany and made possible the wider victory of the Allies. In imposing relentless terroristic repression to enforce implementation of the colossal war effort, both civilian and military, in embodying the patriotic fight to liberate the Motherland, in close direction of the successful course of the war from 1942 onwards, and in negotiating major territorial gains for the Soviet Union, his personal leadership had been indispensable. As the war ended, his prestige, at home and abroad, was at its apogee.

LAST YEARS

On 24 June 1945 Stalin stood on the balcony of the Lenin Mausoleum, the conquering hero soaking up the adulation of a vast euphoric crowd. Marshal Zhukov rode into Red Square on a white stallion, followed by the serried ranks of Red Army regiments who saluted the great leader and threw down before him the captured banners of the defeated enemy.[55] It was a moment of glory and unbounded rejoicing. But it was no more than a fleeting distraction before the immense effort began to rebuild a country utterly devastated by war. Stalin's last years were to inflict further huge hardship and suffering on his country. The dictator himself did not dwell on past glories. His personality, his instincts, his ingrained suspicions were unchanged. And so, in essence, was the system over which he had presided before the war – and turned into a personal despotism.

Victory now took the already grotesque cult of the great leader into new realms of absurdity. Stalin protested at its excesses, though did nothing to diminish them. Though he professed to be Lenin's pupil, he was now placed by ubiquitous propaganda on an even higher pedestal than the legendary Bolshevik leader. Memories that might sully the heroic aura were dangerous. When Anna Alliluyeva, sister of Stalin's second wife Nadya, published in 1946 – with official approval – memoirs that gave harmless though unflattering details of his early life, she was sentenced to ten years in the Gulag for defaming him.[56] The cult masked the actual detachment of the dictator from his people in his last years. He hardly appeared in public, gave few speeches, retreated behind his impenetrable walls of personal security and practically vanished from the view of ordinary citizens.

His iron grip on all centralized levers of power in party and state, security policy and the army – the key props of his rule – remained nonetheless intact. So did his reliance on reports reaching him from agencies of the Ministry of State Security (MGB), and from individuals throughout the institutions of rule ready to turn personal rivalries and jealousies into denunciation or damaging political criticism. His suspicion stopped at no one. Even the homes of members of the Politburo were bugged. No one, especially those in high places who might have posed a threat, could rest easily. The great military hero Marshal Zhukov, whose exploits were seen to pose a threat to Stalin's own popular standing, was consigned to a posting in faraway Odessa and in early 1947 dismissed altogether. Beria was removed as head of state security, where he could have become dangerous to the dictator, and given responsibility for work on developing the atom bomb.[57] Molotov, Mikoyan, Zhdanov, Malenkov, Kaganovich and Beria all had reason to fear the dictator's unpredictability in his final years.

Repression was stepped up. The slave labour camps expanded again. Their 5 million prisoners included over a million soldiers returning from horrendous conditions in German captivity, their only 'crime' to have fallen into enemy hands, causing distrust of their loyalty. As before, material benefits and privileges were used as sweeteners to buy the commitment of the agents of the relentless coercion. There was no return to the Great Terror of 1937–8. But a localized purge of the Leningrad party leadership in 1949 was an indicator that the dictator's unpredictable wrath could be incurred at any time. Wider purges were feared in the top echelons of the party just before his death. In his last months, Stalin once more saw threats at every turn. His paranoia was if anything magnified. He imagined that Molotov and Mikoyan, two of his most loyal acolytes, were agents of foreign powers, and that Kremlin doctors (with Jewish-sounding names) were engaged in a plot to kill him.

The fears even of his closest entourage were only ended by his death on 5 March 1953, following a serious stroke and massive stomach haemorrhage. The struggle for the succession which followed ultimately led to Khrushchev's ascendancy and the denunciation in 1956 of the leader he had served so willingly for so long, and in whose crimes against humanity he had so readily participated.

LEGACY

No sooner was the dictator dead, than his former henchmen strived to introduce reforms to the regime.[58] The battle for power only gradually subsided, with Khrushchev eventually the winner. After disavowing Stalin's personality cult in 1956, he relaxed the suffocating stranglehold on society of the Stalin era. Over 4 million prisoners returned from camps and penal colonies. Life became far less insecure. Living standards improved, though remained modest compared with those in the West. The final official break with the Stalin cult came in 1961 with the removal of the former dictator's body from its place alongside Lenin's in the mausoleum.

But was it a break with Stalinism? Some leading experts have argued that Stalinism was 'a system in its own right', a radical deviation from the aims of Bolshevism.[59] It seems more plausible to see in the Stalin dictatorship less a separate 'system' than *one* possibility that was implicit in Bolshevism which took extreme, radical form in conditions of a permanent state of emergency (fear of internal and external enemies, the growing threat of war). It was not an accidental development, a deviation from a 'true route' of Bolshevism. But nor was it an inevitable offshoot of the Bolshevik Revolution. More than one route was conceivable after Lenin's death. If Bukharin had become leader, the route taken would have been different from that followed by Stalin. Collectivization and industrialization could have occurred without Stalin's extremes, and doubtless with much accompanying brutality – if not on a Stalinist scale. The reduction of the structures of rule to vehicles of personal despotism (backed by an extravagant personality cult) and destruction of party cadres were not predestined to follow from Lenin's style of leadership. Terror was an inbuilt part of Lenin's system, but Stalin gave it an altogether new dimension. Lenin had not turned it against the party itself. Stalin did precisely that. The preconditions for Stalin's rule had indeed been established under Lenin.[60] That they could give rise to Stalin's tyranny was built into the system that he inherited. The extremes to which Stalin took the system that he inherited, however, are such that they amounted not to a new system or break with Leninism, but nevertheless to a distortion which plainly bore his personal imprint.

The speed with which change was introduced as soon as Stalin died itself indicates how deeply the system of rule had become infused during his long years in power with the traits of his paranoid personality. Once he was dead, it could free itself of the distortions. With his death and the traumatic reckoning with his personality cult that followed under Khrushchev the – horrific – dynamism oozed out of the system. Yet in its structural essentials the system remained in place. Under Brezhnev it turned into repressive, but stable, conservative authoritarianism. Though there was no return to mass terror, it remained recognizably the system of government that had taken its form under Stalin. To adapt Marxist terminology, Stalin mutilated – and in part destroyed – the superstructure, but retained the base. As soon as he was dead, the superstructure could be refashioned on a base that remained in all essentials solid until the collapse of the Soviet state nearly four decades later.

At Stalin's death the Soviet Union was no longer a backward peasant society and a weak state open to the threat of invasion from enemy countries to the east as well as the west. The war had been the crucible from which the Soviet Union had emerged as a nascent superpower. This was obviously not solely Stalin's achievement. But he certainly had more than a little to do with it. Could the Soviet Union have industrialized, militarized and organized so rapidly to defeat Hitler's armies had Stalin not been in power? It seems highly unlikely. At barely imaginable human cost, a phenomenal social and economic transformation had taken place. By 1953 the Soviet Union, in possession of a burgeoning nuclear arsenal, was a rival to the USA, a giant on the global stage and soon capable of sending a man into space. The transition from peasant society to superpower was not the least important part of Stalin's legacy.

The Cold War was, of course, part of the same legacy. The mutual distrust between the Soviet Union and its former wartime allies was inevitable, and quick to develop. The countries of central and eastern Europe that fell within the Soviet sphere of influence soon had Stalinist puppet governments, intensifying western fears of Soviet expansionism. Churchill's famous 'Iron Curtain' speech in 1946 sharpened the focus on the responsibility of the Soviet Union for the division of Europe. Western anxieties grew. But Stalin's priority in Europe was a secure buffer zone, not expansion. So, for instance, he did not help the Greek communists to gain power. Nor did he give tangible support to the sizeable communist parties in France and Italy. (In the Far East it was different: his support was important in the communist rise to power in China.)[61] In the immediate post-war years he was anxious not to provoke the West, aware that his devastated country could not compete with American military strength, and fearful that the United States might use its initial nuclear advantage to attack the Soviet Union. The early mutual distrust of the former allies hardened and from 1947 became set in stone. Once Stalin had refused Marshall Aid for the Eastern bloc countries that year – to accept would have undermined Soviet dominance in its satellite states – the Cold War took its defining shape. It would pose a threat to world peace for over forty years.

The personal impact of Stalin on the rule of his Eastern bloc minions was evident. As long as he lived, the leaders of the states within the Iron Curtain were in his thrall, their peoples ruthlessly subjugated by the repressive agencies of police and party. After his death the climate changed abruptly. Within three years risings against Soviet rule took place in the German Democratic Republic and Hungary, and there was serious unrest in Poland. But even after Stalin the systems whose construction he had so strongly influenced proved powerful enough to sustain themselves – with varying degrees of difficulty – until the 1980s.

For decades after his death, judgement on Stalin's place in history was almost entirely and universally negative. Western Soviet apologists sought to portray Stalin as an aberration in Soviet history. The Soviet Union itself tried to airbrush him out of its history. Neither attempt worked. Stalin has come increasingly to be seen as an integral part of Soviet history, not a break in it – a product of unique conditions in the 1920s whose despotism wrought a terrible price on his country but steered it to a historic victory, leaving a legacy that shaped the country until its end. Gorbachev rightly condemned Stalin as one of history's greatest criminals. Yeltsin continued the denigration. Putin, however, altered the tone by praising the achievements of the Soviet state in Stalin's era, though without rehabilitating Stalin himself, and by invoking continuities of Russian and Soviet past greatness.[62] Putin's strategy of restoring Russia (the main legatee of the Soviet Union) as a global great power and reshaping attitudes towards the Soviet past has affected attitudes towards Stalin. In 2003, on the fiftieth anniversary of the dictator's death, an opinion survey of 1,600 Russians registered a 53 per cent approval rating for Stalin. Only 27 per cent agreed that he was 'a cruel, inhuman tyrant responsible for the deaths of millions'.[63]

Such views represent the vagaries of manipulated opinion. But, despite the vast array of material that has become available since the end of the Soviet Union, historical assessment of Stalin – how he was possible, how he could exercise such terroristic control over a huge country for so long, how to assess his achievements – has in many respects become less straightforward and more open to differing interpretation. Whichever way the arguments lean, what seems clear, however, is that Stalin, though a horrific personality who drenched his country in killing and bloodshed, made a deeper mark on European history in the twentieth century than anyone else, perhaps apart from Hitler. Given a unique context that offered the necessary structural conditions, Stalin provides a self-evident case of the importance of the individual in history.

Churchill on the deck of the battleship HMS *Prince of Wales*, during the Atlantic Conference off the coast of Newfoundland in August 1941, at which he discussed war strategy with President Roosevelt. The two leaders agreed British and American goals for the post-war world, laid down in the Atlantic Charter.

5

WINSTON CHURCHILL

Britain's War Hero

Probably no politician in a European democracy has wielded more power than Winston Churchill did between 1940 and 1945. Certainly none has had such accolades bestowed on him. He has frequently been portrayed as the quintessence of historical greatness, the saviour of his nation – even more: the saviour of liberty in the western world. The force of personality has seldom if ever been elevated to such a determining role in history – in a positive way, as contrasted with the catastrophic impact of the personality of dictators.

Yet Churchill was in the main a political failure before 1940. And his leadership in the decade after 1945 – the years of political opposition until 1951, then as Prime Minister again until 1955 – would not have resulted in the effusions of undiluted praise for a political titan had it not been for what preceded them. The assessment of personality and power depends heavily in this case, therefore, on the judgement of Churchill's role during the Second World War. No one was more aware of this than Churchill himself, who consciously sought to shape the way posterity would view his wartime leadership in his six-volume war memoirs. *The Second World War*, published between 1948 and 1954, reached a global readership of millions.[1]

PERSONALITY AND
STYLE OF LEADERSHIP

It was in the exceptional conditions of British democracy at war that Churchill's personality played a vital role. The personal qualities that before the war had so often proved ineffective and after the war were subordinated to economic and geopolitical determinants that Churchill was unable to control, were tailor-made for the emergency conditions of the war. They operated in a democracy – though one transformed by crisis into an unusually malleable vehicle for the leadership of a commanding personality.

Churchill was extremely egotistical – highly opinionated with the innate self-confidence typical of the British aristocracy into which he had been born. His social background also gave him a strong sense of duty and purpose, with that inbred feeling of entitlement and authority that belonged to a member of the ruling elite. His temperament exuded belligerence. He instinctively looked to aggression, not defence. He was resolute and ruthless, physically courageous. He was given to bold, quick decisions – a characteristic that had long brought him the reputation of being reckless, of lacking sound judgement. He possessed unshakeable self-belief, a restless disposition and ingrained authoritarian tendencies. He used his sharp wit and quick, often sarcastic repartee to cutting effect in debate. And it took much to counter his strength of conviction and powers of persuasion. His innate energy and dynamism were accompanied by impatience and outbursts of bad temper. Even his wife, Clementine, felt it necessary in 1940 to upbraid him for his 'rough, sarcastic & overbearing manner', his 'irascibility & rudeness'.[2] But he could also be generous-spirited and magnanimous. He evoked deep affection and loyalty in those around him. 'Action this day' became his watchword. He drove the government relentlessly forward.

With everything subordinated to the war effort, the scope of agencies of democratic control on the executive powers of the government through parliamentary scrutiny and, especially, public opinion was curtailed. Parliament, of course, still sat, Cabinet committees met, newspapers appeared, the radio was more important than ever. But censorship, official and – even more important, perhaps – 'self-censorship', meant the suppression or omission of anything sounding unpatriotic.

As the main body of government, the Cabinet met regularly. But Churchill wasted Cabinet time by not reading relevant papers beforehand or verbose disquisitions on something that had just caught his attention. The crucial decisions were taken by a small War Cabinet, at first of only five members, later eight. Churchill was the dominant figure, quickly and completely asserting his authority. He listened to advice and often took it. There was a widely held and justified view, nevertheless, that he was over-dependent on the counsel of two personal cronies, Lord Beaverbrook (in charge of war production) and Brendan Bracken (Minister of Information), who did not belong to the War Cabinet.[3] There was also resentment at the strong influence of his chief scientific adviser, Professor Frederick Lindemann (an Oxford physics professor). Wartime crisis-management gave full rein to his inbuilt dictatorial tendencies. What had once been seen as impulsive or reckless could now be regarded as decisive and dynamic.

As Defence Minister as well as Prime Minister, the direction of the war was his domain. Foreign affairs were in principle the business of Anthony Eden, appointed Foreign Secretary in December 1940 to replace Lord Halifax (dispatched to Washington as British Ambassador). In practice, however, Churchill effectively ran foreign policy, too. He was little interested in domestic affairs and depended here heavily on the Labour politicians he incorporated in his government: Clement Attlee, the Labour leader and highly efficient coordinator of home affairs, Ernest Bevin, whom Churchill appointed to the key position of Minister of Labour, and Herbert Morrison, from October 1940 Home Secretary and Minister of Home Security. The vital work they carried out on the home front gave Churchill the freedom to devote his copious energies to running the war.

His strategic thinking was, however, often flawed and needed the corrective of his service chiefs of staff. In the second half of the war his power declined as he was forced to yield increasingly to American imperatives, both in strategic and in geopolitical planning. In fact, when it came to the 'Big Three' conferences that were to lay down the post-war order in Europe, the real power was wielded by neither Churchill nor Roosevelt, but by the Soviet dictator, Joseph Stalin. What counted was less personality than military realities.

THE LONG, WINDING ROAD TO POWER

Winston Churchill was born on 30 November 1874 at Blenheim Palace, near Oxford. The palace had been granted to his illustrious ancestor the Duke of Marlborough (whose biography he would write) following the famous victory over the French at the battle of Blenheim in 1704. Winston's father, Lord Randolph Churchill, rose to be Chancellor of the Exchequer and was regarded as a future Prime Minister until recklessness and political mistakes ended his career. He died in 1895 aged only forty-five, probably of a syphilis-related illness. Winston's American-born mother, Jennie Jerome, a socialite of noted beauty, had a number of lovers (including the Prince of Wales) and two further marriages after the death of Lord Randolph, dying in 1921. His parents were distant figures who placed career and socializing before the relationship with their son (and his younger brother, Jack). Winston sought love and attention in his sad and plaintive letters home during his unhappy years away at boarding school; his behaviour at Harrow (one of England's leading public schools) was unruly, and his academic performance undistinguished. Most of his letters went unanswered. What replies he did receive were cold and dismissive. It was appalling emotional cruelty. Winston nevertheless drew closer to his mother over the years. His father he idolized, though he tried in vain to win his approval. The need to emulate, then surpass, his father's achievements stayed with him. Late in life he was still justifying himself to the dead father who had been convinced that his son would be a failure.[4]

The forty-five years that followed his father's death, down to 1940, were indeed hardly an unqualified success. As a young army officer and war correspondent, he was keen to see action and became well known after escaping from captivity during the Boer War. After entering politics in 1899 his precocious talent was quickly recognized, and he had the connections in high places to further his advancement. In 1907 he was prophesying that he would be Prime Minister in little over a decade.[5] Already the previous year he had become a government minister as Under-Secretary of State for the Colonial Office in the Liberal administration. (As a devotee of free trade, he had defected in 1904 from the Conservatives over the introduction of tariffs on goods imported from outside the empire.) He joined the Cabinet as President of the Board of Trade in 1908, was Home Secretary in 1910, and First Lord of the Admiralty in 1911 (a post he particularly cherished). In 1917 he was appointed Minister of Munitions, in 1919

Secretary of State for War and Air, and briefly in 1921–2 Secretary of State for the Colonies. Between 1924 and 1929 he held the high office of Chancellor of the Exchequer in the Conservative administration – he had rejoined the Conservatives in 1924.

His long years in government before entering opposition at the defeat of the Conservatives in the general election of 1929 had given him unusually wide experience. But accusations of lack of judgement dogged him. Stanley Baldwin, three times Prime Minister between 1924 and 1937, had privately remarked:

> When Winston was born lots of fairies swooped down on his cradle [with] gifts – imagination, eloquence, industry, ability, and then came a fairy who said 'No person has a right to so many gifts', picked him up and gave him such a shake and twist that with all these gifts he was denied judgement and wisdom.[6]

The view that Churchill, though possessing great ability, lacked sound judgement was widely held and followed him throughout most of his career. It seemed likely, until the dramatic shift in external circumstances in the late 1930s, to prevent him ever attaining his ambition to be Prime Minister.

His headstrong temperament had indeed contributed to serious mistakes. He stepped down from his cherished post as First Lord of the Admiralty, humiliated by the heavy responsibility he bore for the ill-fated naval operation to force a passage through the Dardanelles in 1915, the prelude to the disastrous Gallipoli campaign which led to over 100,000 casualties. A Conservative newspaper described him that year as 'a danger to the country'.[7] As Chancellor of the Exchequer his decision in 1925 to return to the Gold Standard was widely seen then and later to have been economically damaging. Churchill later came even to agree with his critics that he had been a poor Chancellor.[8] The rich promise of his early years had not been fulfilled.

Nothing suggested, even so, that he would be out of government for a decade. His years 'in the wilderness' (as he called them) seemed to mark the end of a career that had begun with such high expectations. He was at least able to devote more time to writing, which included work on the fourth volume of his *Marlborough* biography, and to his numerous hobbies such as painting, bricklaying and bee-keeping. Even without his ministerial salary, his prolific literary output earned him a sizeable income. But his extravagant lifestyle, and the costs of maintaining and renovating the house and estate at Chartwell in Kent (his home since the early 1920s), of lavish entertainment, of the salaries of fourteen serving staff, and of the upkeep of his family (his wife, Clementine, and their four by now grown-up expensive offspring), meant that he had no difficulty in spending it, and more besides.

Central to Churchill's character was his sense of history. As a scion of the English aristocracy, steeped in the values of the Victorian and Edwardian eras, he saw history as the progress of human civilization that had reached its apogee in Britain's parliamentary institutions and in the British empire – at its height as he approached adulthood. In some ways he belonged more to the nineteenth century than to the twentieth century.[9] He imbibed as a schoolboy the deeds of the great heroes of England's past who had led Britain to pre-eminence. His belief in the empire was the cornerstone of all that he did, defence of the empire his key motivating force. He shared the views of most people at the time – and certainly of the ruling class – that the 'white race' was superior to the 'natives' of the empire, towards whom he felt a sense of paternalistic duty. Throughout his life he regularly used racist expressions that future generations would regard as repellent.[10]

His already dated imperialist mentality lay behind his diehard rejection of even limited constitutional reform in India, which put him at odds with most of his party. He was again on the wrong side of government orthodoxy in his strong backing for Edward VIII at the Abdication Crisis of 1936. But what chiefly brought him mounting unpopularity was his repeated demand for urgent, extensive rearmament. The information reaching him from a number of unofficial but reliable confidential sources on the scale of German rearmament alarmed him deeply. His warnings fell largely on deaf ears, however, as the government, mostly backed by the opposition, moved from a policy of disarmament to one of appeasement, if belatedly backed by rapid rearmament. No one doubted Churchill's eloquence. But his speeches in the House of Commons condemning British defence policy were ineffective. His views remained those of a small minority. His speech in the debate that followed Chamberlain's return in seeming triumph from the Munich Conference in 1938, at which Britain had yielded to

Hitler's demand for the annexation of the Sudetenland region of Czech-oslovakia, was delivered to a mainly hostile House of Commons.

Churchill's denunciation of Nazi Germany had been consistent since Hitler's takeover of power in 1933 (and his early admiration for Mussolini dissolved as Fascist Italy allied itself with Germany). His long-standing hatred of Bolshevism had by the late 1930s given way to recognition that a Soviet alliance was necessary to counter appeasement and prevent war. But his advocacy of a 'grand alliance' that included the Soviet Union was in vain. Only when the Germans occupied the rump of what had been Czechoslovakia in March 1939 did the recognition dawn in Britain that war in Europe was almost certain and that Churchill had been right all along about the danger posed by Nazism. On 3 September 1939, the day of the British declaration of war on Germany, Churchill was recalled to government, once again as First Lord of the Admiralty, the post he had left in humiliation nearly quarter of a century earlier.

Had he died before 1939, Churchill might have been known 'as the man who got the Royal Navy ready for the Great War'.[11] More likely, he would have been best remembered for the Dardanelles disaster.

PRECONDITIONS OF POWER

Churchill certainly introduced new energy and a sense of urgency into naval planning. It was unlikely, however, that he would replace Neville Chamberlain as Prime Minister. He had become an outsider in his own party. As late as July 1939 four-fifths of Conservative backbench Members of Parliament did not even want him in the Cabinet.[12] Even after he had returned to government at the start of the war, senior figures in Whitehall thought his lack of judgement ruled him out as a future Prime Minister.[13] Churchill, however, was instinctively drawn to power. He saw himself as a 'man of destiny'. Of the moment he was appointed Prime Minister, he later wrote: 'It felt as if I were walking with destiny, and that all my past life had been but a preparation for this hour.'[14] It was, however, chance, not destiny, that brought him to the premiership in 1940.

Chance operated, though, within a structural framework determined by the sharp deterioration in international relations during the preceding two decades, the rise of German power, the growing threat from Japan in the Far East and Britain's imperial overstretch in maintaining defence spending and facing colonial independence movements. Policies of disarmament, and then, when they had obviously failed, appeasement, were shaped by this context.

What had begun under Baldwin had been pursued by his successor, Neville Chamberlain, to the point at which Britain's political, economic and military weakness had been laid bare and the threat to the country was all too obvious. Churchill's consistent opposition, which had brought him so many brickbats during the 1930s, was now lauded as prophetic. Attitudes towards him were starting to change. Nevertheless, there was no great threat to Chamberlain's primacy during the strange months of the 'phoney war'. He was still extremely popular within the Conservative Party, and the structures of power that supported his premiership remained intact. It needed more than just the failed appeasement policy to topple him.

Change came from an unexpected turn of events. Chamberlain's foolish remark on 4 April 1940 that Hitler had 'missed the bus' by not invading France and Britain quickly came back to bite him. Five days later, German troops invaded and swiftly overran Denmark and Norway. This pre-empted British plans, which Churchill had strongly promoted, to mine Norwegian waters in order to cut off German iron-ore supplies being shipped from Narvik. Initial naval battles (with losses on both sides) were the prelude to a disastrous land campaign in northern Norway that ended ignominiously with the evacuation of Allied troops. Tactical mistakes, organizational problems and intelligence failures all played their part. There was much rancour within the British military command, much of it rightly directed at Churchill, the architect of the Narvik expedition. Some advocated his dismissal. Had that occurred, any chance of succeeding Chamberlain would have disappeared. As it was, public fury at the debacle largely bypassed Churchill and turned on the head of the government, Chamberlain.

The heated debate on Norway in the House of Commons on 7–8 May saw Chamberlain under fire as never before. The entire debate centred on the question of confidence in the Prime Minister. And the humiliation in Norway was now linked to long-term failings and strategic errors on rearmament and appeasement (with the effect that the spotlight was deflected from Churchill's role in the Norway campaign). Explicit demands were made for a change of leadership. Churchill remained overtly loyal towards Chamberlain. But his friends in the House sang his praises. The government won the vote (though forty-one Conservatives voted against the government, and around a further fifty abstained).[15] It was a fatal moral defeat for Chamberlain.[16] It quickly became clear that he had no way out. Only the timing of his resignation and the question of his successor remained open.

It was far from certain that his successor would be Churchill. In fact, this at first appeared unlikely. Some in the House of Commons even spoke of the possible recall of David Lloyd George, who had been Prime Minister during the First World War.[17] That was wild talk. The favourite to become the next Prime Minister was, however, not Churchill, but Lord Halifax, the Foreign Secretary. Halifax was preferred by Chamberlain and most of the Conservative Party. Labour opposition leaders, who rejected any participation in a government led by Chamberlain, had made it plain that they were ready to serve in a Halifax administration. An obvious problem was that Halifax had no seat in the House of Commons, though neither Chamberlain nor King George VI (who also favoured Halifax) saw that as an insuperable obstacle. The bigger issue was whether Halifax actually wanted to be Prime Minister. The very thought of it gave him stomach ache. He was acutely aware of his lack of military expertise and feared he would be little more than a cypher in an administration dominated by Churchill, who would take charge of defence and would in practice be running the war effort anyway. Halifax's diffidence – or was it a hidden calculation that Churchill was bound to fail? – and Churchill's assertiveness proved decisive. Halifax did not want the heavy responsibility; Churchill wanted nothing more. So when Chamberlain visited Buckingham Palace on the afternoon of 10 May to tender his resignation as Prime Minister, it was to recommend Churchill, not Halifax, to assume the highest office in the land.[18] Four men – Chamberlain, Churchill, Halifax and the Chief Whip, David Margesson – had between them determined who would lead Britain in the worst crisis the country had ever faced.

THE CRITICAL DECISION

Britain's history – indeed, the history of Europe and the western world – would have been very different had Lord Halifax, not Churchill, directed the country's fortunes that year. Halifax had many qualities. But, as he himself recognized, they were not those of a war leader. He would not have been a suitable Prime Minister in 1940. His modest, self-effacing character and coolly rational manner would in many circumstances have been regarded as significant attributes. At a time of great national crisis, however, they were not what was needed. Halifax lacked the capacity to inspire. And he had been a central figure in the government that had pursued the failed policy of appeasement. Churchill, in contrast, was now seen generally to have been right all along in his largely isolated frontal opposition to that policy. His ebullience, indomitable spirit of defiance and pugnacious dynamism were precisely what was required to uphold, then raise, morale when the outlook was at its bleakest. He had the capacity to instil hope. His emotional patriotism, expressed in his inimitable oratory – magnificent cadences, literary flourishes of (somewhat archaic) language – proved inspirational. Rational assessment and cool analysis could not match it in the prevailing circumstances. Churchill's traits of character had at times in his long career been a handicap. But at this juncture, his personality was decisive.

It is hard to conceive of worse conditions in which, at the age of sixty-five, Churchill assumed power. The German offensive in western Europe began the very day that he was appointed Prime Minister, 10 May, advancing with breakneck speed towards the English Channel. Within two weeks Holland had surrendered, Belgium was on the verge of doing so, and the fall of France was looking certain. Britain's main continental ally, up to now still reckoned to be a great power, was facing calamitous defeat. By 25 May the British Expeditionary Force was trapped as it fell back on Dunkirk. The military leadership offered little hope of evacuation. The army and its equipment were presumed largely lost. Even worse was contemplated: British Intelligence thought a German invasion probable in the near future. Establishing air superiority was deemed to be the only real chance of avoiding it. Never had Britain stood in such extreme peril. Voices of despondency, if not outright defeatism, could be heard among those fully aware of the dire situation. There was talk of the final defeat of Britain, the end of the British empire, that everything was finished.

As the great crisis raged, Churchill was not as dominant as he would soon become. He himself plainly recognized his dependence on Chamberlain (who remained the leader of the Conservative Party until his death from cancer in November) and also on Halifax, kept on as Foreign Secretary. The other members of the small War Cabinet that Churchill had immediately set up on becoming Prime Minister were the Labour leader, Clement Attlee, and Arthur Greenwood (deputy Labour leader). Archie Sinclair (the Liberal leader and Secretary of State for Air) was sometimes invited to attend.

It was here that arguably the most critical decision in British history took place in late May 1940.[19] At stake was whether Britain would take soundings about a possible negotiated peace or would despite its evident military weakness fight on. It was a question at this extraordinarily perilous moment not of fighting on to final victory, but of holding out and hoping that Britain's fortunes would improve over the coming months.[20] Discussion on whether to seek terms went on at the War Cabinet during successive days between 25 and 28 May. Lord Halifax favoured exploring Italian brokerage of a peace conference, possibly leading to a negotiated settlement to end the war. Some territorial concessions (including perhaps Malta, Gibraltar and Suez) would doubtless be necessary, though if Britain did not like the terms, argued Halifax, it could always reject them. Halifax was as patriotic as Churchill. Like Churchill, he aimed to preserve Britain's independence. But, coolly rationalizing Britain's military weakness, he looked not unreasonably to a diplomatic solution.

Churchill's temperament was entirely different. He spoke with passion and emotion, instinctively favouring defiance and readiness to fight on in the hope that America would come to Britain's aid before it was too late. Still, he blended emotion with reasoned argument. Any approach to Mussolini would undermine Britain's fighting potential, he declared. Hitler would be sure to impose terms which would drastically weaken Britain. None that might be offered would be acceptable. The country still possessed the power to resist. Showing

Hitler that he could not conquer or break Britain was the only sensible option. To fight and be defeated would result in no worse terms than were currently on offer. He rejected Halifax's approach, therefore, as futile and dangerous.

Discussion was at times heated. Halifax thought 'Winston talked the most frightful rot' and despaired at his 'passion of emotion when he ought to make his brain think and reason'.[21] Nevertheless, Churchill's assessment was accepted by Attlee, Greenwood and, eventually, Chamberlain too. Halifax became isolated in the War Cabinet, even more so after Churchill had addressed the remainder of the Cabinet and received warm backing for his defiant stance. The Foreign Secretary eventually bowed to the collective decision, unwilling to undermine unity. He accepted the decision not to seek terms, and to fight on.[22] Churchill had played the central part in reaching a resolution of fundamental importance.

Only a week after the conclusion of these momentous debates in the War Cabinet, the evacuation from Dunkirk was completed. Beyond all expectations, and when all had been thought lost, 338,000 British, French and Belgian troops were brought across the Channel. On 4 June, Churchill could report the 'miracle of deliverance' at Dunkirk to the House of Commons. His patriotic, defiant speech became justly famous. He succeeded in turning a humiliating defeat into a national triumph. His own standing soared. His authority as Britain's unchallengeable war leader was completely established.

There are few instances where the impact of personality in a decision of vital consequence is so clearly demonstrated. Had Lord Halifax, a man of ability, intelligence and the utmost integrity, as anxious as Churchill to do the best for his country, been Prime Minister in May 1940, Britain's fortunes would surely have been altogether different. Pursuing terms to end the war would have been tantamount to a defeat. The morale of the population would have sunk like a stone. Hitler, as Churchill argued, would have imposed damaging terms in any settlement, guaranteed to ensure Britain's permanent subordinated status. A reasonable speculation is that Britain's fate would have been similar in fashion to that of France following the armistice signed on 21 June. Independence and freedom would have been lost. Britain would have become in effect a satellite of Germany. The armed forces would have been either taken over or neutralized. Halifax, his job done in facilitating peace negotiations, would have been removed – possibly imprisoned or worse. A puppet government, perhaps under the British fascist leader Oswald Mosley or the former wartime leader and Hitler-admirer David Lloyd George, would have been set up. Possibly ex-King Edward VIII would have been reinstalled as monarch. Occupation of the country, or part of it, would probably have been unnecessary, given a government ready to toe the line laid down in Berlin, including implementation of racial legislation.

The empire would not have been destroyed, though there would have been significant territorial concessions, and what remained would have been subjected to German interests and influence. The royal family would probably have been spirited away to Canada. Churchill, had he not been captured and executed, might have gone, too, and tried to rally resistance from abroad. The likelihood of any help to an occupied, at any rate defenceless and pro-German, Britain from the USA would, however, have disappeared. With Britain as well as France out of the war, and American supplies of arms ruled out, Germany would have been victorious in western Europe, and Hitler would have been free to turn all his attention to the war he actually wanted, against the Soviet Union. A pro-German government in Britain would have supported the war and most likely been implicated in the horrific crimes against humanity that accompanied it, and in implementing the Holocaust. A British contingent could have found itself fighting on the side of Germany in the icy wastes and endless steppes of Russia.

That this fate was avoided, and that Britain emerged from the Second World War not as a defeated, conquered and subjugated nation, but among the victors, is in part at least owing to the power of personality – the fact that Churchill, not Halifax, was Prime Minister in May 1940.

WAR LEADER

Although the threat of invasion receded after the Battle of Britain in September, and the almost nightly bombing of London and other cities eventually ended (before beginning again in the last year of the war), there were many setbacks and bad times ahead before war fortunes irreversibly turned towards the end of 1942. In this long, dark phase of the war it is difficult to imagine that any British politician could have been capable of matching Churchill's ability to stimulate and uphold the will to fight.

His main contact with the general public was through the BBC. Between a half and three-quarters of the population listened to Churchill's major broadcast wartime speeches. Many were indeed moved, roused, exhilarated, emboldened by his soaring rhetoric.[23] But the impact of the speeches should not be exaggerated. [24] Surveys of responses showed that the Prime Minister's high-flown style of oratory was far from universally admired. As many were frightened as inspired by his speech on 19 May 1940, delivered during the relentless German advance through western Europe. And more than half responded negatively to his speech on 15 February 1942, announcing the fall of Singapore. People in each case were reacting to dismal news, rather than specifically to Churchill's delivery of it. Criticism of his speeches rose when he had bad news to convey after military reverses and was far lower when he could report military successes. Reaction to the speeches, positive or negative, was in any case short-lived. The popular mood was boosted by a well-received speech, but not for long.

German assessments of their own wartime propaganda distinguished between 'mood', which it was accepted would fluctuate in accordance with positive or negative news, and 'morale', which they claimed (with decreasing truthfulness) remained high. Something similar could be said of Britain. However transient the response was to individual speeches that reflected war fortunes, Churchill's stance and demeanour, his conviction that the British people would overcome adversity, his unshakeable belief in victory, the spirit of defiance through solidarity that he conveyed did contribute substantially to strengthening and maintaining morale. And the speeches built trust in Churchill's leadership.

His physical appearance – short, squat, with a face that advertised pugnaciousness – seemed to embody the readiness to fight. And he let himself be seen by his people (unlike Hitler, who shied away from public appearances and speeches once the war turned sour for Germany). He paid morale-boosting visits to areas that had suffered greatly from bombing, and visited troops at the front. Hoisting his homburg hat on his stick, the omnipresent cigar in his mouth, displaying the V for Victory sign at every opportunity, he epitomized the fighting spirit. He wanted to be close to the action and had to be held back at times from exposing himself recklessly to danger. The King himself had to forbid him from accompanying the D-Day landings in 1944. His popularity was astonishing. Almost throughout the war, around four-fifths of the population approved of his wartime leadership; at times his popularity rating was over 90 per cent.[25] The overwhelming majority of the British population plainly, and with good reason, thought Churchill was the right man to lead the war effort.

Whether he was the right man for post-war reconstruction was a different matter. Expectations of what would follow victory were raised by the publication of the Beveridge Report, which outlined the framework of a future welfare state. The Labour Party seemed, in the eyes of a majority of those questioned in opinion surveys (which began in June 1943), more likely than the Conservatives to implement the far-reaching changes. For the last two years of the war, Labour was ahead of the Conservatives on voter intentions.[26] The often effective administration of domestic policy by Labour ministers in the wartime coalition was an advertisement for the party's potential as a government. The Tories, on the other hand, remained besmirched by memories of appeasement. Churchill's election defeat in 1945 was less surprising than it appeared.

Just after the war ended Churchill voiced irritation at the suggestion that his speeches had been the decisive factor in Britain's war effort. He emphasized instead that he had 'made all the main military decisions'.[27] As Prime Minister (and also Minister of Defence), the decisions were plainly his to make. But does his claim understate the part his military leaders played in reaching those decisions? Did he override or implement military advice?

His personality, military knowledge, keenness to be involved in all stages of strategic and operational planning and his intervention even in the smallest details of preparation meant that conflict with his military advisers was preordained. He did not hesitate to dismiss generals, even those he knew well and liked personally, where he adjudged that new leadership was necessary. Among the generals he removed were

Ironside, Gort, Dill, Dowding, Wavell and Auchinleck. Revitalization of the fighting forces through replacement of commanders worn down by pressure and lacking the requisite dynamism lay behind the changes. Of course, the decisions followed close advice from the military high command, in particular General Sir Alan Brooke, commander of the home forces in 1940–41, thereafter Chief of the Imperial General Staff, but they were hard personnel choices, and responsibility lay indubitably with Churchill himself. The changes were mainly justified. The replacement of Auchinleck by General Sir Harold Alexander in August 1942 as commander-in-chief in the Middle East, then the appointment days later of General Bernard Montgomery to take command of the demoralized Eighth Army were significant in turning the tables on Rommel in the desert war in north Africa.

The appointment of Brooke himself showed that Churchill did not want 'yes-men' as his military leaders. Brooke was not only an able strategist and excellent organizer, but forthright, stubborn and strong- and independent-minded, ready to confront Churchill's forceful opinions with those of his own.[28] Their clashes were frequent and tempestuous. Brooke's diary entries reveal the extent of their regular conflict and at times paint a coruscating picture of Churchill's war leadership. In September 1944, for instance, he wrote of the Prime Minister's 'ridiculous arguments', that he 'knows no details, has only got half the picture in his mind, talks absurdities and makes my blood boil to listen to his nonsense'. Most of the population, Brooke went on, imagined him to be a strategic genius, with 'no conception [of] what a public menace he is and has been throughout this war'. Despite his anger, Brooke acknowledged Churchill's stature and unique attributes. 'Never have I admired and despised a man simultaneously to the same extent,' he wrote in the same diary entry.[29]

Churchill had a fertile and inventive mind. Some of his suggestions, such as that in 1942 to build 'floating harbours' for use in a future Allied landing, were of the greatest value.[30] He was prepared to be utterly ruthless in the pursuit of military objectives. In July 1940, supported by the War Cabinet, he ordered the destruction of the French fleet moored at Mers el-Kébir, the military harbour at Oran in Algeria, to prevent it falling into German hands, killing 1,297 French sailors.[31] However brutal, the action has generally been adjudged regrettable but justifiable. More controversial has remained the effectiveness, not to mention the moral justification, of the shift in February 1942 to a policy of relentless bombing of the German civilian population. Churchill gave the new commander-in-chief of Bomber Command, Arthur Harris, a free hand – grasped with alacrity – to devastate German cities, only getting moral qualms following the destruction of Dresden in 1945.[32] Churchill more than once considered the use of poison gas, but desisted when advised against doing so (on practical, not moral, grounds) by his military staff.[33]

He was extremely forceful in advancing his military preferences. But he did not always get his way. Major-General John Kennedy, Director of Military Operations for much of the war, remarked that 'many of his ideas are wild and unsound and impracticable', though 'in the end they are killed if they are not acceptable'.[34] One such decision where Churchill bowed to the advice of the service chiefs was in rejecting urgent French requests to send more planes to help in the defence of France in 1940.[35] They would certainly have been lost, and with them the potential to survive in the subsequent Battle of Britain. His overpowering, rash manner of decision-making, however, brusquely dismissing even tentative questioning, led to the mistake – which he himself later admitted – in dispatching troops to Greece in spring 1941.[36] He blamed the error on the Chief of the Imperial General Staff at the time, General Sir John Dill, though in fact it had been his own idea, which Dill – a different character than his successor, Brooke – had too pliantly agreed with. So had General Sir Archibald Wavell, commander-in-chief in the Middle East, whose army was seriously weakened by detachments being sent to Greece, and who felt disparaged and under pressure from Churchill.[37]

Dill had earlier given way, against his own preference for reinforcing the Far East, to Churchill's insistence – a bold decision in July 1940 at a time when Britain faced an immediate threat of invasion – on strengthening the British army to attack the Italians in north Africa.[38] Eventual victory in north Africa, after some serious setbacks, owed much to Churchill's determination to make that the crucial theatre of war in 1943. Backing the advice of his chiefs of staff, Churchill was adamant in rejecting American demands for a bridgehead in France as preliminary to the opening of a second front in France that year. His insistence on Operation Torch – the combined Allied landings in north Africa – led to the Allies winning supremacy in the Mediterranean (though the subsequent Italian campaign would bog down their advance for months to come).[39]

As strategic primacy passed to the Americans in the last years of the war, Churchill was forced to yield to the US President, Franklin D. Roosevelt, as supreme war leader. He had to bow to American interests in the planning of D-Day and to back down from his own preference for increased commitment to the Italian campaign. He remained unenthusiastic about Operation Overlord – the Normandy landings – until it happened.[40] He also had to give way on the landing in southern France that the Americans demanded, and he had to abandon the push northwards through the Balkans that he himself strongly favoured.[41] The American strategy was correct in both instances, Churchill's own propositions flawed.

As the war progressed and the incessant, extreme pressure on him took its toll, Churchill was more than ever prone to outbursts of temper. It was psychologically difficult for him to acknowledge that his own war leadership was counting for less. After the entry of the USA into the war in December 1941 Britain was gradually but inexorably reduced to playing second fiddle to the Americans. Churchill's own mistakes contributed to increasing American distrust in his judgement. The Americans refused, for instance, to back operations in the Aegean that Churchill, against Brooke's advice, insisted upon carrying out in October 1943 and which ended in humiliating defeats.[42] Churchill gave the impression, one of his private secretaries remarked towards the end of the war, that he was 'losing interest in the war because he no longer has control of military affairs'. He added that Churchill had earlier seen himself as the 'supreme authority to whom all military decisions were referred', but in the meantime he had become 'little more than a spectator'.[43] It evidently rankled.

Churchill had assiduously courted President Roosevelt in the first years of the war in the attempt to persuade the USA to enter the conflict. He was privately often critical of the US President, and became increasingly resentful of his junior status in their partnership. Still, they developed a bond of friendship as well as mutual respect, whatever the inevitable stresses. It initiated what is still regarded as Britain's 'special relationship' with the USA. Their extensive correspondence reflected the weighting of the relationship; Churchill sent 373 more messages than he received from Roosevelt.[44] They met on nine occasions during the war, the first of these the historic meeting in August 1941 on board ship in Placentia Bay, Newfoundland, when they agreed the principles for the future foundations of a free post-war world. Churchill recognized from the outset that American intervention was necessary for victory. His entreaties were unsuccessful, however, whatever Roosevelt's personal inclinations, in persuading the USA to enter the war until Japan bombed Pearl Harbor on 7 December 1941 and Germany declared war on America four days later. But the Lend-Lease programme, proposed by Roosevelt and agreed by Congress in March 1941, was already by then starting to provide Britain with vital goods and equipment.

Once the Soviet Union began in autumn 1942 to get the upper hand in the horrifically barbarous war on the eastern front, Churchill also had to adjust to the increasingly strong position of Stalin. At his first meeting with the Soviet dictator, in Moscow, in August 1942, with the situation looking grim as the Germans advanced towards the oilfields of the Caucasus, Churchill was assailed by a truculent Stalin about the absence of a second front in the west (a regular Soviet grievance before the Normandy landings in 1944). Yet over a late-night meal and a good deal of drink in Stalin's own apartment, the two leaders from such different backgrounds and political systems ended by establishing a basis of at least functionally friendly relations. In fact, in one-sided fashion it went beyond merely functionally friendly. Even knowing – since Stalin told him – of the Soviet dictator's responsibility for the mass killing of his own people, Churchill left Moscow actually liking him.[45] Despite knowledge of his heinous crimes, Churchill still admitted to liking him three years later.[46] He was taken in by Stalin's always cynical bonhomie. It suited Stalin to show his best face to Churchill. In reality, he continued to regard Churchill (and Roosevelt) with dislike and extreme distrust.

The conferences of the 'Big Three' between Tehran in November 1943 and Yalta in February 1945 revealed Churchill's increasing weakness as a world leader. Already at Casablanca in January 1943 (a meeting Stalin did not attend) Roosevelt was plainly in the ascendancy. Though consulted in advance, Churchill did not like the policy of 'unconditional surrender' which the President announced.[47] Yet Roosevelt went ahead, plainly in the driving seat. By Tehran, Churchill's junior role was barely disguised. Not the 'Big Three', but the 'Big Two and a Half' was one disparaging assessment of the meeting.[48] He was opposed by both Roosevelt and Stalin in his preference for the Mediterranean front over a landing in France, and duly gave way. Not well supported by Roosevelt (who was keen to ingratiate himself with Stalin) and aware that at the end of the war Stalin would 'be able to do as he pleases', Churchill felt 'appalled by his own impotence'.[49]

In his one meeting alone with Stalin at Tehran, Churchill already suggested moving Poland's borders westwards and indicated when he met Stalin in Moscow in October 1944 that the post-war border of Poland was 'settled'.[50] In fact, it was not finally settled until the difficult negotiations at Yalta, although the result was little different from what had been effectively agreed months earlier. Yalta showed more plainly than ever the basic reality that the advances of the Red Army had given Stalin the whip hand in any negotiations. Churchill and Roosevelt – the President was by now physically frail, in the last weeks of his life – were nevertheless over-ready to trust Stalin and to reach an accommodation with him. And, as at Tehran, Roosevelt was prepared to be privately critical of Churchill and to deal separately with Stalin when it suited him – as it did in agreeing conditions for the Soviet Union to enter the war against Japan and then simply presenting the agreement for Churchill to sign.[51]

Churchill achieved relatively little at the three-power conferences. He negotiated with vigour and as a practised card player played his relatively poor hand as well as possible. But his strong personality ran up against two other strong personalities, each of them heading far greater military powers. Conceivably, Clement Attlee, Churchill's successor as Prime Minister whose undemonstrative, uncharismatic, unassuming personality was the direct antithesis of Churchill's, yet acquitted himself adequately (in contrast to Churchill's own poor performance) at the Potsdam Conference that immediately followed the end of the war in Europe, would have done just as well in the negotiations. Churchill perhaps kept the Soviets out of intervening in Greece (in line with the secret arrangement he had made with Stalin during the visit to Moscow in October 1944). But more likely the Soviets had already decided that it was marginal to their interests to intervene in Greece.[52] And at Yalta he was successful in persuading Roosevelt and Stalin to give France a zone of occupation in post-war Germany, though this was not a matter of overwhelming importance to the emerging superpowers. Otherwise, his main achievement may well have been an indirect one: to ensure that Britain, well beyond the duration of the war, was treated as a great power when, in reality, its claim to that status was in steep decline.

Churchill's unique contribution as a war leader was unquestionably in sustaining the war effort and upholding morale during the darkest days of 1940.[53] For the remainder of the war, the singular dynamism and restless energy that he engendered in every aspect of the mobilization of forces were invaluable, even if his decision-making was often flawed, his interventions at times counterproductive, and his overbearing manner oppressive to those who had to deal with him on a regular basis. It is hard to imagine that anyone could have matched what he did. He provided direction, motivation and hope. His constant endeavours to persuade the Americans to provide funding and essential materiel eventually paid rich dividends, though in the second half of the war his importance diminished as the roles of the USA and USSR expanded. He made a major contribution to Allied victory – though by the end it was ultimately a subordinate one.

FADING POWERS

On 8 May 1945 the immense crowds in London celebrating the end of the war in Europe cheered Churchill as the hero who had led the country to victory. Less than two months later, in the general election of 5 July 1945, with the war against Japan still unfinished, he was voted out of office. To the outside world this was a shock. But the election had marked a return to some semblance of conventional party politics. It was a verdict on the Conservative Party, not on Churchill as a war leader. And Churchill, in a poorly led campaign, cast off the unifying mantle of the national war leader, becoming again a divisive party politician. He even absurdly as well as insultingly alleged that a Labour government (whose leaders had for five years sat with him in the War Cabinet) would resort to 'some form of

Gestapo'.[54] Such comments were unlikely to endear Churchill to the many in the industrial working class who had heartily disliked him before the war and associated him and the Conservatives more generally with the extreme hardship of the Great Depression. Many men, still in uniform, had not fought to return to an unlamented past, while younger voters hoped for a better future. Despite Churchill's wartime popularity, his electoral defeat as a party leader in 1945 was far from a bolt from the blue.[55]

He was, of course, fêted wherever he went in the world, regarded for the next twenty years as 'the greatest living Englishman'.[56] But, despite his unrivalled international prestige, his powers faded inexorably – a reflection of age and growing infirmity, but also of Britain's lesser role in global politics. His immense part in European and world history rests heavily on his leadership over five years of the war, not what came later. In 1946, however, he did make two important speeches, at Fulton, Missouri, on 5 March, and at Zurich on 19 September.

In his Fulton speech he spoke memorably of an 'Iron Curtain' that now divided Europe – a division that he and Roosevelt had in essentials agreed to, in fact, at Tehran and Yalta. The speech became famous. At the time, however, it was critically received in the USA and had no practical effect on the Cold War that was to set in fully the following year. Churchill's ingrained hatred of communism, suspended while the Soviet Union was Britain's wartime ally, fully returned once the war was over. In fact, he had been moving towards a policy of confrontation with Moscow even before hostilities ceased.[57] His wartime liking for Stalin was a bizarre anomaly. Like Roosevelt, he thought he 'understood' the Soviet dictator. His grotesque misreading of character was far from explicable by the needs of the wartime alliance. It amounted to an inexcusable blot on Churchill's record of belief in liberty and humanity, confined though this belief was to the western (especially Anglo-Saxon) world.

In his Zurich speech Churchill looked to European unity centred upon friendship between France and Germany, which he underlined as the essential basis of future peace. In a visionary declaration, voicing sentiments that he had first aired as early as 1930, he urged the creation of a 'United States of Europe'. His speech was inspirational for many in countries devastated by nationalist enmity and war. But it was ambiguous in meaning, a symbol of hope rather than a blueprint for action. He recognized that some merger of national sovereignty would be necessary in a future Europe. But that would not apply to Britain. His view was still, as in 1930, that 'We are *with* Europe but not *of* it'. The future 'United States of Europe' would not include Britain.[58]

Churchill gave further important speeches on European unity, at The Hague in 1948 and a year later in Strasbourg, at the foundation of the Council of Europe, which he had been instrumental in creating (and gave rise to the European Convention on Human Rights). But the Council was not the beginning of supranational federalism, rather an association of nation-states to promote democracy, human rights and the rule of law. The ambiguity in Churchill's future vision of Europe remained.[59] It gave encouragement to the federalists – though Churchill was not one of them. He was ultimately too wedded to a belief in British exceptionalism, in the empire and in the primacy of the Atlantic bonds of the 'English-speaking nations' to see Britain politically and economically integrated in the new Europe.

Churchill was not a greatly successful leader of the opposition, though he benefited from the growing unpopularity of the Labour government's stringent austerity measures as it sought to address the damaging costs of the war. Churchill had never won a general election as Conservative leader and was determined to do so. He narrowly failed in 1950, but when another election proved necessary the following year, on 26 October 1951, a month short of his seventy-seventh birthday, he was returned to 10 Downing Street with a comfortable majority (despite winning fewer votes than Labour). Politics was like a drug to him. He could not resist the chance to direct the country's affairs again. In some ways this was a pity. The last years as Prime Minister were not greatly distinguished, even though his administration – which largely continued Labour's social and welfare policies – flourished as the beneficiary of global economic growth, laying the basis for increased prosperity. Domestic politics did not greatly motivate him. They would have been scarcely different whoever had been Prime Minister. His interests were largely directed at foreign affairs (also essentially a continuation of Labour foreign policy). But Britain's actual status as a world power was by this time greatly diminished, and, despite his incomparable international prestige, so was the scope for Churchill to exert strong personal influence on international affairs. In any case, Eden, not Churchill, was effectively running British foreign policy by this time.[60]

Churchill was, like so many leaders who have tasted the elixir of power, unwilling to let it go. This was much to Eden's chagrin. He had long been the 'crown prince' awaiting with increased impatience the moment to succeed. Given his disastrous mishandling of the Suez crisis only a year after becoming Prime Minister, it was, however, perhaps a blessing that Churchill kept him waiting so long.

In June 1953 Churchill suffered a serious stroke which incapacitated him for over a month, though the public was left unaware that the government was functioning without a Prime Minister. He recovered, with some memory loss. Accolades, including the Nobel Prize for Literature in 1953, continued to come his way. His wartime achievements ensured his continuing popularity in Britain and elsewhere. But age was catching up with him. Amphetamines helped keep him going. Still he resisted the growing pressure to make way for Eden. He had almost to be prised out of Downing Street, finally departing from the scene of former glory on 5 April 1955 with a misplaced feeling that he was being hounded out of office.[61]

He remained a Member of Parliament until 1964, though seldom appearing in the House of Commons in his last years. His astonishing literary output had not come to a halt. He now had the time to complete a four-volume work that he had begun in the 1930s, *A History of the English-Speaking Peoples*, which reflected his view that history depended on the achievements of 'great men'. Much of his time was now spent at Chartwell, where he continued to entertain liberally, and on lengthy sojourns in the warmth of the Mediterranean or on luxurious cruising holidays. The potential for a nuclear war made him pessimistic about the future. He was oppressed, too, by the belief that Britain was in decline – its international weakness laid bare by the Suez crisis of 1956, its empire, whose defence had formed the essence of his own political career, visibly crumbling. His memory started to fade after a bad fall in Monte Carlo in 1962, and his remarkable physical powers of endurance finally waned.

He died on 24 January 1965, two weeks after suffering a major stroke. As many as 112 countries were represented at his state funeral on 30 January 1965 – an extraordinary spectacle of solemn grandeur watched by 350 million people around the world.[62]

LEGACY

Churchill's greatest legacy was in helping to preserve liberty, democracy and the rule of law in the western world. This has rightly ensured his lasting renown. The role of the individual in history has never been more clearly demonstrated than in the critical events of 1940. Without him history would have taken a different course.

Liberty, democracy and the rule of law are, however, susceptible to differing interpretations. Beneath the carapace of western civilization, how much of Churchill's legacy has stood the test of time? Perhaps a distinction should be drawn between the elements of his 'world-view', which proved transient, and the lasting impact on how Britain, especially, has viewed the Second World War.

Churchill's funeral marked in some ways the end of an era. The age of empire was ending, the age of European great powers already over. The world that Churchill had been born into ninety years earlier was already distant. The world of his political life and his grandest achievements was changing fast. But his own view of the world had largely been unaltered since the First World War.[63] His political aims were born of that time. His legacy was in this sense, therefore, bound to be short-lived.

He had fought to save the empire. But it was like putting a plaster on a gaping wound. By the time of his death the colonial empire – long since rebranded the Commonwealth, though Churchill preferred the old terminology – was close to its own demise as the unstoppable growth of independence movements forced imperial retreat. He had been pained at the granting of independence to India in 1947, and at the accompanying immense bloodshed that he had long foretold would be the inevitable consequence. By the late 1950s it was proving impossible to hold on to the overseas possessions. By the time he died only remnants of the one-time world empire were left. Perhaps this was in his mind when in his later years he said he had achieved nothing.[64]

When he died, Britain was still far from becoming a multicultural society. The numbers of immigrants then entering the country were small. Churchill's views on race had not materially altered since his youth. He foresaw problems arising 'if many coloured people settle here', he told the Cabinet in 1954. Another time he recommended 'Keep Britain White' as a good slogan.[65] Many people in the country, probably even a majority, shared such views at the time. Even so, attitudes towards race were already starting to change. The views he expressed to the Cabinet would before long mean the end of any mainstream politician's career. Despite extensive popular support for his views, Enoch Powell was sacked as a government minister the day after he had made a racist speech in 1968 and never held office again. Within three years of his death, Churchill's own views would have been publicly equally untenable. And despite the continued existence of racial prejudice, they would come to be regarded as repugnant by the vast majority of society.

Churchill's racial views were not the only part of his world-view that belonged to a rapidly fading age. Gender equality, sexual behaviour, declining deference, weakening class allegiances and 'green' politics were all changes, still in their infancy in the years following Churchill's death, which would gradually gather pace. The values held by Churchill were soon in retreat. In the political sphere, his emphasis on 'Tory democracy' – his brand of conservative paternalism – would be replaced from the 1980s onwards by a more thrusting, shrill and harsh doctrine of something more akin to nineteenth-century liberal individualism.

The question of Britain's relationship with Europe, posed by Churchill's Zurich speech of 1946, would long remain, however, a lingering but uncertain part of Churchill's legacy. He saw Britain, he had said in 1949, as 'an integral part of Europe'. He invariably gave priority, however, to the relationship with America (essential in his eyes to preserving Britain's diminishing role as a great power) and with the Commonwealth (whose economic importance to Britain was already in decline by the 1950s).[66] This was in accord with the policy towards Europe of both major parties during the 1950s. By the early 1960s the European Economic Community, established by the Treaty of Rome in 1957, was already shaping the process of European integration along lines different from those envisaged by Churchill in 1946. The Conservative government, though like the party divided on the issue, had come to see economic advantage for Britain from membership of the European Economic Community. Two years before de Gaulle vetoed Britain's application for membership in 1963, Churchill had written to his constituency chairman expressing his view 'that the Government are right to apply to join the European Economic Community'.[67] He was also, however, heard to voice exactly the opposite opinion, protesting about Britain's proposed entry.[68] As Britain's membership of the European Union became a more poisonous issue in British politics long after his death, Churchill was selectively quoted to support both sides of the argument. Britain's own standing in the world had changed dramatically by the time Europe became the central concern of British politics. How Churchill's own views might have changed in accordance with developments long after his death can only be the purest guesswork. As Hugo Young put it, Churchill was 'the father of misunderstandings' about Britain's part in Europe, the 'prime exponent of British ambiguity'.[69] On Europe, ambiguity was indeed his chief legacy.

Perhaps Churchill's most lasting impact, however, has been on British attitudes towards the Second World War and the part this has played in defining subsequent public consciousness. 'Standing alone', 'fight them on the beaches', 'never surrender', 'their finest hour' are sentiments that have become an intrinsic part of how Britain continues to view itself. The imagery is inextricable from Churchill's central role in the events at the time, largely built on the version he tells in his six-volume history of the war. A television poll in 2002 (with the customary absurdity of such 'league tables') declared Churchill to be the greatest Briton who ever lived. He is enshrined in the British view of the past and the present.[70] Churchill stands for the way the British see themselves. There was, of course, true valour in the fight against the odds in 1940. But over subsequent decades never-ending media preoccupation with the Second World War has produced enduring distortions of history. Churchill represents the 'myth' of British defiance and indomitability in the Second World War – the public memory of an epic story: that of greatness subsequently lost and followed by lengthy, irreversible national decline. This has not helped a medium-sized European power to come to terms with its place in the modern world.

De Gaulle in the midst of a large crowd during his first visit to Algiers in June 1958. His return to power the previous month had been occasioned by the belief that he alone could resolve the crisis in Algeria. Four years later he agreed to Algerian independence, making bitter enemies of those who had looked to him to save 'French Algeria'.

6

CHARLES DE GAULLE

Restoring France's Grandeur

For three decades, between 1940 and his death in 1970, Charles de Gaulle left an indelible mark on France and on Europe. Especially during the Second World War, his actions had global significance. He played a decisive role in French decolonization, especially ending the long and brutal war in Algeria. And the constitution he created in 1958 still exists today. In every respect he was a towering personality on the European and world stage.

From 1940 onwards he saw himself as an irreplaceable leader engaged on a sublime, historical mission: to save France. His habit of referring to himself in the third person, as 'de Gaulle', was suggestive of a distance between the actual person and the historic personage. The 'de Gaulle myth', established during the Second World War, was sustained when the wartime leader withdrew from political life amid the turmoil of post-war France, and reinvoked when he returned to power amid the crisis of 1958 to found the Fifth Republic. The historic image of de Gaulle represents a figure of national unity and greatness. The living de Gaulle was, in contrast, a person who engendered enormous loyalties but also enormous hatreds – a highly divisive figure who to both his friends and his enemies remained an enigma.

PERSONALITY AND IDEALS

Part of the enigma arose from the inner contradictions and paradoxes that made up this extraordinary personality. De Gaulle – born in November 1890 to a well-to-do bourgeois family, steeped in Catholic and patriotic values, with royalist leanings – was deeply conservative. He admired much about the ancient regime and would probably have felt at home as France's military leader under Louis XIV. His idealized vision of the past was shared by many French conservatives. But de Gaulle was far from rigidly adhering to a romanticized past or simply rejecting the France that had resulted from the Revolution. History gave him inspiration. But he recognized the need to accommodate the new and the modern – especially technological change. He was traditionalist and reactionary, yet also a modernizer – in military weaponry, the economy, political institutions and technology (using the new medium of television, for instance, to brilliant advantage). He was an imperialist, yet liquidated the French empire, a nationalist who nevertheless helped to embed France in the supranational framework of the European Community. He was dogmatically inflexible, yet tactically subtle. For many who had to deal with him, he was insufferable – arrogant, intolerant, abrasive, often curtly dismissive even of loyal supporters. But at the same time he could exude charm and attract deep devotion. He was an authoritarian who believed in the constitution, an opponent of party politics and democracy who adapted his instinctive authoritarianism to both. Left-wing opponents often mistakenly labelled him a fascist. He remained too wedded to constitutional rule for that. But he did want to make the constitution serve his form of authoritarianism – as it did after 1958.

A centrepiece in the complicated scaffolding of his mind was his elevated notion of the French state. For him, the state was the supreme political entity, the embodiment of the nation and its general interest, but intrinsically fragile since it was weakened and threatened by the competing interests of political parties. He saw service to the state 'as the most noble and important action that exists in the temporal order'.[1] The state, however, in this philosophy, could not be based upon equality. Rather, the state stood above society. Its rulers had to personify France's historic greatness. De Gaulle was an intellectual, well versed in the deeds of the heroes of antiquity – and of course the heroes of French history. He had no difficulty in placing himself in the line of French heroes that ran from Charlemagne through Joan of Arc and Napoleon to Clemenceau.[2] His elitism, however enveloped it was in romanticized patriotism, did not include a high regard for the

French people.[3] One member of the Resistance commented, indeed, after an evening in de Gaulle's company in the middle of the war on his 'immense contempt for humanity'.[4]

The clue to the enigma of de Gaulle lay in his inimitable vision of France's historic grandeur. 'To me, France cannot be France without greatness,' he wrote.[5] This, in his view, had been lost as second-rate politicians had presided over long-term decline into mediocrity, culminating in the national disaster of 1940. Remarkably, in a schoolboy essay in 1905 he had envisaged France being saved by a 'General de Gaulle'.[6]

The notion that the nation in peril needed a national hero to save it later drove him as an adult. His mission, as he saw it, was to restore France's lost grandeur. He was not shy of comparisons, however absurd they seemed, with Joan of Arc.[7] Saving France meant above all else expunging the ignominy of the disgraceful surrender in 1940 and effectively eliminating from French history what he always saw as an illegitimate Vichy regime. 'Vichy was always, and remains, null and void,' he declared, on his return to Paris in 1944.[8] Liberation was for ever captured in the famous photograph of de Gaulle, head and shoulders taller than all around him – at 6 feet 4 inches, he was nearly a foot taller than the average French citizen of his day[9]– as he strode through the Arc de Triomphe and down the Champs-Élysées on 26 August 1944. Liberation meant for him revival, restoration and renewal. It was not, however, a new France but a continuity with the Republic that had been betrayed in 1940. At the same time, the Liberation demanded overcoming what had been so harmful to France, including the divisiveness of party-politics. Saving France meant standing aloof from the daily divisions of political life, embodying the nation in all its grandeur and glory – and leading it.

Whatever his elitist ideals and lofty sense of his own qualities, de Gaulle would probably never have been heard of outside French military circles and the Defence Ministry had it not been for the devastating defeat of France in 1940. The French capitulation to the Germans was the first precondition that guaranteed de Gaulle's place in history. A second would come long after the war, in 1958.

PRECONDITIONS OF LEADERSHIP

Total military defeat and national crisis enabled de Gaulle to step out of obscurity and, from a highly unpromising position in exile in England, begin to establish himself as the face of the determination to free France from German occupation. These were the essential preconditions of his – initially weak – claim to be a national leader. Had the former Prime Minister Paul Reynaud (who chose not to leave for London and was soon afterwards arrested by the Pétain regime) been available after the fall of France, the British government would almost certainly have preferred him to de Gaulle as the face of 'free France'. Whether anyone else other than de Gaulle could have achieved what he did is, however, highly improbable.

As France collapsed in May and June 1940, de Gaulle had no concept of himself as a political leader. Nor had anyone else. Nothing in his career to that point had suggested that he would play a decisive political role. He had been a military man through and through, since qualifying in 1909 to join the military academy at Saint-Cyr. After serving as a decorated officer in the First World War (and spending some time in German captivity), he gained a reputation as an independent thinker on military tactics and the conduct of war, but also as an arrogant, 'difficult' individual. By 1932 he had been promoted to lieutenant colonel and during his time as a staff officer developed and published his ideas on the future importance of tank warfare – ideas that failed to commend themselves to his superiors. He had an elevated opinion of his own abilities and judgement. But it looked as if he were destined to climb no higher than the position of a high-ranking French officer.

His military promotion to the rank of brigadier-general – recognition for his command of an armoured division which had acquitted itself reasonably well amid the looming calamity – only took place on 23 May 1940. His first involvement in government came on 5 June, when he was appointed Under-Secretary of State for Defence by the Prime Minister, Paul Reynaud, but it was a junior post and the government was on its last legs. His position nevertheless brought him into contact with Winston Churchill, British Prime Minister since 10 May. His indomitable fighting spirit must have made an impact. At any rate,

Churchill was favourably impressed by de Gaulle, whom he thought likely to be involved in the military command of potential resistance in the French colonies.[10] Evidently, de Gaulle did not hide his light under a bushel. Visiting London on 16 June, with France on the verge of defeat, he was 'strutting about' among British ministers, prompting some to ask – presumably sarcastically – whether he was a new Napoleon. 'Yet he is only a Major General just recently discovered,' commented Churchill's secretary, John Colville.[11]

On his return from London that day, de Gaulle learned that Reynaud's government had resigned. Marshal Pétain, the hero of the valiant defence of Verdun in 1916, had been asked to form a new administration which would seek an armistice. De Gaulle had admired Pétain's military leadership in the First World War, but their initially good relationship had subsequently deteriorated. Pétain's willingness to enter into an armistice with Germany was for de Gaulle an unforgivable act of treachery and dishonour. He felt that France should continue fighting. It still had armed forces, even if they were in some disarray. It could fight on, directed if necessary from outside France. The following morning, with one close aide and 100,000 francs which Reynaud had supplied him with from government funds, he left for exile in London.[12] It would be four years before he returned to Paris.

BUILDING A FOLLOWING

De Gaulle's future in London did not look bright. He had no following, no organization and no reputation. His recent promotion to the rank of general was fortunate. Had he remained a colonel, it may well have been more difficult for him to gain British recognition as France's leader in exile.[13] Britain, facing likely invasion, in any case did not regard defeated France as a high priority. So de Gaulle faced a struggle to establish himself both with his British hosts and with the French public, to whom he was as yet completely unknown.

The evening after his arrival in exile, 18 June, announcing himself as 'I, General de Gaulle, currently in London', he made his legendary appeal via the airwaves of the BBC to all who could to join his cause to assure them that victory would eventually be theirs. At least, the appeal later *became* legendary – a foundation stone of the 'de Gaulle myth'. At the time, his short address was heard by few French men and women – and most of those had no idea who he was.[14] The following months of his exile in Britain were highly frustrating for de Gaulle. He had difficulty in gaining the backing of even the relatively small numbers of French soldiers and sailors who had found themselves in England at the fall of France. And those who met him were sometimes repelled by the cold, distant personality of the individual they encountered – and by someone, one recruit recalled, whose physical appearance reminded him of a heron.[15] Exiled French writers could still in November ignore de Gaulle in claiming there was no one 'with authority' to tell the French 'the fight must go on'.[16] On the other hand, most – though there were significant exceptions – of those who joined de Gaulle in the wake of France's capitulation not only stayed with him throughout but served him and the French cause with great loyalty.

Some of them became important advisers and indispensable associates in their work for the Free French, often continuing to serve de Gaulle both after Liberation and when he returned to power in 1958. But there was no question of who gave the orders, who provided the directives, who took the decisions, who was the undisputed leader. De Gaulle's dominant – and domineering – personality gave focus, drive and dynamism to the movement for 'Free France'. He alone held together the fractious, heterogeneous and ill-coordinated group which formed the early inner circle of leadership in London.

While de Gaulle was visiting French Equatorial Africa – France's empire stretched over much of north, west and central Africa – for several weeks in autumn 1940 as he tried to rally support in the colonies, organization in London was left to three individuals who proved as a triumvirate to be hopelessly dysfunctional. Jules Antoine's background in business administration could not compensate for his abrasiveness and extreme right-wing views. Admiral Émile Muselier's unstable temperament, and belief that he, not de Gaulle, should be running things, made him impossible to work with even before he broke with de Gaulle in September 1941.[17] And André Dewavrin, later known by the codename 'Passy', given the role of building an Intelligence service, lacked the weight to hold the other two in check.[18]

Others among his entourage in the early months gave him excellent support. Geoffroy Chodron de Courcel, his closest aide and trained as a diplomat, had accompanied him on the flight to England on 17 June. René Cassin, a lawyer, helped negotiate the formal British recognition of de Gaulle's organization on 7 August. Maurice Schumann was the voice of the Free French most frequently heard in France. And not the least important of his early following was René Pleven, a young and talented businessman with good contacts in the USA who would go on to be Prime Minister of France in the 1950s.[19]

The task of de Gaulle's small and inchoate entourage at first consisted of no more than trying to gain support and to establish their legitimacy as the authentic representation of France. A loose semblance of an embryonic political organization was first obtained when de Gaulle established in October 1940 a nine-man Council for the Defence of the Empire (Conseil de Défense de l'Empire). In theory, the Council had powers that a state would normally exercise. In practice, it was no more than a loose consultative body with powers of decision reserved for de Gaulle himself. It was superseded in September 1941 by the National Committee of the Free French, composed of twelve members, including Pleven in charge of economic affairs and Cassin of legal matters. This had the appearance of a government in exile. But de Gaulle as its president held all the reins of power.[20] It was not a one-man show, but it was not far off it.

There was no hiding the fact that de Gaulle and his initially small but dedicated following faced an uphill struggle. The vast proportion of the French armed forces remained under Vichy's command. The devastating British attack on the French fleet at Mers-el-Kébir in July 1940 was scarcely a good advertisement for de Gaulle. And the empire was overwhelmingly loyal to Pétain. When the failure of a British-backed attempted landing by the Free French at Dakar in Senegal in September offered a gift for Vichy propaganda, it was easy to portray de Gaulle as a traitor to France.

Relations with his British hosts soon turned fractious. The British government provided financial support for the Free French and in August 1940 formally acknowledged their military forces as co-belligerents. De Gaulle was able to use the BBC to deliver twelve speeches and appeals to the French during June and July.[21] But the text of his speeches was subject to amendment by the British. In fact, the British controlled whether he was allowed to speak at all, and when.[22] For the British government, still unsure about how to deal with de Gaulle, the Free French were, given the magnitude of the defeat of France, in these early months not much more than a sideshow in a war now centred on Britain's own fight for national survival.

De Gaulle bitterly resented his subordination to the interests of the British and, once the USA joined the war in December 1941, increasingly to those of Roosevelt and the American administration. But his own obstinacy, haughty demeanour and frequently abrasive manner alienated and infuriated those he came into contact with. For de Gaulle, it was always and invariably a case of 'France First' and over all else. That unavoidably collided at times with the broader war strategy of the Allies. And a clash of temperaments between de Gaulle and Churchill was inevitable.[23] Churchill's respect for France and concern for its future were outweighed by its military insignificance. As the war progressed, Churchill's early admiration for de Gaulle often gave way to angry outbursts at his obduracy, while Roosevelt was from the outset largely dismissive of the leader of the Free French. For the first two years of the war, the Allies regarded de Gaulle and the Free French as a somewhat marginal and often irritating element in their planning. That started to change when the fortunes of war themselves began to swing in the Allies' favour from late 1942 onwards.

In the early part of the war, de Gaulle had struggled to gain support in the French empire. But despite the serious rebuff to his hopes in the Dakar fiasco, he had at least won the support of French Equatorial Africa and tiny French enclaves in India and the Pacific region – chiefly because of their economic dependence on Britain.[24] Most of the colonial empire only rallied to de Gaulle after November 1942. That month the strategically vital British-American landings in north Africa took place. To his fury, de Gaulle had been kept out of the planning, and the Free French had been allocated no role in the operation, in which Vichy forces had fought against the Allies.

The Allied success in north Africa was nevertheless to offer entirely new opportunities to de Gaulle, even if these were not immediately apparent. The German response to the landings had been to occupy the previously 'free zone' of France, leaving the Vichy regime as an altogether obvious puppet of Nazi Germany. This cleared a path for de Gaulle eventually to gain control of surviving elements in the French army – the navy scuttled itself in late November to prevent the Germans taking it over – which was nearly five times the size of his Free French Forces. He also had the chance gradually to gain the backing of the large remainder of the colonial empire. But at first there were blockages in the way. The USA had been among the countries to recognize the legitimacy of Vichy (hoping that the regime would avoid support for the Axis war effort). So Roosevelt's administration, still holding de Gaulle in scant regard, had initially placed its bets on Admiral François Darlan – vehemently Anglophobic and for long the strong man of the Vichy regime – who signed an armistice with the Allies in north Africa. When Darlan was conveniently assassinated in Algiers on Christmas Eve, the Americans transferred their favour to General Henri Giraud, who had dramatically escaped from German imprisonment the previous April and never tired of reminding anyone prepared to listen of his heroic exploits. It took months for de Gaulle, having moved his headquarters in May 1943 to Algiers, to assert his ascendancy over Giraud, whose incompetence and mistakes undermined his own pretensions to leadership.[25] Only towards the end of the year did de Gaulle secure Allied recognition of his outright supremacy as French political as well as military leader. By this time, the building of the 'de Gaulle myth', of which de Gaulle himself was the prime architect, was well underway.

EMERGENCE OF THE NATIONAL HERO

De Gaulle was never a 'man of the people', though he certainly learned how to exploit the popular acclaim that he encountered. His only weapon at first in gaining popular support was the spoken word. And at that, like Churchill, he was a master. His rhetoric, like Churchill's, had an old-fashioned ring to it. But it was perfectly judged to stir patriotic emotions – at first of only a small minority of the French population, though later most of those who looked to the day of France's liberation. De Gaulle became the voice of Liberation long before French people knew what he looked like.

Before 1940 he had been little known in France outside the military academy, the headquarters of the general staff and the corridors of power in Paris. He was certainly regarded, for better or usually for worse, as an extraordinary personality during his early stay in London. But no one, even in his own entourage, thought of him at that stage as a charismatic hero with magnetic popular appeal. The first time that de Gaulle himself realized that 'people were counting upon a man named de Gaulle to liberate them' and that 'there was a person named de Gaulle who existed in other people's minds and was really a separate personality from myself' was when he was met by cheering crowds on his visit to African colonies in autumn 1940.[26] Around the same time, regular broadcasts by French journalists based in London began to spread recognition of his name – a name which itself appeared (from its proximity to 'Gaul') to symbolize his country's early history – more widely in France itself. And there were the first indications of his association with the fragmented pockets of resistance to German occupation.[27] But organized resistance was slow to develop. There was no coherent movement for two years.[28] And, in any case, before 1942 de Gaulle had few expectations of its potential.

The major shift in his involvement with the Resistance which took place that year was largely the work not of de Gaulle himself, but of Jean Moulin, until 1940 prefect of Chartres but soon the key figure who linked together separate embryonic resistance organizations. In October 1941 Moulin travelled incognito via Lisbon to London, met de Gaulle and persuaded him of the potential of coordinated, armed resistance in France. Moulin was supplied with funding. De Gaulle insisted on overall leadership. From January 1942 Moulin was acting formally as de Gaulle's 'delegate'. He regarded de Gaulle as symbolically vital to the building of an effective resistance movement but left a question-mark over his later suitability for government.[29] He faced great difficulties in forging any semblance of unity out of the disparate organizational and ideological positions of the resistance movements. But the complete subordination of the Vichy regime to German demands, especially after the introduction of the compulsory-labour order of February 1943 (aimed at supplying French workers for the German war effort), acted as a great recruiting sergeant for the Resistance.

The common goal of liberation eventually allowed Moulin to bring together representatives of the different resistance movements in a National Council of the Resistance, which first met on 27 May 1943. This agreed that de Gaulle should be foreseen as leader of a provisional government, though unity of the resistance movements remained superficial.[30] His role in the Resistance was still far from de Gaulle's prime concern. At this time he was largely preoccupied from his new base in Algiers with manoeuvring to secure his leadership against the challenge from Giraud. Only from autumn 1943, once de Gaulle had established control over the French Committee of National Liberation (which at first he had jointly led with Giraud), did he gain general recognition as the symbol of French resistance.[31] Even then, the communist resistance especially was wary of conceding too much authority to someone it viewed as a reactionary conservative if not a fascist. De Gaulle, for his part, remained concerned that he might lose control over the resistance movement to the communists. Meanwhile, the courageous work of Moulin had ended tragically with his capture in June 1943 and then torture and death at the hands of the Gestapo.

De Gaulle was by the end of 1943 being increasingly seen by his compatriots and by the Allies as the future leader of liberated France. He adjusted pragmatically to the necessity of collective future planning by the National Liberation Committee (which saw itself as the forerunner of the future French government), but he insisted that the Committee was merely consultative. Any semblance of democracy was purely a façade. He retained control and powers of decision in all significant matters. His ingrained authoritarianism remained undiluted. So did his difficult relationship with Allied leaders. The Allies recognized by now – not always with great enthusiasm – that he alone possessed the authority to speak for 'Free France'. But de Gaulle angrily resented being kept out of their plans for D-Day and was distrustful of what they had in mind as France's future government, imagining – not without justification – that they envisaged keeping the country under Allied control.

He was in a tetchy mood when he met Churchill on 4 June 1944, just before D-Day, after returning to London from Algiers, and a furious exchange about France's (and Britain's) subordination to American interests in plans for the liberation of France took place over lunch. Churchill's choleric outburst was a sign of his own tension (fuelled by alcohol), and a somewhat better-tempered meeting followed with the Allied commander-in-chief General Eisenhower in which de Gaulle complained bitterly about the lack of French involvement in the landing.[32] By D-Day itself, de Gaulle had recovered his poise to deliver a ringing, patriotic address to the French people on the BBC airwaves. But to Churchill's irritation, he spoke of 'the directives given by the French government', as if an actual government already existed. Churchill could not resist pointing out to Roosevelt that the speech was remarkable, since de Gaulle 'has not a single soldier in the great battle now developing' (a soon outdated jibe since a French armoured division, commanded by General Philippe Leclerc, fought as part of the Allied force in Normandy from 1 August 1944).[33] Whatever Churchill's testiness, to large numbers of French men and women de Gaulle had by then come to embody the Liberation itself – and with it the restoration of France's honour.

The 'de Gaulle myth' – the heroic image of the deliverer of France – was further embellished when, after a four-year absence, de Gaulle stepped back on French soil on 14 June. His address to the people of Bayeux, the largest town liberated at this point, in a well-rehearsed visit was largely a propaganda exercise. The reception was enthusiastic, though less euphoric than de Gaulle later claimed.[34] De Gaulle was establishing a basis for political power after liberation. His big step was his triumphant entry to Paris, where he returned on 25 August. The city had by then been liberated – in the final act of the drama by the French themselves. Days earlier the Resistance had orchestrated an uprising in the capital, as elsewhere in France. And the military glory of fighting their way into Paris had been granted by Eisenhower to General Leclerc's forces. French units entered the city on the evening of the 24th. The German surrender followed the next day.

When de Gaulle gave a moving address that evening, 25 August, at the Hôtel de Ville in Paris, he spoke of Paris 'liberated by itself, liberated by its people with the help of the armies of France'.[35] His brief thanks to the Allies for their help amounted to the barest recognition of what they had actually done to make France's liberation possible. But only one thing counted for de Gaulle: to glorify France itself through the image of self-liberation. This was in itself of great importance to the rebuilding of a traumatized nation.

And there was no doubt who was portrayed as the hero of Liberation, the saviour of the nation. De Gaulle took pride of place at the head of the victory parade down the Champs-Élysées the following day. The vast joyful crowd waved banners that they had been given out in advance. They bore the words 'Vive de Gaulle'.[36]

FAILURE

De Gaulle's leadership had been a product of war. The task of building an organization, winning a following both in France and in the empire, sustaining contacts and constructing an army in exile while struggling for recognition with the Allies demanded particular qualities of leadership. De Gaulle's personality suited them. His strength of will, aloofness from day-to-day political squabbling, imperious manner, insistence on autocratic control in a type of military command structure proved invaluable in the emergency conditions of war. These qualities were, however, not well fitted for democratic government in the collective task of post-war reconstruction.

Following the triumphant parade down the Champs-Élysées, de Gaulle began how he meant to continue: by imposing his own authority on the government he had appointed, and – in so far as it was possible to do so – on the country at large (parts of which had still not been liberated). The government incorporated all parts of the political spectrum, including communist representatives. But de Gaulle firmly held the reins of power.

His unique prestige guaranteed him initial successes. He exploited his own personality cult in playing down the role of the Resistance, whose elevation might have posed a challenge to his own authority. He regarded the disillusionment of many who had taken huge risks to fight against occupation and had seen him as the symbol of their future hopes as, effectively, collateral damage. A sense of national unity, drawing a line under the recent, painful past, could be evoked in the trial and punishment of collaborators and representatives of the Vichy regime. And de Gaulle's visit to Moscow in December 1944 for bilateral talks with Stalin (leading to a fairly meaningless treaty of mutual assistance) went down well at home in signalling that France was returning to its presumed rightful great-power status.[37]

How illusory this was soon became clear. De Gaulle was highly piqued by France's exclusion from the deliberations of the 'Big Three' (Stalin, Roosevelt and Churchill) both at Yalta in February 1945 and after the end of the European war at Potsdam in August. Roosevelt retained his dislike of de Gaulle, while Stalin was little more than contemptuous about a country that in 1940 'had not fought at all'. But Churchill wanted to bolster France's position as Britain's most important ally in western Europe. His advocacy was largely behind the agreement – 'only out of kindness', Roosevelt and Stalin indicated – to create a French zone of occupation of Germany.[38] France was also given membership of the Allied Control Council and a permanent seat on the newly formed United Nations Security Council.

It was at home, however, that de Gaulle faced his major challenge. Party politics quickly took shape again, most significantly in the reconstituted Communist and Socialist Parties and a new Christian democratic party, the Mouvement Républicain Populaire (MRP, Popular Republican Movement). Prominent in the MRP's leadership were figures closely associated with de Gaulle, including Georges Bidault, who had headed the National Council of the Resistance after the death of Jean Moulin, and Maurice Schumann, the most regular broadcaster of the Free French in London from summer 1940. In the first post-war elections, in October 1945, the three main parties won almost equal levels of support. Awkward coalition government in a tripartite alliance followed, though there was, in fact, a good deal of cross-party support in the early stages of economic planning to meet the urgent needs of rebuilding the economy.

De Gaulle was re-elected to head the government. But his ideas of how France should in future be governed and those of the political parties – especially those on the Left – soon led to a predictable clash. De Gaulle had always prevailed in asserting his control during the war. Now, however, the power of the parties proved stronger. Under the proposals for a new constitution, government power was to be even more constrained than it had been under the Third Republic.

De Gaulle had been insistent that the provisional government he led after Liberation was a direct continuation of the Third Republic, that the Vichy regime had been no more than an illegitimate interruption. But although he emphasized constitutional continuity, he also signalled the need for political transformation. The constitution of the Third Republic had favoured parliamentary power to control government. The President had a largely ceremonial role. The result had been weak governments, repeatedly made and broken by the power of the National Assembly, itself reflecting divisive party allegiances. This weakness had, for de Gaulle, been a major reason for the collapse of 1940. France, he was certain, needed strong government – which he was the person to deliver. A presidential regime based on popular appeal was what he had in mind.[39]

The parties of the Left had from the outset been suspicious of de Gaulle's intentions and unwilling to give him strong executive power. The proposed constitution ran diametrically contrary to what he wanted. Already contending with difficulties in managing the National Assembly, he was unable to get his way. On 20 January 1946 he peremptorily resigned.[40] Possibly he expected this dramatic act by the national hero to concentrate minds and compel his recall. If that was his hope, it was to be dashed. For the first time since June 1940 he was no longer running things.

De Gaulle did not see himself as a dictator (though many were less sure). But how he depicted himself and envisaged his role amounted to a form of charismatic leadership (as Max Weber had defined it), based upon his achievements as France's war hero and national saviour.[41] Yet this was scarcely compatible with the divisiveness of pluralist party politics which in any form of democracy – and this had been emphatically so in the French system under the Third Republic – constricted and controlled the executive power of government. Precisely this had been de Gaulle's intrinsic dilemma when he took power as head of the provisional government after Liberation. He needed the parties and favoured their restoration both to limit communist influence and to demonstrate the extent of his popular backing – even though the Left (and most of all the communists) were hardly easy bedfellows.[42] On the other hand, even the parties of the Left could scarcely do without him; they, too, had to acknowledge his unique standing. The tension of combining 'charismatic' politics with the divisiveness of parliamentary democracy was obvious and insurmountable. De Gaulle's unwillingness to subordinate his own 'charismatic' authority to the constraints of party politics ultimately resulted in twelve years of political failure. As a war leader he had been unique and indispensable. As a peacetime leader he faced divisions that he could not transcend. A would-be dictator might well have sought to destroy the political structures that stood in his way. De Gaulle's way, in contrast, was to retreat from politics altogether to await the fundamental crisis of the system that, he was certain, would eventually occur. Then the hero would be needed once more. He would return to save France anew.

After resigning in January 1946, he was not gone for long. Within months he was back in the public eye – if not in government. With his well-cultivated sense of theatre he chose Bayeux, scene of his return to France in 1944, to deliver a speech on 16 June in which he laid out his argument for an elected president with executive powers. He saw the government's strength emanating from the head of state (clearly the role he pictured for himself), who would appoint members of the government, though stand above routine administration, reserving for himself the right to promulgate laws and decrees. In times of national danger, the President would guarantee the country's freedom.[43]

His plea fell on stony ground. In October 1946 the French people approved – somewhat half-heartedly – the constitution for the Fourth Republic. It was – as the Third Republic's constitution had been – a recipe for weak government and political instability. Governments depended upon fragile majorities in the National Assembly. None survived long. There were twenty-two governments between 1945 and 1958, lasting from under a week to fifteen months.[44] The inability of government to govern scarcely matched de Gaulle's notion of France's 'grandeur' and was the antithesis of his vision for the country's future. He gloomily foresaw catastrophe again for France, and even, with notable exaggeration, compared the mood in the country with that of June 1940.[45] He was preparing to save France anew. In April 1947 he made another comeback.

The Rassemblement du Peuple Français (RPF, Rally of the French People), which he launched that month, to a rapturous reception, claimed to be a 'movement' not a party, to stand above the parties for the nation. In reality it was, however, another party, which would contest elections on its own platform. It was even so a party with a difference – in essence, a vehicle for de Gaulle's charismatic leadership

and for the form of government he envisaged for France. Its membership soared at first, helped by intensified anti-communism as the Cold
War set in. But it never came close to gaining majority support and, in
fact, split the right-wing vote in weakening the MRP. The Gaullist
Right and communist Left – the communists had been ejected from
government in 1947 – simply formed opposite ends of the political
spectrum, with unstable coalitions between them that struggled to
form lasting administrations. In 1951, at the first general election
since its formation, the RPF won 22 per cent of the vote, though only
came second to the Communist Party (with 26 per cent). De Gaulle
claimed, implausibly, that this relative success gave him the right to
form a government with the intention of altering the constitution, but
was flatly rebuffed by President Auriol.[46] Two years later, in May
1953, with the RPF suffering internal splits and haemorrhaging electoral support, de Gaulle declared that if he were to govern France it
could only be if he could take power and change the regime. 'It means
that or nothing at all,' he declared.[47] It looked like being nothing at
all. He retired again – this time, it seemed, for good.

RETURN OF THE HERO:
THE ALGERIAN CRISIS

Without a fundamental crisis of the Fourth Republic, de Gaulle had
no chance of ever returning to the pinnacle of French politics on terms
he would accept. His political career looked to be over. In his sixty-
third year, he withdrew to his relatively modest country home at
Colombey-les-deux-Églises in the Champagne region of eastern
France, which he and his wife Yvonne had owned since 1934, and
where he worked on his war memoirs. He had begun these in 1946,
though his political involvement had for long limited his time for
writing. Now he could devote himself to leaving for posterity the history of his heroic struggle to bring salvation to France after the depths
of the country's fall in 1940. The huge publicity that attended the
appearance of the first two volumes in 1954 and 1956 – the third
volume was published in 1959, after he had returned to power – embellished de Gaulle's legendary status as France's saviour. And it burnished

the image of the redeemer, ready again to return from lonely isolation should France once more need him.[48] By 1958, it did.

Crises of government came and went during de Gaulle's self-imposed retreat, as they had done since the foundation of the Fourth Republic. Given the nature of the constitution, that was bound to be the case. But governmental instability was compatible with a stability of the underlying state system itself, and with a thriving economy. What was needed as the precondition of de Gaulle's 'second coming' – and the concession to his ambition to bring about lasting, transformative change – was not just another crisis of government, but this time a crisis of the French state itself. This occurred in 1958. What caused it was the inability to solve the problem of Algeria.

Colonial empires were crumbling everywhere. But Algeria was unique – a colony that was not a colony. Although de facto a French colony since 1830, with a caste of mainly French settlers (a tenth of the population) ruling a subordinate Muslim population, it was jurid-ically an integral part of France itself. Losing Algeria was therefore tantamount to losing part of France. In November 1954 the Front de Libération Nationale (FLN, the Algerian National Liberation Front) had begun an armed struggle for independence, which soon turned into a prolonged war of relentless savagery on both sides. Unstable, short-lived French governments could find no answer to the intract-able problem. When French settlers (known as *pieds-noirs*), backed by the army in Algeria, rebelled against the government, pressure mounted for de Gaulle to intervene. De Gaulle let it be known that he was ready to form a government, on condition that he would be empowered to change the constitution. He reminded the French pub-lic that he had in the past led the country to salvation, and that the 'extremely grave national crisis' could bring 'a kind of resurrection'.[49] Both to the army and the *pieds-noirs*, saving France meant saving French Algeria. They trusted de Gaulle to do what no one else was capable of doing.[50]

De Gaulle did ultimately, after four further years of terrible blood-shed, bring the Algerian conflict to an end – though not as the *pieds-noirs* had wanted or expected.[51] That he was able to succeed where the governments of the Fourth Republic had failed flowed from the enhanced powers he had attained through the major change to the constitution. Reappointed as Prime Minister at the end of May 1958 amid high political tension, he had quickly secured parliamentary support to submit a new constitution to the approval of the people. In September his proposals won the support of 79 per cent of the voters. On 21 December he was elected under the new constitution by an electoral college to a presidency which now possessed strong executive powers, formally taking office on 8 January 1959. Constitutional reform was already being mooted and would probably have materialized at some point even had de Gaulle not returned to office the previous year. Governmental paralysis and failure to resolve the Algerian crisis had left the public wanting the restoration of order and made the political elites open to constitutional change. But the specific constitutional arrangements of the Fifth Republic were de Gaulle's achievement, a reflection of his unique authority and prestige.

De Gaulle's handling of the crisis, leading to Algerian independence in 1962, looks in retrospect like a strategic masterpiece. In practice, although his political high-wire act was carried out with consummate skill, it was a pragmatic adjustment to an inexorable defeat for the advocates of 'Algérie française', rather than single-minded pursuit of a clear strategy. It amounted to cutting the losses of a conflict that could not be won.[52] His statement, 'I have understood you', delivered before an ecstatic crowd in Algiers on 4 June 1958, was a masterly expression of studied ambiguity.[53] His listeners wrongly took it to mean that he was on their side, that Algeria would remain French. But he evaded pinning himself down. Although the French had military superiority, they proved incapable of defeating a determined guerrilla force fighting a war for national independence. Moreover, the brutal French conduct of the war proved counterproductive in alienating opinion both at home and internationally. Gradually and cautiously, de Gaulle edged towards recognition that the only feasible outcome was Algerian independence. Acceptance of that meant making enemies out of the *pieds-noirs* and the army in Algeria, the very groups that had looked to him to rescue them. De Gaulle looked upon that outcome with equanimity. It was a far lesser evil than continuing an unwinnable war. He shed no tears over the *pieds-noirs*. It was time to look to the future, not hold on to the dying past.

Pressure for independence would surely have made the retention of

Algeria as a colonial possession impossible for any French government. But de Gaulle alone, in all probability, had the personal authority to turn potential civil war into a general recognition that Algeria could not be retained. He had long realized that he held none of the aces in his hand in resolving the Algerian War. Secret negotiations with the FLN began in secret in autumn 1961 and by 18 March 1962 had led to a ceasefire which on 8 April was approved by 90 per cent of the French electorate (and on 1 July by 99 per cent of voters in Algeria).[54] Algerian independence was declared on 1 July. Hundreds of thousands, the vast majority of them non-white Algerians, had been killed or maimed in the terrible conflict. Most of the *pieds-noirs*, harbouring a lasting sense of betrayal, left for France. De Gaulle had little sympathy for them and none at all for the tens of thousands of Harkis, Algerian Muslims who had fought with the French in Algeria and after independence had fled to France to avoid terrible reprisals at home.

Algeria overshadowed everything in de Gaulle's first years in power. Ending the war and avoiding prolonged civil unrest were in themselves achievements. But his international standing, as well as his domestic authority, brought tangible successes in other arenas. In stark contrast to the unique situation of Algeria, winding up almost all of the rest of the French empire was accomplished swiftly between 1958 and the end of 1960. For someone born into the age of empire, who had viewed France's colonial possessions as an intrinsic component of its status as a great power, de Gaulle was both quick and dispassionate about accepting their liquidation. He accepted it as unavoidable; he did not welcome it. He was dismissive of the newly independent countries, and their people. 'I know that decolonisation is disastrous,' he commented privately in 1962, 'that most of the Africans are hardly at the stage of our Middle Ages' and would soon again 'experience tribal wars, witchcraft, cannibalism'.[55] Nevertheless, he presided over the process of decolonization and helped to ensure the relatively smooth transition to independence, though usually preserving French economic interests. His achievement should not be exaggerated. The global pressure for decolonization was so strong that it would have happened anyway, whatever the character of the French government. Still, without de Gaulle's leadership it could well have been a far more thorny path.

IN POWER: THE IMPRINT OF PERSONALITY

The Fifth Republic was constitutionally structured to accommodate the personal exercise of power by the President to the modern demands of parliamentary pluralist representation. As such, it was a curious hybrid, somewhat more akin to the American presidential system than to British parliamentary democracy, but a uniquely French creation. In certain ways, his position resembled the marrying of charismatic leadership and management of representational politics that Bismarck had mastered in Imperial Germany – though of course Bismarck had still been answerable to the Kaiser. De Gaulle accepted, recognized as necessary, even welcomed popular participation in politics – as long as it was on his terms. In France, de Gaulle was an executive head of state, answerable to no one, not a dictator, but able to use the referendum to gain popular backing for his personal power and as a means of manipulating parliament. Under de Gaulle, politics in France bowed to his personality and to the extraordinary prestige that his historic achievements bestowed on him.

In theory, the President directed foreign and defence policy (and had the right to assume quasi-dictatorial powers in a national emergency), while domestic affairs were the province of the Prime Minister and government, responsible to parliament. In practice, there was no sphere of policy outside de Gaulle's purview. He was well served by some of the outstanding politicians that he appointed to high office, prominent among them Michel Debré, Georges Pompidou (successive Prime Ministers), Maurice Couve de Murville (Foreign Minister) and André Malraux (Culture Minister). But, crucially, ministers were solely dependent upon him, not on parliament. He severed the connection between ministers and any parliamentary power-base. Parliament itself was greatly weakened. Even so, the new Gaullist party, the Union pour la Nouvelle République, established in 1958, ensured strong parliamentary representation for de Gaulle's policies.

De Gaulle dominated all significant policy discussions, also on home affairs. He intervened personally, too, to steer the resolution of economic issues, such as the financial stabilization plan of 1958 (devised by the economist Jacques Rueff) and measures to tackle inflation in 1963.[56] He jealously guarded his prerogative and took all the key decisions. He showed, for someone in his seventies, remarkable drive and energy in pushing through the implementation of policy, even where he was not directly involved. This had been a hallmark of his governance since his return to power in 1958. His high work-rate, ability to listen, grasp of detail, close questioning of ministers and extraordinary memory were features of his style of governing and underpinned his instinctive authoritarianism.[57] The weekly meetings of the Council of Ministers (the equivalent of the Cabinet in Britain) merely heard ministerial reports and rubber-stamped decisions already agreed by ad hoc committees chaired (and completely dominated) by de Gaulle.[58] One thing was abundantly clear: de Gaulle decided.

De Gaulle strengthened his personal power still further in 1962, exploiting a failed assassination attempt by fanatical opponents of Algerian independence, members of the OAS (Organisation de l'Armée Secrète), to amend the constitution in his favour. He sought to reduce the need for parliamentary support through the election of the President by popular vote, not, as in the 1958 constitution, through an electoral college. The move was highly contentious; it was seen, not just on the Left, as the route to a new type of Bonapartist dictatorship. But the change was approved (though by only 62 per cent of the votes cast, with 23 per cent of voters abstaining) in a referendum in October.[59] Three years later, in 1965, he was re-elected as President, gaining 55 per cent of the vote. He had, however, been forced into a rerun against his main opponent, François Mitterrand, the candidate of the Left, after winning only 45 per cent of the popular vote on the first ballot. Far from underlining de Gaulle's pretensions to be a leader who stood above parties and embodied national unity, the election had shown him to be a divisive figure who, in other than times of deep crisis, reflected rather than transcended the normal split along Left–Right lines.[60]

As empire faded in the new age of the superpowers, de Gaulle sought new ways to assert France's great power status. His pursuit of an independent foreign policy bore a distinctly personal imprint. His ingrained anti-Americanism – a legacy in part of the way Roosevelt had snubbed him years earlier – led him to seek good relations with the Soviet Union and communist China. He rejected the American offer of Polaris missiles and poured resources into a French nuclear programme (which, in fact, had already been initiated during the Fourth Republic). In the face of growing opposition from the Left, France acquired hydrogen bombs by 1968 – for de Gaulle, an indispensable symbol of national prestige. Withdrawing from the American-led NATO military command in 1966 had been a further step in underlining French independence in defence and foreign policy. Both independence and the implied great power status were nonetheless largely a mirage. De Gaulle indeed made France more of a presence for non-aligned countries (those which would commit to neither of the superpowers).[61] But the days of anything approaching genuine independence for a middle-ranking European nation-state were long gone (as Britain, too, had discovered).

Unlike Britain, France had already found a new role for itself in the European Economic Community (EEC) by the time de Gaulle took office. De Gaulle had never liked Jean Monnet, or his supranational ideas of European integration. Here, too, his own views were anchored in a past of independent, rival European states. But he was a realist. The EEC brought big benefits for France – notably in the Common Agricultural Policy, which disproportionately favoured French farmers. And de Gaulle acknowledged that peace in Europe depended upon close relations with West Germany, which he sealed with the symbolic Franco-German Friendship Treaty, signed with Chancellor Konrad Adenauer in 1963. But French dominance of a 'Europe of nations' ('Europe des patries') was what he wanted. The policy of 'France First' determined that Britain – regarded as a threat to French interests in Europe – had to be kept out of the EEC. This, however, merely postponed British entry (and the inevitable friction between British and EEC interests, which de Gaulle foresaw) for some years. De Gaulle's insistence on the primacy of French interests also led to a seven-month French boycott of European institutions over an extension of the supranational powers of the European Commission, which ended in an awkward compromise in 1966. This summed up the uneasy balance between French national interests and the EEC's supranational aims – a tension that it was impossible to overcome, certainly as long as de Gaulle remained in power.

What de Gaulle was unable to do was to bend to his brand of authoritarianism the forces of modernization and cultural transformation which were coursing through France and the rest of Europe in the 1960s. When student protests, initially at conditions in universities, galvanized a level of upheaval across France that for a while in May 1968 threatened the political order, de Gaulle was caught unawares. His initial response – to leave for a four-day state visit to Romania, leaving Prime Minister Pompidou in charge – showed him to be mistaken in his assessment of the situation and out of touch with the mentalities of the younger generation. Only towards the end of a month of violent disturbances did he regain the initiative – and only then after he had mysteriously disappeared for a few days without even informing his Prime Minister. The cause of his disappearance was to cross the West German border to obtain assurance from General Jacques Massu, head of the French forces in West Germany, that he could rely upon the backing of the military. He then went on the offensive, warning the nation of the danger of dictatorship and the threat of communism, while an orchestrated march through Paris of half a million loyalists demonstrated their support. Pompidou then played the major role (as he had done throughout the crisis), through concessions and promises of reform, in bringing about the gradual restoration of order.

Elections a month later resulted in a huge vote of confidence in de Gaulle. But the tide was turning against him. When he put his proposals for government reforms to the popular vote in a referendum on 27 April 1969, the people rejected them. De Gaulle viewed the referendum as a test of confidence in his leadership. He drew the obvious consequence from the result, therefore, and promptly resigned, without any song and dance. He had told one of his closest advisers: 'If the French do not want to listen to me, well, I will go, and afterwards people will see that I was right.'[62]

The truth was, he was no longer in tune with the times. In two crises, in 1940 then again in 1958, his personality had been crucial to shaping France's destiny. But the May events of 1968, even though they left few immediately tangible results, showed that France had moved on from the peculiar brand of personal power of de Gaulle. He recognized that, in his inimitable way. The French, he implied privately, had not lived up to his vision of grandeur. They had chosen 'mediocrity'.[63] In reality, his successor, Georges Pompidou, was anything but a mediocrity, while de Gaulle's vision of a restoration of French grandeur had never been anything but an illusion. He retired once more, first for a holiday on the remote west coast of Ireland, then to the seclusion of Colombey-les-deux-Églises, where he worked assiduously on what he intended to be a three-volume set of memoirs on his time in office since 1958. This time his retirement was final. The de Gaulle era was over. Little over a year later, he was dead.

LEGACY

Revisiting the dramatic decades of French history in which de Gaulle left such an indelible mark – from the 'hollow years' of the 1930s,[64] through the trauma of the war and liberation, the turbulence of the Fourth Republic and the Algerian War, to the remarkable stability of the Fifth Republic – the obvious question poses itself: could anyone other than de Gaulle have achieved such a remarkable transformation? It can surely be answered in the negative.

Some achievements, as we have seen, can easily be exaggerated, or at least require qualification. France's liberation was won primarily by American and British armed might, not by de Gaulle's Free French or the unquestionable high courage of the Resistance. But de Gaulle's vision of 'another France' was nonetheless crucial, as a rallying point both in France itself and in the empire and in upholding the view, accepted by Churchill though not readily by Roosevelt, that France should be treated after the war still as a great power. His vision allowed the France crushed in 1940 to regain its self-respect after its liberation.

Algerian independence, and decolonization more generally, would certainly have come about anyway, though de Gaulle's personal role in the actual process was decisive. He also provided a distinct flavour to the construction of an independent French foreign and defence policy. As an achievement, this needs qualification. Plans to build nuclear weapons already existed before he came to office. And time has diluted both the pretence of being a great power and the value of an independent defence policy (as France's reintegration in NATO has shown).

Reconciliation between France and (West) Germany owed more to the early steps taken by Robert Schuman, Jean Monnet and Konrad Adenauer than to de Gaulle and was already well established by 1958, though de Gaulle symbolically sealed the new relationship in the friendship treaty he signed with Adenauer in 1963. His desired 'Europe of nations' never supplanted Monnet's vision of supranational integration. But the converse has also not happened. The uneasy balance of the national and the supranational within the European Community (then the European Union) has continued. Yet, in certain respects developments have moved in a direction that de Gaulle would have favoured. The key decision-making body since 1974 has been the European Council, representing the individual member-states. And the primacy of national interests has generally prevailed, especially at times of crisis.

Finally, France's economy unquestionably thrived under de Gaulle. But there had been extraordinary economic growth – despite governmental instability, inflation, the cost of the Algerian War and periodic crises of public finances – during the Fourth Republic.[65] De Gaulle was lucky in his timing in inheriting an intrinsically strong economy when the difficulties were becoming more manageable. Nor did the growth cease when de Gaulle left office. It was sustained until major changes in the global economy affected France, as they did other countries, during the 1970s to bring the 'thirty glorious years' (les trentes glorieuses) to a close. De Gaulle's personal role here was secondary to impersonal economic forces that outstripped national control. And the modernization that accompanied the economic boom ultimately undermined the France of de Gaulle's vision. The Common Agricultural Policy of the EEC certainly helped French farming. But the peasantry – the heart of the traditional image of France – disappeared, as it did all over Europe. And, meanwhile, the modern lifestyles and mentalities that were emerging from rapid economic change did not conform to de Gaulle's patriarchal style of leadership.

De Gaulle had outlived belief in national 'heroes'. He was the last in the lineage of European political leaders who thought of themselves as 'great men'.[66] Democratic pluralism, civil liberties and human rights, as they established themselves across western Europe, especially after the 1960s, made notions of political 'greatness', so prevalent in the nineteenth and early twentieth centuries, seem archaic. More stable conditions and changed mentalities were not compatible with forms of 'charismatic leadership' that were a product of crisis and which presented the 'genius' of the 'great leader' as the solution to immensely complex social and political problems.

Nevertheless, his style of personal leadership produced de Gaulle's most significant, and lasting, achievement: the remarkable constitution of the Fifth Republic. This was designed to accommodate his demand for power. Blending authoritarianism and democratic pluralism in a unique structure, the constitution has stood the test of time. Recent years have arguably exposed the weakness at times of crisis of a constitution that depends so heavily upon the (perceived) qualities of the President. Still, although politics in France seldom lacks drama, there is no clamour for the constitution to be changed – something that could be said of no period of French history between the Revolution and de Gaulle.[67]

De Gaulle was certainly a leader of remarkable qualities and extraordinary achievements. What has far outlasted his personal role is, however, the 'myth of de Gaulle' – the legendary image of greatness. The heroic image of de Gaulle has successfully transcended the vagaries of French politics in the decades since the war (if proving at times a mixed blessing for his successors). De Gaulle is widely regarded in France as the most important figure in French history – far ahead of Napoleon. Paris's main airport is named after him. More symbolically, the Place de l'Étoile in the heart of Paris, with the Arc de Triomphe at its centre and site of the tomb of the Unknown Soldier, bears the name 'Place Charles de Gaulle'.[68] So do hundreds of other squares in French towns and cities. Today's France has moved on in so many ways since the time of de Gaulle. It is nevertheless unthinkable without his legacy.

Konrad Adenauer (right) is accompanied by the Mayor of West Berlin (and later Federal Chancellor) Willy Brandt and the American President John F. Kennedy, who was rapturously greeted by enormous crowds during his visit to the city on 26 June 1963.

7

KONRAD ADENAUER

Building West Germany

Not the least remarkable thing about Konrad Adenauer is that his major contribution to public life began only at an age when most people were already enjoying retirement. He was mainly known only as a provincial Rhineland politician before he came to prominence in the early years after the Second World War. By the time he became the first Chancellor of the new Federal Republic of Germany (FRG) in 1949 he was seventy-three years old. Few imagined he would still be Chancellor fourteen years later, finally resigning at the age of eighty-seven. And by the end of his Chancellorship in 1963 he was renowned internationally – acknowledged generally to have been one of western Europe's outstanding statesmen of the early post-war era.

Adenauer was centrally involved in the profound transformation of Germany and Europe for nearly two decades after the end of the war. But what, precisely, was his personal role? How much did the establishment of West German democracy, the binding of the Federal Republic to the West and the establishment of an integrative European Community owe to his individual decisions? Did he make history, or was he largely the vehicle of the forces of international politics and economics that he channelled but at best only partially controlled?

PERSONALITY, EARLY CAREER
AND POLITICAL AIMS

The young Konrad Adenauer clearly showed the traits of personality that would shape his later Chancellorship and would make him such a formidable leader, even in his eighties. The values he had imbibed from childhood – he was born in Cologne in 1876 to a middle-class, devoutly Catholic family – gave him a pronounced sense that the responsibilities and duties of each individual were rooted in the tradition and legacy of Christianity in western Europe. The importance of duty, hard work, reliability and public service in a society built on order and rationality was ingrained in his character.[1] He shared the political views of most citizens of his social class (and religious affiliation) in Wilhelmine Germany. He was proud that Germany had become a great power and had acquired a colonial empire. His Catholic upbringing instilled in him a fear of the growing power of 'atheistic' social democracy. The social doctrine of the Catholic Church in the late nineteenth century (which sought to improve conditions for the poor but avoid class conflict and attacks on private property) shaped his political consciousness and was later adapted to his form of Christian democratic conservatism.

To these general principles he added personal characteristics. Not least of these was ambition. He had been drawn to politics soon after completing his law studies and beginning work in Cologne's courts. In 1906 – by now married with a young child – he had joined the Zentrum (the Centre Party, the main voice of political Catholicism), which, alongside the Liberals, was the dominant political force in the city. It was the route to advancement. The same year he had been elected to the city's council and within three years was made deputy mayor. When the First World War broke out severe bronchial problems made him unfit to join the army – they had already years earlier excluded him from military service. By then his work in the administration of a major city close to the western front was in any case sufficiently important to warrant exemption. His ability in ensuring the provisioning of Cologne during the war was a major stepping-stone to becoming in 1917 the youngest lord mayor (*Oberbürgermeister*) in the whole of Prussia. As lord mayor throughout the Weimar years, until the coming of Nazi rule in 1933, he introduced modernizing improvements to the amenities of Cologne and gained invaluable political and administrative experience. The position of lord mayor of a large city gave the incumbent extensive executive authority and a significant base of power – so much so that Adenauer was more than once in the 1920s considered as a possible Reich Chancellor. Cologne was the essential crucible for what came later.

The coming of the Nazis brought a sudden end to his long period of office as Cologne's mayor. Years of difficulty and anxiety followed. He had long been in the Nazis' sights as the key local figure in the Zentrum, the party which posed a major obstacle to their break-through among the Catholic population of Cologne and the wider Rhineland. Their campaign against him – including accusations that he was sympathetic to Jews, or even Jewish himself – was vicious and prolonged. Nazi thugs even went round collecting money 'for a bullet for Adenauer'.[2] Like others, he was prepared to consider Nazi partici-pation in the Reich government as a way out of the crisis of state, but such a misjudgement did not reflect his support for Nazi values, which he found abhorrent. He continued to speak out for the Zentrum's advocacy of 'truth, freedom and law' in the weeks after Hitler had become Chancellor on 30 January 1933.[3]

His deposition as lord mayor was inevitable when the Nazis seized control of Cologne in March. Bleak years followed. He was deprived of his home and his livelihood. He took refuge for some months in the monastery of Maria Laach in the Eifel region. His second wife, Gus-sie, and his (by now) seven children – his first wife, Emma, the mother of his three eldest children, had died in 1916 – moved temporarily into a Caritas home in Cologne. Until his pension was restored in 1937 – civil law still functioned in part – he had to rely on financial support from friends. From 1935 onwards he was allowed to live with his family in seclusion in Rhöndorf, a village on the right bank of the Rhine, to the south of Bonn. The three older children from his first marriage had by this time left home, though Adenauer retained a close relationship with all his children. The family provided him with an oasis of stability and support during such troubled years. The Nazi regime did not lose sight of him. He was twice arrested but he had kept his distance from the conspiracy to kill Hitler in 1944, and, with some good fortune, he and his family survived the Third Reich. Gus-sie, however, never fully recovered from a blood infection she had contracted while she herself had been imprisoned in the last weeks of the war and died in 1948.

The German capitulation of 1945, as unpromising as the situation initially seemed, gave Adenauer the chance to restart his own political career and to acquire a national, not just regional, profile. His name was at the top of a 'White List' drawn up by Allied leaders in early 1945 of persons who could be useful to them.[4] The Americans reinstalled him as lord mayor of Cologne on 4 May 1945.[5] When the British took over the occupation some weeks later, however, they blamed Adenauer for doing too little to prepare the city for the coming winter and in October dismissed him for incompetence – a spectacular misjudgement.[6] Within three months they realized their mistake and came to see Adenauer as an important figure in building a new political party, the Christian Democratic Union (CDU), in their zone of occupation. Adenauer shared a widely held view in conservative circles that a party resting on principles of Christian renewal but capable of transcending the division between Catholics and Protestants was necessary to overcome the stain of Nazi criminality and counter the threat of 'Godless' socialism and communism. He had been involved since August 1945 in the construction of the CDU in the Rhineland and by March 1946 was the party's leader in the whole of the British Zone.[7] This paved the way for his ascendance to the Chancellorship of the Federal Republic of Germany at its establishment in 1949.

Meanwhile, his ambition had become plain. 'I want to be Federal Chancellor,' he declared.[8] He had a high level of self-discipline and – even in advanced old age – a Stakhanovite capacity for hard work. He would prove unshakeably loyal to his colleagues and advisers. Neither in appearance nor in public speaking did he exude natural charisma. He instinctively conveyed authority, however, whether running the affairs of Cologne or later managing his Cabinet in the government of the Federal Republic.

He was unusually strong-willed, with distinctly authoritarian tendencies. Already in the Cologne years some thought he had the style of a dictator. His left-wing opponents called him a 'German Mussolini' or 'the Duce of Cologne'.[9] People joked that he enjoyed more power in Cologne than the King of Prussia or the German Kaiser had ever had.[10] He believed in democratic government. But democracy in his view needed steering, guiding, directing. Not for nothing was he later often accused of running a 'Chancellor democracy' (*Kanzlerdemokratie*). His style of government, it has been said, was a bridge between a patriarchal state and a multi-party democracy.[11] He had a finely attuned sense of the political realities that underpinned power. He could be ruthless and Machiavellian in his manoeuvring and machinations. He looked to the long term, though was adept at making whatever short-term adjustments and compromises were necessary in order to achieve his objectives. Prominent among these were building a democratic, economically stable West Germany that was committed to western values, ready to work cooperatively with its European neighbours and closely allied to the USA. Once set on a course of action, he followed it with determination, was hard to shake from it and was ready to fight for it. Coupled with his detailed mastery of a proposal, his clarity of mind and powers of persuasion made him a formidable political operator.

His outright priority in his first years as Chancellor was the ending of Allied occupation and the attainment of sovereignty for the Federal Republic. He totally rejected the aggressive nationalism that had led to Nazi criminality and the destruction of Germany. But he was deeply patriotic and placed the welfare and interests of his country beyond all other political considerations. He naturally (like almost all his compatriots) wanted Germany once again to be a united nation-state. Privately, he accepted that the former eastern provinces beyond the Oder–Neisse Line, overrun by the Red Army towards the end of the war and since the war part (mainly) of Poland, were lost. Publicly, he had to hold to the fiction that the borders of Germany were still those of the German Reich in 1937. His political realism led him, moreover, to the early conclusion that for the indefinite future unification even on the 1945 borders – agreed at the Potsdam Conference that year – would be impossible. Only at some distant and currently unforeseeable future point would it become realizable – and then only if the West were militarily far stronger than the Soviet Union.

A second leitmotiv reinforced his first. In his early years his Catholic upbringing instilled in him his first intense dislike of socialism. And before the First World War, like many other Germans, he had feared the might of Russia. Both translated later into his lasting intense detestation of Soviet communism and anxiety about the Soviet nuclear threat. That meant, inexorably, that he saw the key to Germany's security in close bonds with the western powers, above all with the USA. Although this ruled out early unification, it did not diminish the sense of national identity in Adenauer's eyes. Rather, it amounted to redefining that national identity as a part of western, liberal, constitutional democracy in stark opposition to the tyranny of Soviet communism.

His strong support for the early stages of west European integration followed from the same premise. Already in autumn 1945, foreseeing a Europe irreconcilably divided between east and west, he thought the future of the non-Soviet zones would be shaped by economic integration with other countries in western Europe.[12] As a Rhinelander it was natural for him to look to close economic cooperation with Germany's neighbours to the west. He had even in 1923, during the French occupation of the Ruhr, toyed with the idea of a separate Rhine republic with industrial, financial and mutual security links to France. Immediately after the Second World War he showed himself open to ideas about economic rapprochement aimed at eliminating the age-old conflict between France and Germany. His swift support for Schuman's proposal in 1950 of a Coal and Steel Community, and for the French suggestion of a European Defence Community, followed from a similar starting-point – that Germany's future was bound up in the integration of western Europe, economically and militarily. But integration was not a goal in itself. Its purpose was to serve German national interests. And rapprochement with France, desirable as it was to remove old antagonisms, would never be enough in security terms to protect Germany from the threat of Soviet communism. For that end, he regarded the continuing support of the USA as indispensable.

Adenauer's motives in driving forward his policy of close bonds with the western powers (especially the USA) and closer economic integration with neighbouring countries (above all France) had a direct impact on his domestic agenda. He aimed at nothing less than the rebuilding of Germany – physically, economically and morally ruined by twelve years of Nazi rule. Integrating a broken society was the crucial imperative, the indispensable base of the process of rebuilding. Damaging and dangerous mentalities bred over the years of extreme nationalist, imperialist and racist dictatorship had to be replaced by commitment to peace, democracy, freedom, the rule of law and friendly cooperation with countries sharing similar values. That would take time. It would necessitate outlawing political movements, Left or Right, which rejected those values. But it also meant for him drawing a veil over the complicity of large sections of society in National Socialism – prioritizing political integration over moral condemnation and reckoning.

Building a new (West) Germany would need help from outside, from the western Allies, and also from other European countries. But above all it needed the commitment by the German population to the new, democratic values. This would be easier if democracy worked in people's interests. Here, good fortune as well as good policy choices proved a bonus in the shape of the 'economic miracle'. Adenauer, who had enjoyed close links with leading industrialists already in the Cologne years, instinctively favoured liberal economic policy over state control. He was lucky to have Ludwig Erhard to guide the economic recovery, and to have the external impact of the Korean War to stimulate a still struggling economy. Even in such a positive economic environment, winning support for highly controversial policies like integration with the West at the expense of any early prospect of national unification took political courage, a high level of determination and the ability to convince doubters through force of argument and power of personality.

PRECONDITIONS

Less propitious circumstances than those facing Adenauer in the early post-war years are hard to imagine. Between 1945 and the foundation in 1949 of the two new states, the Federal Republic of Germany and the German Democratic Republic, 'Germany' consisted of no more than the zones of the four occupying powers (Great Britain, the United States, France and the Soviet Union). What confronted Adenauer when he emerged as the most significant German political leader in the three western zones was not a state crisis, but the daunting task of constructing a state completely afresh. He was free of complicity with the Nazi regime. But he had to begin from a position of complete subordination to the occupying forces in a country where Nazi values were still widely prevalent.

Between 1946 and 1949 Adenauer swiftly built up the CDU's organization in the British zone. The American Zone had no unified leadership, and Bavaria, its largest state and overwhelmingly Catholic, where political Catholicism had been represented in the Weimar Republic not by the Zentrum but by the Bavarian People's Party, was establishing its own variant of Christian democracy, the Christian Social Union (CSU). Berlin, under Four-Power rule but situated deep in the Soviet Zone, which was by 1946 firmly under communist control, was deemed unsuitable as the location of national headquarters. So Adenauer's strong base in the British Zone in north-western Germany proved advantageous in widening his control over the nascent party. When, in June 1948, amid heightened Cold War tension, the western Allies agreed to create a new state in western Germany, Adenauer was in prime position to win election as President of the Parliamentary Council (Parlamentarischer Rat), established in Bonn that September to draft a constitution (promulgated in May 1949). It was a stepping-stone on the way to seeing himself not merely as a party leader, but potentially a head of government.[13]

On 14 August 1949 Adenauer led the CDU in the elections to a federal parliament (*Bundestag*). Victory by a narrow margin over the Social Democratic Party (SPD) was enough to determine that the new state – founded on 20 September 1949 (the foundation of the German Democratic Republic followed on 7 October) – would be built on principles of a liberal market economy, not the planned socialist economy that the SPD had wanted. Opposition to the SPD enabled Adenauer to construct an anti-socialist coalition in which the CDU was joined by its sister party, the CSU, the recently-created market-orientated Free Democratic Party (the Freie Demokratische Partei, FDP) and the Deutsche Partei (DP). When the coalition wrangling was over, there was still the question of the Chancellorship to be decided. A majority of members of the Bundestag was necessary. And the opposition parties were almost as strongly represented as the governing coalition. When the votes were counted on 15 September, Adenauer had been elected Federal Chancellor by one vote – his own. Declaring his readiness to serve as Chancellor, Adenauer had said, 'My doctor tells me that I would be able to carry out this office for at least a year, perhaps for two.'[14] As it was, he lasted fourteen years.

COMMITTING TO THE WEST: THE ROUTE TO SOVEREIGNTY

That the Federal Republic in 1955, after a decade under Allied occupation, became a sovereign country – scarcely imaginable six years earlier – owed much to Adenauer's personal leadership. His chief advisers on foreign policy, the State Secretary at the Foreign Office Walter Hallstein and the experienced diplomat Herbert Blankenhorn, were instrumental behind the scene. But direction unmistakably came from Adenauer himself, who – reflecting the extraordinary importance of West Germany's external relations at the time – was Foreign Minister as well as Federal Chancellor between 1951 and 1955.

The rapid attainment of sovereignty was possible because in the early 1950s Adenauer decisively bound the new Federal Republic to the West. With the passage of time, the fundamental turn to the West seems unremarkable, even inevitable. It was not so in the early 1950s. Huge opposition was articulated most powerfully – though not solely – by the Social Democratic Party, which favoured early political unification of a neutral, demilitarized country and a socialized economy. The turn to the West meant, in contrast, accepting the seemingly permanent division of Germany, commitment to a capitalist economy and participation (including rearmament) in the West's military alliance.

Few issues were more sensitive than German rearmament – deeply divisive within the Federal Republic itself and understandably highly unwelcome to France, which had been invaded three times from across the Rhine between 1870 and 1940. An attempt to defuse it was the French initiative of a European Defence Community (EDC), which would include small West German troop contingents in a system controlled (it was tacitly assumed) by the French. Adenauer welcomed the initiative, seeing membership of the EDC as a step towards recognition of sovereignty for the Federal Republic of Germany. This goal edged a little closer with the start of talks in autumn 1951 to work towards a 'General Treaty' to revise the terms of occupation by new relations with the western Allies and give the Federal Republic extensive sovereign powers. This was the background against which, alarmed at the moves towards closer political and military ties with the western powers, Stalin launched his own initiative on 10 March 1952.

Stalin's 'Note' to the western Allies proposed a Four-Power conference to prepare a peace treaty with Germany based upon the country's reunification on the borders agreed in 1945 (meaning west of the Oder–Neisse Line), neutrality, 'free activity of democratic parties and organizations' and military forces necessary for self-defence. Stalin's initiative was a plain attempt to wean the Federal Republic away from the embrace of the western Allies. Smelling danger, Adenauer's negative reaction was unhesitating. He told the Allied High Commissioners that the 'Note' would have no influence on the federal government's policy. In their diplomatic exchanges with the Soviet Union over subsequent weeks, the western powers went on to pose conditions – for instance, on holding free elections and terms for a peace treaty – that Stalin was not prepared to meet. Adenauer's own position was unbending: only when the West was stronger than the Soviet Union would the time for negotiations have arrived. That would not be any time soon. Meanwhile, the moves towards EDC and, above all, towards concluding the 'General Treaty' needed to be accelerated.[15]

He worried understandably, however, about popular reactions in West Germany. Superficially, what Stalin was offering was far from unattractive. There were powerful voices in favour of at least exploring the possibilities – among them Kurt Schumacher, the well-respected leader of the SPD, and Jakob Kaiser, an old adversary of Adenauer within the CDU and now a member of his Cabinet as Minister of All German Affairs. Adenauer authorized a press communiqué, however, that was strongly negative in tone, emphasizing the threat Stalin's initiative posed to Germany's exposure to Soviet influence (given its inability to defend itself) and the certain and permanent loss of the eastern provinces. Opinion surveys showed that his stance enjoyed much support with the public.[16]

Had Germany taken up Stalin's 'offer', its future path would have been different. It was a turning-point at which West Germany did not turn. The question has, unsurprisingly, been asked ever since, therefore, whether a historic chance was missed already in 1952 to create a unified, peaceful and free Germany. The 'what ifs' of history can of their nature never be conclusively answered. But almost certainly no historic chance was missed.[17] The imposition of Soviet power over the countries of central Europe hardly instilled confidence in Stalin's safe-guards for Germany's future. Nor was the example of the communist stranglehold in the Soviet Zone of eastern Germany a good augur. Whether Stalin would have kept his word on the terms of the 'Note' was obviously questionable. In any case, 'free elections' and 'democracy' did not mean for the Soviet Union what they meant for the West. There was a big risk – one certainly not worth taking – that the whole of Germany would eventually have fallen under Soviet control. The position of the western Allies – most notably the United States – would have been gravely weakened, and western Europe accordingly left exposed. Within Germany itself, Adenauer would surely have resigned or been forced from office. German government would most likely have become more favourably disposed towards the Soviet Union, offering a firm foothold for the Communist Party. If the dangers of Soviet control needed emphasizing, they would soon be well advertised by the brutal suppression through military force of the uprising against communist rule in East Germany in June 1953.

It is in any case clear that the western Allies would not have accepted the Soviet proposals, whether or not Adenauer had been Chancellor. They were determined to integrate the Federal Republic into the western alliance. The Americans were resolute: withdrawal of US forces from Germany was inconceivable, which meant there could be no neutral Germany, no agreement with the Soviet Union and the indefinite continuation of the division of Germany and Europe.[18] Soviet domination of the whole of Germany was a danger they could not contemplate. However, a government more amenable to exploring Stalin's 'offer' would have posed problems for the western powers. At the very least, they would have faced greater difficulties without Adenauer's strong leadership and a less determined pro-western stance by the federal government.

The 'Stalin Notes' – there were three further 'Notes' in 1952, though the substance was not materially different from that of the first – hastened rather than retarded progress towards the crucial General Treaty between the Federal Republic and the three western powers. Preparation of the Treaty involved Adenauer in months of complex negotiation with the Allies. Strikingly, he kept even his Cabinet largely in the dark about their progress.[19] The Treaty (meanwhile renamed the Germany Treaty – Deutschlandvertrag) was signed in Bonn on 26 May 1952. There was a lengthy delay, however, before the Federal Republic finally became a sovereign state on 5 May 1955. It was caused by growing opposition in France to the EDC, and ultimately the French rejection in August 1954 of their own proposal to establish it. But what was initially a grave disappointment to Adenauer opened the door to NATO membership – for him a still better solution.[20] This followed on 9 May 1955. The Federal Republic was granted permission to form an army of half a million men but (on Adenauer's own initiative) was expressly forbidden to manufacture atomic, biological or chemical weapons.[21]

The British and, especially, the Americans had moved sharply in the early 1950s to seeing the integration of a sovereign Federal Republic in western defences as vital to the West's military strategy. The failure of the EDC meant the French had to accept what they had earlier sought to avoid. Instead of being a junior partner to the French in the EDC, West Germany was of practically equal standing in the western alliance. The interests of the western powers were the overriding determinant. Adenauer's wishes chimed with these interests completely. But Adenauer's adroitness, clear-sightedness and determination were of inestimable value in pursuit of goals that both he and the western powers sought to attain. Had another West German politician been leading the government of the Federal Republic, the task would almost certainly have been more difficult. The Social Democrats wanted a different policy altogether. Even within his own Cabinet Adenauer had to contend with opposition. The structural determinants of western strategy in the Cold War certainly shaped the foundations. But following the path needed Adenauer's sure guidance.

FRIENDSHIP WITH FRANCE: FOUNDATIONS OF A NEW EUROPE

On 8 May 1950 Adenauer privately gave a warm welcome to an initiative launched the following day by Robert Schuman, which marked the inauguration of the Coal and Steel Community (comprising

France, West Germany, the Benelux countries and Italy). Four decades later this would eventually evolve into the European Union. The removal of the centuries-old hostility between France and Germany, Schuman had stated, was the premise of a new Europe.

Adenauer made his first trip abroad as Chancellor to sign the treaty establishing the European Coal and Steel Community on 18 April 1951. Ratification by the Bundestag followed on 11 January 1952, despite opposition from the Social Democrats, whose leader, Kurt Schumacher, rejected the Coal and Steel Community as a capitalist conspiracy directed against organized labour.[22] But, boosted by the demand for steel caused by the Korean War, the West German economy boomed during the early 1950s, drawing in exports from the rest of western Europe,[23] so that direct opposition became more difficult to sustain. By 1956, when the Bundestag authorized Adenauer to enter negotiations to establish a common market and a common policy on nuclear energy, there was general bipartisan agreement that European integration was vital to future stability and security.[24]

After the failure of the EDC in 1954, Adenauer had at first been anxious about the prospects of success of another big French-inspired European project – understandably given the continuing political instability in France. And his own Economics Minister, Ludwig Erhard, who more than any single individual had engineered the 'economic miracle', favoured a system of international free trade over a European customs union. Erhard and the Minister for Nuclear Energy (and from 1956 Defence Minister) Franz Josef Strauss, objected, too, to the plans for a common atomic-energy policy, which they argued would be disadvantageous to the nascent German atomic industry. But, persuaded by the former Belgian Prime Minister, the driving force of the integrative process, Paul-Henri Spaak, Adenauer overcame his doubts about the merits of a common market. Writing in April 1956 to Erhard, he emphasized the value of European integration to the Federal Republic's international standing. He regarded it as necessary both for Europe and for the Federal Republic. He especially stressed that the United States viewed integration as the basis of its policy towards Europe, adding that he regarded 'the help of the United States as absolutely necessary for us'.[25]

However, divisions remained within the Cabinet. Nor were France and West Germany in agreement on either the prospective atomic treaty or the creation of a common market. Relations with France were further complicated by the Suez crisis, caused when British, French and Israeli troops invaded Egypt on 5 November 1956 in a botched attempt to regain control over the Suez Canal (which had been nationalized by the Egyptian leader, Gamal Abdel Nasser). The breakthrough came with a visit by Adenauer to Paris during the Suez crisis itself. Agreement with France was reached during meetings on 6 November with the French Prime Minister, Guy Mollet, and a basis for future close cooperation between the two countries established. The path was now clear. On 25 March 1957 Adenauer was among the signatories to the Treaty of Rome – backed by both major West German parties – which established the European Economic Community and the European Atomic Energy Community. He had told journalists a few weeks earlier that it might amount to 'the most important event of the post-war era'.[26]

That the Treaty of Rome had come to fruition was, of course, a collective enterprise – hardly Adenauer's own work. If one man deserves singling out, then it was Spaak. Even so, without Adenauer's skill in defusing the tensions within his own Cabinet and negotiating agreement with the French – sweetened by a substantial German contribution to the EEC's development fund, from which France was set to benefit – the major step towards European integration would most likely not have been taken in 1957.

A side-issue in broader European politics, but of importance for West German opinion and touching directly on Franco-German relations, was the reversion to German sovereignty of the Saar. The important industrial area with a mainly German population had been a 'protectorate' administered by France since 1947. This was highly unpopular in the Federal Republic, but the French were keen to hold on to the Saar. When put to the test in a plebiscite held on 23 October 1955, however, more than two-thirds of voters chose to unite with West Germany. The French had little choice but to accept the result, and on 1 January 1957 the Saarland became part of the Federal Republic. The outcome removed a sore point in relations between France and the Federal Republic. Adenauer's government was given the credit by citizens of the Federal Republic.[27] In fact, however,

Adenauer, keen not to upset the French and in the interests of European integration, had actually been ready, if necessary, to let the Saar remain with France.[28]

Franco-German relations had improved greatly during the 1950s. But a deeper rapprochement was established only after Charles de Gaulle had come to power in France in 1958. It rested on the common strategic interests of France and the Federal Republic. Closer bonds between the two countries were for de Gaulle a key part of limiting American influence in Europe. His priority was to build French primacy in a European defence strategy that would be independent of the USA and Great Britain and would reach a modus vivendi with the Soviet Union. Replacing the Federal Republic's dependence on the USA as the basis of western Europe's security by alignment with France was never likely to be a winning formula in Bonn. Neither Adenauer nor the German Foreign Ministry thought in such terms. Their misgivings were linked to the question of European integration. And here West German and French ideas differed. For de Gaulle, the supranational aims of the EEC (which he intensely disliked) were to be subordinated to French national interests. For Adenauer, German interests could only be served by their sublimation in those of a more integrated western Europe.[29]

Over the five years following their first meeting in September 1958 Adenauer and de Gaulle met on a number of occasions. In July 1960 – France became a nuclear power that year – de Gaulle sought to persuade Adenauer of the value of deepened integration of defence and foreign policy of France and the Federal Republic which would greatly reduce (if not altogether supplant) security dependence on NATO. The EEC in this vision would be limited to economic cooperation. Future political integration would be off the agenda. Politics, for de Gaulle, was the affair of national governments. As Adenauer clearly saw, however, the interests of the Federal Republic were deeply wedded to the advantages to be accrued from the European Economic Community on the one hand and the security provided by NATO, backed by the power of the USA, on the other.[30]

In 1962 de Gaulle proposed a bilateral relationship with the Federal Republic, though still within the framework of the EEC and NATO. 'Hopes of uniting Europe', he declared, depended on the solidarity of France and Germany.[31] This solidarity saw its expression in the 'Élysée Treaty' signed amid great pomp and ceremony by Adenauer and de Gaulle on 22 January 1963 in which France and the Federal Republic agreed to close consultation, especially on foreign and defence policy.[32] The sealing of Franco-German reconciliation was a final foreign-policy success for Adenauer, whose Chancellorship would end that same year. But in truth the Treaty was stronger on symbolism than content. And it masked rifts at the heart of the EEC.

De Gaulle's proposed way forward for Europe was designed not only to reduce the influence of the Benelux countries, but also to exclude Britain from membership. His veto of British entry on 14 January 1963 was a logical consequence. But it was a blow to the other EEC members, who had favoured Britain joining. Adenauer had at one time seen Britain's involvement as important to Europe's reconstruction, though negative British attitudes towards the EEC had meanwhile tempered his views. And by 1963 he thought de Gaulle was right to veto British membership, regarding it as not advantageous to the EEC and sharing the French President's view that Britain was too close to the USA (whose uncertain long-term commitment to the defence of Europe worried him at the time).[33]

His party, the CDU, on the other hand, had been keen to see Britain join and, as Adenauer's authority ebbed away at home, some of its prominent members publicly criticized the opposition to British EEC membership that had flowed from the overriding commitment to the bilateral relationship with France.[34] Erhard spoke of the rejection of British membership as 'a black hour for Europe'.[35] Within months, Erhard would succeed Adenauer as Chancellor. Before then, the Bundestag would in May ratify the Élysée Treaty, though only after Adenauer's critics had forced him to accept a preamble stating the Federal Republic's adherence to partnership with the USA, its commitment to NATO and its support for the EEC as the vehicle for Europe's unification.

A unilaterally introduced preamble to an already signed international treaty was an extraordinary procedure.[36] It signalled Adenauer's time as Chancellor was almost up. It was obviously an affront to de Gaulle. But it was the French President's policy that had brought the EEC to an impasse. Unable to proceed along de Gaulle's lines, but unable to develop further without French engagement (which for a time in the mid-1960s was completely withdrawn), the EEC would largely stagnate for years to come.

Adenauer had surmounted serious opposition to make possible the creation of the EEC in 1957. But although the West German economy continued to thrive as its most dynamic component, Adenauer's prolonged and close bilateral relationship with de Gaulle after 1958, driven primarily by considerations of defence strategy, helped to block progress towards the political integration of the EEC for nearly a quarter of a century.

STABILIZING DEMOCRACY

At its foundation, only four years after the end of the Third Reich, the Federal Republic of Germany was a highly fragile democracy. One in two Germans, according to opinion polls, thought National Socialism had been a good idea, just badly carried out (and preferred it to communism). Asked in 1951 about Germany's best time in the twentieth century, over four-fifths of the population pointed to either the years before 1914 (when the Kaiser still ruled) or the pre-war years of the Third Reich between 1933 and 1939 (under Hitler). Only 7 per cent thought the best time had been under Weimar democracy. And a mere 2 per cent thought it was the present. A third of those questioned in 1951 were critical of the members of the Resistance who tried to kill Hitler in 1944. The following year a quarter of the population still had a 'good opinion' of Hitler. A majority thought – remarkably and presumably thinking only of what they saw as 'good times' before the war – he had done more for Germany than Adenauer (yet to benefit from the uplift of the 'economic miracle').[37] By the mid-1950s, however, there had been an extraordinary turn-around. Adenauer was by now regarded as second only to Bismarck in the public's estimation of the leader who had done most for Germany. By the time he left office in 1963, he had even overtaken Bismarck. More than half of the population already ranked him in 1958 as 'among the really great men of our century'.[38]

When Adenauer resigned as Chancellor during a fourth successive term in office, multi-party parliamentary democracy – though conservative, patriarchal and elitist in essential character – was well established, even if still not entirely sure of itself. Unlike the Weimar Republic, which had never been accepted either by most of the political elite or by a large part of the electorate, the Federal Republic, from uncertain beginnings, had won overwhelming backing at both levels. Whatever the political divisions, there was as good as complete acceptance of a constitution resting upon principles of personal liberty and the rule of law and strengthened by learning lessons from weaknesses of the Weimar constitution. The Weimar Republic had been destroyed by its inability to cope with the long, multi-faceted crises that almost brought down democracy in the early 1920s, then did so a decade later. The Bonn Republic, in contrast, was beset by no prolonged internal crisis and enjoyed strong backing from the western Allies (especially the USA). Unlike the aftermath of the First World War, there was no imposition of what had been widely viewed as unjust reparations, which had helped to poison Weimar politics. And, of course, instead of devastating economic crisis, the Federal Republic was soon experiencing a boom that brought rapidly increasing levels of prosperity. More than anything else, the 'economic miracle' of the 1950s underpinned the consolidation of democracy. Millions of West Germans had become better off and felt their lives more secure. Adenauer certainly played a major part in shaping the political framework for the astonishing explosion of economic growth. But the architect of the 'economic miracle' was not Adenauer, but Ludwig Erhard, who successfully used the state to establish the framework for a burgeoning liberal market economy linked to principles of social welfare.

The two often did not see eye to eye. By the early 1960s Erhard, as noted earlier, was openly criticizing the implications for relations with the USA and for the development of the EEC entailed by Adenauer's close alignment to France and the rejection of British membership. Adenauer, for his part, was by now letting it be known that he did not think Erhard was fit to replace him as Chancellor. It had throughout been a marriage of convenience. But it had worked well for West Germany, largely because Adenauer left Erhard to run economic affairs without interference.[39] In the crucial area of the economy, decisive in stabilizing democracy, Erhard had been more important than Adenauer.

The importance of Erhard to the key economic policy is an indicator that even a head of government as assertive and directive as Adenauer was dependent upon the vital contribution of effective ministers. Besides Erhard other ministers played a significant role in the early development of the Federal Republic and were far from mere rubber-stamps for Adenauer's policies – among them Heinrich von Brentano (Foreign Office), Gerhard Schröder (Interior Ministry, then Foreign Office), Theodor Blank (Defence, then Labour Ministry) and Franz Josef Strauss (Defence). But the Chancellor's Office (Bundeskanzleramt) formulated the key decisions. And Adenauer, with single-mindedness and consummate political skill, drove them through.

Unlike foreign affairs, in the major issues of domestic policy (leaving aside the question of German unification) Adenauer more often than not swam with the tide of public opinion rather than against it. His pronounced anti-communism, for instance, fitted the public mood. That the Iron Curtain ran down the middle of Germany, and that the German Democratic Republic was a glaring example of a system that was abhorrent to most West Germans, were of inestimable value to Adenauer. The outrage at the crushing of the 1953 uprising by Soviet armed might helped him to a resounding electoral victory that year. The date of the uprising, 17 June, was swiftly turned into an annual public holiday in West Germany, a regular reminder of the horrors of Soviet communism.

Anti-communism was the ideological cement of West German society. It united all but the far Left (and the already electorally insignificant Communist Party was banned in 1956). It increasingly helped Adenauer as he walked the tightrope of policy on German unification. By the mid-1950s, the Soviet Union had come to accept the failure of its endeavours to reunite Germany and to recognize that the division of the country was unalterable. By 1960 the earlier conflict about western integration versus national unification was over. That year the Social Democrats altered their previous stance on unification, accepting western integration, rearmament (though emphatically rejecting West German possession of nuclear weapons) and membership of NATO.[40]

When the last major crisis over Berlin between 1958 and 1961 ended with the building of the Berlin Wall on 13 August 1961, visibly sealing the division of Germany, Adenauer's political antennae for once failed him. He lost popularity when he announced that his government would do nothing to damage relations with the Soviet Union or endanger the international situation. And taking nine days after the Wall went up to visit Berlin did not help. But the Wall now defused the issue of German unification. Whatever the hopes for the long term, for the foreseeable future Adenauer's policy of integration with the West had won the day.

His strongly anti-Soviet, pro-western conservatism was able to attract many who might otherwise have drifted towards a revived nationalism on the extreme Right.[41] The lethal anti-Bolshevism of the Nazi years mutated into the anti-communism of the Adenauer era. The Wehrmacht's war in the east could be portrayed as honourable. Public opinion strongly backed the early release of former high-ranking officers who had been condemned for war crimes by the Allies. And one of Adenauer's most popular attainments was, during his visit to Moscow in September 1955, negotiating the release of thousands of German prisoners still held in the Soviet Union.[42] The Wehrmacht, people were more than happy to accept, was 'clean'. Nazi criminality could be laid fully at the door of the SS. Even this distinction generally excluded, also by many supporters of the Left, the 900,000 or so members of the Waffen-SS (the military wing of the SS). According to the SPD leader, Kurt Schumacher, they had 'committed no crime' and deserved 'the opportunity of making their way in what for them is a new world'.[43]

Adenauer's approach to the Hitler years was perfectly attuned to a society more anxious to look to future peace, prosperity and stability than to rake over the crimes of the very recent past.[44] Drawing a veil over the Nazi era suited most people, who were more than ready to look no further than Hitler and the Nazi leadership for those to blame for the disaster that had befallen Germany. The punishment meted out at Nuremberg to leading Nazis was generally seen as justified, according to opinion surveys conducted in the American Zone. These did not tell the whole story. Many at the time, and since, thought the trials were just 'victors' justice'. The Soviets had perpetrated heinous crimes, it was pointed out, and the western Allies had mercilessly bombed the civilian population, but now they sat in judgement on the Germans. And there was declining interest in the trials as they progressed. Everyday economic issues often outweighed concern about the fate of former Nazi leaders.[45] But the small fry were a different matter altogether. Millions of Germans had been members of the Nazi Party and its various sub-organizations, and countless others had also cheered Hitler or been complicit in one way or another in Nazism. Whatever the level of earlier commitment to Nazism, few were prepared to admit their own guilt for what had happened. They rejected, too, the collective guilt that they saw as an unjustified Allied verdict on the entire society. Most felt they had been misled by propaganda and repressed by a totalitarian police state.

The Allied denazification programme was, unsurprisingly, an almost complete failure. And when the Germans themselves took it over it descended into little more than farce. So, with nationalist feeling still strong and resentment at the slur of collective guilt, Adenauer had most of the public on his side when he introduced amnesties for all but the small number of those convicted of the worst offences in the Nazi era. Pressure for a general amnesty had come in part from former Nazis, some of them with a very murky past, who had infiltrated Adenauer's coalition partners, the FDP. It also came from the increasingly influential expellee organizations, representing the millions of Germans who had been driven out of Czechoslovakia, Poland and elsewhere.[46] Any possible resurgence of Nazism was, however, stamped out in 1952 with the banning of the Socialist Reich Party (Sozialistische Reichspartei), which had attracted ex-Nazis and the previous year made disturbing headway in parts of north Germany, acquiring a membership of around 40,000. The danger soon passed. In the 1953 general election, with Adenauer's popularity buoyed by the flourishing economy, the extreme Right won under 1 per cent of the vote.[47]

By then, large numbers of those who had served Hitler's regime – sometimes in significant positions – had been reintegrated into the civil service and legal system. A law passed in 1951 granted reinstatement in former or equivalent positions, with full pension rights, for former civil servants and career soldiers who had been dismissed as a consequence of denazification. For instance, over a third of high-ranking civil servants in the Foreign Office in 1952 had belonged to the Nazi Party.[48] Judges who had passed death sentences for political offences in the Third Reich returned to office. The degree of continuity in personnel with those who had served Hitler's regime was striking.[49]

Nowhere was this more controversial than in Adenauer's closest entourage, in the figure of Hans Globke, who served between 1953 and 1963 as state secretary (the top civil servant beneath the minister) in the Federal Chancellery. Globke had daily direct contact with the Chancellor, sitting like the 'spider in the web' of all personnel issues and imposing 'the stamp of Adenauer's will' in extensive areas of government.[50] Highly able and efficient, he became indispensable to Adenauer. But his past was a major problem. Although never a party member, as a civil servant in the Reich Ministry of the Interior he had helped to formulate anti-Jewish legislation and had co-authored the commentary on the Reich Citizenship Law (part of the notorious Nuremberg Laws of 1935). It was politically embarrassing.[51] But Adenauer never withdrew his support for Globke despite the heated public criticism, especially on the Left.[52] It did not affect his popularity. The Globke issue was, paradoxically, a matter of heated political debate yet seems hardly to have registered with the vast majority of the German population. Three-quarters of those asked in 1960 claimed they did not even know who Globke was.[53] Perhaps it was a case of not wanting to know.

An even more overt case of the rehabilitation of former Nazis was the inclusion in Adenauer's government after 1953 of Theodor Oberländer, who in 1923 had participated in the Hitler Putsch and had been involved before the war in racial planning for eastern Europe. Adenauer acknowledged that Oberländer had been a dyed-in-the-wool Nazi. But Oberländer was a leading representative of the sizeable refugee lobby.[54] So when the All-German Bloc/League of Expellees and Dispossessed (Gesamtdeutscher Block/Bund der Heimatvertriebenen und Entrechteten) won twenty-seven parliamentary seats in the 1953 election, Adenauer appointed him Federal Minister for Displaced Persons, Refugees and Victims of War without great popular outcry. When the League's vote fell in 1957, leaving it without seats in the Bundestag, Adenauer still retained Oberländer, who had meanwhile opportunely joined the CDU. By 1960 as criticism of former Nazis in government mounted, especially among students, Oberländer, by now an unnecessary liability, resigned. But Adenauer stuck by him to the last, declaring that he had 'never done anything dishonourable'.[55]

Adenauer's popularity was by this time starting to sag. He had won an astonishing victory at the 1957 general election, when the Christian Union (CDU and CSU) gained an absolute majority of votes, 50.2 per cent – a unique attainment in the history of the Federal Republic. His election slogan, 'Keine Experimente' ('No Experiments'), chimed perfectly with the mood of the times, reflecting the growth in affluence. He had offered the electorate a highly attractive extension of social benefits in a guarantee of pensions index-linked to the cost of living, which was supported by the Social Democrats.[56] But 1957 was the apogee of his popular appeal. The 1961 general election brought for the first time since 1949 a drop in the Christian Union's vote, down 5 per cent compared with 1957, with a loss of twenty-six seats.

A marked sign that Adenauer was losing touch with the changing mood in the country was the 'Spiegel Affair'. An article in the news magazine Der Spiegel on 10 October 1962, attacking the Defence Minister, Franz Josef Strauss, and pointing out deficiencies in the country's defence capability, led to a police raid on the magazine's office in Hamburg and the arrest of its editor and several others. Adenauer denounced what he said was the magazine's treason. But a storm of protest, led by students and intellectuals, at the attack on press freedom and what were seen as Nazi methods eventually forced the resignation of Strauss (who returned to his Bavarian stronghold, where his popularity had not suffered). Adenauer was damaged by the affair, his authority left weakened. Some CDU ministers had refused to serve alongside Strauss, and five FDP ministers had resigned. In a wider sense, the affair was the first clear indication that public feeling was starting to turn against the forms of authoritarian conservatism that had characterized Adenauer's long Chancellorship.[57]

Adenauer had already indicated before the end of 1962 that he would resign as Chancellor in autumn 1963. Leading politicians inevitably started looking to a future without him. There was even talk of the social democrats joining a 'grand coalition' – something unthinkable only a few years earlier, but soon to become reality. Within his own party, succession planning became urgent. Adenauer failed in his attempts to block the obvious and favoured candidate to replace him and, unwillingly, on 15 October 1963 had to make way for a successor he thought not up to the job.

LEGACY

Endless effusive tributes, at home and abroad, accompanied Adenauer's departure from office. 'Adenauer need not be afraid of the verdict of history,' pronounced *Die Zeit*, a liberal newspaper that had often been among his critics. 'He was the greatest of our time.'[58] Further eulogies appeared at Adenauer's death (aged ninety-one) in 1967. His reputation lasted across the decades. In 2003, 3 million Germans voted him 'the greatest German of all time' for his achievement in pulling Germany from the ashes and giving it a place on the world stage.[59] But if we turn away from the vacuous enquiry about 'greatness' to the more tangible, if still difficult, question of personal impact on historical development, a more nuanced assessment presents itself.

The part that he played personally in committing the Federal Republic to the western alliance in the early 1950s was arguably the most important part of his legacy. The future of Germany, at the epicentre of the Cold War, was at that time completely uncertain. Backed by the social democratic opposition and elements of his own party, the pressure for early unification could have unwittingly destabilized both Germany and Europe and might have led to Soviet penetration of the entire country. Probably the western Allies would have prevented this, whoever had been Federal Chancellor. But conceivably the political constellation in Germany, had it favoured taking up Stalin's offer of 1952, would have rendered this difficult, even impossible. Adenauer was instrumental in ensuring that the Federal Republic looked to the West, and in particular to the United States, for its future security. Whatever the vagaries of international politics since then – and there were some bumps in the road in relations with the USA in Adenauer's own time – the integration with the West continued across the decades to serve the Federal Republic well. Without Adenauer, the history of Germany and of Europe could have turned out very differently.

Adenauer was important, too, in recognizing that the future of the Federal Republic had to be as part of a more integrated western Europe based upon mutual interests, friendship and close cooperation. He keenly supported the early French initiatives to establish the Coal and Steel Community and European Defence Community. And he lent his weight to the creation and growth of the European Economic Community from 1957 onwards. But in his later years he became over-enamoured by de Gaulle, and his emphasis on the bilateral relationship with France threatened to split the Community and posed difficulties for the process of European integration.

Adenauer's legacy to the Federal Republic itself was not straightforward. There were major achievements. He played an indispensable role in the stabilization of democracy in West Germany (though the 'economic miracle', its strongest pillar, was primarily Erhard's work). From early frailty, democracy there had come to rest on solid foundations. And Adenauer, through his visits abroad and his meetings with international leaders – including Churchill, Eisenhower and de Gaulle – built respect for the Federal Republic and its new democracy throughout the western world. This rested in no small measure on the personal respect he had won, which transferred itself to the Federal Republic, even in Israel after he had personally (and, characteristically, without authorization from his Cabinet) agreed in December 1951 to substantial financial compensation for Nazi crimes against Jews.[60]

The character of early West German democracy reflected the imprint of Adenauer's authoritarian personality. This accorded with the dominant public mood in a society that still placed great store on political authority, looked to firm leadership and wanted to draw a line under the Nazi past. But Adenauer's rehabilitation and integration of former Nazis in the new democracy was the most questionable part of his legacy. Was the appointment of Globke wholly unavoidable? Certainly, Globke was a highly able aide to Adenauer. But could no other state secretary have been found, equally good but lacking the moral stigma? And was it absolutely essential to give a place in his Cabinet to Oberländer, who had been a Nazi of the deepest hue, and to retain him in government even when the importance of the refugee lobby declined?

The strong continuity with the Third Reich in the personnel of the civil service, judiciary and medical profession, and among teachers, academics and others, was without doubt a chequered part of Adenauer's legacy. He deemed their skills indispensable for the Federal Republic. Even more importantly, he regarded their integration as vital to the process of consolidating democracy as quickly as possible, without its being torn apart by ferocious conflict about the very recent past. Critics, at the time and subsequently, have seen the rapid rehabilitation of so many with a highly unsavoury past – even some who had been members of the Nazi security police – as morally reprehensible. It has without doubt left an enduring stain on Adenauer's reputation.

Drawing a curtain on a recent harrowing past in order to build a new political system through integration rather than confrontation has been far from confined to West Germany. It was, in fact, the norm in most west European countries (and Japan) after the Second World War, and was also the case in post-Franco Spain. However, practically everywhere it merely postpones the reckoning with the past. In the Federal Republic it began with the Eichmann and Auschwitz trials in the early 1960s and took off in the student protests of 1968. Often heated public debates about the Nazi past were to recur periodically over subsequent decades. Already as Adenauer left office, the values he reflected were losing currency. Stuffy, authoritarian conservatism was starting to give way, at first tentatively, to more liberal norms – part of the social change that was taking place across Europe.

This was politically reflected in the exclusion from government after the 1969 election of Adenauer's party, the CDU, for the first time since the foundation of the Federal Republic twenty years earlier. The social democrats, under the charismatic Willy Brandt, headed a government that symbolized a new era. An important aspect of this was the reversal of Adenauer's policy on relations with the German Democratic Republic, with direct implications for the question of German unification. In 1955 Adenauer had laid out the policy, which became labelled the 'Hallstein Doctrine' (named after Walter Hallstein, his chief adviser on foreign policy and later the first President of the EEC Commission). The aim of the 'doctrine' was to prevent international recognition of the German Democratic Republic and to uphold the claim of the Federal Republic to be the sole representative of the

German people within the borders of 1937. But Adenauer's hard line towards the GDR lasted only until the introduction of Brandt's *Ostpolitik* (eastern policy) in 1970. Despite heated conservative opposition, this led to recognition of the GDR, established diplomatic relations between the two German states, and, in accepting in principle that the Oder–Neisse Line now permanently marked Germany's eastern border, therefore recognized the loss of the former German provinces to its east (though this was legally confirmed only in 1990).

Such a long political career in such turbulent times inevitably left a legacy not free of ambivalence. There were unquestionably some negative aspects, chief among them the rehabilitation of prominent former Nazis. Yet Adenauer's achievement in extraordinarily difficult circumstances in establishing a peaceful, democratic West Germany and anchoring it as an essential part of a western network of states committed to pluralism and the rule of law was enormous. Winston Churchill, no less, described Adenauer in May 1953 as 'the wisest German statesman since the days of Bismarck' and 'greatly admired the perseverance, courage, composure and skill with which he has faced the complex, changing, uncertain and unpredictable situations with which he has been ceaselessly confronted'.[61] Adenauer combined ideological single-mindedness with great tactical acumen, managing the constraints of a democratic system with a shrewd combination of political manipulation, self-assuredness and authoritarian direction. Without him, history in Germany – and, more widely, in Europe – would have taken a different course.

Franco is acclaimed (with apparently differing degrees of enthusiasm) by nationalist leaders as Generalísimo and Head of State on 1 October 1936 in Burgos. Within a year he was officially designated 'Caudillo' (Leader) of the 'Movement to save Spain'.

FRANCISCO FRANCO

Nationalist Crusader

Franco, it is tempting to think, is too peripheral a figure to be ranked as a 'maker of twentieth-century Europe' – central to Spanish history of the era, naturally, but not necessarily of wider importance. It is, of course, obvious that Franco's wider impact scarcely compares with that of Hitler and Mussolini, or Lenin and Stalin. He presents a case-study in the role and impact of the individual in history at the lower end of the scale. And it is fair to say that for much of the twentieth century Spain was on the periphery of the key developments in Europe. It has been adjudged that Franco 'at best influenced world history somewhat during the 1930s. But the twentieth century would not have been much different without him.'[1]

Such an assessment is too dismissive. European as well as Spanish history would certainly, if in indefinable ways, have been different had the republic survived after 1936. That it did not survive owed without doubt much to Franco's leadership in the Civil War. Moreover, the importance of that war was such that it drew in – in different measure – Europe's major powers and attracted the participation of volunteer fighters from across the continent. Franco's dealings with the Axis powers during the Second World War and then with the West during the Cold War also give his long dictatorship a significance not confined to Spain. Moreover, the character of the subsequent transition to pluralist democracy, and the impact of Franco's era on Spanish memory and political culture and on the divisive question of regional separatism in one of Europe's biggest countries, additionally make Franco a figure of relevance to European, not just Spanish, history. Not least, Franco illustrates how an individual with recognized qualities as a military commander but no experience of political leadership could benefit from the historical conditions that made his assumption of power possible in the first place and enabled him to go on to 'make his own history'.

PERSONALITY

Francisco Franco Bahamonde's upbringing pointed towards a military career.[2] Born in 1892 in El Ferrol, a naval base in Galicia, nearly 400 miles from Madrid, into a well-to-do military family, he seemed set to follow in the footsteps of his father and grandfather, both of whom had been high-ranking naval officers. His father, Nicolás, was away a good deal – probably just as well, since at home he was a despotic presence, given to outbursts of rage and to beating his wife and children. Francisco, the second of five children, wholly lacked affection from his domineering and dismissive father, who, with a track-record of philandering and gambling, moved out of the family home in 1907 to take up a post in Madrid (and leave behind an unhappy marriage). The relationship with his father never improved. He was, however, attached to his piously Catholic, deeply conservative mother, Pilar Bahamonde, who did her best to compensate for his tyrannical father and, despite stretched finances after her husband had left home, ensured that he had a good education. Just before his father moved out, Francisco passed the examination in 1907 to enter the military academy in Toledo.

There he soaked up military values – rigid discipline, a strong sense of duty, bravery, stoical acceptance of physical hardship, and belief in the glories of Spain's past. His record at the academy was undistinguished, and between 1910 and 1912 he was not sufficiently well qualified to apply for the posting he wanted in Morocco (one of the few remaining Spanish colonies). But he was determined. And after nearly two years serving back in his home town, he succeeded in obtaining a transfer to serve in the Spanish Army in Morocco. This is where he showed outstanding military prowess.

During brutal colonial wars that aimed to suppress insurgent Berber tribesmen he proved to be an officer of bravery, tactical skill and coolness in combat. His bravery and leadership brought him rapid promotion: to first lieutenant in 1912, to captain in 1914, to major in

1916 (leading to a posting back in Spain), lieutenant colonel in 1922 (and the following year command of the Spanish Legion in Morocco), and in 1926 at the age of only thirty-three to the rank of brigadier-general. He had meanwhile married, in 1923, María del Carmen Polo, from a well-connected family in Oviedo, who gave birth three years later to a daughter, Carmen, his only child. But his family life came second to his burgeoning military career. His victories in Morocco over rebellious indigenous tribal forces won him great prestige and made him something of a celebrity in Spain. King Alfonso XIII bestowed the prestigious Military Medal upon him in 1923 and made him one of his elite body of military courtiers. Flattered by the adulation already being heaped upon him, Franco started to see himself as of some national importance, though still primarily in the military rather than the political sphere.

His ideological formation had begun at an early age. A heavy feeling of national humiliation was long prevalent in military circles after Spain's disastrous defeat by the USA in a short war in 1898 that led to Cuban independence and the loss of almost all Spain's colonial possessions. The young Franco grew up in this atmosphere, deeply imbued with a sense of national shame and the belief that the military had been let down by the politicians. He soon saw Spain beset by enemies abroad and at home. He detested the anarchists and socialists who in 1909 launched a week-long violent protest against Spain's colonial war in Morocco and approved of their ruthless suppression by armed force. His life-long paranoid belief that international Freemasonry was behind Spain's subversive elements – a loathing that was as irrational, all-pervasive and enduring as Hitler's hatred of Jews – seems to have dated back to this time.[3]

In personality, Franco was self-contained and detached, emotionally cold, cautiously calculating, not spontaneous, driven by an overweening sense of duty, discipline and obedience, seldom revealing outward emotion and merciless towards defeated enemies. And he was ambitious. He approved of the atrocities of his brutal legionaries against captured Moorish villages in the colonial wars in Morocco. He later showed the same lack of humanity in his treatment of political enemies in Spain. Cold revenge against his enemies, external or internal, was a trait that ran through his character. And the long list of internal enemies amounted to all in his eyes who were ruining Spain – the revolutionary Left, anti-monarchists, anti-militarists, pacifists, liberals, those determined to destroy the Catholic Church and the separatists in Catalonia and the Basque Country who dreamed of breaking away from the centralized Spanish state. Behind them he came to see hidden backers – Moscow, Jews, but above all international Freemasonry, which, in his eyes, was responsible for Spain's plight.[4]

PRECONDITIONS

Franco was unquestionably a product of exceptional circumstances, even if these were in some respects the Spanish manifestation of a widespread and deep-seated malaise in interwar Europe. The searing social, political and ideological convulsions that beset Spain during the hugely turbulent five years of the Second Republic from 1931 to 1936 resulted in devastating civil war, which elevated Franco to the position of military leader of the nationalist rebellion. Without the Civil War there was no chance that Franco would have become Spain's head of state.

He was the beneficiary of long-festering ulcers in Spain's body politic. Under the constitutional monarchy from 1874 down to the abdication of King Alfonso XIII in 1931, Spain's political system functioned largely in the interests of a massively corrupt ruling class. Even following the expansion of industry in the Basque Country, Asturias, Catalonia and around Madrid, local 'notables' – usually long-standing powerful family dynasties – dominated politics and controlled elections through clientelism and patronage. Corruption at every level of society was extensive and endemic. The central state was weak, though it could rely upon the self-interested cooperation of local bosses to repress any signs of social upheaval or rebellion. Industrialization brought the growth of a manufacturing and commercial bourgeoisie, but the sector's influence remained small in relation to that of the major landholders, who, alongside the monarchy and the Catholic Church's hierarchy, retained a stranglehold on political power until the major challenge to their interests posed by the ousting of the King and establishment of a republic in 1931.[5]

The vast majority of the population had no political representation. Poverty was deep and widespread. For agricultural workers living in primitive conditions and engaged in back-breaking work on the estates of big landowners in wide swathes of central and southern Spain, and for a growing industrial proletariat living and working in miserable, impoverished conditions in Madrid, Barcelona and parts of the north, the state represented an alien, hostile and threatening entity. Socialism and membership of trade unions offered industrial workers an ideological and organizational basis to challenge the power of the state. In the north, class conflict blended into Catalan or Basque regional hostility to the central government in Madrid. In the poor agricultural south, anarcho-syndicalism, often involving sporadic anti-state violence, gained much support among landless labourers. Strikes, riots and localized insurrections against state power and 'bourgeois rule' were an increasing feature of Spanish politics.[6] Anticlericalism also fused with class conflict as another element in the gathering storm. The industrial working class and the agricultural proletariat viewed the representatives of the Church, with much justification, as part of the system of economic and political oppression. Attacks on Church property were no rarity even before they escalated drastically during the Second Republic.[7] At the same time, especially in rural Spain, most of the population was still wedded to Catholic beliefs and traditions, seeing these as central to whatever sense there was of national identity and as threatened by dangerous forces on the Left.

The cleavages in Spain's society and political system deepened still further following the First World War (which brought huge economic disturbance, even though the country had remained neutral).[8] A rapidly growing socialist movement, and now a Communist Party with an outrightly revolutionary doctrine, faced a weakened political oligarchy of liberal and conservative elites determined to hold on to power.[9] The coup of 1923, when General Miguel Primo de Rivera took power – backed by practically all sectors of conservative Spain in the face of ineffective and neutralized working-class opposition – was just the latest in an array of military takeovers stretching back to the early nineteenth century. It pointed to a fundamental divide between the army leadership, which saw itself as the sole guarantor of national unity and social order facing powerful internal enemies on the revolutionary Left, and a working class that hated the army as the state's most important agent of repression.[10] Primo's counter-revolution was of short duration, though ideologically its legacy carried through to the Franco dictatorship.[11] In 1930 mounting economic problems in the wake of the Wall Street Crash and growing popular unrest forced his resignation and retreat to exile in Paris. King Alfonso XIII left Spain months later, and elections in April 1931 inaugurated a new democratic republic. Spain's extreme reactionary forces, temporarily defeated and demoralized, were forced on to the defensive. But they were soon reorganizing and preparing to mount their assault to restore their power and destroy democracy – they hoped for good.

Victory for the republican Left in the 1931 elections was less impressive than it looked. The foundations of democracy were built on shifting sands. Rural Spain – most of the country – largely still supported the monarchy. Many people offered little more than lukewarm, conditional support to the new system. The republic's leadership received solid backing only from the relatively small industrial working class, though this was confined to big cities and specific regions – Catalonia, Asturias, the Basque Country – and was divided in its political allegiance between socialists, anarchists and Moscow-orientated communists. The government, a coalition of moderate socialists and largely middle-class liberals, lacked a coherent, radical agenda. Its limited reforms to agriculture, improved worker protection and curtailment through separation of Church and state of the social power of the Catholic Church – notably over education – were not radical enough for many of its own supporters. But they hugely antagonized the dominant elites while leaving their power, wealth and influence largely intact.[12] The readiness to accept an autonomous status for Catalonia in 1932 was a special source of antagonism in relations between the republic and the army, wedded to a centralized Spanish state and further angered by plans to reduce its size and influence.[13]

Within two years the republic was on the back foot. The Left suffered a heavy defeat in new elections in November 1933. The last two years of the republic brought a hardening of the class conflict and set the tone for the catastrophe that followed. Landlords, employers, the military and the Catholic Church saw their social power bolstered by the electoral triumph of parties of the Right, and the earlier reforms were reversed by the new right-wing government. The driving force was the newly formed CEDA (Confederación Española de Derechas Autónomas; Spanish Confederation of Autonomous Right-Wing Groups), led by José María Gil Robles, an enormous mass movement of 735,000 members, fascist in all but name, and claiming to defend Christianity from Marxism.[14] The Left responded by calling for a general strike in October 1934, which in Asturias, in northern Spain, turned into a full-scale insurrection that lasted two weeks. The insurrectionists, mainly working-class and led by striking miners, occupied a number of towns, seized large quantities of mainly small arms, killed a number of priests and seminarians and destroyed churches and convents in the capital, Oviedo.[15]

It was at this juncture that Franco first stamped his imprint on Spain's deepening crisis. He had been appointed director of the new General Military Academy in Zaragoza in 1928, but the establishment of the republic in 1931 saw his career stall. The fall of the monarchy in 1931 had been a matter of regret for him, though he pragmatically adjusted, holding his nose and swearing the oath of loyalty to the republic. It was purely nominal loyalty. He was viewed with some suspicion by the government's leaders, who looked to keep him well away from the centre of power. He was posted to La Coruña as a brigade commander in 1932 and in February 1933 dispatched as military commander of the Balearic Islands. The change of government following the 1933 election revitalized his career. The new Minister of War, Diego Hidalgo, was greatly impressed when he met Franco, promoted him to major-general and made him his personal military adviser.

It was in this capacity (and effectively serving as unofficial Chief of the General Staff) that he was charged with the suppression of the revolt in Asturias. Backed by a declaration of martial law, Franco brought in units of hardened Moroccan mercenaries, who savagely crushed the uprising. Over 1,100 civilians were killed, around 4,000 injured and more than 15,000 imprisoned.[16]

Franco's prestige soared on the conservative Right.[17] But despite talk of a coup he did not see the time as ripe for military intervention against the republic. His reward for Asturias was to be made commander-in-chief of the Moroccan army, though he was soon back in Spain, promoted by May 1935 officially to the position of Chief of the

General Staff. Rumours of a coup persisted in a climate of extreme volatility. The army might well have attempted one before long in any event, though a move to overthrow the government became more likely following the next elections, held in February 1936. Reflecting a country completely riven, these resulted in a victory – narrow in votes, large in parliamentary seats won – of the left-wing Popular Front. Fears on the Right were magnified. They reached fever-pitch as strikes, land-occupation and church-burnings were depicted as precursors of communist revolution. In fact, there was no prospect of that, though the perception of danger on the nationalist Right was real enough, and political murders perpetrated by the Left and Right reflected a land in enormous turmoil. The social, political and ideological polarization was unbridgeable. Whether the republic could have survived is questionable. Powerful forces, especially in the military, were determined to destroy it. The leaders of the Right now began to conspire with urgency to stage a military coup.

The government was largely in the dark about the growing conspiracy.[18] It did take the precaution of removing Franco from his post as chief of staff and dispatching him to the Canary Isles. He was already being talked about as a likely leader of a coup. But for weeks he remained hesitant and was little involved in the preparations. His instinctive caution made him doubt whether a rising against the government would succeed. In an ambiguously phrased letter to the Prime Minister, Santiago Casares y Quiroga, in June 1936 he appears to have preferred a military government that upheld order in the republic to a risky uprising. The Prime Minister ignored his letter. Whatever Franco's motivation had been, he now soon joined the plot to overthrow the republic.[19]

Among the conspirators, General José Sanjurjo, a monarchist, veteran of colonial wars in Morocco and former head of the Civil Guard who had been living in exile in Portugal following his part in a failed coup in 1932 (which Franco had kept well out of), was envisaged as Spain's future leader, while the chief organizer of the developing plot was General Emilio Mola, based in Pamplona in northern Spain. Mola had earmarked Franco for command of the rising in Spanish Morocco. But as late as the end of June he was still uncertain about whether Franco would participate. Even when he finally committed himself, Franco did not initially see himself as Spain's leader-in-waiting. His hope was to become High Commissioner in Morocco.[20]

The assassination on 13 July 1936 of José Calvo Sotelo, a charismatic figure on the monarchist Right, who had favoured government under an authoritarian monarchy and had been tipped to play a major role after a successful coup, was the moment when Franco decided he could no longer stay aloof from the planned rebellion.[21] Four days later, 17 July, the rising began in Morocco. Franco flew there from the Canaries the following day to take command of the Army of Africa, the most hardened and brutal soldiers in the Spanish armed forces.

IDEOLOGICAL WARRIOR

Franco scarcely looked the part of a great national hero. He was far from an imposing figure. Small in stature (he was only 5 feet 4 inches in height), prematurely balding, a little portly and possessed of an unappealing high-pitched droning voice, he lacked any obvious charismatic nimbus. Unlike Mussolini or Hitler, he had no demagogic powers and had built no mass movement around a personal following. He had not, in fact, engaged at all in party politics (though he had very briefly flirted with the idea in May 1936).[22] But he did have outstanding military ability and inspired deep loyalty and admiration among the troops he commanded, most notably in the Army of Africa, where he was revered for his victorious leadership in the colonial wars during the previous decade. Once the military uprising had commenced, he soon became ambitious to lead it. But fulfilling that ambition depended on factors beyond his control. There were other contenders. Nevertheless, he rapidly rose to take supreme command of the nationalist forces. And once he gained recognition as the leader of the uprising, he quickly came to be spoken of as Spain's head of state. He owed this swift rise in status to strokes of good fortune as well as his unquestionable and proven military prowess.

The good fortune was the chance elimination of all potential rivals. General Sanjurjo, the prospective leader of the uprising, died three days after the start of the rebellion when the light aircraft carrying him back from Portugal crashed on take-off. Convenient though it was for Franco, it was an accident, not foul play. Two other military leaders who might have rivalled Franco, General Joachín Fanjul and General Manuel Goded, were executed after the initial failure of the rising in Madrid and Barcelona. General Mola, the only remaining challenger to Franco within the military, soon turned out to be in a relatively weak position. The forces in northern Spain under his command were unable to impose any decisive breakthrough, while after their arrival from Morocco Franco's Army of Africa made rapid progress in the south. Moreover, Mola also managed to alienate strongly monarchist officers who started to look to Franco as their prospective leader. Most crucially, Mola proved far less adept and energetic than Franco in gaining foreign arms supplies.

Among potential civilian leaders, Gil Robles had fallen into discredit after the poor showing of the CEDA in the 1936 elections. And Sotelo, as noted, had already been assassinated before the uprising began. José Antonio Primo de Rivera (son of the former dictator), the charismatic founder of the Falange – the radical fascist movement which from modest beginnings had rapidly grown in the last months of the republic (when it won over especially younger former supporters of the CEDA) – had been imprisoned in March 1936 and was executed in November. That left Franco.

His ascendancy was, however, far from just down to good fortune. At the age of forty-three when the Civil War began, Franco was the youngest general in Europe since Napoleon.[23] Outside military circles, the Right in Spain had held him in high regard since his ruthless suppression of the Asturian rising. And he was both astute and well connected. He acted swiftly, using personal contacts and notable initiative, to obtain aid from abroad. Mussolini and Hitler both quickly committed themselves to supplying the vital aircraft needed to transport the Army of Africa to the Spanish mainland. By the end of August 1936 around 30,000 hardened fighters – 'regulars' being indigenous Moroccans, and 'legionaries' mainly Spaniards – had landed in Spain.

The arrival of the feared Army of Africa transformed the fortunes of the nationalists in southern Spain while Mola struggled to surmount strong republican forces in the north. The Moroccan troops spread terror in their wake – a calculated part of Franco's strategy – massacring prisoners and raping women as they advanced.[24] The levels of ingrained violence in the ideologically torn society were already so great that such outrages were as acceptable to one side as they were detestable atrocities to the other. By mid-August north and south had joined to form a single nationalist zone. Franco's early successes ensured that he, not Mola, was soon seen as the dominant commander – and the one personally favoured by the Germans as the recipient of the vital supplies of arms.

On 21 September a meeting of leading generals voted – some with distinctly muted enthusiasm – to make Franco the supreme commander (Generalísimo) of the nationalist forces. A week later, Franco achieved a major propaganda triumph, winning euphoric acclaim on the nationalist side, when his Moroccan forces diverted from the logical path of an assault on the capital, Madrid, to end – amid huge bloodshed – the republican siege of the formidable Alcázar fortress at Toledo, built by Emperor Charles V and a symbol of Spain's former glory. Another meeting of the generals next day led to the reluctant acceptance on the part of Mola and others of a proposal that as supreme military commander Franco would be head of government 'as long as the war lasts' and 'assume all the powers of the new State'. On 1 October, in a solemn ceremony and applauded by ecstatic crowds, Franco was handed 'the absolute powers of the State'.[25]

Within days, nationalist propaganda was styling him the Caudillo – 'the leader', a title linking Franco with the heroes of the Spanish past.[26] This adulation pandered to Franco's already outsized ego. He devoured the clamour of nationalist propaganda and declarations by Church leaders which portrayed him at the head of a crusade for the defence of Spain and the Catholic faith against the atheism and barbarism of the republic.[27] It matched his belief that he had an overriding, God-given patriotic mission. He felt he had been singled out by divine providence as Spain's saviour.[28]

The army, in Franco's world-view and that of the military caste generally, stood between the revolutionary anarchy a feeble government was incapable of preventing and Spain's salvation. The poison had to be drained from Spanish politics. The enemy within had to be not just defeated, but destroyed. Only then would Spain's glory return. That the army would determine Spain's destiny was axiomatic to him. The turmoil of the Second Republic after 1931 confirmed this in his eyes.

Expectations that the uprising in 1936 would bring a swift military takeover of power nevertheless rapidly evaporated. An intensely brutal struggle began that would last for three long years. It bore Franco's hallmark.

Franco's determination to eradicate, not simply defeat, those he saw as Spain's inner enemies contributed to lengthening the cruel conflict. He wanted no quick but merely superficial victory. His forces advanced slowly, relentlessly – and mercilessly. Terrible atrocities were perpetrated by both sides, though by far the majority by the nationalists.[29] Beyond the million or so thrown into jails and labour camps (from a population of around 25 million), Franco's forces executed tens of thousands of republicans. He personally read through and signed many death sentences.[30]

The desperate republican defence gradually but inexorably weakened. The imbalance in supplies of arms from abroad proved decisive. The flow of arms from the Axis powers (aimed at blocking any Bolshevik inroads into Spain and testing their military technology, including the bombing of civilians) gave the nationalist rebels a great advantage, magnified by the non-intervention policy of the western democracies.[31] Soviet aid to the republic was too little to turn the tables, and in any case Moscow's involvement was divisive. The international dimension of the conflict stretched beyond the corridors of power in Europe's capitals. Some 30,000 volunteers from across the European continent travelled to Spain to fight fascism, many dying in the valiant effort. But their contribution was too little to tip the balance of an increasingly uneven war. By early 1939 the end was in sight as republican defences in the major strongholds crumbled one by one. On 28 March the nationalists, nearly three years after their initial, failed attempt to take the city, entered Madrid. On 1 April, Franco declared the war over.

Including the hundreds of thousands who had died on the battlefields, the tens of thousands executed by each side and the half a million or so republicans who fled into exile (many of whom died of disease in French internment camps), the victims of the Civil War on both sides perhaps numbered over a million.[32] The killing did not stop with the end of the war. Retribution, and the drive 'to bring about the total extirpation of our enemies' (as the president of the Tribunal of Political Responsibilities, Enrique Suñer Ordóñez, appointed by Franco put it in

1938) ensured that the terroristic purging of the demonized Left went on into the mid-1940s.[33] One of Franco's press officers, an army captain and landowner, Gonzalo de Aguilera, even spoke in 1939 of a 'programme' designed as a work of purification 'to exterminate a third of the male population of Spain' in order to 'clean up the country and rid us of the proletariat'.[34] No such programme was ever created. Even so, around 20,000 republicans were executed after the end of the Civil War, thousands more dying in prisons, camps and forced-labour battalions before the bloodletting at last subsided.[35]

What was Franco's personal contribution to the nationalist victory? He had had little personally to do with the outbreak of a civil war in Spain. His ideological preferences were plain. His deep antipathy towards the republic, readiness to act with great ruthlessness against the Left and sympathies with the militarist Right, which he knew was preparing a coup, were evident. But his ideological hatreds were widely shared on the Right, and he was still on the fringes of the conspiracy when the rising began. His vital early contribution was in engineering the help from Italy and Germany that enabled the transport of the Army of Africa to Spain. Thereafter he condoned where he did not actively encourage the barbarous conduct of the war. But had a nationalist general other than Franco been in command, say Mola (who in the event died in plane crash in June 1937, again convenient for Franco but apparently an accident), a descent into barbarity would still have taken place.

Mola shared Franco's ideological obsessions, including his hatred of Freemasonry and Jews. He favoured extreme violence, terror and exemplary punishment in the pursuit of internal enemies and the 'purification' of Spain.[36] Whether the thirst for revenge, so characteristic of Franco, would have been so vicious and lasted so long after the Civil War under another military leader cannot of course be known. Franco's military skill undoubtedly played a significant part in defeating the republican forces.[37] Without the supplies of arms from the Axis powers, however, Franco's prowess as a commander would most likely not have been enough. And with those arms, another nationalist general might well have attained victory. So Franco was in certain respects fortunate to receive all the victory laurels. By the time victory was won, however, there were few in Spain prepared to argue the point.

The victory of the nationalists marked the point at which the manufacture of the Franco cult went into overdrive. By this time he had, extending far beyond the military, a political mass movement in place to spread and uphold the aura of the great leader. In 1937, the various factions of the Right had been united in a restructured and reinvented Falange that now included monarchists, conservatives, many one-time CEDA members and other rightists. Franco had played little or no direct part in this, though he was now the object of their unquenchable adulation. The once tiny movement had become a vast state party of the new regime, its hundreds of thousands of members the main vehicle of acclamation of the Caudillo.[38]

Its huge serried ranks formed part of the spectacular propaganda display, of a kind familiar from Fascist Italy and Nazi Germany, staged in Madrid over three days from the evening of the 18th until the 20th of May 1939, to celebrate the nationalist victory and, above all, bolster the image of the Caudillo as Spain's glorious hero. Franco's triumphant entry into the city was consciously designed to evoke visions of the legendary medieval Spanish hero El Cid. Next day he presided over a five-hour victory parade, followed by a speech in which he warned against 'the Jewish spirit which permitted the alliance of big capital with Marxism'. On 20 May a vast pageant celebrated Spain's medieval crusade against the Moors and the country's glorious military past. The accompanying solemn High Mass conveyed the Catholic Church's gratitude for Franco's victory.

For three years the Spanish Civil War had held much of Europe in thrall – the prelude, it seemed, to an increasingly inevitable wider conflagration. In the event, when that greater, European-wide, then global, war broke out, it had little to do with Spain. Franco's conquest nevertheless had consequences not confined within Spanish frontiers. Germany and Italy had exploited the opportunity to try out terror bombing. Through their policy of non-intervention, western democracies had further demonstrated their weakness, something not lost on the Soviet Union as well as the Axis powers. They saw victory for Franco, however distasteful his methods, as preferable to the triumph of communism in Spain. The Left, not just in Spain, was defeated and demoralized. But as most of Europe was gripped by what would soon become world war, Spain fell out of view, no longer central to the events consuming the continent. Even so, both during the Second World War and the Cold War

Franco played a part, if a minor one, in the grander strategic plans of major powers. It was just not the part that he had envisaged.

WORLD WAR AND COLD WAR: FRANCO'S TWO FACES

Throughout the Spanish Civil War, Franco had been in awe of Mussolini and even more so of Hitler. During the first years of the Second World War while the Axis powers seemed to be heading for victory Franco courted both dictators. He felt ideologically in tune with them. More than that, he saw advantages for Spain from the war itself, and from what he took to be the certain defeat of western democracy by Fascist Italy and Nazi Germany. He wanted Spain to join the Second World War as a belligerent power and to share in their imagined triumph.

That was, naturally, not the image he wanted to portray either to the Spanish people or, more importantly, to the victorious Allies once the Second World War was over. As the war began to turn against the Axis powers and their defeat became ever more certain, Franco's early enthusiasm wilted. At the same time, Spanish propaganda began the process of reversing the public image of the Caudillo from avid supporter of the Axis to wise leader whose brilliant diplomacy had skilfully kept Spain out of the war and nobly preserved the country's neutrality. It marked the start of the attempt in the immediate post-war world to overcome the hostility of the West and to end Spain's pariah status in international relations. But the strategic demands of the Cold War, not Franco's own abilities or efforts, brought the break-through to Spain's partial rehabilitation. During both the Second World War and the Cold War, external factors, not Franco himself, were the key determinants in shaping Spain's international relations. Franco represented their contradictory public face.

There is no doubt that Franco took the decisions that defined Spanish policy. The ultimate responsibility was his. But nothing indicates that he took them 'against the grain', that he was doing other than giving expression to the collective voice of Spain's power-elites. The decision, moreover, not to enter the war simply reflected Spain's economic and military weakness. An alternative decision was scarcely possible. Had another military dictator been in charge of Spain's fortunes, policy would most likely have been identical, or at least very similar. Franco was not a weak dictator, since he held real power and his authority was accepted by the whole of Spain's ruling class. But his actions were constrained by non-personal determinants. Left to Franco's personal choice, Spain would have found itself a belligerent nation, fighting on the side of the Axis.

Franco regretted that war in Europe had come too soon for Spain, which was in no state, militarily or economically, to join in the fighting. His confidence that Britain would soon have to seek peace was accompanied by the decision, taken on the recommendation of his economic 'experts', to cut off Spain's economy from the West in favour of autarky (self-sufficiency). The result was to intensify the already acute hardship felt by most of the population and create disastrous shortages in food and other everyday necessities.[39] The demand for massive German economic aid to alleviate the dire state of the economy as well as extensive military supplies was one of the two central issues on which Franco's desire to take Spain into what he presumed would be a victorious war were to founder. The other was Franco's claim, after France had been defeated in June 1940, that Spain should be given French Morocco. His expectation that, ultimately, the British would cede Gibraltar to Spain was not a hindrance to a potential deal with Hitler's Germany, though from a German perspective that, too, necessitated Spanish entry into the war and, therefore, hinged on resolution of the other two factors – both of them the focus of the fruitless diplomacy in the summer of 1940. Germany's refusal to countenance Spain's exorbitant 'wish-list' rested on the assessment that Spanish belligerence, even though it potentially offered the opportunity to take Gibraltar and seal off the Mediterranean, was of negligible value – simply not worth the price Franco was demanding in return for it.

The German view of Spain's low military value to the Axis – based on the calculation that a Spanish war effort could only be of limited strength and extremely short duration – was established even before the conflict began and never substantially altered. Nevertheless, strategic considerations in Berlin in summer 1940 included – alongside Hitler's directions to prepare for a war against the Soviet Union the following spring – a 'peripheral strategy' to push Britain out of the

Mediterranean. Control of Gibraltar, involving Spain's participation in the war, was, therefore, an obvious issue. So Germany was prepared to test the waters with Spain. But talks in Berlin in mid-September 1940 between the German Foreign Minister, Joachim von Ribbentrop, and Ramón Serrano Súñer, married to the sister of Franco's wife and the most powerful man in the regime beneath the dictator himself, and then the following month between Hitler and Franco, at Hendaye, on the Spanish border, led nowhere. Franco was disappointed by the outcome, but undeterred in his expressions of support for the Axis.

However, military setbacks for the Axis in the Mediterranean and the inability to force Britain out of the war made him begin to doubt an early German victory. His military advisers warned him that it would be dangerous to contemplate Spanish belligerence until the Axis powers captured Suez. From Germany's perspective, plans for an assault on Gibraltar were hazardous without Spain's intervention in the war. Preparations for the attack on the Soviet Union led to the final abandonment of these plans in February 1941, after Franco had made economic, military and territorial demands so exorbitant that they were regarded in Berlin as no more than an excuse to avoid Spain's entry into the war. As the course of the war turned inexorably against the Axis from autumn 1942 onwards, and once the Allies within the following year controlled the Mediterranean and north Africa, Franco, backed by his leading generals, spread his bets. He tried, unsuccessfully, to exploit Spanish neutrality to obtain German armaments to resist the Allies while making the first overtures to the British and Americans towards a rapprochement.[40]

The Blue Division, formed in the enthusiasm of summer 1941 and attracting a total of 47,000 Spaniards to serve the German cause on the eastern front (with around a 50 per cent casualty rate), was withdrawn from the front in October 1943 and officially disbanded the following month – though a small number of fanatics fought on as the Blue Legion for several months before the remaining few were incorporated in the Waffen-SS.[41] The tide had by then well and truly turned. By autumn 1944 Franco was proposing to Churchill an Anglo-Spanish alliance against the Bolsheviks and soon afterwards, despite his private fantasies about American-based Freemason conspiracies, putting out tentative feelers to Roosevelt's administration. Both overtures met with a hostile response.[42]

Franco's power in Spain was undiminished, though his image was now reconstructed to emphasize his wartime non-belligerency and to play down the fascist colouring of the regime while underlining its Catholic and monarchical credentials – the latter reinforced when Spain was declared a monarchy (if without a king) by the succession law of 1947. The extravagant Caudillo cult retained its full measure of absurdity. The official press in 1949 rated Franco higher than Alexander the Great and Julius Caesar, describing him as 'the man of God', 'champion of the forces of heaven and earth', 'star of the entire world', who was owed 'the mobilisation of the Vatican, of Washington, and of the entire world'.[43] If the Vatican gladly lent its continued backing to the extreme anti-communist defender of Catholic Spain,[44] Franco remained ostracized by most of western Europe during the immediate post-war years. This soon started to change, however, under the impact of the Cold War.

Franco had little or nothing to do with the circumstances that were to end Spain's international isolation and pariah status. The onset of the Cold War meant that the Americans – the new guarantors of western security – were anxious to prevent any spread of communism in southern Europe. Western Europe, though more hesitant than the USA, soon followed suit. In 1947 the Americans had still regarded Franco as a pariah and excluded Spain from the Marshall Plan. By 1949, however, the Cold War had hardened into a deep freeze, the Soviets had exploded their own atom bomb and Mao had established a new communist regime in China. A year later, the Korean War began. American attitudes towards Franco changed in accordance with the assessment of international dangers. Whatever the dislike of Franco, no end to his regime was in sight, and Franco's quasi-fascism was regarded as preferable to the prospect of communist infiltration of southern Europe. From 'fascist beast', Franco had become 'sentinel of the Occident'.[45] The need to acquire military bases in Spain superseded any moral and political objections. By 1951 agreement was reached on the leasing of bases in Spain, bringing valuable financial aid from the USA. Two years later, the deal was finalized, and trumpeted in Spain as a great victory for Franco. He was now a valued ally of the United States. In 1955 Spain joined the United Nations. Spain had come in from the international cold.

In the process, the aim of Franco's regime had subsided into little more than ensuring long-term survival. Its fascist elements diluted, whatever dynamism it had once possessed faded. It was still highly repressive, though no longer outrightly terroristic, as it had been in the first years after the Civil War. And there was a complete shift in economic policy, beginning the alignment of Spain with the rest of western Europe and with the international economy.

Unsustainable economic crisis – a severe balance of payments deficit and inflation taking the country close to bankruptcy – forced the change of direction despite Franco's initial disagreement.[46] The policy of economic self-sufficiency was abandoned in 1959. It had inflicted abject poverty on the vast bulk of the population, left with no choice but to accept the poor standard of living and constraints of dull but unchangeable dictatorship while most of post-war western Europe had undergone an astonishing transformation and recovery from the ravages of world war.[47] By the end of the 1950s, however, Spain – now itself experiencing strong growth – was incorporated in the Organization for European Economic Cooperation (from 1961 the Organization for Economic Co-Operation and Development), and accepted as a member of the World Bank, the International Monetary Fund and the GATT framework of foreign-trade regulation. Under a new 'Stabilization Plan', drastic reforms were introduced and implemented by new economics experts (labelled 'technocrats') closely associated with Opus Dei, a theologically conservative but economically liberal elitist Catholic lay organization, the well-educated members of which were closely connected with business and finance.[48] Their incisive restructuring and liberalizing of the economy brought swift rewards as Spain belatedly shared the unprecedented levels of growth experienced by most of Europe.[49] Foreign tourism soon magnified the growth in Spain's burgeoning economy.[50]

None of these fundamental structural changes owed much to Franco's personality – still a negative factor in international assessments of Spain – or to his talent. They were part of the modernization that came to Spain initially from external pressures, not from within – meeting at first, indeed, with the Franco's disapproval.[51] And, as conditions for much of the population began to improve greatly, modernization increasingly showed Franco and his regime to be obsolete leftovers from a bygone age, even if political transformation had to await the dictator's death.

THE POWER-CARTEL

Before 1939 Franco had been a military commander with only embryonic political responsibilities. He subsequently had to adjust to a new role as head of state. A law issued on 8 August 1939 gave him supreme, unrestricted legislative powers. There were no constitutional constraints.[52] He did not see himself as a dictator, though he viewed government as a matter of command, much like the army.[53] But how did Franco actually rule Spain for more than three decades following the end of the Civil War? Did he actively and personally dictate policy? Or was he in effect giving voice to powerful interests that shaped policy and sustained his regime? And in what ways did these change during the long existence of the dictatorship? How, quite especially when Franco was old and increasingly infirm, did his personal rule continue to function? Put more abstractly, did the individual determine the course of Spanish history, or was this shaped by wider, more impersonal, political, economic and cultural structures and pressures?

The nationalist cause during the Civil War had been supported by most of the ruling classes that had traditionally formed Spain's power-elites – the military, landowners, big business, the hierarchy of the Catholic Church. The same forces formed the backbone of the regime once the Civil War was over. The elites had entrusted power to Franco, much as those in Italy and Germany had done with Mussolini and Hitler, and were broadly content with his rule as long as it served their own interests.[54] In Italy and Germany the ideological dynamic of the regimes had brought increasing friction with the interests of the conservative elites. The Francoist regime, however, although there were significant changes over the duration of the dictatorship, led to no commensurate undermining of the conservative pillars of support.

In this sense, his regime could be depicted as a power-cartel, though not one of equal parts. Industrial bosses and landowners backed the regime, though without having direct input into policy-making.

Industrialists were happy with the destruction of socialism and removal of worker rights through the abolition of independent trade unions. They welcomed the establishment of a corporate state along the lines of that of Fascist Italy which strengthened their control over industrial relations. Landowners benefited from agricultural protectionism and state backing for their extended power over their labourers. In a country where Catholic piety was so deep and widespread, Church leaders provided indispensable ideological legitimation. They recalled the times during the republic when churches had been destroyed and the clergy attacked. They gave thanks for a leader whom they saw as shielding them, a defender of religion from godless atheism and upholder of their traditional social power. The state bureaucracy, as in many other parts of Europe, warmed to the task of implementing policy directives under the authoritarian regime while the agencies of enforcement – police, judiciary, Civil Guard – relished the chance to exploit their wide coercive powers. The Falange, the crucial bearer and transmitter of the Caudillo cult, served on account of its size and omnipresence as an important vehicle of everyday surveillance, mobilization and control, if with limited influence on policy-formulation. The military were the beneficiaries of the regime they had in large measure been responsible for creating, which could be relied upon to look after their interests.

Policy-making was dominated by a relatively small number of military officers and civilian ministers, all selected by Franco and dependent upon his continued favour. Family members were also influential.[55] In the early years, the most important figure was Ramón Serrano Súñer, who was chiefly responsible for the unification of the various nationalist factions into the single 'Spanish Falange' party in 1937 and subsequently its effective head. He played a major part in constructing the apparatus of the authoritarian state at the end of the Civil War. As Minister of the Interior, and then from October 1940 Foreign Minister, he was second in importance only to Franco himself. But his regular access to the dictator was the true base of his power. When Franco removed his favour, as he did in September 1942 following a serious clash between Falangists and monarchists, Serrano Súñer was dismissed – and the Falange significantly weakened, to the benefit of the military component of the power-cartel.

Government and administration permitted, of course, no official forms of opposition to the head of state. Ministers were nevertheless allowed considerable autonomy – though it was *relative* autonomy, always subject to Franco's overriding and recognized personal authority.[56] Meetings of the Cabinet – the Council of Ministers – often lasted for hours, on occasion lasting from morning until, following a long lunch break, the early hours of the next day. (Franco's bladder-control was extraordinary; until December 1968 he never paused the meetings to go to the toilet – much to the distress of some of his ministers.) In the early years Franco's meandering addresses were the dominant feature of Cabinet meetings. By the end he was saying little. He let his ministers speak at length without any fear that they might challenge his authority. Where there were disagreements – which were never of a fundamental nature – decisions were deferred until agreement was somehow reached.[57] But the Cabinet was devoid of real power. Most important decisions in any case bypassed the Cabinet and followed deliberations with Franco's inner circle of trusted generals, particular favourites and other cronies among the clique that frequented the seat of the dictatorship in Madrid's El Pardo palace. The hundred members of the Falange's supreme body, the National Council of the Movement, in theory offered an important voice for the Falange leadership. In practice, the National Council was weak and, even before its total emasculation in later years, gave the Movement no more than representation without genuine power. There was also a parliament – of sorts: the Cortes, established in 1942, provided, however, merely a façade of legitimation but without power to challenge, let alone constrain, the government.

Franco stood entirely unchallenged at the pinnacle of the power-cartel. He immersed himself in the early years in the detail of policy, making alterations to drafts of laws and decrees. He appointed and dismissed ministers as he thought fit. And the ultimate decisions rested with him. But at no point was there any significant breach with the fundamental basis of support on which his regime rested. He was certainly astute enough to manipulate to good effect the often conflicting interests of competing individuals or rival sectors of the regime. He was particularly skilful in keeping the monarchists on side, promising through the Succession Act of 1947 the eventual restoration of the monarchy while avoiding any specific time-frame and retaining in his own hands the power to choose who should eventually become the next monarch. 'Divide and rule' was a maxim that served him well over the years.

The promise of advancement, together with the almost unlimited potential for enrichment in a system that relied upon colossal bribery and corruption, was a vital sweetener, a significant element in binding the elites to Franco.[58] The power-elites, allowed to enrich themselves without restraint or retribution, had everything to gain from keeping the regime in place. The security, espionage and armed services were financially well looked after, and so could be relied upon to ensure the regime remained intact and keep in check any who were not reconciled to it.

From the mid-1960s onwards Franco delegated the daily business of government to Luis Carrero Blanco, a naval officer (by this time with the rank of admiral) and arch-loyalist who had been his most trusted lieutenant since 1941.[59] But he ceded none of his powers. Undynamic authoritarianism was firmly entrenched. The police and Civil Guard clamped down rigorously on dissent. Opponents were largely forced into apathetic compliance. The National Movement – the name 'Falange' was removed in 1970 – still helped to ensure quiescence at the grassroots. Stirrings of independent civil society began to emerge even so, particularly among industrial workers and students, though they were far from sufficient to break the strong grip of the regime. This was starting to loosen, nonetheless, as Spain gradually experienced the economic, social and cultural changes that were affecting the whole of western Europe. The armed struggle for Basque independence was a speciality of Spain, though forms of home-grown terrorism were soon to manifest themselves elsewhere in western Europe. When Basque separatists assassinated Carrero Blanco in 1973 it triggered a last spasm of violent repression in Franco's Spain. But by this time the regime was plainly living on borrowed time. The dictatorship was crassly out of step with unstoppable demands for liberalization and democratization. As long as the dictator lived, however, genuine transformation remained impossible. This, as much as anything, signified the importance of the individual to Spanish, and European, history in the twentieth century.

LEGACY

Franco was unquestionably an outstanding military leader, as he showed in the 1920s in Morocco and then later in directing the nationalist forces in the Civil War. But his qualities of political leadership were invisible before the late 1930s. Without the specific conditions prevailing in Spain at the time they would almost certainly have remained so.

He was given the opportunity to gain power by the class equilibrium in Spain during the Second Republic, when neither the forces of Left nor those of the Right could prevail.[60] The Civil War then propelled him to military leadership of the nationalist rebels. For over three decades as head of state, his main ability was the skill to sustain his own hold on power by dividing and manipulating the component sectors of the power-cartel. His unchallengeable authority was immensely bolstered by the 'heroic' personality cult that was manufactured around him. Whether or not belief in Franco was genuine or contrived, a sizeable (if unquantifiable) proportion of the population bought into the Caudillo cult, as did – often cynically, no doubt – the elites who stood to gain from the dictatorship. The public image hid the reality: a personality which in a different era would have left no mark on history.

After the war, maintaining power, more or less for its own sake – along with accruing the vast wealth that he amassed in the process in a system that depended on corruption on the grand scale – was what the dictatorship largely amounted to. There was no longer any great ideological dynamic behind it once the internal enemies had been ruthlessly and vengefully destroyed. A belief in patriotism, religion, unity and order was what remained.[61] Franco had admired and identified with Mussolini and Hitler. But his enthusiasm for the Axis was officially erased once the increasingly inevitable victory of the Allies rendered it counterproductive. His fantasy about the international Masonic conspiracy persisted, but, whatever its reflection of Franco's weird mind-set, had no practical implications.[62] When circumstances demanded a rapprochement with the USA, the centre in his eyes of nebulous Masonic power, his personal paranoia played no part in a policy-shift determined by the needs of pragmatic adjustment to geopolitical realities.

As the years, then the decades passed, Franco's own energies for ruling faded even while he held on tenaciously to power. His interest in the daily grind of government diminished and he spent increasing amounts of time indulging his hobbies of hunting, deep-sea fishing and, in the final years, when he was increasingly beset by ill-health, watching television and doing the football pools (which he sometimes won).[63] The dictatorship continued to function, however, not least because it still served the interests of Spain's ruling classes, while the compliance of the bulk of the population was underpinned by increased living standards resulting from the belated economic growth. And Franco retained the well-rewarded loyalty of the military and security apparatus.

It was increasingly obvious, however, that the forces of modernization were overtaking the outmoded authoritarianism of the system. This was recognized by all sections of the power-elites. So they were ready to move to a new kind of relationship with the state once Franco had died, though they sought to ensure that pluralist democracy under the restored monarchy continued to serve their interests.

Weeks of mounting medical crisis finally brought Franco's death on 20 November 1975. Henry Kissinger had said in 1970 that Spain was 'waiting for a life to end so that it could re-join European history'.[64] With Franco dead, the process of rejoining could begin, although the transition to democracy was only consolidated after the failure of the last attempted coup, by members of the Civil Guard in 1981. Franco's chosen successor, King Juan Carlos, played a significant role in the crucial process of establishing a durable democracy.[65] During the 1980s Spain was run by a socialist government for the first time since 1936. It joined NATO. And it became a member of the European Community (soon to be the European Union). But Franco had left an indelible mark on Spanish history. As Spain underwent its transition from dictatorship to democracy, the wounds of division from Franco's time were too deep to be risk being opened up anew.[66] Democracy was still fragile. The police, judiciary and Civil Guard were still largely unreformed. Fears on the Left of a new dictatorship, even of a return to civil war, lingered.[67] Political practicalities of creating some form of political consensus took precedence over a reckoning with the past (much as they had done in Germany during the 1950s).

Only after the millennium did 'the recovery of historical memory' begin in earnest.[68] Statues of Franco started to be demolished. In 2006, seventy years after the outbreak of the Civil War, the 'year of historical memory' brought intensive public debate about the Franco era.[69] Gradually, the scale of the killing, suffering and repression in the Civil War and many – though far from all – of the atrocities perpetrated under the dictatorship were brought to light. After 2008 the socialist government supported the search for mass graves of people executed under Franco.

Residual support for Franco had not, however, disappeared. The graves of Falangists who had fought with the Germans on the eastern front were maintained, with some support from Spain's conservative government after it had returned to power in 2011.[70] Franco's tomb in the basilica in the Valley of the Fallen – a memorial to the dead of the Civil War erected by thousands of prisoners during the 1940s – was the site of annual pilgrimages by Franco loyalists and ex-Falangists until political rallies in honour of the former dictator were banned in 2007. It was closed by the socialist government in 2009, but reopened by the conservative administration three years later. Franco's remains were, however, finally exhumed from the Valley of the Fallen in 2019, following years of political wrangling that showed the divides of the Civil War were far from healed. The interment of Franco in the family mausoleum away from public view could, of course, scarcely bring decades of division and confrontation over his legacy to an end. It marked, even so, a closure of sorts.

What had it all been for? During the long years of his dictatorship, Franco's military, police and judiciary had imposed order on Spanish society. It was an order favoured by the many who had applauded the suppression of the Left and had feared the threats of anarchism and communism. For the rest of Spanish society it had been order sustained by the iron fist backed by rigorous social control, censorship of the mass media and orchestrated mobilization of support. Franco's disastrous autarky policy had condemned most of the population to lasting poverty until the 1960s, while Spain's ruling class enriched itself as never before. By the time of Franco's death in 1975 Spain was slowly beginning to catch up with economic progress elsewhere in Europe.[71] The impressive economic growth of Franco's later years owed little or nothing, however, to his own initiatives, but reflected international trends and 'catch-up' after the long era of economic backwardness.[72] The advances were the offshoot of liberalizing policies and necessary modernizing reforms that discarded his own long-held beliefs in fascist-style autarky. Even his reactionary brand of Catholicism was by the end long out of tune with the liberal reforms of the Catholic Church (though the Church continued to protect its own interests).[73] And within a decade of Franco's death, Spain had become a pluralist democracy and rapidly developed into a 'normal' west European state.

Franco's long shadow had not altogether been dispelled.[74] Over three-quarters of Spaniards asked in 2000 thought that little or nothing of Franco remained as a legacy.[75] But even beyond the controversies over historical memory Spain could not wholly escape the colouring of its Francoist past. Corruption in high places, some of it connected to figures in the conservative party, the Partido Popular, was far from eradicated.[76] And the crisis over independence in relatively prosperous Catalonia, prompting an aggressive reaction by the conservative Spanish government, roused memories of the ruthless suppression of Catalonian identity under Franco and his regime's imposition of an extremely centralized state based on Spanish hyper-nationalism. Nevertheless, Spain had changed dramatically since Franco's day. Whatever the problems that arose from the deep impact of the financial crisis of 2008, rifts over Catalan independence and the rise of populism, Spanish society remained overwhelmingly wedded to European values – the antithesis of all that Franco had stood for. That Spain had turned into a pillar of the European Union was not the least of the unintended consequences of Franco's long dictatorship.

The memory of the dark years of dictatorship could not even so be fully erased. It remains in its own way, like the enduring legacy of the Nazi era in Germany, an unavoidable part of the present – a 'past that will not pass away'.[77] Franco left an indelible imprint on twentieth-century Spain. His role in the Civil War, long dictatorship and legacy were also part of the making of twentieth-century Europe.

Tito looks bored as he and the Soviet leader Nikita Khrushchev relax while cruising on the Adriatic during Khrushchev's visit to Yugoslavia between 20 August and 3 September 1963. Friendly relations between Yugoslavia and the Soviet Union had been restored after Stalin's death, though Khrushchev's visit was not altogether harmonious.

JOSIP BROZ TITO

Uncrowned King of Socialist Yugoslavia

Josip Broz was known throughout the world in the post-war decades simply as 'Tito', a name he first began to use in 1934. Like other political activists he had previously used other pseudonyms to avoid arrest. 'Tito', he said, had no special significance for him.[1] But it stuck. Just how crucial Tito was to Yugoslavia's existence as a multinational federal republic is shown by how quickly after his death the edifice that he had built was torn apart by nationalist and ethnic conflict.

He first came to international prominence during the Second World War as the indomitable leader of the Partisans, who, uniquely among resistance movements, with little external military assistance liberated their country from enemy occupation. He then, through political skill and ruthlessness, kept tight control of the reins of power in Yugoslavia for thirty-five years, dying in office in 1980. He successfully defied extreme pressure from Stalin in 1948, keeping Yugoslavia out of the Soviet bloc and ensuring that it was the only European communist country to preserve its independence from Moscow. As a consequence the Soviet Union was prevented from extending its domination throughout the Balkans. Through subtle diplomacy Tito ensured Yugoslavia's international importance as the pivot between East and West in the Cold War, able to exploit and play off the conflicting interests of the Soviet Union and the United States of America. He was instrumental in constructing, effectively under Yugoslav leadership, the Non-Aligned Movement as an umbrella organization for countries in Asia, Africa and South America that did not want to commit allegiance to either superpower. Abroad, Tito's standing far outstripped what might have been expected from the leader of a European communist country lacking both economic and military power. At home he alone proved capable of sustaining national unity in a state whose strong centrifugal tendencies even he at times barely held in check.

How could Tito make such a profound impact, both on his own country and internationally? What qualities of leadership, in war and in peace, made him such an outstanding figure? What conditions enabled him to take power and to consolidate it? And how did he keep power for so long? What structures of rule lay behind his outright dominance? Not least, why was the state he built so dependent upon him personally? Why did it collapse so violently barely a decade after his death?

PERSONALITY

Josip Broz was a striking personality – intelligent, self-confident, resolute, a dynamic man of action. He exuded a natural authority and won support by personal example. He was, as his wartime exploits showed, physically, as well as politically, courageous, able to withstand hardship and to inspire endurance in others.

According to Milovan Djilas, one of his closest associates until he broke with Tito in the 1950s, he was 'lively, spontaneous, folksy', not aloof. He was not a notably good speaker. But he was able to put ideas into simple, direct language, and to deliver his message through his own conviction, drive and decisiveness. He evoked confidence and trust. He convinced his followers through his sense of historical mission and of his personal destiny to shape it. What most impressed those who saw him at close quarters were his political instinct and 'a shrewd and insatiable drive for power'.[2] In his last years Tito recalled what Churchill had told him towards the end of the war: 'What counts is power, and power again, and power once and for all.'[3]

His thirst for power was inevitably laced with another ingredient that is an essential component of the personality of dictators (and to some extent of all political leaders): ruthlessness. He did not possess the psychotic cruelty of Stalin. But leadership of the Partisans necessitated uncompromising harshness towards enemies. Victory brought savage retribution. In the notorious massacres at Kočevski Rog in

May 1945 Tito's men summarily executed around 10,000 collaborators, returned by the British forces in Austria. Tens of thousands more, mainly prisoners of war, were killed before the year's end. And in the early years in power after the war he felt no compunction about seeing 'internal enemies' dispatched to a concentration camp erected by the new state. When he felt it necessary, he peremptorily dismissed from post even close associates. He accepted to the end that those who fundamentally opposed the system of rule in the one-party state should be severely punished. Maintaining his power and upholding the aura of his own authority carried with them the indelible callous stain that underlay his superficial joviality and bonhomie. But the harsh core of his personality was not immediately visible.

Fitzroy Maclean, head of the British Military Mission dispatched to the Partisans in 1943, found Tito, at the age of fifty-two, an imposing figure: 'He was of medium height, clean-shaven, with tanned regular features and iron-grey hair. He had a very firm mouth and alert blue eyes.' He was 'perfectly sure of himself' and, though open to argument, ready 'to take a decision there and then'. Maclean was struck by his organizational ability, but also by his 'never-failing sense of humour; his unashamed delight in the minor pleasures of life', and by his 'natural friendliness' and convivial manner. But he also witnessed 'a violent temper, flaring up in sudden rages'.[4]

Tito's power and prestige, as well as his good looks and charm, attracted women to him, and he had a strong sexual appetite even in his advanced years. He was married three times and had two further long-standing relationships and numerous affairs. He was particularly drawn to women much younger than he was himself (something he shared with both Hitler and Stalin). Whether a 'trophy-wife' appealed to his vanity, whether there was some other psychological reason or whether it was merely the physical attraction of sensual young women it is impossible to say. His first wife, Pelagiia, daughter of a St Petersburg worker, was only fourteen when he married her in 1918. Of their five children only a son, Zarko, survived. They divorced in 1936, and Tito married a twenty-two-year-old German woman, Elsa Johanna König (otherwise known as Lucie Bauer), who only a year later was arrested by Stalin's secret police, falsely accused of being a Gestapo spy and executed.[5] Tito never mentioned her in later years. Whether, as an ardent Stalinist, Tito willingly accepted the alleged reasons for her execution cannot be known. Within two years, in any case, he had a new partner: the twenty-five-year-old Herta Haas, daughter of an Austrian lawyer, who gave him another son, Alexander (known as Miša), before they separated in 1941. By then he had taken up with his secretary Zdenka – the nickname of Davorjanka Paunović – who died of tuberculosis in 1946 aged only twenty-seven. Tito's last wife, Jovanka Budisavljević, from a peasant background, joined the Partisans in 1942 aged only seventeen and within five years, at less than half his age, was Tito's lover. She was glamorous (at least at first), but strong-willed, jealous and interfering – soon alienating almost all around Tito by her haughty, rude behaviour. They married in 1952 and, perhaps as he became more suspicious about even his closest associates, he came increasingly to depend upon her, fractious though the relationship was. It gradually became so acrimonious, however, that it led to their formal separation in 1977. Jovanka, detested by most who encountered her, outlived him.

THE MAKING OF A POLITICAL LEADER

Josip Broz was a political leader before he became a military leader. The path to leadership was long and winding. He was initially drawn to socialism from his experience of discrimination and hardship at work, only gradually finding his way to an ideological interpretation. His political beliefs had not been imbibed at home, or come from deep study of classic Marxist texts. Eventually, Marxism came to provide him with an explanation of social misery and the prospect of a better future. But there was no 'Road to Damascus' conversion en route to becoming a deeply committed communist. There were a number of steps on the way.

He had been born in 1892 in the village of Kumrovec in the district of Zagorje, a poor region of western Croatia, close to the border with Slovenia, still at that time part of the Austro-Hungarian empire. His father was a smallholder, given to heavy drinking, and with too little land to support a large family. His mother, a pious Catholic and mother of fifteen children, eight of whom had died in infancy, had a hard job feeding the household. By the age of eighteen Josip had found employment in Zagreb as a metalworker. He had started to show interest in politics and in 1910 joined the Metalworkers' Union and the Social Democratic Party. It was the beginning of his political awakening. But there were no signs of socialist or pacifist misgivings about serving four years later as a sergeant-major in the Austro-Hungarian army. When, fighting on the Carpathian front, he was wounded and taken into Russian captivity in 1915, it began a second stage in his ideological radicalization. He did not suffer great hardship as a prisoner, and after a year mainly in hospital recovering from his wounds he worked first in a flour mill then on the Trans-Siberian Railway. By 1917 he was a Bolshevik sympathizer. In the chaos following the overthrow of the Tsar he was able to make his way to Petrograd, experienced the revolutionary ferment there, took part in demonstrations in July, was imprisoned for a time, then managed to escape from a train carrying him back to the Urals and to reach Omsk in Siberia, where he joined the Red Guards. He was forced to flee once more during the Russian civil war when the White counter-revolutionaries temporarily took power in Omsk. But in 1920, by now a fervent communist and after almost six years away, he was able to return to his homeland.[6]

The persecution of the Left that he encountered in the newly created, highly unstable Kingdom of the Serbs, Croats and Slovenes (in 1929 renamed Yugoslavia) was a third stage in his political emergence. Repression and violence punctuated the political scene. The newly formed Communist Party was banned by the royalist government in 1921. Years of underground activity followed as party members faced arrest and imprisonment. Broz had thrown himself into political activity and in 1928 became secretary of the party's Zagreb branch. That year he was arrested and put on trial with five others for illegal communist activity, including possession of two bombs (which he claimed had been planted by the police). He gave a bravura performance of defiance but was sentenced to five years' hard labour.

During his years in prison the corrupt monarchist regime in Yugoslavia became an outright dictatorship. The banned Communist Party lost support, and its organization was largely destroyed. Immediately on leaving jail, Tito (now starting to use that alias among others) turned to the hazardous attempt to rebuild the party. Towards the end of 1934 – he was by now an elected member of the party's Central Committee and Politburo – it was decided to send him to Moscow to work in the Comintern (Communist International) on Yugoslav affairs.[7] It would be the last important stage on his way to becoming the leader of the Communist Party in Yugoslavia.

He arrived in Moscow in February 1935 at a notably dangerous time to be in the Soviet Union. Big purges were starting to sweep through the country after the murder the previous December of the Leningrad party boss, Sergei Kirov, a close associate of Stalin. The menacing atmosphere of suspicion and distrust was all-pervasive. Foreigners, including those working for the Comintern, were particularly exposed, suspected of being spies or – just as bad – Trotskyites. As the Great Terror reached its peak in late 1937, three-quarters of Yugoslav communists in the Soviet Union fell under suspicion of being Trotskyites.[8] Hundreds were arrested and summarily executed, among them the General Secretary of the Yugoslav Communist Party, Milan Gorkić. Tito was fortunate to be out of the Soviet Union.

He had witnessed the beginning of the show trials in Moscow before leaving in autumn 1936 to begin over two years of clandestine travel and organizational work abroad, presumably financed by the Comintern. He spent time in Vienna, Paris, returned to Yugoslavia to try to rebuild the weakened party and was briefly in Madrid during the Spanish Civil War (which may have involved collaboration with the Soviet secret service in the liquidation of Trotskyites).[9] Living under false names, travelling with forged papers, moving between different addresses, managing inner-party factions and rivalries was exhausting and perilous – though perhaps less perilous than staying in Moscow would have been.

By the time he was recalled to Moscow in August 1938 to face criticism about the state of the Yugoslav party from a hostile five-man commission, the high-point of the purges had passed. Nevertheless, his position was precarious. He almost certainly avoided disastrous – perhaps fatal – consequences through support behind the scenes from the head of the Comintern, Georgi Dimitrov. He had to deal with a second threatening issue. In 1936, shortly before he left Moscow that October, Tito had, as noted, married Lucie Bauer, a young German communist who had been sent to Moscow in 1934 to be trained for illegal party activity back in Germany but in 1937 had been arrested, accused of spying and executed. This put Tito in danger when he was questioned by the commission. He did not defend Lucie Bauer (which would have been suicidal), but confessed that he had not been sufficiently vigilant in trusting her and admitted that it was a black mark against him.[10] As was the case for some in the Soviet hierarchy, abandoning his wife meant he passed the test.[11] He emerged intact from the ordeal.

Thanks, again almost certainly to Dimitrov's influence, he was formally confirmed as General Secretary of the Yugoslav Communist Party on 5 January 1939.[12] Dimitrov told him he was 'the only one left' and ordered him to root out factionalism and rebuild the party, otherwise it would be dissolved. Tito promised to 'clear out the filth'.[13] Stalin would have approved of the sentiment. What he thought of the appointment, or of Tito personally at the time, is, however, unrecorded; he did not know Tito personally – the two would meet for the first time in 1944.[14] At any rate, Tito was allowed to leave the Soviet Union and return to Yugoslavia.

How Tito, unlike many of his comrades, evaded the clutches of the Soviet secret police (the NKVD), especially after the arrest of his wife, is unclear. Was he tacitly working with the NKVD? Whether, and if so to what extent, he was implicated in the purges has never been ascertained. Djilas inferred that he had been involved, but that his 'participation in the purges was limited'.[15] By the time he was writing Djilas had long broken completely with Tito. And he had not been with Tito in Moscow during the purges. Certainly, however, Tito offered no support to his Yugoslav comrades and voiced no word of criticism of the Stalinist terror. As Djilas pointed out, complete loyalty to Stalin was imperative to survival. Tito was at that time a committed Stalinist. He had already been a strong supporter of Stalin's Soviet Union before he went to Moscow in 1935 and seems to have acknowledged later that, even if taken to excess, the purges were in principle correct.[16] Indeed, though not with the savagery of Stalin, he showed no compunction in resorting to purges when he later held power in Yugoslavia.

Back in Yugoslavia, as the storm of war came ever closer, Tito set about the radical reform of the disorganized and disunited party. With enormous energy, relentless determination and intolerance of opposing factions, he gradually turned the party into a highly centralized, nation-wide, Stalinist organization, ideologically wholly committed to the Moscow line. He insisted, though, that it become financially independ-ent, mainly through members' contributions from their meagre earn-ings. He brought the Central Committee back from its foreign exile to Yugoslavia. And he created an inner leadership core of new, young revolutionaries, committed to the cause represented by Stalin's Soviet Union but also loyal to Tito himself. Three of them – Edvard Kardelj, Aleksandar Ranković and Milovan Djilas –would form his closest band of support, not just during the Partisan struggle, but also in the power-structure of the new Yugoslav state after the war.[17]

The party had no more than about 6,500 regular members (and another 18,000 members of the youth organization) by autumn 1940. And it was still a proscribed organization. Tito was impatient to encourage an uprising against the state, but was restrained by Mos-cow. An attempt to overturn the government would, the Comintern convincingly argued, lead to certain disaster. Nevertheless, as the external threat to Yugoslavia grew, Tito led preparations for armed revolt in what by now was a disciplined, and growing, party. The situ-ation soon changed dramatically. On 6 April 1941, in response to a military coup in Belgrade to thwart Yugoslav plans to join the Tripar-tite Pact (Germany, Italy and Japan), the Germans invaded.

The Yugoslav army collapsed without a fight. Nearly 350,000 men, the majority of them Serbs, were taken captive, though another 300,000 escaped. The government and royal family fled into exile. Yugoslavia was dismantled. The Germans controlled Serbia. Their allies, the Italians, Hungarians and Bulgarians, occupied other parts of the dismembered country. On 10 April an Independent State of Croatia was established, run by the fascist Ustaše, who extended their control to Bosnia-Herzegovina and for the remainder of the war imposed a reign of indescribable terror, murdering over 300,000 Serbs and tens of thousands of Jews and Roma.

Tito was forced to move from Zagreb to Belgrade just before the border between Croatia and Serbia was closed, and to operate in condi-tions of utmost secrecy. He was soon to start a peripatetic existence, often through Yugoslavia's remote mountainous areas, that would last until the end of the war. Some in the party argued that it could do little beyond undertaking acts of sporadic sabotage. But once the German invasion of the Soviet Union began on 22 June 1941, Tito was able successfully to press the case for armed struggle. On 27 June the party's Politburo established a General Staff of Partisan Units, ready to engage in a guerrilla war for the National Liberation of Yugoslavia. Inevitably, as party leader Tito was named as its commander-in-chief.

PRECONDITIONS OF POWER

War made Tito's rule possible. Without the war, the invasion, the dismembering of the country, the cruel German and Italian occupation, the horrific Ustaše terror and the splintering of resistance between the communist-led Partisans and the monarchist Chetnik movement, Tito would almost certainly never have been in a position to take power in Yugoslavia. Before 1941 the communists were a small movement and lacked widespread popularity. The ethnic divisions and rival nationalities made it almost impossible to build an overriding Yugoslav class identity. The potential for a revolutionary uprising, as was recognized in Moscow, did not exist. Without an invasion, a unitary communist state would have been barely conceivable. More probably, Yugoslavia – a largely patched-together construction after the First World War – would have broken apart at some point into a number of small nation-states.

Of those examined in this book, Tito was the only leader who came to power as the victor in both a world war and a simultaneous civil war. Lenin, Mussolini, Hitler (indirectly), Churchill and de Gaulle all came to power as a consequence, at least in part, of a world war (and de Gaulle had to contend with the rival claims of the Vichy regime). Franco owed his power to victory in a civil war but did not participate in a world war. But only Tito had come to power after fighting a civil war within a world war – and not from a relatively secure headquarters away from immediate danger but from the front line itself of the ferocious struggle. His Partisans had to reckon not only with the mighty and lethal force of the German (and Italian) occupiers, but also with the barbaric atrocities of the Ustaše and the pitiless attacks of the Chetniks, a royalist and Serbian nationalist force led by a colonel in the defeated Yugoslav army, Draža Mihailović. Brutality bred brutality. The Partisans perpetrated their own atrocities. Tito personally ordered the liquidation of all spies, fifth columnists and 'active opponents of the people's liberation struggle'.[18]

The Partisans numbered only about 40,000 at the start of the civil war in Serbia. The cruelty, persecution, reprisals and atrocities they faced daily, while hugely intimidatory, served as a recruiting sergeant for the fanatical minority ready to sacrifice everything for the Partisan cause: liberation of the homeland from fascists and imperialists. By 1943 Tito commanded around 150,000 Partisans. The number doubled by the end of the year as people saw the war was turning inexorably against the invaders. At the liberation of Belgrade in October 1944 this had risen to no fewer than 800,000.[19] Behind these figures lay the growing numbers of those, including family members, who, while not among the fighters themselves, sympathized with and provided help and succour for the Partisans.[20]

Tito was bitter at the minimal backing from the Soviet Union, itself needing all the resources it could muster for the titanic showdown with Hitler's forces. Nor, until 1943, did the Partisans have any tangible support from Britain or the USA. Churchill's sympathies initially lay with the Chetniks, but what counted for him was the defeat of Germany, and, gradually, he realized that he had backed the wrong horse. There was collaboration between the Chetniks and the Germans and Italians. And they were losing popular support. Although the Americans continued to pin their hopes on them because of their vehement anti-communism, Churchill committed increasing British resources to helping the Partisans. By the time of the Tehran Conference in November 1943, the Allies were prepared to recognize the Partisans as the Yugoslav national liberation force. Churchill, the British leader of aristocratic descent, made a direct contribution to the making of the communist leader, Tito. Aided by supplies of British armaments, the Partisans were by 1944 tying down fifteen German divisions in the Balkans.[21]

Tito was far from flawless in his military command (as Djilas later pointed out).[22] But he had good subordinate commanders. And he was an inspiring leader – decisive, calm in danger, ready to share the hardships of his men, upholding discipline, exuding strength of will and confidence in victory. He built a staff of about thirty who accompanied him in his constantly shifting headquarters, criss-crossing hundreds of miles of Yugoslav territory.[23] But he took the key decisions himself. All the lines of control ran through his hands. His authority was unquestioned.

For more than three years as commander of the Partisans he led such an extraordinary existence that it reads today like a 'Boy's Own' fictional adventure story. But this was real. In March 1943, for instance, through a highly risky manoeuvre, he led his Partisan army, including the sick and wounded, across the River Neretva to safety, avoiding its certain destruction at the hands of a large force of armed Chetniks. More than that: the Partisans were then able to turn the tables on the Chetniks, though greatly outnumbered. The Chetniks never recovered. It was a decisive defeat for their leader Mikhailović.[24] In June, amid intense fighting, Tito narrowly avoided death and was wounded in his left arm by a grenade which exploded nearby and still managed to evade encirclement near the River Sutjeska. Over 7,000 Partisans were killed, but again Tito managed to escape into the woods of eastern Bosnia. In May 1944 he and his close comrades, trapped in a cave during a big German offensive, followed a dried-out river bed and were eventually able to flee into the mountains. Such exploits were later embroidered to construct a powerful image of the legendary Partisan commander, an intrinsic component of the Tito cult.

After Tito had flown to Moscow in September 1944, Stalin agreed to send troops to help in the liberation of Yugoslavia. Around 400,000 Red Army soldiers fought alongside the Partisans in the final assault on Belgrade, though their rapacious behaviour – reportedly 1,219 rapes, 111 murders and 1,204 cases of looting – was deeply alienating.[25] The Soviet military assistance at this stage was far from insignificant.[26] The Partisans had also, as mentioned, benefited for a year or so by then from British arms supplies. Nevertheless, for the best part of three years the Partisans had fought effectively alone, against initially long odds, defying the Germans, the Italians, the Ustaše and the Chetniks. Their claim to have liberated their own country was in large measure justified. Unlike everywhere else in eastern Europe, the Red Army had played only a belated and subsidiary role.

Five days after the Partisans had entered Belgrade, following intense fighting, on 20 October 1944, Tito returned to the capital – now as the triumphant war leader and liberator of Yugoslavia, a hero with an unchallengeable claim to the post-war leadership of the country.

TITO'S AUTOCRACY

Welding together the fissiparous parts of Yugoslavia, torn by war for four years, into a unitary state would have been inconceivable without Tito. He was the founder, inspiration and fulcrum of the Yugoslav state, its indispensable focus of integration until his death.

The framework of a government and future constitutional arrangements had been laid down already at a meeting of 142 delegates to the second Antifascist Council on 29–30 November 1943. The future Yugoslavia, it determined, was to be a democratic federal state. The exiled government would be barred from power. Almost a year later, on 1 November 1944, a provisional government was formed, with Tito as Prime Minister but incorporating some pre-war 'bourgeois' politicians who were not compromised through collaboration with the enemy.[27] Over the following months, however, any hopes that the western Allies had of a pluralist government and democratic freedoms disappeared. By November 1945, when elections to a Constituent Assembly took place, the only party on the ballot-sheet was the Popular Front, led by Tito – in effect, the Communist Party – and it duly won 96 per cent of the vote.[28] The monarchy was abolished. By then (as already mentioned), there had been a brutal reckoning with former collaborators, thousands of whom, with Tito's express approval, had been shot (though thousands more – including Ante Pavelić, the unspeakable Ustaše leader – had escaped to find refuge first in Austria, later elsewhere abroad, including Argentina, Spain and the USA). The Chetnik leader Mihailović would be executed in July 1946.[29] Tito's rule was founded not only on his war leadership, but also on his utter brutality in ordering or condoning the atrocities of the immediate post-war months.

According to the constitution, which came into effect that year, the new Yugoslavia was to be a federation of six republics (Serbia, Slovenia, Croatia, Bosnia and Herzegovina, Montenegro and Macedonia) with autonomous status granted to the Serbian provinces of Vojdodina and Kosovo, both of which had large non-Slav minorities.[30]

There was, even in theory, to be no western-style pluralistic democracy, and whatever autonomy existed constitutionally was constrained in practice by the fact that Yugoslavia was a one-party state, run on Stalinist lines by the Communist Party.

During the war the Communist Party had become the only political force that aimed to recreate a unified state of Yugoslavia. Dwindling numbers of royalists hoped, of course, for a different future for Yugoslavia under a restored monarchy. But the Chetniks had fought for a 'greater Serbia'. And the Ustaše had wanted an ethnically cleansed state of Croatia. Meanwhile the organizations of both the Chetniks and the Ustaše had been destroyed. But the communists were far from universally welcomed. They had to tie their claim to be the ruling party for the whole of Yugoslavia to Tito's enormous popularity. The beginnings of a Tito personality cult – the indispensable foundation of the new state's legitimacy – were plainly on show in the huge outpouring of adulation on his birthday, 25 May 1946. A propaganda barrage lauded the leader as war hero, statesman and simple 'son of the people'. Three weeks earlier, 70,000 people had marched through Belgrade carrying red flags and shouting 'Tito-Stalin', 'Long live the Red Army' and 'Long live the Communist Party'.[31]

Very soon, however, Tito and Stalin could no longer be jointly acclaimed. The relationship between the two – long deteriorating – dissolved into lasting acrimony. Control over the Balkans was the key issue. Stalin wanted Yugoslavia to become a pliant satellite of the Soviet Union as part of a 'Balkan Federation'.[32] Tito's diplomatic moves to extend his influence over Bulgaria, Albania and Greece were intolerable to Moscow. In addition, Tito's insistence on a Yugoslav five-year industrialization programme did not fit in with Soviet plans to keep the Balkans, including Yugoslavia, as chiefly agricultural economies which would help feed the Soviet Union itself and other industrialized parts of their bloc. By early 1948 Stalin's patience was wearing thin. In March he sent Tito a long letter, accusing him of 'revisionism' and Trotskyite tendencies. Tito was undaunted. He presented his lengthy, unyielding reply to a meeting of Yugoslav party leaders and gained almost unanimous approval. Stalin did not constrain his anger in two further letters. He demanded that Tito attend a meeting in Bucharest of members of Cominform (the Communist Information Bureau, founded in October

1947 as successor to the Comintern to coordinate international communist parties under Moscow's aegis). It was obvious to Tito that if he attended the meeting he would be forced into line, possibly with dire consequences. In his absence he was accused of being an 'imperialist spy', and it was decided that the Yugoslav Communist Party had excluded itself from the family of fraternal parties.

In the contest of strong wills, Tito held his ground. He had refused to be intimidated by the infinitely more powerful Soviet Union and had shown personal as well as political courage. The Soviet press poured vitriol on him. There were even Soviet attempts to assassinate him. But Tito would not bow to Stalin's bullying. Stalin kept a note from Tito in his desk drawer, found only after his death: 'If you don't stop sending killers, I'll send one to Moscow, and I won't have to send a second.'[33]

There were genuine fears in Yugoslavia that the Red Army would march into the country and subjugate it to Soviet rule. But for all his threats Stalin did not want to risk a world war over Yugoslavia – or anywhere else at this time, when tensions with the western Allies were becoming acute (and the Americans were still the sole power in possession of an atomic bomb). Perhaps most importantly, Stalin had witnessed the successful Partisan guerrilla war against the Germans. An invasion, even with his far superior forces, would have risked a protracted war against committed, patriotic guerrilla fighters. So Tito prevailed. And within Yugoslavia, his defiance of Stalin sent his already high prestige soaring.

After victory in the war, victory over the Soviet Union was the second foundation of Tito's charismatic appeal. Not only had he liberated Yugoslavia in the war. He had now established the country's independence. It made him a national hero even to those who until then had not been won over to Tito and were at best opportunistic or simply conformist in their support of communism.

Although communism in Yugoslavia would soon develop along different lines from the Soviet bloc – yet another source of deep alienation in Moscow – the split with Stalin strengthened the Yugoslav party organization. At first – the tendency later weakened somewhat – the Yugoslav Communist Party actually became even more monolithic (and totally focused on loyalty to Tito). Tito himself took the decision to have two leading critics, Andrija Hebrang (the Economics Minister, thought to be Stalin's favourite to succeed Tito) and Sreten Žujović (the Finance Minister and firm Stalin supporter) stripped of their posts, expelled from the party and imprisoned as 'enemies of the people'. A propaganda campaign was launched to root out 'enemies' within the party. Over 55,000 Moscow sympathizers were purged. Tito approved the proposal to establish a concentration camp on the Adriatic island of Goli Otok, where between 1949 and 1956 some 13,000 prisoners endured forced labour in hellish conditions. Thousands of others were 're-educated' in labour camps.[34] The gaps in party membership were easily and quickly filled. Almost half a million new members were recruited within a few years of the split with Moscow – all Tito loyalists, many owing careers and material benefits to their commitment to him. Regional parties were subordinated to Belgrade. Important positions at all levels of government were held by party members. So Tito's autocracy filtered down through hundreds of thousands of loyalists to all parts of the Yugoslav state.

Within the all-dominant Communist Party, the twelve sections of the Central Committee implemented government policy. The key forum of power, however, was the Secretariat of the ten-man Politburo, which had only three members besides Tito himself: Kardelj, Ranković and Djilas. Kardelj was in charge of foreign policy, Ranković internal security, and Djilas propaganda and intellectual life. This 'quartet' (as Djilas called it) determined policy, the Politburo confirmed it, and the lower levels of the party – mainly formed of young, former Partisan zealots with little education but fervent belief in Tito, implemented it.[35] Within the Secretariat itself there was no question of who really wielded power. Kardelj, Ranković and Djilas had all served alongside Tito in the war; they knew how he operated, recognized his right to leadership and bowed to his incontestable authority.

Whatever the constitutional theory, in practice this was an autocracy. 'I'm responsible for Yugoslavia! I decide here!' Tito made plain.[36] It was not an idle boast. He would take important decisions with little or no consultation.[37] And once he had decided, there was no going back. He had been used to giving unquestioned orders as Partisan leader. He could now turn his unique prestige as war hero into authoritarian leadership of the state. His opulent lifestyle exuded absolute power and authority. It was an intended statement of his untouchable supremacy. Long used to coping with harsh living conditions, he relished luxury all the more. It was a grotesque parody of socialist ideals. Money was no object. He treated state finances as his private revenue (and, after starting modestly, paid himself a handsome salary as well). He turned himself into a pseudo-monarch, a mini-Louis XIV enjoying socialist-style splendour attended by his retinue of courtiers who were corrupted by proximity to power and access to material privileges. One-time revolutionaries became the nouveau riche – avidly joining in the appropriation of wealth and property.

Tito immediately moved into one of the royal palaces, had another refurbished for lavish state receptions and before long added further former royal residences and huge hunting estates to his collection. A favourite was his summer residence on the island of Brioni, where he had an extravagant new villa and spacious accommodation for his government and party officials constructed by prisoners. He even set up his own zoo there. He soon came to possess an armour-plated Mercedes, a Rolls-Royce, a sumptuously equipped ocean-going yacht and an extensive array of works of art. He was vain about his stature. He gloried in the title of marshal, bestowed on him in 1943, and on public occasions invariably appeared in his garish marshal's uniform and decorations. His ostentatious vulgarity reminded some of a Latin American dictator.[38]

His position as head of state, commander-in-chief of the armed forces and party leader was unchallengeable – and would remain so until his death in 1980. His power rested on the triad of the party, the army and the security forces. Many party loyalists also served in the Yugoslav army, which, building on the Partisan movement, had strong personal bonds with Tito. Practically all officers were party members. Ideological formation was part of military training for the half a million soldiers who served in the army in the early 1950s. Tito made sure that the army was well paid and had privileged access to state housing. Its loyalty was never in doubt.[39]

The security police (under the direction of his close associate, Minister of the Interior and subsequently Deputy Prime Minister, Aleksandar Ranković), ensured conformity and punished political deviance. The 'inner enemy' was, as in all dictatorships, a device to promote integration and allegiance, with the arbitrary arrest and punishment of supposed 'traitors' aimed at ensuring compliance. The security police (the UDBA) could bug buildings, intercept post and listen to phone-calls. They never came close to matching the level of terror deployed in the Soviet Union. But opposition to Tito's regime was nonetheless severely punished through imprisonment or internment in labour camps. Most ordinary citizens, whatever their private views, understandably conformed with a system they could not alter.

This was not, however, a regime that was sustained only by coercion and intimidation. Tito's was for many years a popular dictatorship. How popular cannot of course be measured. And that popular legitimacy was in part at least manufactured by controlled mass media and by indoctrination in the party and army is obvious. No stone was left unturned in embellishing the rapidly ubiquitous Tito cult. Huge portraits of him adorned public buildings. Streets and town-squares were named after him.[40] The aura of the heroic leader totally dominated the political scene. No other political figure came remotely close to the popularity of the 'people's hero'. However important the role of propaganda manipulation, it would be misleading to deny that Tito enjoyed genuine personal popularity, particularly in the early years, when he could bask in the glory of his legendary wartime exploits and his defence of the nation against the Soviet bully. He epitomized national pride. And it was not just a psychological uplift. Enormous social and political energy was unleashed. New buildings, construction sites and big infrastructural projects were physical signs of major change. There were noticeable improvements in living standards – modest, certainly, by comparison with the wealthiest parts of western Europe, let alone the USA, but higher than anything most people had ever experienced, and offering hope of a still better future. The 1950s saw huge state investment and impressive economic growth (from low beginnings): an annual rise of 13 per cent in industrial production and a rise in income of almost 6 per cent. It meant a big shift from agriculture to industry. But the initial drive to collectivized farming (though without Stalin's murderous brutality) was reversed by 1953, since it had proved so unpopular and was not economically viable. Unproductive cooperatives were wound up, the land returned to the peasants, and more invested in agriculture – bringing higher returns and growing contentment among the large agrarian population.[41]

Following the break with the Soviet Union there were changes in running the economy which at least at first seemed promising and attractive. Kardelj (the party's chief theorist), Boris Kidrič (a leading Politburo member, in charge of the economy) and Djilas (the propagandist) persuaded Tito in 1949 to adopt a new mode of industrial relations. 'Self-management', at least in theory, allowed workers' councils to direct the running of factories and mobilize the building of socialism 'from below', not through 'top-down' direction by the state as in the Soviet Union. Problems in practice mounted soon enough, but initially the system seemed attractive to workers, as well as to the government. For Tito, never dwelling on theory as Kardelj in particular did, the political and propaganda advantages of the system outweighed the narrowly economic. Crucial for him was that the party's overall control – largely synonymous with his own – was not undermined by 'self-management'. There was an obvious tension. But ultimately Tito insisted that the party's monopoly of power remained uncontested. Democratization had its limits.[42]

This was plainly demonstrated when, in 1953, Milovan Djilas, thought by some to be Tito's likeliest successor, publicly criticized the system that he himself had helped build up. When, instead of retreating, Djilas intensified his criticism – which he published in the party's main newspaper, *Borba*, no less – recrimination was certain. He was dismissed from his offices, forced to resign from the party and eventually imprisoned for a total of nine years. He was later amnestied and able to write of his experiences with Tito. But once he did not serve Tito's interests, he was expendable. As Tito told him, he was 'politically dead'.[43] At least he was not actually dead, as he would certainly have been under Stalin.

By the 1960s Tito's absolutist power was at its zenith. But below him rifts in the leadership widened between the Slovenian system-reformer Edvard Kardelj and the Serbian conservative hardliner Aleksandar Ranković, the two main contenders for the succession (after Djilas' hara-kiri the previous decade). At first, as the problems – inefficiency and corruption – of the 'self-management' system that he had promoted became increasingly evident, Kardelj was the main target of Tito's ire. He survived in no small measure through tactical guile and because of the support he enjoyed in his Slovenian homeland (the richest and most advanced part of Yugoslavia). By the mid-1960s, the position of Ranković was the more exposed. He had been Tito's hatchet-man, loyally carrying out his dirty work. He presided over a repressive apparatus that had collected files on millions of citizens. And he had another powerful position as the party's Organizational Secretary.[44] But he had made enemies even among his Serbian party colleagues. Moreover, Tito had become deeply suspicious not only about the intrigues and infighting in the top echelons of the regime, but about his own safety and whether the security services were plotting against him. It did not prove difficult to persuade him that his private residence, even his bedroom, had been bugged by the secret service. The listening devices were connected to Ranković's villa. Ranković was browbeaten into submission at a meeting of the Central Committee in June 1966, accepted his responsibility (though privately he thought he had been framed) and subsequently resigned from all his offices. He was later pardoned (in contrast to what would have been his certain fate under Stalin) and disappeared from public life, secretly accusing Tito of betrayal.[45]

The security service was purged of Ranković's erstwhile supporters and decentralized (apart from the vital sphere of counter-intelligence). Control of security passed to the individual republics – though reports on any subversive behaviour were still sent on to Belgrade. Whatever danger – more imaginary than real – the security services had come to pose to Tito was excised, its outright loyalty re-established. The party, despite suggestions that it should be less centrally controlled, stayed essentially unchanged as a vehicle for Tito's power. The army, as ever, remained the most crucial bastion of his power. And Tito had kept a firm grip on the military intelligence service (KOS).[46] The Defence Minister, General Ivan Gošnjak, a former Partisan commander with a close working relationship with Tito, had always ensured its firm loyalty. When their relationship cooled in the wake of demands for change following the Ranković affair, Tito replaced him with General Nikola Ljubičić, another former Partisan commander and arch-loyalist.[47]

Yugoslavia, thanks to Tito's international standing and the internal reforms that he had overseen, was by far the most popular European communist state in the eyes of the world in the 1960s. It seemed a more attractive version of communism than that of the Soviet bloc. Its economic growth won admiration in the West. Investment poured in. Mass tourism swelled the state coffers. The partial liberalization of culture was attractive to foreign visitors. Tito's prestige, abroad as well as at home, was at its height. Yet all was not as it seemed. Cracks were appearing that would widen greatly in the following decade. Economic growth was slowing, unemployment and inflation rising ominously, the trade deficit increasing, and dependence on foreign loans a hostage to future prosperity.[48] Steps towards modest liberalization were leaving the economy more, rather than less, exposed to international market forces. Tito, powerful as he was, could do nothing to halt, let alone reverse, the structural problems. In the 1970s these would be magnified and, in their train, so would the difficulty of holding the separatist nationalist tendencies in check. Tito, now as before, was the very symbol of Yugoslav unity. His authority cemented the entire foundations of the multinational socialist state that he had built. He still held the country together. But Yugoslavia was in many respects a flawed construct, and had been since its beginnings after the First World War. Tito turned eighty in 1972. How long would unity last after his death?

BETWEEN THE BLOCS:
THE GLOBAL STATESMAN

Only Tito could have made Yugoslavia – an economically weak, medium-sized country with a proud wartime record but modest military strength – into a key factor in international affairs. He was courted by both superpowers, and able through sometimes slippery diplomacy to play them off against each other by exploiting Yugoslavia's strategic importance. As he skilfully manoeuvred between them, he engineered Yugoslavia into the position of leader of an amorphous group of countries, scattered across the globe, which formed the loosely organized Non-Aligned Movement, operating between the big power-blocs, committed neither to the USA nor to the Soviet Union. Especially from the mid-1950s onwards, Tito made himself a central player on the global stage. From initial isolation following the breakdown of relations with the Soviet Union, he single-handedly put Yugoslavia on the world map. His diplomatic travels reached epic proportions. He made 169 state visits to 92 countries between 1944 and 1980, and held receptions at home for 175 heads of state, 100 prime ministers and hundreds of other notable political figures.[49]

The split with Stalin was the basis of his new-found international leverage. As Stalin seethed and threatened in the Kremlin, Tito became the focus of American attention – seen as a vital wedge in the Soviet bloc of eastern Europe. Strategically, Yugoslavia held the key to the Balkans. With Yugoslavia under its aegis as a satellite, the Soviet Union would potentially have been in a position to widen its influence over much of southern Europe. As it was, Yugoslavia provided an open door to western penetration of the communist-dominated half of Europe. Through the door came – mainly American – financial aid ($553.8 million between 1950 and 1953), which fed the booming Yugoslav economy. As the Korean War sharpened anxiety about Soviet expansionist aims, the USA's aid also went to fund armaments in the hope of drawing Yugoslavia into western defence plans.[50] In later years, when the economy was under growing pressure, American finances helped to keep Tito afloat – though at the price of increasing Yugoslav dependence on western aid and adding to growing levels of foreign debt.

Especially in the USA and in Great Britain – after the war still an international force to be reckoned with and with bases all around the eastern Mediterranean – Tito was recognized not just as a remarkable wartime commander of the Partisans, but as an extraordinary leader who alone had shown the strong nerve, iron will and ruthless determination to fend off Stalin and the might of the Soviet Union. This gave him a major advantage in his dealings with the West. He exploited it skilfully, at the same time ensuring that Yugoslavia – once Khrushchev had taken the initiative after Stalin's death to heal the breach – also utilized the greatly improved relations with Moscow, while still keeping the Soviet Union at arm's length. Financial aid (and technical cooperation) was negotiated with Moscow as well as Washington.[51]

There were numerous bumps in the road of relations with both East and West. Relations with Moscow, for instance, nosedived for some months following the Hungarian uprising in 1956, when Tito had both accepted the need for the intervention and criticized the continuation of Stalinism in the Soviet Union and its satellites as the cause of the trouble.[52] Tito's siding with the Arabs in the wars of 1967 and 1973 with Israel went down badly in the West. Diplomatic relations with Belgrade were broken off by West Germany for a time following Yugoslavia's recognition of the German Democratic Republic in 1957. De Gaulle was angered by Tito's supply of arms to the Algerian Liberation Movement. And the Soviet Union was greatly alienated by Tito's condemnation of the invasion of Czechoslovakia in 1968. In each case, however, the geopolitical interests of both Moscow and Washington on the one side and the economic interests of Belgrade on the other meant that damaged relations were repaired.

In the face of Soviet anger after 1968, Tito turned demonstratively to the USA. President Nixon was invited to Yugoslavia in October 1970 and the following year Tito was fêted during a state visit to Washington, returning with finance credits worth nearly a billion dollars in his pocket. Just before Tito travelled to America the Soviet leader, Leonid Brezhnev, had swallowed his pride and in October 1971, though still in high dudgeon, gone to Belgrade. The atmosphere during the discussions with Tito was frosty. But when Brezhnev left, it was after providing credits for $540 million.[53]

The opportunity for Yugoslavia to escape the diplomatic isolation that ensued from the break with the Soviet Union and give the country undue weight in the international arena arose from the policy of forging close relations with countries that did not align themselves with either of the superpowers. The new policy was not Tito's own initiative. It first emerged as an indirect product of the good personal relationship at the United Nations between the Indian and Yugoslav representatives on the Security Council. Diplomatic relations were established between Belgrade and New Delhi, and the Yugoslav ambassador, Josip Djerdja, was soon attracted by the belief of the Indian head of state, Jawaharlal Nehru, that a 'third force' between the superpower blocs had potential. Djerdja put the case to Kardelj, at the time still Foreign Minister, in 1951, and Kardelj took it further to an initially unenthusiastic Tito. Following further persuasion, Tito warmed to the idea and then fully embraced it.[54] The first fruit was an invitation to visit India, which Tito eagerly accepted, becoming, in November 1954, the first European head of state to make an official state visit.

That was the start. Tito was soon embarking on his foreign tours, many of them including lengthy voyages on his luxurious state yacht,

Galeb (Seagull). He was the first communist leader to visit sub-Saharan Africa and Latin America, as well as extending his connections with Asian countries. The personal diplomacy was important. He established good relations especially with leaders of newly independent countries who had risen to power through their role in anti-colonial movements. Among the more important, apart from Nehru, were Sukarno in Indonesia, Gamal Abdel Nasser in Egypt, Kwame Nkrumah in Ghana, Julius Nyerere in Tanzania and Emperor Haile Selassie in Ethiopia. Some were notably unsavoury characters like the Ugandan President Idi Amin and the dictator of the Central African Republic, Jean-Bedél Bokassa. The doctrine that bound the disparate political systems together was 'peaceful coexistence', the aim to create a 'third force' that would exert influence on world politics and counter the dominance of the two superpower blocs.[55] As tension rose between the superpowers in September 1961, Tito expounded the principles – condemning both NATO and the Warsaw Pact – to representatives of twenty-five countries at a conference he had called in Belgrade.[56] It marked a high-point of his leadership of what had come to be called the 'Non-Alignment Movement'.

However strong the rhetoric, the effectiveness of the disparate grouping of states was limited. It had no substantial impact on superpower relations and did little or nothing to diminish the tensions of the Cold War. But, for Yugoslavia, Tito's prominence brought dividends. It not only raised the international standing of the country, but also opened export markets that swelled Yugoslav finances by around $1.5 billion a year. Internally, it helped to gloss over the inherent division between the westward-looking Slovenia and Croatia and, traditionally drawn to Russia, Serbia. It was attractive, too, to Bosnian Muslims because of the connections with Islamic culture.[57] Not least, international renown brought reflective glory for Tito at home. His prestige was sky-high, his position untouchable.

FADING POWER

Even in old age Tito cut an impressive figure and did not contemplate giving up power. He showed remarkable energy in keeping up his representational activity abroad – which provided the opportunity for extended luxury holidays in the sun. He travelled in the 1970s to the Indian sub-continent, Syria and Latin America (apart from official visits to European countries), and participated in the globally import-ant Conference on Security and Cooperation in Europe in Helsinki in 1975. His health was, however, declining; those close to him saw the visible signs of ageing.[58] His decades in power as the vital integrative force in Yugoslavia were plainly drawing to a close.

The system that he had built and sustained was already creaking at the seams long before his death. Tito's personal power was unable to halt, let alone reverse, the inherent structural problems of the economy – increasing national debt, inflation and unemployment as productivity levels dropped. The intrinsic difficulties were massively exacerbated by the impact of the 1973 oil-crisis and the now ruin-ously higher costs faced by all countries dependent on the import of oil. In the second half of the 1970s there was an almost five-fold increase in borrowing and a three-fold increase in the interest on repayment. There was less available for the import of foreign con-sumer goods. Prices inevitably rose.[59] So did economic inequality. In its wake, national tensions and separatist tendencies intensified. Croatia and Slovenia objected to 'their' money being siphoned off to finance the poorer parts of the country. Serbia and the economically weaker republics were antagonized by the wealthier regions benefit-ing disproportionately. Economic and social resentment brought a more shrill and corrosive emphasis on cultural differences and national identity. Conversely, the sense of Yugoslav state identity was faltering.

Yugoslavia was not immune to the liberalizing pressures that spread across Europe in the late 1960s. When student unrest flared in 1968, Tito headed it off with promised – if unfulfilled – concessions that, amid fears of a Soviet incursion (greatly magnified by the invasion of Czechoslovakia), helped to calm the unrest.[60] More worrying were big nationalist demands for Croat independence by Zagreb students in 1971. Tito responded with the big stick. He forced the Croatian party leadership to resign.[61] Nearly 200 arrests were made, hundreds more purged from the Croatian party, and extensive purges undertaken in the other republics of those who harboured nationalist feelings. In 1972 more than 5,000 liberals in the Serbian economy and media were forced to resign. In 1973 significant restrictions on press freedom were introduced. Some films and magazines were banned. A number of professors from Belgrade University were suspended from their posts. By the middle of the decade Yugoslav jails held around 5,000 political prisoners.[62]

There was not only the big stick of repression. There was a carrot, too, in the plans to devolve more power to the republics. The hope, clearly, was to defuse the tensions that were starting to threaten Yugoslav unity – and the regime's survival. The commission of a new constitution (which came into effect in 1974) was Kardelj's work. Tito disliked it, insisting that guarantees be included to safeguard the pre-eminence of the party and the army, and on confirmation that he would be President for life (already granted to him in the 1962 revised constitution).[63] In practice, the unwieldy new constitution did nothing to dilute separatist tendencies and prevent the country's growing fragmentation. Yugoslavia's unity was becoming increasingly fragile. Only the army and security police remained under federal control, but as throughout these were crucial loyalist institutions and, together with the party, the pillars of Tito's power. Tito had no doubt that he would always be able to rely on the army. He still held the levers of power. And like many other leaders – not just dictators – he was unwilling to let go of them. But he worried about the future of the country when he was gone.[64] He was well aware that he was increasingly the sole bulwark against the disintegration of Yugoslavia.

Though the problems mounted during the 1970s, Tito's autocracy remained intact until his death on 4 May 1980 at the age of eighty-seven. The last surviving European dictator who had come to power during the terrible decades of the 1930s and 1940s was gone. In his final years his long-standing diabetes had worsened to the point when his left leg had to be amputated, and towards the end his condition had drastically deteriorated. There was an enormous outpouring of national grief at the news of his death. His international standing was reflected in the representation of foreign dignitaries from 128 countries at his funeral.[65]

LEGACY

Seldom has a statesman held power for so long and in death been saluted across the globe, only for his life's work to crumble within a decade. It is, therefore, difficult to speak in any meaningful way of a lasting legacy. Rather, the collapse of Yugoslavia in the terrible ethnic conflict of the 1990s more vividly demonstrates how monumental Tito's achievement had been in building a political system that could hold together for so long despite its intrinsically centrifugal forces. For some thirty-five years he had been the focal point of integration for peoples of different ethnic, linguistic and religious backgrounds, and different levels of economic development. At the same time, the speed of the collapse illustrates the inherent structural flaws in his construct, which inevitably produced the tensions and divisions, already well apparent by the 1970s, that would ultimately split the country apart.

Without Tito, the attempted complex balancing act of the 1974 constitution did not work. The army was increasingly the only institution left that was anxious to sustain a federal, unitary state. And by the late 1980s Gorbachev's impact was dramatically altering the international balance of power, and as an indirect consequence deflecting concern at the growing threat of disintegration in Yugoslavia.[66] Tito was a maker of history. But he was powerless to prevent impersonal forces – mounting and ultimately uncontainable pressures of nationalism and separatism – undermining, and then finally sweeping aside, the Yugoslavia that he had built. His personal impact on historical change was, therefore, significant – but transient.

Tito's actions did not only affect Yugoslavia. His defiance of Stalin had important European and even global consequences. His engagement with developing countries was also of worldwide significance. For almost four decades Tito unquestionably took the crucial decisions himself that shaped his country's fate. He played a unique personal role. No one else could have emulated it. He was completely indispensable to the construction and sustaining of the socialist state in post-war Yugoslavia, as he had been earlier to the triumph of the Partisans.[67] His personality and his achievements brought him the loyalty and unified support of a potentially fractious leadership corps.

Tito was, in Max Weber's sense, a 'charismatic leader', backed by a 'charismatic community'. It was the core of what endless products of the state propaganda machine turned into the full-blown 'Tito cult' – the basis of his popular legitimacy and making his position of power unassailable.

Tito's 'charismatic' nimbus lasted until his death. Soon afterwards, however, it began to fade. His years in power started to be re-examined and seen in a different light. His private life, his hankering after luxury, his vanity and lust for power were starkly contrasted with the socialist ideals that he had preached. Both socialism as a political system and the national unity of Yugoslavia's multi-ethnic state were increasingly discredited as a result. Even his wartime record was called into question as a more complex picture of the struggle against fascism was painted – one which partially rehabilitated the Chetniks and revealed the extent of Partisan atrocities.[68] Turning Tito from a national idol to a figure of heated political and historical dispute was part of the onset of Yugoslavia's tragic disintegration. Little more than a decade after his death, streets and squares in Croatia named in his honour were being given new names, statues to the Partisans demolished. In a post-communist, ethnically divided former Yugoslavia, splintered cultural identity left no room for veneration of a communist dictator who had through force of personality and through ruthless repression insisted on the unity of the socialist state and abhorred the nationalist enmities that threatened to destroy it. Tito had avoided grooming a successor. And indeed no leader capable of maintaining the integrity of a multi-national Yugoslavia followed him. Instead, the 'strongmen' who within a few years were building their power-bases were leaders who poured oil on the fires of ethnic divisions: Slobodan Milošević in Serbia, Franjo Tudjman in Croatia, Alija Izetbegović in Bosnia-Herzegovina, and Radovan Karadžić among the Bosnian Serbs.

The governments that took over in the separate states of what had formerly been Yugoslavia did all they could to discredit Tito and to turn their backs on the era that was synonymous with his name. Tito symbolized a past that they wanted to erase. During the four decades since his death, Tito has become the central figure in a highly conten-tious history. Only older citizens in the successor states to Yugoslavia still remember him as the country's leader. They may well still recall the inextricably intertwined positive and negative features of his long years in power.

Tito has become little more than a distant remnant of the past, of no real significance for the daily lives of most people, who see political history dating back only to the foundation of the current nation-states that were once part of Yugoslavia. A mythical image of Tito remains: the symbol of lost unity. Only a minority are gripped by this nostalgia.[69] That is all that is left of a political titan who made history, but whose legacy proved to be remarkably short-lived.

Margaret Thatcher, with (from left to right) Nigel Lawson (Chancellor of the Exchequer), Norman Tebbit (Chairman of the Conservative Party) and Paul Channon (Secretary of State for Trade and Industry), on the eve of the 1987 General Election. Making Britain 'great' again was Mrs Thatcher's underlying political aim.

MARGARET THATCHER

National Regeneration

Margaret Thatcher is the only woman to be included among my selected case studies of political leadership. This reflects the fact that politics in twentieth-century Europe was overwhelmingly a man's world. It is also, however, testimony to her standing in Britain, Europe and the wider world during the 1980s. To what extent did Mrs Thatcher personally shape Britain's undoubted transformation during almost twelve years of her premiership? Was she largely steering change which was coming about anyway? Or did she succeed 'against the grain', in the face of powerful opposition? How should her personal role be evaluated in reshaping the British economy, in the military victory in the Falklands and in the defeat of the miners' strike? And how important was her mark on the twentieth century beyond British shores?

PERSONALITY AND POLITICAL EMERGENCE

Having to contend in a socially elitist male-dominated political milieu with snobbery about her provincial, lower-middle-class background and condescension about her gender probably helped to shape Margaret Thatcher's steeliness, toughness, even aggression. It encouraged the feeling that she had always to prove herself, to show that she was more able, more industrious, more decisive, more in control than anyone else. Hardness, competitiveness, abrasiveness are not usually seen as feminine characteristics. But in a macho political environment she had to – or

felt she had to – display characteristics men would value. Yet she combined her domineering personality with an overtly feminine side, which
she used to advantage. She could turn on her considerable charm, play
on emotions, show a soft, sensitive aspect of her character. She could
even appear sexy. The reputed remark of President Mitterrand of France
that 'she has the eyes of Caligula but the mouth of Marilyn Monroe' is
one, slightly odd indication of her feminine appeal.[1] It was feminine,
but not feminist. Her own attitude towards gender was traditionalist. She emphasized the woman's role as housewife and mother. She had
no truck with the demands of the feminist movement: in her view
women had every right to succeed on merit, but deserved no favour on
grounds of gender. She felt she had fought her way to the top as the best
person for the job, not because she was a woman.[2]

She was unusually sure of her views. The certainty that she was right,
allied to a quick mind, sharpness in debate and adamantine refusal to
compromise, made Mrs Thatcher difficult to combat, let alone defeat,
in a political argument. The certainty drew largely upon her instincts
and long-held values, formed in her early years. She had been born in
1925 in the Lincolnshire market town of Grantham. Her father, Alfred
Roberts, was a preacher in the Methodist Church, an austere, largely
self-taught man who became a pillar of his community, a local councillor and eventually mayor of Grantham. Margaret seldom spoke of her
mother, Beatrice. 'After I was fifteen we had nothing more to say to each
other,' she commented in 1961.[3] In stark contrast, she said later 'I owe
almost everything to my father' (though she saw remarkably little of
him after the age of eighteen).[4] She imbibed his essentially Victorian
values: order, thrift, self-reliance, hard work, duty, patriotism. These
values remained an intrinsic part of her character, unchanged through
her years studying chemistry at Oxford University and her subsequent
qualification as a barrister. They were reinforced after her marriage in
1951 to Denis Thatcher, a successful and well-to-do businessman, who
helped to ease her path into conservative circles in the heartlands of
south-eastern England. Their twin children, Carol and Mark, were
born in 1953. Comfortable financial circumstances allowed her to
combine family life with pursuing her career in politics.

In 1959 she was elected as Conservative Member of Parliament for
Finchley, in north London, and before long was making her mark in

her party. During her first decade in parliament she advanced to become the Conservative opposition's spokesperson for transport, and then, after the Conservative victory in the 1970 election, joined the Cabinet as Secretary of State for Education and Science. It was already mooted in some circles that she might become Britain's first woman Prime Minister. She later claimed to have been dismissive of such notions, and that the height of her ambition had been to become Chancellor of the Exchequer.[5] Even that was to aim extremely high.

PRECONDITIONS

By the mid-1970s long-standing structural problems in the British economy (including poor industrial relations and low rates of investment), sharply exacerbated by the impact of the oil crisis in 1973, had engendered an unholy combination of high inflation (27 per cent in 1975) and high unemployment (over a million by then). What was labelled 'stagflation' seemed uncontrollable. Government expenditure was worryingly high, and the soaring cost of imports since the oil crisis had led to a trebling of the spending deficit. In 1976 the Labour government suffered the humiliation of having to ask the International Monetary Fund for a big loan, necessitating a reduction in public spending. But the powerful public sector trade unions understandably refused to accept pay awards that were substantially below the rate of inflation, as this would have reduced their members' standard of living. Chronic unrest continued to bedevil industrial production, culminating in the notorious 'Winter of Discontent' in 1979, when strikes brought public services to the point of near complete breakdown. Between 1974 (a year of two general elections in the shadow of the turbulence following the quadrupling of oil prices after the Arab–Israeli War of 1973) and 1979, when Mrs Thatcher became Prime Minister, neither of the two main political parties had been able to establish firm stability or had shown the capacity to master the seemingly intransigent economic problems.

Edward Heath, Prime Minister since 1970, had a torrid time trying to cope with the industrial unrest. In February 1974, during a damaging miners' strike in which the country was reduced to a three-day working week, Heath lost an election that he had called on the question 'who governs Britain?' When, amid political and economic turbulence, further elections followed in October that year, the Conservatives were again defeated. But still Heath would not stand down as party leader. He stubbornly clung on when political failure made his resignation inevitable. This was the fateful element of chance that opened the door to Mrs Thatcher's becoming leader of the Conservative Party.

Mrs Thatcher had not been seen as Heath's likely successor. Following the defeat in February, Heath, now leader of the opposition, had made her spokesperson for the Environment in the Shadow Cabinet, tasked with preparing a new housing policy.[6] It was an unlikely position in which to shine. But she came up with radical proposals, including the right of tenants to buy their council houses. Her remit covered financial issues, in particular the question of the unpopular local government property tax – 'the rates'. Strikingly, she proposed that the next Conservative government should abolish the rates and reduce local taxation. During the second election campaign of the year, she proved to be the Conservatives' star turn, with a natural aptitude for performing on television.[7] The Conservatives still lost the election. But Mrs Thatcher had propelled herself into the limelight. And opinion polls showed that her proposed policies were popular. As Heath desperately held on, Mrs Thatcher exploited a new position he had given her, as spokesperson for Treasury matters, to enhance her standing in the party through forceful attacks on the Labour government's economic policy.

By early 1975 the inevitable challenge to Heath could be delayed no longer. Many wanted a move to the right. Even more simply wanted Heath to go. But the candidates who sought to replace him dropped by the wayside. Sir Keith Joseph, a cerebral, somewhat other-worldly figure, emerging as an ideologue on the party's Right, soon proved unsuitable, and Edward du Cann, the ultimate party wheeler-dealer, withdrew to concentrate on his business interests. Most of the party bigwigs, in fact, still felt duty-bound to stand by Heath. If he had promptly resigned after the election defeat, the party leadership may well have fallen to Willie Whitelaw, a north-country landowner imbued with the paternalistic values of 'one-nation' conservatism. But Whitelaw's strong sense of loyalty meant that he would not stand against Heath. Mrs Thatcher had no such reservations and, once

Joseph had vacated the field, put herself forward for the leadership as a candidate for radical change. Backed by a well-organized campaign, she comprehensively defeated Heath on the first ballot. Heath finally resigned, and Whitelaw then entered the second round of the contest. But Mrs Thatcher, with the wind in her sails, was by now unstoppable. Whitelaw's chance had gone. He bore no grudges, attuned his political inclinations to the new order and became an utterly dependable pillar of support for Mrs Thatcher, the outsider who, it was remarked, happened to be 'opposite the spot on the roulette wheel at the right time'.[8]

Mrs Thatcher was driven by the need for action. She was neither a theorist nor an original thinker, but she was a quick and ready learner. Her guru in the mid-1970s, Sir Keith Joseph, had adjusted to his own lack of leadership qualities to become the prime theorist of a radical shift in economic policy. Joseph had been a minister in the Macmillan and Heath governments but had undergone a Damascene conversion and had come to reject entirely the economic principles based on the theory advanced in the 1930s of John Maynard Keynes, who had advocated government intervention to stimulate demand as the route to economic recovery. Until the fall of Heath's government Keynesian theory had underpinned every post-war Conservative administration. Joseph had, however, swallowed wholesale the monetarist ideas first advanced in the USA by Milton Friedman, professor of economics at Chicago University. These ideas rejected state expenditure to stimulate demand. Inflation, not unemployment, was seem as the chief economic evil. Friedman's central thesis was that control of inflation flowed from control of the money supply. All followed from that premise.

Other key figures were John Hoskyns, a former army captain and businessman who had made a fortune in computers, Sir Alfred Sherman, a founder of the Conservative think-tank Centre for Policy Studies and an influence on Joseph himself, and Professor Alan Walters, who had held the chair of economics at London School of Economics, then at Johns Hopkins University, before taking up a position as economic adviser to Mrs Thatcher. It is doubtful that Mrs Thatcher fully grasped the intricacies of monetarist theory.[9] She was hardly alone in that. But she could distil her economic philosophy into apparent common sense – homilies about the need to restrict government spending in the same way that a housewife had to manage the family budget. In this, as in almost everything else, her 'world-view' went back to the values of her Grantham childhood. She had the singular ability to grasp 'how a broad stratum of Middle England felt because she felt the same way'.[10] By the time the crisis had deepened in Britain in the late 1970s, Mrs Thatcher had completely distanced herself philosophically from the politics of her post-war predecessors and was armed with a fervently held (if inconsistently applied) set of convictions that offered her the answer to the structural economic and political problems at the root of Britain's widely perceived national decline.

The growing unrest during the 'Winter of Discontent' prompted the Labour government's defeat, by a single vote, in a motion of no-confidence on 28 March 1979. That meant a general election. The Prime Minister, James Callaghan, had decided not to risk an election the previous October, which, before the winter crisis, he might well have won. Had he done so, Mrs Thatcher might never have come to power.[11] As it was, the Conservative Party was galvanized by the campaign under a dynamic leader whose ideas struck a chord with so much of the grassroots membership. Labour was on the back foot, unpopular with much of the electorate and mired in insuperable problems.[12] In the general election on 3 May 1979 the Conservatives swept to power with a majority of forty-three seats. Mrs Thatcher entered Number 10 Downing Street as Prime Minister promising radical transformation in a country that had experienced a decade or more of political and economic turbulence, and widely perceived national decline.[13]

IMPOSING CONTROL

The fundamental principles behind the Thatcherite mission for change were: limiting the money supply to control the economy, cutting state expenditure, reducing the power of the trade unions, freeing the economy from the constraints imposed by 'socialist' governments (allowing it to be shaped more by market forces) and ending the high level of welfare dependency. As she started out in government, her entire political and economic programme amounted, as she envisaged it, to an ambitious aim to halt Britain's decline and to restore the country's greatness.

Her view that only strong leadership, needed to implement radical political change, could reverse the relentless decline of a once-great nation resonated with many people. The economic and political turmoil of the 1970s seemed ample confirmation of national decline. There was a subconscious more than overt lament for the loss of global power, for the times when Britannia had 'ruled the waves' and the country's industrial pre-eminence had made it the 'workshop of the world'. There was barely concealed resentment, too, that Britain had 'won the war, but lost the peace', having been overtaken in prosperity by the defeated countries, Germany and Japan. The perception of decline was widespread. But, notwithstanding the serious issues of the 1970s, national decline was more mirage than reality. Other countries had caught up, certainly, but that was merely part of the spread of global modernization. Britain had lost its colonies. But the empire had long drained rather than amplified Britain's resources, quite apart from moral considerations of colonial rule. And whatever its undoubted problems, Britain had since the war become a more prosperous country, with a far better standard of living for the majority of its population than in the imperial era. Moreover, as a small country even its residual global influence was still impressive.[14] Still, perceptions can outweigh reality. And Mrs Thatcher tapped into the rich vein of deep pessimism about Britain's future.

She presented a public image of strength and indomitability with skill, agility and clarity. She was more cautious, however, at least in the early years, than she appeared to be to the party and the public. In practice, principles were subjected to tactical adjustments and accommodated to political realities. But what amounted to an ideology remained in its essence unchanged. It was later compressed into a simple slogan of great force: THERE IS NO ALTERNATIVE, invariably abbreviated to TINA.[15]

At first, despite her election victory in 1979 and her big parliamentary majority, Mrs Thatcher had to tread carefully in persuading her Cabinet to adopt widely unpopular and divisive policies. Practically all her Cabinet – entirely male other than herself – had served under Heath. While they saw the need for change, few were firmly wedded to the radical break with former conservative policies envisaged by Mrs Thatcher. More were apprehensive, even fearful, of the consequences for the electoral prospects of the Conservative Party and of possible social disorder arising from government policies aimed at drastic cuts to public spending and entailing increased unemployment. Those with such reservations, generally proponents of a more traditionally paternalistic, less confrontational brand of Conservative politics, would soon become dubbed the 'Wets', among them some highly experienced and well-regarded party grandees.

Mrs Thatcher enjoyed, however, several notable advantages that underpinned her increasingly untouchable supremacy. The intrinsic power that any British Prime Minister enjoys has been aptly termed an 'elective dictatorship'. It gives an inbuilt dominance of the executive over the legislature.[16] Short of a unified revolt of senior members of the government, a Prime Minister who presides over a substantial parliamentary majority cannot be deposed. Moreover, the power of patronage is a formidable weapon. There is never a shortage of politicians prepared to sacrifice principles for a taste of power, and its emoluments.

Only resolute and united opposition within government can deflect a Prime Minister who refuses to alter course. The Thatcher Cabinet during her critical early years was anything but resolute and united in its opposition. Some of the 'Wets' were damper than others. They formed no united phalanx of opposition to government policy and lacked any semblance of a clearly defined alternative policy. Other Cabinet ministers were in any case prepared to swallow whatever reservations they might have. And there were those who were wholehearted in support of the Prime Minister's course. Gradually, but inexorably, the 'Wets' were replaced. The Cabinet came over time to be built far more in the Prime Minister's own image.

Given the divisions, a great strength enjoyed by Mrs Thatcher lay in her ideological clarity and her steely determination to drive through her policies whatever the reservations. Her inner doubts – and soon after becoming Prime Minister she publicly admitted to some – never weakened her will to persevere, whatever the obstacles, nor her belief that she was right. When others wavered in their resolve, Mrs Thatcher remained unbending. She advertised this, to enormous acclaim from the faithful gathered at the Conservative Party Conference in October

1980, when, in one of her few memorable rhetorical flourishes, she outrightly rejected calls to get her to change course. 'You turn if you want to, she declared. 'The lady's not for turning.'[17]

She was actually more cautious, adaptable and pragmatic than her inflexible public image implied. The exercise of power in a democracy invariably demands some concessions and compromises. Nevertheless, Mrs Thatcher conceded less and compromised on less than any other recent British Prime Minister. Opportunistic adjustment fitted into, rather than contradicted, her ideological drive.

Her style of government gave her another advantage. Rather than seek consensus – she detested the very word – Mrs Thatcher thrived on abrasive argument and combative dispute. Her workaholic habits – reading government papers until late in the night, mastering the detail in all briefings, involving herself in the minutiae of administration – along with an excellent memory and the forensic interrogative powers of a trained lawyer equipped her very well to carry her case against Cabinet colleagues who were less well prepared or more submissive in character. Some felt hindered by traditional upper-class male civilities from countering her hectoring, intimidatory style with equal aggression. 'You bully your weaker colleagues,' ran a withering critique of her leadership style by John Hoskyns in August 1981. 'They can't answer back without appearing disrespectful, in front of others, to a woman and to a Prime Minister.'[18]

She could, therefore, increasingly impose the level of control on her government that enabled her to determine her desired direction of policy, helped by a Civil Service that, certainly at first, welcomed the clarity of policy direction. She was reinforced in her judgement and its public presentation by her two most important aides, her private secretary (nominally for foreign affairs) Charles Powell and her press secretary, Bernard Ingham (a crucial link to the tabloid newspapers). And, in the central sphere of economic policy, Mrs Thatcher had from the outset shown political astuteness in appointing to key economic positions those who could be relied upon to follow her precepts.[19] Her most important appointment was that of Sir Geoffrey Howe. As Chancellor of the Exchequer, the key post after that of the Prime Minister, Howe was the loyal manager of the Prime Minister's economic policy in the early 1980s. Other Thatcher loyalists were placed in key positions in the Treasury, and the departments of trade, industry and energy. Force of personality, refusal to deviate fundamentally from the course embarked upon (whatever the temporary deviations and even subtle U-turns), and, not least, support from those in charge of the crucial economic ministries gave her the essential platform to continue as she had set out, whatever the obstacles.

RESHAPING THE ECONOMY

Measured against her vaulting ambitions for restructuring the British economy, Margaret Thatcher's first term of office was in many respects a failure. A steep recession in 1980–81 was partly the consequence (as in other countries) of the second oil crisis that followed the Iranian revolution in 1979. It was partly, though, the product of the very policies pursued – cuts in state spending, increased interest rates and as an indirect result of the discovery of North Sea oil a rise in the value of sterling, making exports uncompetitive. Howe's highly unpopular budget in 1981, which tightened the financial squeeze, deepened the economic misery.[20] But by 1983 the economy was recovering from the recession, helped by revenues from North Sea oil.[21] And the big prize – control of inflation – had been won, if at a very high price. Inflation dropped from 22 per cent in May 1980 to under 4 per cent in May 1983, a success loudly trumpeted, of course, by the government.

Otherwise, the record looked dismal. Gross domestic product had fallen, manufacturing output had gone down, unemployment had nearly trebled (seen by monetarists as a necessary by-product of controlling inflation), taxes had risen instead of falling in line with the government's professed aim, and, ironically, the money supply had grown in the face of monetarist dogma rather than declined. Most striking of all: state spending was actually higher in 1983 than the level inherited four years earlier from the previous Labour government.[22] *The Economist*, broadly supportive of the Thatcher government, disdainfully summed up its first-term performance: it had failed to honour 'its promise of structural radicalism', had backed away from reforming welfare and, whatever the rhetoric, had not taken bold, strategically driven decisions.[23]

The cost of high unemployment made the intended reduction in government spending difficult to achieve in practice. Only in Mrs Thatcher's last two years in office did it significantly fall as a proportion of gross domestic product. Adjusted for inflation, in fact, spending even slightly rose in the Thatcher era.[24] Monetarism had turned out to be an unwieldy and unsatisfactory device for rigid control of the money supply.[25] Even so, the Thatcher years fundamentally altered the entire basis for framing economic policy.

The state was no longer to intervene in the running of industry. Ailing firms could expect no financial support from government. (At least that was the theory; it took time to turn it into practice. In the first two years subsidies for the struggling car and steel industries even went up.)[26] The power of the trade unions was curbed by legislation that limited picketing and outlawed political strikes.[27] Control of inflation was deemed more important than maintaining full employment. Inflation, according to monetarist theory (and the 1970s seemed to support the theory), would inevitably prompt demands for higher wages – strengthening trade union power while weakening that of the state – which would lead to further price rises in an unending spiral that undermined both economic management and national prosperity. So, the theory ran, only rigorous control of the money supply to bring down inflation would bring economic recovery, even if the short- to medium-term consequence was a steep rise in unemployment. The ideological implications of the theory went further. The public sector of the economy was denigrated as monopolistic, limiting choice and freedom, costly and inefficient. Privatization of nationalized industries and public utilities began (and was soon to go much further). The sale of shares and previously rented council houses turned many citizens into small-scale holders of capital.

Market forces played a far greater role in shaping society than they had done previously, intruding now – largely through new forms of 'market oriented' management – into territory such as welfare and education (though these were not privatized). The financial deregulatory 'Big Bang' of 1986 brought the growing pre-eminence of London as a world banking centre. This saw new wealth come to Britain's capital, but with it came a crass increase in inequality. Finance, focused on the City of London, was replacing industry and manufacture as the focus of the British economy, greatly accelerating a decline in manufacturing that was already underway when Mrs Thatcher took office.[28] The doldrums of the 1970s had been left far behind. The wealth was becoming, however, increasingly centred in London and the south-east of England.

Whole swathes of Britain felt the cold winds of post-industrial dereliction. Britain's coal-mining, steel and shipbuilding industries were in steep decline, tens of thousands of their workers facing an uncertain future, whole communities feeling a deep sense of alienation from the government. The palpable and lasting anger in such communities at their treatment by the Thatcher government contrasted starkly with the adulation in which the Prime Minister was held in wealthier, conservative-voting parts of the country. In Scotland, and to some extent in Wales, the Thatcher years saw the Conservative Party – no longer the patrician one-nation party of the pre-Thatcher era – lose support it would never regain, and intensified the pressures for devolved government that would come to fruition nearly a decade after Mrs Thatcher had left office.

Substantial economic change would have taken place over time whoever was Prime Minister. By the 1970s international post-war economics was no longer working. The trend away from the economic framework of the first post-war decades had begun in the USA – Britain's main model – in 1971 with the break from fixed currency relations. The oil shocks of 1973 and 1979 were so severe that they marked the end of Keynesian economics. The changes experienced in Britain were felt in most of western Europe in the 1980s. This was in reaction to global economic forces, not a copy of Thatcherite methods. Deindustrialization and financial retrenchment were necessary adjustments to new economic realities. But they were introduced elsewhere in western Europe without the traumas that accompanied the transformation in Britain. Germany's ability to sustain its major industries indicates that the extensive destruction of the manufacturing base that Britain experienced was not the only route possible.

The abruptness, rapidity and severity of the transformation singled out Britain. This owed much to the depths to which the British economy, in international comparison, had sunk by the 1970s. It was also a consequence of the alacrity with which the British government – in contrast to other major economies in western Europe – seized with ideological zeal upon the American model of monetarism, outdoing even the Americans in its application. Mrs Thatcher's personal part in this was to give her government clear direction and to hold the line – subject to necessary pragmatic and tactical adjustments – whatever the weighty objections and despite the cost, in the early stages, of political dissent and social unrest.

THE FALKLANDS WAR

At the end of 1981 under a quarter of voters thought Mrs Thatcher was doing a good job as Prime Minister.[29] But at this juncture her political prospects were transformed by a stroke of fortune. The Argentinian invasion of the Falkland Islands could have gone very badly for her. As it was, her own actions helped to ensure that war over the Falklands became a great triumph. It was a turning-point in her premiership.[30]

The Falklands, deep in the South Atlantic, had been a British possession for a century and a half. Their population comprised fewer than 2,000 inhabitants, mainly of British descent. The islands, though, were still claimed by Argentina, now ruled by a military junta under General Leopoldo Galtieri. The invasion on 2 April 1982 was followed the next day by the annexation of South Georgia, a remote Falklands dependency, where the Argentinian flag had been illegally raised on 19 March. The response in London was outrage and a sense of national humiliation. But there had been warning signs. The act of aggression ought to have been anticipated. The fact was that the Thatcher government had been asleep on the watch.

The government had soon after taking office developed plans to transfer sovereignty to Argentina with a long-term leaseback to Britain. The Falklands were a low priority for the Foreign Office – a minor but troublesome leftover from the colonial era. A leaseback arrangement seemed like an elegant way out of the territorial dispute. But Mrs Thatcher shared the anger of the Conservative Right at this readiness to hand over the British possession. The possibility of a leaseback solution completely vanished once the belligerent General Galtieri had seized power in Argentina in December 1981. By then, the British Ministry of Defence, as part of its commitment to expenditure cuts, had removed the armed survey ship HMS *Endurance* from service in the South Atlantic. Even before Galtieri took power, the Argentinian government had correctly interpreted this as a sign of waning British interest in the Falklands. In 1981 and early 1982 the Falklands barely figured on the British government's agenda. Only in March 1982, immediately prior to the invasion, did the government – and the Prime Minister herself – wake up to the danger signs.[31]

To have tolerated the flagrant aggression against a British possession would almost certainly have brought down the government.[32] In any case, supine acceptance did not come into question for the Prime Minister. She swiftly took the navy's advice that military action to recover the Falklands was possible, if risky. Without hesitation, she ordered the assembly of a naval task force to set out for the South Atlantic. This order preceded an emergency sitting of the House of Commons on Saturday, 3 April 1982, at which the sense of outrage ran from jingoistic right-wing Conservatives to the Labour Left. The House of Commons, not Mrs Thatcher, that day made war in the South Atlantic almost inevitable by the decision to dispatch the task force. Two days later flag-waving crowds waved it off as it left Portsmouth. It did so with the overwhelming backing of the British people.[33]

The sailing of the task force did not in itself mean war, likely though that prospect now was. The six weeks taken by the task force to reach the South Atlantic gave ample time for negotiations. That these led to nothing was largely owing to the intransigence of the Argentinian junta. But it also reflected differences in the Cabinet in London. Usefully deflecting criticism from the Prime Minister, Lord Carrington had resigned as Foreign Secretary, accepting blame for the debacle of the invasion (though this more actually attached to the Ministry of Defence and some to Mrs Thatcher herself). As his replacement, the Prime Minister appointed Francis Pym, an old-style 'one-nation Tory' who had served in the Second World War and had long experience of foreign affairs, both as Shadow Foreign Secretary before 1979, and most recently as Defence Secretary. It was an obvious move to make him Foreign Secretary, though still a somewhat reluctant one, taken after advice.[34] Pym was, in fact, by temperament and inclination, the antithesis of Mrs Thatcher, the dove to her hawk. Where Pym looked to avoid the horror of war, which he had experienced at first hand, Mrs Thatcher increasingly embraced the prospect. A negotiated compromise, even if attainable, became synonymous with appeasement – with all the historic connotations of that term.[35]

During the long journey of the task force, and during the subsequent war itself, Mrs Thatcher was in full accord with her military leaders. She took the key decisions. But the military, more than the small inner (or War) Cabinet itself (which included Pym), called the shots. The five politicians beyond Mrs Thatcher in the seven-strong War Cabinet (Foreign, Defence and Home Secretaries, alongside the Party Chairman and Attorney General), whatever misgivings they might have entertained, followed the Prime Minister's lead. She herself took the advice of the military, voiced in the War Cabinet by Admiral of the Fleet and Chief of the Defence Staff Sir Terence Lewin. Primarily through Lewin and First Sea Lord Sir Henry Leach, the military knew they could rely completely on the Prime Minister's backing.[36]

The close relationship between Prime Minister and military leadership was cemented by the opening act of the war. This clearly shows the decision-making process. The sinking by a British submarine of the Argentinian cruiser *General Belgrano* on 2 May (with the loss of 363 lives) outside the agreed Exclusion Zone around the Falklands followed a request by the commander of the task force, Rear Admiral J. F. Woodward, presented to the Prime Minister by Lewin. She immediately agreed. The vital decision was unquestionably hers, consented to without objection – Pym was away – by the War Cabinet.[37]

Mrs Thatcher never doubted that it was the right decision, despite much international opprobrium and domestic criticism. It set the tone for her defiant resolve throughout the short war. The outcome was far from a foregone conclusion, and Mrs Thatcher was more than aware of the proximity of disaster, especially when HMS *Sheffield* was hit by an Exocet missile and sank with the loss of twenty-one lives and many serious injuries. The weeks between the landing of British troops on the Falklands on 21 May and the surrender of the Argentinians on 15 June were extraordinarily tense. But she held her nerve. In the end it was a complete military victory.

It brought her a big political dividend. In the month following the Falklands victory her popularity ratings doubled, to 51 per cent.[38]

Party critics were silenced. The divided opposition looked hapless. Her international reputation as the defender of the democratic rule of law against dictatorial aggression had soared. Admiration for Mrs Thatcher's courage was extensive. In the USA, especially on the Republican Right, she was eulogized. Her friendship with President Reagan was cemented, even though his administration had only gradually come round to supporting fully the British position on the Falklands.

There was a noticeable, though fairly short-lived, psychological uplift in Britain from the victory in the Falklands. Popular morale, badly dented over the previous decade, received a boost. The years of Britain's decline, the government proclaimed, were now well and truly over. 'The Great is back in Britain,' proclaimed one newspaper.[39] Euphoria cannot be bottled. Soon, everyday concerns again preoccupied people. The Falklands victory nonetheless had a lasting legacy. It revitalized and prolonged the British (and specifically English) sense of exceptionalism. The country that had not been conquered since 1066, that had repelled the Spanish Armada, Napoleon and Hitler, was – the victory seemed to imply – still a military force to be reckoned with, ready to defend its interests, withstand aggression and overthrow bullies; the empire might be long gone, but Britain remained a major player on the world stage.

A year after her Falklands triumph, Mrs Thatcher fought a second general election. Fortune again smiled on her: the opposition was fatally undermined by a deep schism. The Labour Party had moved sharply to the left after the election of a new leader, Michael Foot, in November 1980. In response, in 1981 a breakaway faction from the Labour Party had formed the Social Democratic Party (SDP). Labour, in the eyes of the SDP's leaders, was heading towards Marxism and in no position to win a general election. Soon, the SDP had a level of electoral support to rival Labour's.

On the eve of the Falklands War the Conservatives were polling little more than 30 per cent. By 1983, with the recession over, inflation drastically reduced, and – electorally the most decisive factor of all – the Left completely split, they would probably have won even without the Falklands triumph. In fact, by the time of the election some of the sheen from the victory had evaporated. Admiration for the Prime Minister's action in the Falklands, which stretched far beyond Conservative supporters, did not outweigh widespread rejection of the economic policies of her government. The country was sharply divided. But the vagaries of the British electoral system worked greatly to the advantages of the Conservatives. Their share of the vote actually dropped slightly, from 43.9 per cent in 1979 to 42.4 per cent. But they increased their majority in the House of Commons, gaining fifty-eight seats (mainly from Labour). Emboldened and with greatly weakened opposition, Mrs Thatcher could continue her mission to transform Britain.

SHOWDOWN WITH THE MINERS

While at university Margaret Thatcher had read Friedrich von Hayek's 1944 book *The Road to Serfdom*, which had forcibly argued that socialism led to servitude; that only the free market, liberated from state controls, brought freedom. She reread Hayek in the 1970s, when monetarist theories were shaping her thinking. By this time, her vision was starting to focus ever more sharply on the need to break the stranglehold that, in her eyes, the nationalized industries in Britain, and at their centre the power of the trade unions, held over the British economy. The unions, for her, were the source of the disease that had eaten into British greatness. Ending their dominance was, to Mrs Thatcher, a moral cause.

Legislation to curb the rights of unions, particularly through limits imposed on lawful picketing, had already been passed by parliament during the first Thatcher administration. In 1984 Mrs Thatcher personally endorsed and resolutely upheld the decision to ban trade unions at the Government Communications Headquarters (GCHQ), despite the predictable outrage of trade unionists and unease – bringing readiness to compromise – among government ministers. That the government eventually prevailed owed much to Mrs Thatcher's unbending determination and readiness, even relish, to fight and defeat union power. The big test was, however, still to come.

The miners were seen as the strongest bulwark of union power. They had broken the Heath government in 1974, a humiliation seared into Conservative consciousness. In 1981 the potential damage from another pit strike had forced the Thatcher government to step away from conflict (while digesting lessons for the future).[40] Meanwhile, the National Union of Mineworkers had elected as its president Arthur Scargill, a Marxist militant who was thirsting to take on the government. Facing him was a hard-nosed Scots-American businessman, Ian MacGregor, newly appointed to head the National Coal Board. He had earlier presided over substantial cut-backs in the steel industry. It was obvious that a showdown with the miners was coming.

Unlike the position in 1981, the government had stockpiled coal at power stations and was equipped to endure a long strike. Scargill gave it the opportunity to do so. Coal-mining was losing money. Challenged by other sources of energy – oil, nuclear power and natural gas – the coal industry was in decline, the number of miners less than half of what it had been in the 1950s.[41] But when twenty uneconomic pits were singled out for closure in spring 1984 (part of a much wider programme of scheduled closures, kept secret at the time), the enormous anger in mining communities prompted unofficial strikes at a number of collieries in Yorkshire. The National Union of Mineworkers was under pressure to make the strike official, and Scargill, fired up with rage at the government, was only too ready to oblige. He refused to acknowledge that the pits were uneconomic.[42] A coal strike in spring and summer was, for the union side, tactical madness. Nonetheless, it went ahead. For Scargill, the fight against pit closures and the loss of tens of thousands of jobs in the mining industry formed part in any case of what he conceived as a revolutionary struggle.[43]

He called the miners out on strike – without a ballot (which he was unsure he would win) to test support for the action. In some parts of the country miners refused to strike, and a union split resulted. The bitterness and rancour of the conflict were enormous. It dragged on, solidly supported in Yorkshire, Scotland and South Wales, but opposed by a breakaway union in the Nottinghamshire coalfields (leading to huge acrimony between striking and non-striking miners). Mass picketing of pits and power stations led to violent clashes with the police, most notably at Orgreave in south Yorkshire. Public opinion divided. Miners had traditionally enjoyed much public sympathy. But most people were alienated by the violence on the picket lines, and also by Scargill's revolutionary rhetoric, which seemed repugnant to many British voters. At the same time, the scenes on television of

mounted police charging into miners at Orgreave and of police officers beating miners with truncheons were repellent, and not just for
the government's opponents.

The strike started to weaken in the autumn, and by March 1985,
after the striking miners had experienced increasing hardship throughout the winter, the union voted to return to work. It was a resounding
defeat for the miners and a victory for the government. But there was
little rejoicing in the country as there had been at the end of the Falklands conflict. Although Mrs Thatcher had sought to link the fight
against the external enemy with the struggle against 'the enemy
within',[44] the sight of the miners, their union banners aloft as they
trudged back to work, stirred no great jubilation.

Nevertheless, the government had broken the back of Britain's most
powerful union. The Prime Minister had again demonstrated her
strength. Her position in Cabinet was unassailable. Those who had
been apprehensive about an all-out showdown with the miners were
now silenced. The Labour opposition was also weakened. It had been
equivocal about the miners' strike, unwilling to alienate its trade
union support but aware too that many potential Labour voters were
themselves alienated by Scargill's extremism.

Mrs Thatcher's own role in the dispute was less overt than the direct and commanding part she had played in the Falklands War. She
certainly set the tone with her militant rhetoric about a battle for freedom against tyranny, a fight to uphold the rule of law against mob
violence. And she had approved the appointment in 1983 of Ian
MacGregor, whose remit was obviously to take on the miners' leadership in a frontal contest over pit closures. It was in her view
MacGregor's job as chairman of the Coal Board, not that of the government, to deal with a dispute in the coal industry. It was a fiction,
but one that the government publicly held to.[45] Presenting the government line to the public was a survivor of the 'Wets' from Heath's time,
the Energy Secretary, Peter Walker, who was completely supportive of
the Prime Minister's unbending determination to crush Scargill but
possessed the communications skills needed to redress the harsh and
abrasive image of MacGregor.

There was no economic case for keeping open loss-making pits.
Coal mines had been closing under both Labour and Conservative

governments since the 1960s and were doing so in other parts of Europe. But the closures could have been handled far less aggressively. The personalities of both Arthur Scargill and Margaret Thatcher contributed to making the confrontation so bitter. Scargill had walked straight into the trap that the government had prepared for him. Mrs Thatcher was waiting for the most opportune moment to tackle the miners. Scargill provided it.

The closures that Scargill had predicted, and which now duly followed the defeat of the union, hollowed out entire communities that had grown up around the pitheads. Even had Mrs Thatcher never existed, coal-mining would have shrunk over time, as elsewhere in the western world, in the wake of post-industrialization, globalization and growing environmental concerns. But the showdown with the miners meant that in Britain the demise of the coal industry was accompanied by a lasting legacy of bitter hatred of the Thatcher government. It was not the work of Mrs Thatcher alone. Her personal imprint was nonetheless undeniable.

ATLANTICISM AND EUROPE

The limits of Mrs Thatcher's power were more obvious in the realm of foreign affairs than in domestic policy. In the early years, especially, she was unable to exert much influence. Events were largely beyond her control. This in itself was a symptom of Britain's decline as a global power. There was, however, an evident personal chemistry between the assertive, workaholic British Prime Minister and the laid-back, easy-going Ronald Reagan, elected President of the USA in 1980. Her attitude towards 'Europe' – meaning, in practice, the European Economic Community – was, in contrast, instinctively less warm, became more chilly and ended by being near icy.

The Cold War was central to her political purpose – her sense of a moral mission to fight for the free world against the evil of communism. She had grown up in the Cold War, and with the memory of the recent defeat of Nazi Germany in the Second World War deep in her psyche. Both the Cold War and the memory of the Second World War militated against Europe. 'Most of the problems the world has faced have come from mainland Europe,' she wrote after leaving office, 'and the solutions from outside it.'[46] The USA, Britain's great ally in the Second World War, was the West's leader in the fight against the 'evil empire' (as Reagan had dubbed the Soviet Union). Her Atlanticism and downgrading of Europe were, therefore, deeply ingrained in her personality and her politics.

The 'special relationship' with the USA remained, nonetheless, asymmetrical. However warm the public images were, and however closely her world-view chimed with that of Reagan, Mrs Thatcher's role was a subordinate one where American national interests were at stake. When, in October 1983, American troops invaded the tiny Caribbean island of Grenada, a former British possession, where the deposition and then murder of the Marxist leader of the government threatened destabilization in the American 'backyard', Britain was not even consulted in advance. Mrs Thatcher was angry and humiliated. She acutely felt what she thought was a breach of trust. But she had to live with the fait accompli.[47] Reagan blithely put Grenada down to a mistake in communications. Mrs Thatcher's sense of affront rapidly subsided. Personal warmth returned. Mutual foreign-policy interests, especially in relation to the Soviet Union, formed the continuing basis of the relationship. Mrs Thatcher's full support for an uncompromising stance in the Cold War was shown by her agreement, despite heated popular protest, to the stationing from 1983 of medium-range American missiles in Britain.

She revelled in her greatly enhanced global stature after her Falklands triumph. And once change was underway in the Soviet Union from the mid-1980s she enjoyed a starring, though subordinate, role in the rapidly thawing Cold War. Mrs Thatcher had invited Mikhail Gorbachev to London four months before he became General Secretary of the Communist Party in March 1985. Despite their diametrically opposed ideologies, she had taken a liking to him and thought she could work with him.[48] The good relations developed once Gorbachev had taken power. This gave Mrs Thatcher the opening to play a more important role on the international stage than hitherto, serving as an extremely valuable conduit in recommending Reagan, whose initial attitude towards the Soviet leader was far cooler than her own, to take Gorbachev seriously in his efforts at rapprochement with the West.

Reagan soon developed his own rapport with Gorbachev. But

following their meeting in Reykjavik in October 1986, where the President had come close to agreeing to the abolition of all nuclear weapons, Mrs Thatcher's vehement opposition to nuclear disarmament helped to end Reagan's brief flirtation with such a prospect. This was welcome to the Pentagon, horrified by the line taken by the President in Reykjavik, though whether her intervention was decisive in any way is doubtful. Almost certainly, pressure from the Pentagon would have held Reagan back from pursuing his impulsive agreement even if he had attempted to take it further.[49]

By the late 1980s, as the astonishing momentum unleashed by Gorbachev was undermining the Soviet Union and its hold over its satellite states of central and eastern Europe, Mrs Thatcher – now into her third term of Prime Minister, her outright dominance in domestic politics completely established – was distancing Britain from embryonic moves towards the closer integration of the European Economic Community (EEC).

She had backed Heath when he took Britain into the EEC in 1973 and had supported membership in the 1975 referendum. But unlike Heath she had no emotional attachment to Britain's membership. She saw the unity of western Europe as necessary in the Cold War, particularly in backing NATO. And she could see economic advantages in membership of the European Common Market at a time when Britain's trade with the Commonwealth and elsewhere was in steep decline. But she thought that the price for Britain's membership was far too high and strongly pressed, already in 1979, for a significant rebate in the British contribution to EEC funds. Community leaders disliked her harangues but had to get used to them. She was effectively forced by her own Cabinet to accept a settlement in 1980 lower than she wanted, but annual acrimonious bargaining continued until, three years later, she attained a larger, permanent reduction in Britain's contribution. In the end, Community heads of government gave in to her ceaseless hectoring and agreed a rebate of two-thirds of the difference between what Britain paid into and received from the Community. She had already by then established Britain's position as the most awkward of the Community's member-states. She nevertheless saw substantial benefits for Britain from closer economic integration, and her government, during her second term in office, played a vital role in the decision in 1986 to establish the Single Market, aimed at harmonizing regulation on movement of goods, capital, services and labour.

The economics of EEC membership were one thing. Closer political integration was another. Once Jacques Delors, the President of the European Commission (whose appointment she had supported), started to push in that direction in the later 1980s, it triggered Mrs Thatcher's forthright hostility to the developing 'European Project'. In what became a notorious speech delivered at Bruges in 1988, she declared her opposition in no uncertain terms: 'We have not successfully rolled back the frontiers of the state in Britain, only to see them re-imposed at a European level with a European super-state exercising a new dominance from Brussels.'[50] The declaration made her the champion of those who would soon be dubbed 'Eurosceptics'.

By the time the Iron Curtain fell Reagan had left office, and Mrs Thatcher was less close to his successor, George H. W. Bush. Britain's relatively minor role in the unfolding drama of 1989–90 reflected, however, less changed personal relations than basic realities of power. Although head of government in one of the four post-war occupying powers in Germany, Mrs Thatcher played no substantial role either in the collapse of the Soviet bloc or in the subsequent reunification of Germany (which, in fact, with her deep-seated anti-German views never far from the surface, she did not like but could not prevent). The key figures were Gorbachev, Bush and the German Chancellor Helmut Kohl. Mrs Thatcher's Britain, like the France of President François Mitterrand, found itself, apart from diplomatic niceties, largely on the side-lines. In late 1990 Mrs Thatcher's own days as Prime Minister were, in any case, numbered – not that she realized this until she was forced to confront the challenge to her authority at home.

ARROGANCE OF POWER

Mrs Thatcher's second term in office, between 1983 and 1987, had not been trouble-free for the Conservatives. There had been some successful policies, to be sure, prominent among them the sale of council houses which gave tenants the chance to become houseowners (and swell government coffers at the same time). The privatization of a number of nationalized industries (British Telecom, British Gas, British Airways and Rolls-Royce) started an irreversible process and, in another apparently successful move towards popular capitalism, millions of individuals rushed to buy shares (which would, however, fairly soon come to be gobbled up by big investors). But people, including many trade unionists, could benefit from such policies without being converted to Thatcherism. There had been no popularity bounce from the victory over the miners, as there had been after the Falklands. The Prime Minister had been generally admired, also by opponents, for her courage and resilience following the IRA bomb attack on the hotel where she was staying during the Conservative Party Conference in Brighton in 1984, though this did not translate into popular liking for her or political support for the government. And in 1985, the government was damaged by a serious dispute over the purchase of Westland Helicopters – whether the near-bankrupt company should be sold to American buyers (as the Prime Minister wanted), or to a European consortium, favoured by the Defence Secretary, Michael Heseltine. The affair led to the resignation of Michael Heseltine from the Cabinet over the governmental style and personal integrity of the Prime Minister herself. The government was viewed unfavourably around that time by a majority of the public, according to opinion polls.

Yet in June 1987 Mrs Thatcher won her third resounding election victory. When it came, the election, like that four years earlier, was held in propitious circumstances for the government. Inflation, no higher than 5 per cent during her second term in office, had been conquered. Real wages had increased. The Chancellor of the Exchequer, Nigel Lawson, who had three months earlier announced a further cut in income tax and increased spending on the National Health Service, was engineering an economic boom. And Mrs Thatcher had been rapturously received on a visit to the Soviet Union, cementing her image as an outstanding world leader.

The Conservatives continued too to be helped by the schism in the opposition. They benefited as well from a largely favourable press, and from successful marketing of their policies by the public relations experts Saatchi & Saatchi. Yet Mrs Thatcher herself was no more popular than she had been all along, except for the brief period of euphoria after the Falklands triumph. There were some indications, in fact, that she might no longer even be an electoral asset to her party. Nevertheless, when the results were tallied, she could celebrate another victory – though the proportion of the vote won – 42.2 per cent – was practically identical with that of 1983 (Labour won 30.8 per cent, the Alliance 22.6 per cent) and even though the Conservatives actually lost twenty-one seats.

Mrs Thatcher's dominance was by now complete. The 'Wets' had been entirely vanquished. The Right of the party was onside. She was eulogized by the party faithful. There was no evident challenge to her leadership in sight. New appointments to public positions were chosen for their compliance. 'Is he one of us?' she is reputed to have asked.[51] Indeed, the Cabinet was compliant, though lurking beneath the surface was the potential for disquiet, as thoughts were given to a post-Thatcher future. The greatest threat, which would prove to be fatal, arose from the Prime Minister's own arrogance of power – growing since the Falklands triumph and by the late 1980s starting to pose its own dangers. Not all ambitious Tory ministers were thrilled when she told the BBC in 1987 that she might go 'on, and on, and on'.[52]

A major policy mistake at home glaringly revealed Mrs Thatcher's waning grip on power. It showed, too, that her antennae had become dangerously ill attuned to what was politically possible. She had carried the day so often in the face of doubt, criticism and opposition that she had acquired a delusional sense of invincibility. In reality, she was losing touch with many of the rank-and-file Members of Parliament in the House of Commons. Arrogance of power made her fatally impervious to all contrary advice.

The issue that brought the mounting unease about her leadership within her own party to the fore was the introduction of the Community Charge, quickly dubbed the Poll Tax. The idea of replacing a local property tax (the rates) with a flat-rate per capita tax on all adults who used local government services had been initially explored in 1984. Mrs Thatcher persisted with this objective, although Nigel Lawson warned that it would be 'politically catastrophic'.[53] Despite weighty opposition from her own side, she supported the necessary legislation in 1988. It was no diktat; there was full scrutiny by the normal Cabinet committees.[54] Nonetheless, the Prime Minister's authority was decisive. The inequalities and social injustice built into the Poll Tax were plain for all to see: since it was based on individuals not the type of property, the poorest and the richest householders paid the same level of tax. When it was introduced in Scotland in April 1989, many people refused to pay, and there were large demonstrations against the tax in English cities the following year. But Mrs Thatcher refused to back down. (The Poll Tax would eventually be abandoned under John Major, Mrs Thatcher's successor as Prime Minister and replaced by a new form of property charge, the Council Tax.) It provided the backcloth, amid renewed problems from an overheating economy, for the downfall of the once all-powerful Prime Minister.

The issue compounded the evident divisions within the Conservative Party over Europe, magnified since Mrs Thatcher's Bruges Speech in 1988. The speech signalled her clear – and as it was to turn out dangerous – opposition to the approach favoured by two of her Cabinet heavyweights, her most long-standing and loyal lieutenant, Sir Geoffrey Howe (by now Foreign Secretary), and the highly regarded mastermind of the economic boom of the late 1980s, Chancellor of the Exchequer Nigel Lawson. Things started to come to a head when the Delors Plan, envisaging control of monetary policy by a European central bank and a single currency, and convergence towards membership of the European Monetary System, was published in 1989.

Both Howe and Lawson favoured Britain joining the European Exchange Rate Mechanism (ERM, a key element of the European Monetary System), involving a managed exchange rate of restricted currency fluctuation, dominated by the German Mark. For Mrs Thatcher this was incompatible with full control of the British currency, which she saw as intrinsic to national sovereignty. As the central part of a major Cabinet reshuffle in July 1989, Howe was removed from the Foreign Office and demoted to the position of Leader of the House of Commons, unassuaged by the added – meaningless – title of Deputy Prime Minister. In October, Lawson resigned, feeling with justification that his position had been undermined by the Prime

Minister's readiness to take the contrary advice on the Exchange Rate Mechanism of the arch-monetarist Alan Walters, recently brought back from the USA as her personal economic adviser.[55] (The unnecessary alienation of such an effective minister was highlighted when Mrs Thatcher finally bowed to much pressure, articulated by her new Chancellor, John Major, and agreed that Britain would after all join the ERM, which it did in October 1990.)[56] The demotion of Howe and departure of Lawson highlighted a crucial division on a central issue of policy at the heart of the government. And, for the first time, it posed a looming threat to Mrs Thatcher's authority.

None other than her most faithful retainer, Sir Geoffrey Howe, long bullied and finally humiliated by dismissal from office, turned the knife in a devastating attack in the House of Commons on the Prime Minister's leadership on 1 November 1990, following yet another show of her defiance of European moves towards further integration. Michael Heseltine, who had broken with Mrs Thatcher over the Westland affair in 1986, now challenged her for the leadership. He was defeated in the ballot that followed, but the Prime Minister had won only a pyrrhic victory. Her Cabinet colleagues individually advised her to resign, though she did so with great reluctance, departing from office in tears and believing that she had been betrayed. 'They sold me down the river,' she bitterly concluded.[57] Her rancour lasted. A phalanx of diehard loyalists sustained the myth of betrayal well into the future, making life difficult for her successor, John Major (whose authority Mrs Thatcher repeatedly undermined). Her stance on Europe, especially, made her a beacon for Eurosceptics within sections of the Conservative Party.

LEGACY

Despite winning three successive elections Mrs Thatcher never won the support of even a half of the electorate. But with the disproportionate allocation of seats in the British electoral system, she enjoyed big majorities in the House of Commons – 43 seats in 1979, 144 seats in 1983, 102 seats in 1987. This gave her an extraordinary opportunity to implement her policies. Domestically, these rested on her early and eager embrace of neo-liberal economic ideas which were to reshape Britain's economy for decades. This was a crucial component of her legacy for Britain.

Britain was certainly a greatly changed country by the time she left office. 'Socialism', with its base in the trade union movement, was weakened, the economic role of the state reduced (though its coercive powers were increased and central government was strengthened at the expense of local government), nationalization rolled back, privatization advanced, the shift from manufacturing to a finance-based economy established, and the dominance of the market everywhere underlined. Her implicit claim (accepted by her devoted followers) that she had practically single-handedly brought about the transformation was, nevertheless, an exaggeration.[58] Less was transformed than she imagined. And in much of what she accomplished, she was swimming with a strong tide behind her, partly through her instinctive ability to attune to prevalent strains of individualism and aspiration. From the Falklands triumph onwards, until she overplayed her hand in the prelude to the final drama, she could reckon with the overwhelming backing of her Cabinet, and of her party in parliament and in the country. It still needed an unusually strong, forceful, determined and courageous Prime Minister to drive through an often radical agenda over such a lengthy period of time. And in a number of crucial issues – for instance, refusing to alter course in industrial and economic policy in the early 1980s, going to war over the Falklands, the insistence on a rebate from the EEC – her personal role was decisive. Imagining these issues under a different figure as Prime Minister, say, William Whitelaw, James Prior or Francis Pym, is to demonstrate the point. British history would have been different had one of these, or anyone else, been Prime Minister. Mrs Thatcher took prime ministerial power to its outer limits in a peacetime democracy (though these limits have been transcended in more recent times).

In one crucial issue, though, she changed hardly anything. Northern Ireland was as dismaying a concern at the end of her term in office as it was at the beginning. Her deep-seated leanings towards the Unionists limited her scope for imaginative flexibility. True, she did, together with the Irish Taoiseach, Garret Fitzgerald, sign the Anglo-Irish Agreement in November 1985 – a modest step in collaboration between the British and Irish governments. Not much of substance followed, however, until secretive advances under her successor, John Major, led to Tony Blair's path-breaking Good Friday Agreement of 1998.

However much Mrs Thatcher can be said to have changed Britain, her global impact can be exaggerated. It is stretching a point to claim that 'her successes were copied across the world'.[59] Her undeniable personal triumph, victory in the Falklands, amounted for much of the world to an anachronistic colonial-style war. It did, however, embellish the aura of the 'Iron Lady', raising her stature on the global stage, and indicated a revitalized Britain, once more capable of punching above its weight in international affairs. Her relationship with Reagan and, subsequently, Gorbachev burnished this image. Her visits to Washington and Moscow kept her in the international spotlight – a leader of evident importance in her dealings with the superpowers. But she played only a subordinate role in ending the Cold War.

Mrs Thatcher left office slightly more than a year before the dissolution of the Soviet Union at the end of December 1991, which led West European leaders to rethink and reconstitute the European project of closer integration. Her dislike of the European Economic Community had intensified over the years. She had become more disparaging of the workings of Brussels, more hostile to what she saw as moves towards a federal European state and diminution of sovereignty for national governments. In the House of Commons she had put on a bravura performance in denouncing the Delors proposals to move in the direction of European political union as she thundered 'No. No. No.'[60] She felt vindicated in her opposition to the Exchange Rate Mechanism by Britain's ignominious forced exit in September 1992. And the agreement at Maastricht to introduce within a few years a single currency and create a common identity through European citizenship in what from now on would be the European Union was, of course, anathema to her.

A crucial part of her legacy was the hostility to the European Union that, in retirement, she helped to foster within the Conservative Party. She had been instrumental in establishing the Single Market. But she had not foreseen the political consequences of the economic step she had embraced. The Eurosceptics remained for long a minority in the Tory ranks. But she served as their unfading champion, the voice of a Britain that, in their eyes, could never again be great as long as it was shackled to Europe. Later events were to convert this minority taste into a groundswell of backing for Britain's exit from the European Union. Mrs Thatcher was, beyond the grave, the godmother to Brexit.

The last years before her death on 8 April 2013 were spent in increasing isolation, suffering from the tragic onset of dementia. Her funeral was held at St Paul's Cathedral in London, something accorded only to outstanding national figures. Sir Winston Churchill's in 1965 united practically the whole country. Mrs Thatcher had, however, been a deeply divisive Prime Minister, who had elicited unusually strong devotion, but had also inspired not just dislike, but hatred, at the other end of the spectrum. Attitudes towards her death and subsequent state funeral duly reflected the polarization. More than thirty years after she left 10 Downing Street for the last time, the name Margaret Thatcher still retains the capacity to engender the full range of emotions. The scars felt by the many who had borne the brunt of her government's economic policies are to this day still not healed.

Charles Moore concluded his monumental three-volume biography by describing Mrs Thatcher as 'the greatest genius ever to direct the affairs of the United Kingdom'.[61] The accolade is surely unwarranted. But, like her or loathe her, she was without doubt an extraordinary political leader.

Mikhail Gorbachev, newly elected as General Secretary of the Communist Party of the Soviet Union, meets Moscow citizens on 17 April 1985. His readiness to listen to the views of ordinary people helped to establish his great popularity, which was eventually undermined in 1989–90 by economic collapse and political turmoil.

11

MIKHAIL GORBACHEV

Breaker of the Soviet Union,
Maker of a New Europe

'By 1990, political leaders and ordinary citizens alike regarded him as one of the greatest statesmen of the twentieth century.'[1] This was unquestionably true of the reputation of Mikhail Gorbachev in the West, where he was fêted as the man who, more than anyone else, was responsible for ending the Cold War. From a western perspective, he had, astonishingly, turned his back on the Soviet past, sought to introduce democracy and endeavoured to eradicate the threat of nuclear war. For citizens of the former Soviet satellite states in central Europe he was the individual who helped to liberate them from over forty years of Soviet domination. In the Soviet Union itself it was a different story. While his popularity soared in the West, it plummeted in his own country – though not until 1990; until then he had been a popular leader there too. By the time he left office at the end of 1991 his reputation at home was extremely low. He was widely seen as having ruined the Soviet Union. He had become the leader of a superpower in 1985. Six years later, the one-time superpower was left enfeebled, impoverished and humiliated.

Whatever the verdict on his leadership, Gorbachev was by any reckoning the towering European personality of the second half of the twentieth century. But to what extent was he in control of the momentous events that took place during the short period of his leadership of the Soviet Union? Do we need to look no farther than his own decisions – his mistakes, as well as his achievements – to explain the epic transformation of Europe at that time? Or was he himself little more than the vehicle of insurmountable pressures inside and outside the Soviet Union that determined his actions?[2] Did he simply assist the unstoppable collapse of the Soviet Union or did he actually cause it? Was the Soviet hold over its satellite states already virtually unsustainable? Or was the revolutionary momentum only unleashed by Gorbachev's own actions? And was his role in international affairs in reality an unavoidable response to American superiority in the nuclear arms race? Or was his personality the crucial component in ending the Cold War?

PERSONALITY AND THE ROAD TO THE TOP

Gorbachev rose to the pinnacle of the Soviet system as an archetypal insider, a conformist, a recognizably able apparatchik of the regime, a true believer in Marxist-Leninist principles. Any other route to the top would have been unthinkable, and impossible. So why did he change so categorically within the few years that he was in power? Was it an acknowledgement that he had been wrong throughout his early life? Was it intelligent recognition that fundamental flaws in the Soviet system meant that it was unsustainable in the face of both external and internal forces for major change? Was he swept away by unrealistic reformist idealism? Or was it simple opportunism – adjustment to chances as they arose? Understanding Gorbachev posed problems for those who knew him well – even for himself.[3]

The astonishing drama within the Soviet Union and in central Europe between 1985 and 1991 is at any rate inexplicable without the enigma of Gorbachev's extraordinary personality. By the time he took power in the Soviet Union his unquenchable self-confidence, together with a naive optimism that his own powers of persuasion and relentless energy could reshape fundamentally a regime in such dire need of reform, were strong traits of his character. They were accompanied by impulsiveness and a readiness to avoid strategic planning and, instead, 'let processes develop'. He also, remarkable for a Soviet leader, had an ingrained reluctance to use force.[4] The attributes and the weaknesses went hand in hand. Together, they formed an intrinsic part of the epochal transformation, not just of the Soviet Union, but of Europe during his years in office.

Born in 1931 to a poor peasant family in the village of Privolnoe, a backwater in the Stavropol district of the North Caucasus, Gorbachev grew up under the dark shadow of Stalinism and the devastating impact of the war. Both his grandfathers had been arrested under Stalin but had survived the Gulag. His father, Sergei, was injured during the war (and was indeed mistakenly reported killed) but returned a decorated hero. He later told his son of the horrors he had experienced. Perhaps this influenced Mikhail's later unwillingness to resort to violence to prop up the tottering Soviet empire. The war was a time of intense fear and suffering, for the Gorbachevs as for every Soviet family. The German invaders, only for a short time in Privolnoe, left the village ruined. But the Gorbachevs were spared the worst. They had survived. Living and working conditions were extremely harsh in the post-war years. Even so, Mikhail's childhood was a happy one. He had a specially close bond with his father, less so with his mother, Maria, a stern disciplinarian.

Mikhail had to grow up quickly during the war. He was effectively an only child – his brother Aleksandr, born in 1947, was sixteen years younger – and he had to work hard physically to help his mother eke out a living while his father was away (involved in heavy fighting at Kursk, Kiev and Kharkov). It helped him develop independence and initiative. He stood out at his local school through his ability. He also showed early signs of leadership. He started, too, to develop a thirst for learning and self-advancement. Both were lasting traits of his character. He grew up a self-confident boy, highly intelligent, extremely determined, with a tendency (one of his friends from school days recalled) to want to prove that he was right, and 'a remarkable talent for subjecting everyone to his will'.[5]

At the age of fifteen he joined the Komsomol (the Soviet youth organization) and quickly became a local leader. Working alongside his father on the collective farm, he gained knowledge of agricultural production. Two years later, in summer 1948, helping his father drive a combine harvester, he won a competition to bring in the biggest grain-yield, which won him the Order of the Red Banner of Labour, signed by Stalin himself. His parents had been near-illiterate. But he was ambitious and soon became aware that education offered him the route to life beyond the collective farm in Privolnoe. His ability, together with his drive and ambition, enabled him to make the break-through. In 1950 he gained admission to the prestigious Moscow State University (where he studied law and met Raisa, later his wife, from whom he was inseparable until her death in 1999). He applied the same year for party membership.

It was the first step on what would become a steep rise to the top – but one which followed an orthodox path of career advancement in the Soviet Union. He quickly learned how to manoeuvre within the system's power-echelons. His tactical skills were necessary to clamber up the treacherous political path. He was not hiding heterodox views; Gorbachev was a dyed-in-the-wool communist. Before his eyes were opened by Khrushchev's denunciation of the former leader in 1956, he was a believer in Stalin and had joined the thousands paying their last respects as the dictator lay in state in 1953.[6] Later, while by now an ardent anti-Stalinist, he continued to express admiration for Lenin.[7]

After university he rose to become party chief in Stavropol city. In 1970, at the young age of thirty-nine, he was appointed by Leonid Brezhnev to head the party in the entire Stavropol region. The previous year, in the wake of the ideological tightening after the invasion of Czechoslovakia (which had met with his approval), Gorbachev had obeyed orders in savaging a book by a colleague in Stavropol which proposed reforms to the system. It was 'foreign to our ideology', was Gorbachev's withering verdict.[8] The ideas were, in fact, not dissimilar to some of those which Gorbachev himself tried to implement much later. His public statements around at this time were suitably con-formist (including effusive adulatory comments about Brezhnev). Privately, however, he was becoming more critical of the harmful consequences of a highly centralized command economy.

Gorbachev's drive, initiative and organizational ability drew atten-tion and praise in high quarters, particularly for his work in improving agricultural output and extending the irrigation system of a region blighted by frequent droughts. He started to cultivate good relations with a number of powerful individuals. It did his career prospects no harm at all that he came to know Yuri Andropov, the head of the KGB, also from the Stavropol area. Soviet leaders liked the health spas in the Caucasian foothills. As the party's First Secretary in

Stavropol, Gorbachev provided the formal welcome.[9] Andropov met Gorbachev during holidays there, as did Alexei Kosygin, Chairman of the Council of Ministers (Prime Minister) until 1980.

In 1978 Gorbachev was summoned back to Moscow as a Central Committee secretary with special responsibilities for agriculture. His meteoric ascent continued. Two years later he became the youngest member of the Politburo. Andropov had recognized Gorbachev's talent and, on becoming General Secretary at Brezhnev's death in 1982, extended his remit from agriculture to the whole economy. After less than two years in office, beset by ill health, Andropov himself died. He had wanted his protégé to succeed him as Soviet leader, but the old guard favoured Konstantin Chernenko, yet another near-invalid, who lasted barely more than a year in the top post. Gorbachev had sometimes chaired Politburo meetings while Andropov was alive, and ran the Politburo and Party Secretariat for much of the time during Chernenko's illness. Although far from everyone's favoured candidate, he had in effect – and in default of any obvious alternative – become the heir apparent. The day after Chernenko's death he was elected unopposed as General Secretary.

PRECONDITIONS

When Gorbachev became its leader in March 1985, the Soviet Union had become weakened both economically and politically. But neither economics nor politics determined that the system was doomed to collapse within a matter of only a few years. Hardly anyone forecast that would be the case. Even experts who were cognizant of the Soviet Union's fundamental structural weaknesses and presumed that the system would ultimately not be able to survive saw no reason why it could not continue for the indefinite future. It did not have a high level of foreign debt, faced no serious internal disorder and could rely upon the backing of the military and the security services.[10] Authoritarian systems of rule, particularly if they are as strong as the Soviet system had been for seven decades, seldom implode so rapidly and spectacularly – and without massive bloodshed. Most Kremlin watchers in 1985 adjudged that the Soviet Union, whatever its internal difficulties, was stable and in no danger of imminent collapse, though it would eventually reach a point of unsustainable systemic crisis. Had someone other than Gorbachev been elected General Secretary in 1985, an unreformed, or only superficially reformed, system could have kept going for some years. As Archie Brown, the foremost analyst of Gorbachev's rule, has emphasized, 'it was radical reform which produced crisis, rather than crisis that dictated reform'.[11] Fundamental reform was neither inevitable nor economically determined.[12] It was a consequence of Gorbachev's actions.

Gorbachev himself later vividly outlined the dismal state of the Soviet economy that he inherited as leader. The imbalance that flowed from the level of military expenditure – no less than 40 per cent of the state budget – was enormous, hugely distorting the overall running of the economy, massively limiting the room for manoeuvre in satisfying civilian demands and undermining the potential for economic growth. Expenditure on research and development was directed overwhelmingly at the military and grossly neglected the civilian sphere. There were few incentives to increase economic productivity. The costs of labour, fuel and raw materials were more than double those in the West – in agriculture, according to Gorbachev, ten times higher. Despite higher levels of production of coal, oil and other materials, the 'end-product' (as Gorbachev put it) was only half that of the USA. Huge inefficiency and technological backwardness compared with the West went hand in hand with shoddy quality. Poor management compounded and reflected the deep underlying problems. Production figures bore little resemblance to reality. Heavy-handed and rigid centralization stifled all initiative. Corruption, bribery, stealing and embezzlement were endemic. And on top of all this, the Soviet Union's unchallengeable political and ideological imperatives imposed their own extreme constraints on originality in thought, on anything that might test existing orthodoxy.[13]

During the 1970s the relative backwardness and ingrained inflexibility of the Soviet economy had been partly hidden by the big rise in the price of oil in the wake of the Arab–Israeli War of 1973. Since the Soviet Union had its own rich oilfields, it benefited at first from the unexpected price-hike. A decade later, however, the Soviet economy was badly hit when oil prices fell almost as steeply as they had earlier risen. At the same time there was a decrease in Soviet oil production. So the prospect of significantly improving the already low standard of living in the Soviet Union disappeared. Economic decline and the potential for social discontent loomed.

Politically, Gorbachev's inheritance was equally daunting. As the economic difficulties mounted, the political system stagnated. Brezhnev's long rule had sapped from it whatever energies had fleetingly shown themselves under his predecessor, Khrushchev. Major reforms were as good as impossible given the sclerotic structures of government and administration. There was a flicker of hope from would-be reformers in 1982 that change would come under Brezhnev's successor, Yuri Andropov, who attempted to rein in corruption and to reimpose work discipline. Andropov recognized the deep underlying problems in the economy and set out to improve living standards. Though surrounded by the conservative old guard in the Politburo, he did promote a number of younger party officials – including Mikhail Gorbachev – to positions in which they could start to deploy their reformist instincts.[14] The reformers represented underlying social trends in the Soviet Union, particularly the shift away from agriculture to a far more urbanized, educated society dissatisfied with economic backwardness and political constraints and open to technological, modernizing change.[15] But Andropov wanted reforms that would pose no challenge to regime orthodoxy. In any case, he was seriously ill. No reforming zeal, plainly, was to be expected from his successor, Konstantin Chernenko, the conservatives' choice – older than Andropov, far less competent and terminally ill himself, dying in March 1985. Even to the other members of the gerontocracy in the Politburo, it was clear that a halt was needed to the succession of old and frail leaders. The demise of three aged and infirm general secretaries within three years meant, moreover, that no obvious candidate from the conservative old guard was still awaiting the call. This was the unpromising background to the election as General Secretary of Mikhail Gorbachev on 11 March 1985.

At that point Gorbachev was fifty-four years old. Only Stalin (at forty-three) had been younger when he became General Secretary. After three elderly and ailing leaders in quick succession, his energy and dynamism stood out. But while Gorbachev recognized the need for reform, it was plain that it would be an uphill struggle. The average age of the ten voting members of the Politburo on Gorbachev's election was sixty-seven, and five of the members were over seventy.[16] The system was run by members of an elderly, conservative elite that was far from anxious to bring about drastic alteration to a system which had served them well. They accepted the need for some changes. Andropov had after all tried to introduce some in his short period of rule. But they neither wanted nor expected anything fundamental. They imagined that, with Gorbachev's election, they would see some reforms. But it was beyond their comprehension that he might do anything to endanger Soviet power, either at home or within the east European satellite states.[17]

Gorbachev was alone in the Politburo in seeking major change. In any case, what did that entail? Gorbachev himself did not know. There was no grand strategy. He had no clear plan in mind. Reform, yes: he was sure that reform was necessary. But every indication is that he aimed at reform *within* the system. He started from the presumption that the Soviet system was capable of being reformed.[18] Political change, in his view, was essential to effecting any meaningful economic change. But in his view that could be achieved constructively, without damaging the basis of the Soviet power-structure. Whatever his intentions, he was forced to start cautiously to avoid any backlash by alienating the conservative 'establishment' in the party and state bureaucracies. Soon, however, the momentum for change – which would ultimately destroy the Soviet Union – gathered pace.

Did it have to develop in the destructive fashion that it did for the Soviet Union? Might not a 'Chinese solution' have been possible? It was asked at the time, and has often been subsequently asked, why Gorbachev did not pursue the line adopted under Deng Xiaoping in China, where the economy was gradually transformed into a new kind of state capitalism but the firm hold of the Communist Party was not in any way diluted. Gorbachev rejected the comparison with the situation in the Soviet Union as naive. He pointed out that the two countries, and their recent histories, were very different. He argued that an 'attempt to drive everyone into some mandatory, uniform model of development' might work for China, with its 'huge population and an ancient civilisation', but that 'the methods of maintaining political stability that are considered possible and essential in China are in many respects not applicable to our conditions'. In the Soviet Union, he was convinced, it was impossible 'to implement economic reforms first and only later take up political reforms'.[19] Deng reputedly thought Gorbachev 'an idiot' for risking the very survival of Soviet communism by trying to reform the political system before the economy.[20] In reality, Gorbachev was trying to do both at the same time. Without political reform, in his view, there could be no meaningful economic reform.

THE STRUGGLE FOR REFORM

Gorbachev was in personality completely different not only from the grey, old men who surrounded him in the Politburo, but from anything the Soviet Union had previously experienced. It was remarkable, in retrospect, that the encrusted, unbending Soviet system could have produced an insider who rose to the top possessed by the desire to change the very framework of power that had made him possible in the first place. But his career trajectory had been orthodox, and he gave no indication that whatever reforms he had in mind would prove so completely corrosive – indeed, he did not intend that to be the case. An accelerated process of learning the full nature of the problems he encountered and the difficulties in trying to combat them through moderate reform would take him over time towards more radical surgery.

In leadership style, too, he stood in stark contrast to what had become the dreary, unchanging authoritarianism of the established political elite. His energy, drive and dynamism struck all who came into contact with him. He had the zeal of a missionary. But he was prepared to listen and to learn, not just to preach and instruct. He coupled ebullience and natural optimism with personal charm, eloquence and self-evident intelligence. He was open to argument in ways that were alien to previous Soviet leaders. He worked through persuasion, not diktat. Politburo meetings were far longer than they had been. He invited discussion and disagreement. He was prepared to amend prepared positions in the light of objections to keep potentially disgruntled Politburo members on side.[21] But he was self-confident, bordering on arrogant, in his presumption that he possessed the intellectual ability, knowledge and persuasiveness to counter any argument and to win over doubters.

At the lower level Gorbachev was keen to enter into direct contact and discussion with the public – and, above all, to listen to what they had to say. This was both novel and popular. His insistence on hearing the views of ordinary people, not just meeting selected representatives and party apparatchiks, deepened his sense of how pervasive the political as well as economic malaise was in the Soviet Union. His early visits to Leningrad, and then to Ukraine, Siberia and Kazakhstan, brought home to him the level of failure in economic policy and reinforced the sense that direct communication, not simple top-down exhortation, was necessary to bring about change.[22]

His outstanding ability, flexibility of mind and expression, and keenness to engage in open discussion rather than simply rehearse well-established party lines, made him an appealing interlocutor also outside the Soviet Union, even working through interpreters. On a visit to Britain in the year before he became General Secretary, the British Prime Minister, Margaret Thatcher, though poles apart from him ideologically, warmed to his personality, which she found such an attractive contrast to 'the wooden ventriloquism of the average Soviet apparatchik'. She liked the way he self-confidently and without recourse to any prepared brief, sharply, knowledgeably and with good humour debated controversial topics of high politics. The excellent impression made by his cultured and highly intelligent wife, Raisa, also helped to make the meeting of such opposites a great success. Mrs Thatcher's famous conclusion was that 'this was a man with whom I could do business'.[23] The qualities that appealed to Mrs Thatcher also paved the way for good, even warm and friendly, relations with other western leaders on the conservative Right, most importantly Ronald Reagan, George H. W. Bush and Helmut Kohl.

Impatient on taking power to introduce political as well as economic change, Gorbachev was well aware that he could not proceed with impetuous haste. Moreover, though committed to systematic, structural reform even before he became General Secretary, his ideas were far from forming a coherent strategy. Also, on attaining power and now fully appreciating how bad the economic situation was, he later accepted that time was lost in attempting at first to 'pull ourselves out of this hole by the old methods, and then begin significant reforms'.[24] So he was left in the early stages of his time as General Secretary with little more than slogans, powerful in themselves but susceptible to widely different interpretation, and directions for action that lacked obvious means of implementation in a labyrinthine bureaucratic system well used to blocking initiatives. In April 1985 he spoke of the 'acceleration of the social and economic development of the country and seeking improvement in all aspects of the life of our society'. No one could have objected to such a vague statement of intent, which was perfectly compatible with traditional Soviet ideals, though scarcely qualified as the 'strategic policy' that Gorbachev claimed it to be.[25]

He clarified his tangible aims, if still in broad terms, a month later. The economy had to be modernized, he stated, by changing management structures, freeing up initiatives from below and restricting central control to strategic direction.[26] But it was at Leningrad (later returned to its old name of St Petersburg) on 17 May that Gorbachev first introduced the term that would soon symbolize his drive for reform: perestroika, meaning 'reconstruction'. 'Obviously, we all of us must undergo reconstruction,' he declared. 'Everyone must adopt new approaches and understand that no other path is available to us.'[27] Looking back, Gorbachev saw his Leningrad speech as 'the first event of glasnost' – another term, meaning 'openness', which came to characterize the remarkable change that the world outside was also coming to recognize in the Soviet Union.[28] Like perestroika, glasnost was to develop an unstoppable momentum. But this was not immediately apparent. In the first two years, Gorbachev struggled to overcome the major roadblocks in the way of substantial change. As he himself later admitted, remarkably few tangible results were attained in this period, least of all in the pressing matter of the economy.

He was more successful during his first few months in reshaping his central power-base, using much tactical finesse to oust the old guard from their one-time positions of strength in the Politburo and replacing numerous lower-tier regional and city officials. He brought in advisers and aides who favoured reform. Andrei Gromyko, the inflexible seventy-six-year-old long-standing Foreign Minister, was replaced by Eduard Shevardnadze, party leader in Georgia, who would prove a crucial and loyal ally in the rapidly improving relations with the West.[29] An essential role in influencing and shaping Gorbachev's ideas on reform and backing them in the Central Committee was played by Aleksandr Yakovlev, an ardent promoter of radical change who had spent a decade as Soviet ambassador to Canada. Nikolai Ryzhkov replaced the eighty-year-old Nikolai Tikhonov as Chairman of the Council of Ministers, with overall responsibility for the economy. Yegor Ligachev, who had been given charge of the Central Committee's important organizational department by Andropov, was now elevated to full membership of the Politburo.[30] Both Ryzhkov and Ligachev later came to oppose Gorbachev as his reforms turned more radical, but in the early years they gave him vital support. Another promotion proved fateful. Boris Yeltsin, party boss in Sverdlovsk (later returned to its old name of Yekaterinburg), was, against Ryzhkov's advice, elected a Secretary of the Central Committee and by July 1985 had replaced the conservative hardliner Viktor Grishin, a powerful blockage to any change, in the crucial position of Moscow party leader. He would turn out to be Gorbachev's nemesis. In 1985, however, he was another strong voice in favour of reform.

Gorbachev had to tread carefully with the military, to which he had never had close ties.[31] But a scandal in May 1987 when a young West German flew his light aircraft through Soviet airspace to land near Red Square offered an opportune moment to make changes to personnel – essential to any hopes of reducing defence spending. The Defence Minister, Marshal Sergei Sokolov, and the Chief of the Air Defences, General Aleksandr Koldunov, were forced to resign, and around a hundred military leaders opposed to Gorbachev's reforms and his overtures towards a new understanding with the USA were pressed to take retirement.

Implementing serious reform in any part of the Soviet system remained, however, an uphill task. Gorbachev depended upon a panoply of party and government bureaucratic institutions to turn intentions into effective action.[32] Exhortations from the top, repeated in Gorbachev's visits to different parts of the country, could not overcome the deeply ingrained conservatism at all levels of the political and economic system.[33] People had had nearly seventy years of making the system work to their advantage. It still cranked and wheezed as it had done for decades. Corruption, inefficiency, falsifying of reports, telling supervisors, managers and party bosses what they wanted to hear, were all endemic to a malfunctioning system capable of resisting all endeavours to reform it. The result was a dismal lack of significant economic progress. Within a year, Gorbachev was dismayed to learn 'that everything was slowed by inertia; the policy of perestroika was making no impact on the life of cities and enterprises'. He recognized that 'perestroika was stuck', that it had 'run up against the gigantic Party and state apparatus, which stood like a dam in the path of reforms'.[34]

And this was before the terrible shock of the Chernobyl nuclear disaster on 26 April 1986, which, for Gorbachev, 'shed light on many of the sicknesses of our system as a whole'. It opened up for him 'the concealing or hushing up of accidents and other bad news, irresponsibility and carelessness, slipshod work, wholesale drunkenness'. It made him even more determined to push forward with perestroika, to bring about fundamental change. It 'was one more convincing argument in favour of radical reforms'.[35] And there was much readiness to accept reform among a population whose belief in the existing system had been seriously shaken by the disaster.

By 1987 Gorbachev's policy of reform had reached a crossroads. Would it subside into a bold attempt that had ultimately failed to make a lasting dent in the entrenched structures of the Soviet Union? Or would it press forwards into the unknown realms of fundamental transformation, with all the risks that entailed? The way forward was unpredictable. Later, as the system was imploding, Gorbachev implied that the very processes of change he had begun removed any choice. He was said to have remarked: 'I'm doomed to go forward, and only forward. And if I retreat, I myself will perish and the cause will perish too!'[36]

Was this an exaggeration? The early changes were popular in the country and supported by the reformers appointed by Gorbachev to significant positions in party and state. He himself still enjoyed the prestige and the enormous power that accrued to the General

Secretary of the Communist Party. There was, however, still a large residue of conservative opposition, including most of the military leadership (major beneficiaries of the existing system), to his reforms. Deposing Gorbachev and replacing him as Soviet leader would have been a difficult and hazardous step to take. But there was still the possibility of Gorbachev himself, and his key supporters, deciding to rein in the reforms, consolidate power, content themselves with relatively minor change and accept that the system of rule could not be fundamentally altered.

Instead, between 1987 and 1989 Gorbachev accelerated and radicalized the drive for change. He had his entourage of supporters, of course. But there is no doubt that he himself took the vital decisions. He was the key driver of change. And he himself was changing. The desire for reform turned into a determination to transform the Soviet system.[37] His view had been that the inbuilt rigidities of both the economy and the underlying structure of power had to be loosened, and that this could only be achieved through a degree of decentralization and liberalization. Once the handbrake had been released, however, moves towards liberalization turned almost inevitably into an increasingly strong push from below for democratization. Gorbachev welcomed this development – intended at first to be *within* the party. But he soon came to realize that democratization meant breaking the Communist Party's monopoly on all positions of power and opening them up to pluralism.

The radicalization of reform began in early 1987. At the Central Committee's Plenum in January, Gorbachev boldly criticized long-standing party doctrine and then pressed the need for perestroika, which would 'choke and suffocate' without democracy to unleash 'socialism's most powerful creative force – free labour and free thought in a free country'.[38] He advocated elections by secret ballot at all stages. To be sure, this was not western-style pluralism. But contested elections of candidates from within the party at all levels itself denoted a sharp break with past practice.

Significant economic reform still proved elusive. There were limited steps towards liberalization. The Law on State Enterprise of 1987 gave factory managers more freedom from central control and powers to set wage levels and product prices, though in practice it resulted in little beyond raising prices for goods of still mediocre quality.[39] The Law on Cooperatives in May 1988 was significant in allowing the creation of what were tantamount to small-scale private companies, though this still made little dent in the state-run command economy.[40] Gorbachev had much besides the economy on his mind. He later admitted that 'in the heat of political battles we lost sight of the economy and people never forgave us for the shortages of everyday items and the lines for essential goods'.[41]

It is doubtful whether he could have achieved more. He still had to tread a tightrope politically. Even important allies like Ryzhkov and Ligachev wanted to apply the brakes to reform. Conservative opposition, even within the leadership, was openly voiced in spring 1988 in a withering newspaper attack on the reformist line. Others, in contrast, wanted to accelerate reform. Foremost among the radicals was Boris Yeltsin. Already, some months earlier, Gorbachev had broken with Yeltsin – arrogant, impulsive, abrasive and power-hungry as well as increasingly insistent on faster, more far-reaching reform. At a Central Committee plenary meeting on 21 October 1987, Yeltsin had criticized the lack of progress on perestroika and attacked what he saw as a revival of the cult of personality – a barb directed, of course, at Gorbachev. Those at the meeting turned on Yeltsin, and Gorbachev did nothing to stem the invective. Yeltsin resigned from the Politburo and was within weeks removed from his powerful position as party boss in Moscow. Gorbachev and Yeltsin had never got on well. But from now on there was outright enmity between the two. Yeltsin would prove a dangerous enemy.

Discussions in Gorbachev's entourage during the months leading up to the Nineteenth Party Conference in late June 1988 sharpened his reformist aims. At the Conference itself he used his authority as General Secretary – probably at its height at this point – to push through changes that were plainly not to the taste of many of the 5,000 delegates attending. He proposed the 'deepening of perestroika', also in foreign policy, and the 'democratization of Soviet society' together with 'reform of the political system'.[42] At the core of the proposals was a reduction in the power of the party and an enhancement of the role of a restructured quasi-parliamentary Supreme Soviet, two-thirds of whose members were to be elected by universal suffrage.[43]

He used the term 'socialist pluralism' to describe the desired democratization of opinion and expression – still far from western
liberalism.[44] By the end of the year the changes to the party's structures and huge cuts in the numbers of apparatchiks were all approved.
A new electoral law and constitutional amendments provided for
elections to be held in the spring of 1989.[45]

During 1988 Gorbachev passed the point of no return. From then
on the momentum that he had unleashed swept along the process of
transformation, and Gorbachev with it. He was no longer in control
of events. The last two and a half years of his power would see a
swelling tide of radical change that would finally destroy the Soviet
Union. Already by 1988 the warning lights were shining brightly.
There were worrying signs of unrest in Kazakhstan and the Caucasus.
The 'nationality question' was becoming serious.[46] Economic conditions were meanwhile visibly deteriorating, ever-longer queues
becoming a regular part of daily life.

REDUCING THE NUCLEAR THREAT

The preconditions for the breathtaking change in foreign relations
which would characterize the following few years were anything but
promising when Gorbachev took power. The Soviet Union had been
embroiled since 1979 in a war in Afghanistan. Relations with the USA
were poor. The West had responded to the Soviet stationing of SS-20
missiles in eastern Europe by stationing its own Pershing and cruise
missiles in western Europe in 1983. That same year, President Reagan,
hawkish in foreign policy and denouncing the Soviet Union as 'an evil
empire', introduced a new American nuclear programme, the Strategic Defense Initiative (SDI), colloquially known as 'Star Wars',
aimed at establishing an impregnable defence system in space. The
shooting down by the Soviets on 1 September 1983 of a Korean air-
liner that had mistakenly entered Soviet airspace and was believed to
be engaged in military reconnaissance was a sign of increased international tension. The Soviet leadership also initially thought that a
NATO exercise in November 1983 was a forerunner to a nuclear

strike.[47] The danger of nuclear war – perhaps unleashed by a misunderstanding – was evident.

Nothing in the dismal scene of superpower relations presaged, let alone predetermined, the extraordinary shift in Soviet foreign policy that was soon to have such a dramatic impact on Europe, and on the world outside. The early reaction in Moscow to what were viewed as dangerous escalatory policies by Washington offered no change of course, but rather a hardening of existing policy. Defence spending was to be increased, not reduced, in order to catch up with American advances in technology. Had the old guard survived in positions of power, there seems no reason to doubt that the Soviet hard line would have continued. In the short to medium term at least there would have been no substantial change to the long-standing priorities of Soviet foreign policy. The vested interests of the military would have seen to that.

Foreign policy offered, however, an arena in which Gorbachev had scope to make a personal mark. Here, he could operate predominantly through the Ministry of Foreign Affairs, which was in the hands of one of his most dependable and like-minded colleagues, Eduard Shevardnadze. Gorbachev's innovative thinking in foreign policy was a breath of fresh air. His willingness to have frequent meetings with other foreign leaders was itself novel. Earlier summits between Soviet and American leaders had been rare events. But in under seven years as Soviet leader Gorbachev had nine meetings with US Presidents, three on American soil, and numerous meetings with European leaders.[48] That he was soon fêted and eulogized on his foreign visits, where he was regarded as a world statesman of undeniable stature, can only have given a further boost to his already unquenchable self-confidence.

In the total recasting of Soviet foreign policy that followed, Gorbachev's personal role was vital. He had the loyal and able Shevardnadze at his side. And he had strong support within his inner circle of policy advisers, notably his closest aide, Anatoly Chernyaev. The conservatives had been weakened and, as with domestic policy, short of a return to the traditional Cold War hard line, had no alternative to offer. The new thinking of his team took shape over time.

But there can be no doubt who was both architect and driving force of the transformation.

Gorbachev had recognized from the outset that the progress of any significant domestic reform depended upon redressing the excessively high level of military spending, which was in turn bound up with the priorities of Soviet foreign policy. The technology gap with the USA, exposed by the introduction of SDI, reinforced in him the urgent need for a novel approach. Rather than trying to compete on defence spending (a competition the Soviet Union had no hope of winning), *reducing* the arms race in nuclear weaponry seemed a logical and far more beneficial policy if it could be achieved. Gorbachev's anxiety about the growing possibility of a nuclear catastrophe should this route not be taken was sharply enhanced by Chernobyl. So the basis of an entirely innovative foreign-policy aim of improved relations with the USA, de-escalation of the arms race and extensive nuclear disarmament by both superpowers soon took shape. Progress towards these aims, Gorbachev was certain, depended upon his personal relations with the American President.

Beginning with his first summit meeting with Reagan in Geneva in November 1985, Gorbachev established a strong rapport with the initially sceptical US President. The personality of both leaders played an important part in helping to weaken ideological differences. The personal chemistry, later also with President Bush, was crucial. Mrs Thatcher had played no small part in assuring Reagan that Gorbachev was a different kind of Soviet leader. The second meeting, in October 1986 in Reykjavik, closed, however, on a sour note. What was remarkable was that both sides came close to agreeing on an extensive mutual reduction in their nuclear arsenals. At one point, following Gorbachev's suggestion of a 50 per cent reduction in 'strategic offensive weapons' by 1991 and elimination of the rest by 1996, President Reagan, according to the American minutes of the meeting, even stated that 'it would be fine with him if we eliminated all nuclear weapons'. Gorbachev readily concurred.[49] So close and yet so far: the summit ended in failure.

The sticking-point was Reagan's refusal to ban work on SDI in space and confine it to the laboratory. Nevertheless, when the dust had settled, Reykjavik had not only increased the mutual respect between Gorbachev and Reagan, but also paved the way for the major achievement at the Washington summit in December 1987: the Intermediate-Range Nuclear Forces Treaty, which removed Soviet SS-20 and western cruise and Pershing missiles from Europe. (The SDI programme was not immediately abolished but lost support in the USA after the end of the Cold War and was officially ended in 1993, having in effect done its work.) The Gorbachev–Reagan meeting in spring 1988 in Moscow was more noteworthy as a demonstration of the new climate of friendship than for any tangible results – though the symbolism of the two leaders of what had for so long been such dangerous adversaries now standing in Red Square with their arms around each other indicated how far things had come in such a short time.[50]

Gorbachev's speech to the United Nations in December 1988 provided a compelling demonstration of his earnest commitment to disarmament and peace. He announced a reduction of half a million men in the Soviet armed forces and the withdrawal of six armoured divisions from central Europe by 1991. He emphasized a 'common goal' for humanity in establishing a peaceful world. There was no mention of class struggle or Marxism-Leninism. 'Breathtaking', 'heroic', 'a speech as remarkable as any ever delivered at the United Nations' were among the plaudits in the American press.[51]

The increasingly warm personal relations that had grown between Gorbachev and Reagan continued with President George H. W. Bush – after a cool beginning before the new American administration's initial scepticism about the Soviet leader evaporated. Gorbachev and Bush developed a close understanding of the great issues that were unfolding. By the time they met for what would prove another crucial summit, on a Soviet ship in stormy seas off the coast of Malta in December 1989, momentous change was underway. Gorbachev had by then taken Soviet troops out of Afghanistan – a long overdue cutting of losses in a tacitly accepted painful defeat. And in Germany the opening of the Berlin Wall a month before the summit had triggered a domino-style collapse of Soviet power in its central European satellite states.

Only a few years earlier the crisis in the German Democratic Republic would have hugely heightened superpower tension, not paved the way for closer rapprochement. As it was, both Gorbachev and Bush were keen at Malta to avoid any misunderstanding about German unification, the issue that was beginning to dominate the agenda in European affairs. Gorbachev gave an assurance that 'the Soviet Union will not under any circumstances initiate a war' and would publicly cease to consider the USA as an enemy. Bush reciprocated the goodwill, offering to cooperate on economic issues and to support perestroika. The summit cemented the increasingly good relations between the superpowers. As Gorbachev saw it, Malta denoted that the Cold War was finally over.[52]

BRINGING DOWN THE IRON CURTAIN

The six countries straddling central Europe – the German Democratic Republic, Poland, Czechoslovakia, Hungary, Romania and Bulgaria – were of immense symbolic importance to the Soviet Union, to which they were bound politically, ideologically, economically and militarily. The 'fraternal brotherhood' of these states was a product of Soviet conquest in the 'Great Patriotic War'. They offered a solidly united bloc facing the hostile bloc allied to the USA on the other side of the Iron Curtain. And they underscored the Soviet Union's status as a superpower.

By the 1980s the central European satellites were, however, contributing to the Soviet Union's already serious economic problems. Gorbachev was made aware that the satellites were a drag on the Soviet economy.[53] Their own economies – heavily burdened with debt, highly inefficient and desperately in need of modernization, which they could not afford – were a poor advertisement for Soviet-style socialism. They had racked up debt to the West in the wake of the oil crisis of the previous decade, which had also increased their dependency on subsidized oil imports from the Soviet Union. When the price of oil eventually fell, so did the revenues coming from the satellites to the Soviet Union. In the satellites as well as in the Soviet Union, therefore, the state of the economy was worrying when Gorbachev came to power. The survival of the satellites depended entirely upon Soviet backing – military as well as economic. Their regimes existed because the Soviet Union had created and sustained them by military force, or the threat of it. By the 1980s, however, military intervention to shore up tottering regimes, as had happened in East Germany in 1953, Hungary in 1956 and Czechoslovakia in 1968, was no longer viewed as feasible. It was discounted in 1981 as a solution to the crisis in Poland. So the satellites were an increasing problem. At the same time, it was unthinkable that they could be let go; that the Soviet bloc could be allowed to disintegrate.

This was not an immediate danger when Gorbachev came to power. By 1988, however, there were ominous signs of an approaching crisis. In October, Gorbachev received a pressing memorandum seeking advice on what should be done if economic bankruptcy or 'social instability' should grip one or more countries in the Soviet bloc. He was encouraged to discuss the issue in the Politburo. Preoccupied by other concerns, he evidently saw no urgency; the mounting difficulties within the Soviet Union itself were his overriding priority. It was four months before an inconsequential discussion took place. Analyses in early 1989 posed alternative scenarios: either 'a new model of socialism' which would sustain communist control or 'the collapse of the socialist idea'.[54] Gorbachev ruled out military intervention, but otherwise took no action.

The countries of the Soviet bloc had reacted differently to the gathering pace of change within the Soviet Union under Gorbachev. Romania, under the unspeakable tyranny of Nicolae Ceauşescu, continued to follow its own path of partial distance from Moscow – a brand of despotic national communism – and was utterly resistant to any notions of reform. Bulgaria paid lip service to reform but only with the intention of retaining the Communist Party's monopoly of power.[55] The hardline leaders of Czechoslovakia, too, were opposed to anything that might threaten their power. Reform was rejected as unnecessary in the GDR. Perestroika did not suit East Germany, according to the lapidary verdict of Erich Honecker, the East German leader.[56] There were stirrings of popular dissent in both Czechoslovakia and the GDR, though, unless Moscow withdrew support from the regimes, the opposition would have been far too weak to topple them. In Hungary and Poland, however, popular opposition had been building for a number of years within the framework of the monolithic communist systems and had now gained new strength through the licensed changes afoot in the Soviet Union. The regimes in both countries had felt compelled to offer concessions.

Gorbachev's early years in office had already begun to undermine the power of the regimes in the Soviet-bloc countries. But that power was still strong. It was wholly undermined only when Gorbachev made plain that the Soviet Union would no longer do anything to sustain it. This crucial rejection of the 'Brezhnev doctrine' of intervention to uphold communist rule took time to sink in, both for the leaders (and citizens) of countries in the Soviet bloc and for western observers. Gorbachev's initially ambivalent comments only gradually became clearer to leaders of the Soviet satellites. The states of the Soviet bloc had 'the right to choose' their own destiny.[57] This was decisive. The people of the satellite states were emboldened, the power-elites weakened.

Pressure for political pluralism had made such headway in Hungary that the Communist Party formally accepted the end of its one-party rule in January 1989. In Poland, political prisoners arrested under the state of martial law of 1981 had been amnestied in 1986 and partial reforms introduced. A sharply deteriorating economy had then provoked a wave of strikes in 1988 that in turn forced the regime's hand and by the following year had led to mounting pressure for democratic change. The most crucial phase across the entire Soviet bloc came in the autumn of 1989, spurred by the dramatic events in the German Democratic Republic. Gorbachev had for two years viewed Erich Honecker, the East German leader, as a political dinosaur who stood in the way of necessary reform. But he did nothing to have him removed from office and indeed remained inactive in the deteriorating situation.[58] It became plain, however, that without Moscow's backing (which had been ruled out) the East German police would not intervene to halt the increasingly huge demonstrations in favour of reform, encouraged by the extraordinary shift in Soviet policy that Gorbachev had articulated. The pressure on the system built up irresistibly until, on 9 November 1989, the symbolic moment arrived with the opening of the Berlin Wall.

By the end of 1989, as communist power in the satellite states collapsed, the Soviet empire in central Europe had gone. In the long run, no doubt, the structural problems of the Soviet bloc would have made it unsustainable. But that the change came when it did, and as quickly as it did, arose from Gorbachev's readiness to embrace it and to remove the shield of Soviet intervention. The ending of forty-five years of Soviet domination of central Europe clearly was the result of the 'Gorbachev Factor'.[59]

One huge issue, of historic and international importance, had resurrected itself as a consequence of the seismic changes in central Europe: the German Question. The weeks following the opening of the Berlin Wall brought unmistakable indications that for the West German leadership – and increasingly for the people on both sides of the country's division – the unification of Germany was turning from a distant dream to an imminent possibility. Gorbachev had two years earlier spoken of the possibility of a united Germany 'in a hundred years'.[60] But the growing prospect of that happening in the near future was highly unattractive to him – and to most Soviet citizens, only too well aware of what horror Germany had inflicted on their country in the recent past. His reaction to Helmut Kohl's speech on 28 November 1989, unexpectedly suggesting the possibility of a 'confederation' of the Federal Republic with the GDR, a step that obviously went in the direction of unification, was emotionally negative.[61] But, one of his aides commented, he was slow to recognize the speed with which events were inexorably moving.[62] The pressure building up from both parts of Germany for unification became by early 1990 impossible to resist. Gorbachev at that point realized he could not hold back the tidal wave.

He firmly ruled out, however, the potential extension of NATO into what had been East Germany, before changing his mind during a visit to the USA at the end of May 1990. Perhaps because of his deepening concerns at home, the Americans found him less 'commanding' than earlier. And, out of the blue, during his talks with President Bush he made the vital concession – that a united Germany could decide itself whether it wanted to belong to NATO. That was the breakthrough, one which astonished Bush and his entourage. It was Gorbachev's own initiative. He had not agreed it beforehand with his advisers around the negotiating table. The Americans imagined long afterwards that Gorbachev might have been able to hold out successfully for a united, but neutral, Germany. He himself later described his concession as simply a recognition that a sovereign people should be able to decide for themselves – a basic principle of democracy.[63] His own thinking had come a long way in a short time. Recognition of Soviet weakness had merged into a genuine and increasingly firm conviction that trying to hold back the popular demand for change was both undesirable and futile. When Kohl visited Moscow in mid-July 1990, offering guarantees that Germany would pose no security risk to the Soviet Union, Gorbachev made explicit to the delighted German Chancellor: 'United Germany can be a member of NATO.'[64]

Money was a lubricant. The desperate financial plight of the Soviet Union made Gorbachev open to the offer of German loans. By September hard bargaining resulted in a promise of 15 billion Marks in credits to finance Soviet troop withdrawals from the territory of the GDR.[65] More was to follow. By mid-1991 German credits, credit guarantees and grants for removing Soviet troops and resettling them in the Soviet Union and covering East Germany's debts have been calculated to have totalled some 60 billion Marks.[66] German unification had meanwhile become a reality on 3 October 1990. By then, Gorbachev's own survival as Soviet leader was hanging by a thread.

DISINTEGRATION

Between autumn 1989 and autumn 1991, Gorbachev's power waned and then finally collapsed altogether. Though he battled to the end, he was in these two years increasingly buffeted by events, not directing them. His unquenchable thirst for reform had unleashed forces that could be neither controlled nor halted. Pandora's Box was well and truly opened.

Economically, the Soviet Union was by 1991 on its knees. The command economy was gravely weakened, but moves in the direction of a market economy had not been penetrating enough to undermine it fully. The old verities had been much criticized. But the structures built on their precepts remained largely in place. In the process of several years of attempted changes, blockages to reforms and much

354

confusion and disincentive, the economy had become grossly dysfunctional. This had led to rationing of foodstuffs and disastrous shortages of fuel, medicines and other necessary commodities – understandably sparking mounting anger at the government and party, and at Gorbachev personally. His popularity, strong in the early years of reform, fell precipitously during 1990.

He tried unsuccessfully between autumn 1990 and spring 1991 to head off growing conservative dissent. He remained squeezed between conservatives – alienated by the reforms that had in their eyes led only to disaster, incensed by the loss of the Soviet empire in central Europe and still hoping for a restoration of the old system – and the radicals who, led by Yeltsin, were sharpening their political and personal attacks on Gorbachev. Yeltsin, emerging as a serious contender to challenge Gorbachev's supremacy, had been greatly strengthened by the election to the Congress of People's Deputies in March 1989 that had seen his candidacy backed by nearly 90 per cent of Muscovites, in the face of the concerted opposition of the official party apparatus. Yeltsin's triumph marked a big step in the direction of turning the Russian republic into the main challenger to the power, ultimately even to the existence, of the Soviet Union.

By 1991 the Soviet Union's chances of survival were also coming under intense threat from the growing clamour for independence of the nominally autonomous republics. The Soviet Union was in practice a federation dominated by Russia to which nearly all the republics had belonged for the best part of seven decades. The Baltic countries (Lithuania, Latvia and Estonia) formed an exception. They had been forcibly incorporated into the Soviet Union by Stalin in 1940 and were by now actively seeking independence. Violent Soviet repression in January 1991 – against Gorbachev's will, though signalling his growing political weakness – led to bloodshed in Lithuania and Latvia and provoked huge popular protests in Moscow as well as in the Baltic countries themselves. There had been violent disturbances, too, in 1990 in Central Asian republics and in the Caucasus, again leading to the brutal deployment of Soviet troops. In Georgia there were big demonstrations in favour of independence. A movement demanding independence even emerged in Ukraine, an integral part of the Soviet Union since its very origins. This spelled acute danger.

The centre of the entire system was by this time starting to implode. The Russian republic was the vital nucleus of the Soviet Union – far and away its largest republic. And precisely here, directed by Yeltsin, the pressure was mounting for Russian national interests to take priority over the interests of the union.

Gorbachev's power had rested on his office as General Secretary of the Communist Party. However, what five years earlier would have seemed unimaginable, became reality in April 1990: the Communist Party lost its monopoly of power. A month earlier, Gorbachev had been elected to the newly created position of President of the Soviet Union. His claim to power now resided in his extensive new rights as head of state. But his actual power was dwindling fast. Gorbachev had chosen a quick route to the presidency: election by the Congress of People's Deputies, not by a people's vote. Yeltsin, by this time plainly Gorbachev's arch-rival, avoided a similar mistake. He made sure in June 1991 that he won a popular mandate by direct election to the Russian presidency.[67] For well over a year Yeltsin had been courting popularity by advancing Russian interests at every opportunity at the cost of the Soviet Union as a whole. He was content to work alongside Gorbachev in 1991 on a treaty to replace the old subordination of the Soviet republics by a new union of sovereign states. But this was a purely tactical move. Time was on his side, not Gorbachev's.

The hardliners and even some of the disaffected among Gorbachev appointees had by mid-summer 1991 had enough. Gorbachev's political dexterity had until this point held off any potential attempt to remove him from office. But opposition was building. He was seemingly blind to the looming danger when a reactionary newspaper published 'A Word to the People', signed by military, economic and intellectual intransigents. The frontal assault on the new politics declared that 'Our motherland is dying, breaking apart and plunging into darkness and nothingness.' It unmistakably meant Gorbachev when it denounced those 'who do not love their country, who kowtow to foreign patrons and seek advice and blessings abroad'.[68]

While he was on holiday in the Crimea in August the plotters struck. The attempted coup, perpetrated by a group of conspirators who had been in Gorbachev's trust – including his Vice-President, Gennadi Yanaev, his Prime Minister, Valentin Pavlov, the Defence and Interior Ministers, the head of the KGB and his own treacherous chief of staff, Valery Boldin – was a short-lived fiasco. Had it succeeded, there might even have been civil war in the Soviet Union. As it was, Gorbachev's resolute defiance, the plotters' own ineptitude and the courageous popular resistance in Moscow spearheaded by none other than Boris Yeltsin doomed the putsch to outright failure within three days. Gorbachev had survived. But he was mortally weakened, now well and truly in Yeltsin's shade. He hung on for the time being. The end, though, was in sight. He had become the prisoner of events.

Yeltsin suspended (and soon banned) the Communist Party in Russia. He formed a new Cabinet, with himself as Prime Minister, which aimed to introduce a fully fledged market economy without delay. Gorbachev's plans to introduce his treaty to create a union of independent states were confined to the waste-bin. The non-Russian republics, one after the other, proclaimed their independence, backed by Yeltsin. The last fatal blow to the once mighty Soviet Union was the overwhelming support of Ukrainian voters for independence in a referendum on 1 December 1991. Russia, Ukraine and Belarus agreed a week later to form a loose Commonwealth of Independent States (which eight other republics soon expressed their readiness to join) to replace the Soviet Union. On 25 December, in a televised address, Gorbachev resigned as President of the Soviet Union – an office from which all power had drained away, representing a country that had almost ceased to exist. His powers were transferred to a triumphant Boris Yeltsin. Six days later the Soviet Union was formally dissolved.

Gorbachev had himself undergone a metamorphosis: from true believer in the tenets of communism to a western-style social democrat. He chose for his people freedom over subservience. But he was slow to realize, if he did indeed ultimately realize, that the structures of the Soviet Union were incompatible with a social democracy that was built upon personal choice, individual liberties and political independence. These were attractive to the great majority of the population – at least until their own living standards collapsed. But over time, and if they were allowed to flourish, as increasingly they were under Gorbachev, they could only, inexorably, dissolve the bonds that held the Soviet political system together.

LEGACY

Without Gorbachev, citizens of the Soviet Union would have remained deprived of basic civil liberties. Without Gorbachev, it is improbable that the liberty of the former Soviet bloc states of central Europe could have been won through (almost) bloodless revolutions. Without Gorbachev, a rapprochement with the USA would have been unlikely and the danger of a nuclear conflict enhanced. The changes, within and outside the Soviet Union, that Gorbachev himself brought about, or that he inspired, were monumental. More than any other single individual he left by the end of 1991 a country and a continent transformed.

At his valedictory address to the Soviet people on stepping down from power on the verge of the Soviet Union's dissolution he was in far from defensive mode. His reforms, he declared, had been necessary and justified. They had overcome totalitarianism, produced democratic pluralism, introduced liberal freedoms and, not least, removed the threat of nuclear war. His list of achievements cut little ice with most Soviet citizens. By the end of 1991 they blamed him for their economic misery, for the loss of an empire, for casting away all that the glorious victory of 1945 had brought (at colossal sacrifice) and for 'selling out' to the West. He had inherited a superpower. Little over six years later it had gone.

In fact, it was Yeltsin, not Gorbachev, who actively destroyed the Soviet Union. Gorbachev had done his utmost to save it. That Gorbachev was extensively blamed by former Soviet citizens for causing the destruction of the Soviet Union is nevertheless understandable. In terms of a medical analogy, Gorbachev's reforms, above all the introduction of contested elections in 1989, had left the patient on life support. Yeltsin pulled the plug.

Gorbachev's immediate legacy in Russia itself was the disastrous Yeltsin era. Yeltsin's recklessly swift deregulation of prices in a liberalized market economy brought soaring inflation in 1992, which wiped out the savings of many Russian citizens. The beginning of rapid privatization the same year handed out enormous state assets at knock-down prices, fostering the emergence of super-rich oligarchs who used mafia-style violence to turn Russia into a criminalized state. Amid economic disarray and mounting political opposition, Yeltsin even used military force in 1993 against his own parliament to bolster his personal power.[69] Yeltsin epitomized Russia's humiliation by his own drunken behaviour and the patronizing contempt in which he was increasingly held by foreign leaders. Different leadership might have offered Soviet citizens a better way forward. But Yeltsin was the only leader on offer at the time. Could the West have done more to help? Possibly, though the support required to bail out the catastrophic ex-Soviet economy would have totally dwarfed that of the post-war Marshall Plan. And whether it would have worked is an open question.

Vladimir Putin, Russian leader from 1999 onwards, offered a reaction to the disorderly, dissolute and disastrous Yeltsin years. The return to 'strongman' autocratic rule (if under a quasi-democratic façade), the evocation of Russian values in a conscious turn away from the West and the intended restoration of Russian great-power status amounted, however, to a reaction not just to Yeltsin, but also to the Gorbachev era. Gorbachev remained utterly contemptuous of Yeltsin for leaving the country in a chaotic state. Towards Putin he was more ambiguous. He praised him for rescuing Russia from Yeltsin's chaos. And he thought 'a certain dose of authoritarianism' necessary after Yeltsin.[70] Though he was more critical of Putin as the descent into outright authoritarianism accelerated, he never wholly withdrew his general support for the Russian President, even backing him over the annexation of Crimea in 2014.[71]

Gorbachev was an extraordinary politician, statesman and leader of the Soviet Union. That the transformation he instigated was not his sole work is to state the obvious. Nonetheless, he was the decisive driving force. Without him, much that did happen would not have happened. Europe – and the wider world – after Gorbachev has certainly experienced grave problems that make for deep anxiety. But given a choice, not many people, especially those who could recall what it had been like, would opt to go back to the era that Gorbachev, more than anyone else, brought to an end. In his case, it can categorically be said that an individual changed history – and for the better.

Helmut Kohl, head of the Christian Democratic Union (CDU), waves to the crowd in Bonn on 23 June 1975. The following year he was defeated by Helmut Schmidt in the Federal Election and several more years of opposition followed before he eventually attained power as Chancellor in 1982.

HELMUT KOHL

Chancellor of Unity,
Driving Force of European Integration

Helmut Kohl, the 'Chancellor of Unity', is assured of his place in German, and in European, history. He served as Chancellor – between 1982 and 1990 of West Germany, and then from 1990 to 1998 of the newly united Germany – longer than any Chancellor since Bismarck. At his death in 2017, aged eighty-seven, the tributes from world leaders offered effusive accolades: 'one of the greatest leaders in post-war Europe'; 'a great European'; 'a great statesman'; 'a great politician in exceptional times'; 'a giant of united Europe'; 'a towering figure in German and European history'.[1] Germany and, more widely, Europe had been transformed by the time he left office. But did he make history? Or did history make him? Had he left office at any point before autumn 1989, his achievements might well have been seen as fairly modest, overshadowed by those of his immediate predecessors Helmut Schmidt and Willy Brandt, let alone by the first West German Chancellor, Konrad Adenauer. Even within West Germany (as it still was then) he would not have been rated as an outstanding Chancellor. Outside Germany up to that point he had made no great mark. The sort of tributes paid at his death would have been unthinkable. His international recognition, his legacy and his lasting outstanding reputation were almost entirely shaped by the transformative events of 1989–90 and by the impact these had on the 'project' of European integration.

Questions about the personal part he played in the transformation might, nevertheless, be fairly posed. What was his personal contribution to the changes that were sweeping over Europe, and specifically Germany, in those dramatic years? What was his role in the accelerated moves towards European integration in and after the Maastricht Conference that followed German unification? Was he little more than the agent of unstoppable forces? Or would history have taken a different course without him?

PERSONALITY AND EARLY CAREER

Helmut Kohl was an unmistakable figure. However crowded the room, he stood out. His huge size – 6 feet 4 inches tall, over 17 stone – gave him an imposing, even at times an intimidating, presence. He was often described as 'the Giant' (*der Riese*). His height and spreading girth led to his being labelled '*die Birne*' (the Pear). His appearance and stature made him a caricaturist's dream.

Helmut Kohl's identity with the region of Germany in which he grew up, the Pfalz (in English, the Palatinate), in the south-west of the country, a beautiful wine-growing area bordering on France, stamped its mark on his personality. An undiluted positive emotion, the feeling of belonging to a particular locality and strong association with its customs and traditions – *Heimatgefühl* – often has deep connotations in Germany. The Palatinate offered him a sense of solidity and security. It gave him his political base. More than that, it played an important part in shaping his mental world.

Much later, as Federal Chancellor and international statesman, he would travel back every weekend to his home at Oggersheim (a well-to-do suburb of Ludwigshafen) in the Palatinate. Prominent guests from all over the world were shown the Palatinate's delights. In his favourite hostelry in Deidesheim, situated at the heart of the Palatinate's wine district, he would regularly hold court in his reserved corner. He gained inspiration from discussion – which he invariably dominated – among close groups of trusted associates. His Palatinate background helped, too, to break the ice and build relationships in his dealings with other politicians, abroad as well as at home.

When he met the East German leader, Erich Honecker, for the first time, in Moscow in 1983, Kohl started by mentioning the names of people in the Palatinate that Honecker had known before the war as a functionary in the communist youth movement in the region. And he joked that they should speak in the dialect of the Palatinate to make it difficult for anyone listening in to their conversation to understand them.[2] His regional accent, his unadorned, sometimes clumsy mode of expression and his liking for basic Palatinate delicacies like *Saumagen* (stuffed and spiced pig's belly) gave him a personal warmth of character. They also invited snobbery from those who thought themselves more sophisticated. The image of being no more than a provincial politician earned Kohl the disdain of his opponents, none more so than his highly experienced, cosmopolitan, worldly-wise immediate predecessor as Chancellor, Helmut Schmidt. Until the events of 1989–90, Kohl remained a largely underrated figure in German politics.[3]

He had been born in 1930 in Ludwigshafen, the Palatinate's only big industrial city, on the left bank of the Rhine, which became the headquarters of the chemical giant BASF. His family was solidly middle class and Catholic. His father, Hans, an officer in the First World War, was a civil servant in the finance office in Ludwigshafen. His mother, Cäcilie, came from a suburb of Ludwigshafen that had retained its rural character even after being swallowed up by the expanding industrial metropolis in the late nineteenth century. Helmut was the youngest of three children, eight years younger than his sister, five younger than his brother.

The Second World War – especially, as for most Germans, its last traumatic months – left an indelible imprint on his character. His father had been called up as a reserve officer and served in the campaigns in Poland and France. He was patriotic, though not a Nazi. The Kohl family's firm adherence to Catholic beliefs was a barrier to full support for the anti-Christian ideology of Hitler's regime. From 1941 onwards Helmut's parents were increasingly certain of Germany's defeat and fearful of what that would bring. Like many others, they increasingly blamed Hitler for the pending disaster. Helmut was only thirteen when Ludwigshafen was reduced to ruins by a massive air-raid on 6 September 1943. By the end of the war the presence of major industry had made it one of the most bombed cities in Germany. Fear of the raids was a part of daily life. It was a great shock to the family in October 1944 to learn that Helmut's brother, Walter, had been killed during an air-raid. Helmut's schooling was, meanwhile, increasingly disturbed by air raids. Like all boys, he was enrolled in the Jungvolk, the compulsory preparatory organization for the Hitler Youth. When the war ended he had to find his way back home from a Hitler Youth pre-military training camp near Berchtesgaden, where he had been sent in February 1945. It took him five weeks finally to reach home, but he found his parents alive and their house still standing.

The experience of these months never left him. The revelations of the Nuremberg Trials in 1946 opened his eyes fully to the catastrophe of Nazism. That year, at the age of sixteen, he helped to found the youth wing of the newly established Christian Democratic Union (CDU). His parents had voted for the Catholic Zentrum party in the Weimar Republic. For them, as for Helmut, the logical post-war step was to support the CDU, the party committed to Christian – now not just Catholic – principles. Helmut's early political mentor, Johannes Finck, a local priest, had himself been a leading figure in the Zentrum in the Palatinate before the Nazi takeover. Finck's influence persuaded him that social solidarity underpinned by Christian ideals was the hope of the future.

Already by 1949, while still at school, he was becoming known in Ludwigshafen political circles. While studying at Frankfurt, and then Heidelberg, during the 1950s he earned money during the university vacations working in Ludwigshafen's chemical factories. But his eye was already on a political career. His energy, drive and organizational ability were quickly acknowledged and made him extremely useful to the local CDU in Ludwigshafen. He was adept at cultivating a net-work of like-minded political colleagues. By 1955 he was part of the CDU's leadership in the state of Rhineland-Palatinate. Four years later he became the youngest member of the state parliament (*Land-tag*). He was earning good money by this time with a well-paid post offered to him by the bosses of the local chemical industry, who saw advantage through Kohl's party connections; he could be a useful lobbyist for their interests. He combined attachment to the chemical industry and political activity until 1969, by which time he had been elected Minister President (Prime Minister) of Rhineland-Palatinate.[4]

Meanwhile, he had married Hannelore Renner in 1960 and had two sons (Walter, born in 1963, and Peter, two years later). He was still under forty years of age, politically successful, highly ambitious and also making a name for himself in the CDU at the federal level. By 1973 he was the party's chairman – a position he would hold until 1998 – and its dominant figure.

The federal system offered possibilities – more difficult in a highly centralized system – of building a solid provincial base that could serve as a platform for the big step into national politics and power. By the mid-1970s Helmut Kohl, who had devoted himself almost entirely for almost three decades to building a political career, was ready to tilt for the major prize: the Federal Chancellorship. For years he had foreseen himself as Chancellor.[5] His difficulty was that the hold on power of the Social Democrats, in government since 1969, seemed solid – as long as the support of their coalition partners, the Free Democrats, held.

PRECONDITIONS

Politically adept and experienced as Kohl was, his personality and leadership of the CDU were not in themselves enough to take him to power. To attain that goal, conditions had to change. West Germany had been buffeted less than practically every other west European country by the oil shock of 1973. But democratic politics often works in cycles. Governing parties lose their way. Confidence in them among influential public bodies, not least within their own ranks, erodes. A momentum for change builds up. This momentum gathered pace at the end of the 1970s, and by 1982 Kohl was on the threshold of power.

He had failed to oust Helmut Schmidt from office in the 1976 election, resigning thereafter as Minister President of the Rhineland-Palatinate to concentrate on leading the CDU opposition in the Federal Parliament. His rival within the Christian Union, Franz-Josef Strauss, the uncrowned king of Bavaria, was chosen as Chancellor candidate in the 1980 election, though after he, too, failed to defeat Schmidt, Kohl's leadership of the opposition to the centre-Left government was unchallenged. When the opportunity came, two years later, he was ready to succeed Schmidt.

Few, whatever their discontents, sought a radical break. Of course, there were problems, among them immediate security issues connected with Baader-Meinhof terrorist activities and longer-term adjustments to the closing of old industries. Renewed fears of nuclear war caused much anxiety. But the West German economy was strong, there was stable government, and the political system was well-established and cohesive, conventional party-political differences were conducted in a mainly respectful and civilized fashion. Democracy stood on firm foundations. The Christian Union enjoyed the support of nearly half of the voters. But it was not enough to form a government. A coalition partner was needed for that. And as long as the most likely partner, the Free Democratic Party (FDP), was not ready to offer the Union its support, the social–liberal coalition under Helmut Schmidt remained intact.

Beneath the surface, even so, difficulties were mounting and would eventually usher Helmut Kohl into the Chancellorship. Both unemployment and inflation levels rose during the 1970s. Though modest, compared with Britain, 'stagflation' resurrected old anxieties in West Germany and was not susceptible to the traditional Keynesian economic remedies. The feeling that a change of course was necessary grew strongly after the second oil crisis of 1979 affected West Germany more strongly than the first had done. As economic growth slumped, unemployment rose, inflation remained high, real wages fell, bankruptcies mounted, and state indebtedness increased sharply, the problems facing the coalition government were daunting. The Free Democrats sought a neo-liberal remedy for the struggling economy in a move to greater reliance on market forces, deregulation and spending cuts. The breach with the SPD (Social Democratic Party) and its traditional emphasis on state intervention and protection of high levels of social expenditure was inevitable. Though re-elected as Chancellor in 1980, within two years Helmut Schmidt had lost the support of his coalition partners.[6] The FDP simply swapped sides in 1982. Its fairly small base of popular support – just under 11 per cent in 1980 – now shifted from the SPD to backing the Christian Union. Through a political manoeuvre rather than a compelling electoral victory, Helmut Kohl became Chancellor of the Federal Republic of Germany.[7] That he would remain Chancellor for sixteen years – longer even than Adenauer – was foreseen by no one.

FEDERAL CHANCELLOR

Nothing in the early years of Kohl's Chancellorship, between 1982 and 1989, pointed at what was later to come. There was little or no indication that Kohl had the making of an exceptional Chancellor. Indeed, he often seemed to live down to the dismissive views of his political opponents – shared by no small part of the population – that he was a somewhat mediocre figure, devoid of charisma and altogether lacking the stature of his predecessors, Willy Brandt and Helmut Schmidt.

He did, however, have an unquenchable thirst for political power. And government was for him a vehicle of personalized power.[8] He was a dynamic presence within his party, energizing the leadership with a sense of purpose and drive, motivating the rank-and-file with speeches which, while no rhetorical masterpieces, gained from an impulsively emotional, even sentimental, manner and expression. He certainly felt the need to renew and revitalize the CDU, to extend its appeal to all sections of society, to modernize German conservatism. Yet, paradoxically, his leadership style was in essence old-fashioned, increasingly authoritarian, drawing heavily on bonds of personal loyalty. As he approached the end of his long Chancellorship he was labelled 'the patriarch'.[9] And, in patriarchal fashion, he condescendingly referred to the woman who would eventually take over his mantle as CDU leader and Chancellor, Angela Merkel, as *'das Mädchen'* (the girl).

His early years saw a sizeable rise in party membership. He built the consensus in his party that underpinned his base of power as Chancellor. As Chancellor, his stance in domestic policy was in practice a conventional middle-of-the-road conservatism, which enabled him to hold together both the more liberal and more conservative wings of his party. He claimed to be offering radical change.[10] In reality, there was no dramatic shift in direction. It was unexciting, though not necessarily on those grounds unpopular. Germans had experienced plenty of drama and anxiety in the recent past. A period of dullness was in a way welcome, as long as there was economic stability and no disturbance to prosperity and its social welfare underpinnings.

Under Kohl's government, the economy, as in much of Europe,

became tilted towards restricting government expenditure, containing the growth of social spending, greater labour flexibility, tax incentives to improve competitiveness and early steps towards privatization. But there was no ideological embrace of the monetarist free-market model espoused in the USA under President Reagan and in Great Britain under the premiership of Margaret Thatcher. Instead, the corporative approach of the tried and tested 'social market economy' – now with a stronger though not overriding emphasis on 'market' – was adapted to the imperatives of the global economy, shaken by the crises of the 1970s.[11] West Germany's industrial economy, necessarily modernized after the war, had brought unprecedented prosperity for the country's citizens. Whatever the current problems, they were in no rush to change its fundamentals – which, indeed, survived the buffeting of the oil shock essentially intact. There was no deep economic malaise similar to that which had exposed the underlying problems of the British economy – lack of investment and innovation, uncompetitive industries and poor industrial relations – during the 1970s. So, there was no sharp break in West Germany with the immediate past under the new conservative-led coalition government after 1982, no descent into the sort of social and political conflict seen in Britain.

Nor were there – at any rate in the early years – serious rifts within Kohl's government. Many of his ministers remained in office throughout the 1980s – all the more remarkable since they did not, for the most part, come from any long-favoured inner circle, and since he had both to accommodate his coalition partners and to find ministerial posts for the CDU's sister party, the Bavarian CSU, in forming his Cabinet.[12] He had able people in key positions. They included his Finance Minister, Gerhard Stoltenberg, the Labour and Social Affairs Minister, Norbert Blüm, and, quite especially, the formidable and, from his time in the Schmidt Cabinet, highly experienced Foreign Minister, head of the FDP Hans-Dietrich Genscher. The CDU's General Secretary, Heiner Geißler, ensured that the party served as a pliant vehicle for the Chancellor. That the Cabinet, whose collective voice became much diminished, had no major fissures owed not a little to Kohl's style of governance. This was an odd combination of near-authoritarian decision-making, control-freakery and the sort of affability that went with the demand for unquestioned loyalty and recognition of who was boss.[13]

The social advances attained during the era of the social–liberal coalition were not reversed. Trade union rights were generally upheld, for instance, though not without a struggle by the unions. After a seven-week-long strike of the metalworkers' union in 1984 about a reduction of working hours to thirty-five hours a week was followed by an employers' lock-out involving a quarter of a million workers, a compromise of 38.5 hours per week was agreed with the government for the metalworkers, setting a pattern for other branches of industry. The unions were not seriously weakened, as the government had hoped. Although the government was successful in reducing the level of benefits for striking workers, there was no undermining of the trade unions' role as an effective, and stabilizing, agent in industrial relations.[14] State subsidies to combat hardship arising from the run-down of mining and steel in big industrial regions were actually increased. Some steps were taken to improve unemployment and child-care benefits, though these were within an overall framework of cuts in social-welfare spending. The pattern was one of modest change tacked on to a strong base of continuity.

West German conservatives had dubbed the change of government in 1982 'the turn' (*die Wende*). Aside from the fact that the same term was subsequently more generally and far more appropriately deployed to capture the impact of the dramatic transformation of Germany and Europe between 1989 and 1991, it was a big exaggeration of what took place under Kohl after 1982. It was at most a half-turn.[15]

Kohl had inherited an economy affected by the global travails of the previous decade but nevertheless inherently strong and in a good position to recover well and swiftly. He had fortune on his side, too. Coincidental with his accession to the Chancellorship, the economic boom that began in the USA in 1982 started to sweep over Europe. Monetary policy reined in inflation in the USA and across western Europe. German exports flourished again, producing greater surpluses than ever by 1989. Little of this was of Kohl's doing. Of course, he can take credit for heading a government that provided the conditions for a thriving economy. But it would have been difficult for any

West Germany Chancellor in the 1980s *not* to have overseen substantial economic growth.

An early election in 1983, aimed at giving the new coalition a mandate, had proved successful for Kohl, who strengthened his position in the federal parliament. His coalition partners, the FDP, blamed by many for the change of government the previous year, were losers, as were the Social Democrats (partly to the new political force, the Greens). Four years later, however, the electorate showed that it was unimpressed by Kohl's first years as Chancellor. Most West Germans by now, according to opinion surveys, did not have a good opinion of Kohl.[16] His party lost seats, though not enough to turn the coalition out of office, since the FDP recovered most of its losses at the previous election while the SPD had further, minor losses and the Greens – beneficiaries of hostility both to nuclear energy and to the stationing of Pershing missiles on German soil – continued to gain support. Kohl remained as Chancellor, therefore, though not on the basis of any resounding electoral success.

There was also much continuity in foreign relations. What stood out before 1989 was the effort Kohl made to build a close relationship with the French President, François Mitterrand, as the crucial basis – recognized since Adenauer – of a new Europe in which cordial relations and close cooperation between European countries would eliminate conflict and enmity. That Kohl, brought up as a conservative and a Catholic, would combine this with a frontal rejection of socialism – and obviously of Soviet communism – was a matter of course. Beyond that, it is hard to define a clear-cut ideological position. His touch could be clumsy and insensitive. Addressing the Israeli parliament, the Knesset, in 1984, he spoke of 'the grace of late birth'. He meant to imply that his fortune at being too young to be complicit in Nazi crimes nevertheless entailed a duty to ensure they could never recur. But the expression caused embarrassment both in Israel and in West Germany in seemingly pointing to a post-war generation that could dispense with the burden of the German past.[17]

As if this were not bad enough, the impression was hardened a year later by the 'Bitburg affair'. Forty years after the end of the Second World War, Kohl was attempting a gesture of reconciliation in visiting a war cemetery in Germany alongside the representative of the wartime enemy, the American President, Ronald Reagan. It followed a moving ceremony the previous year in which Kohl and President Mitterrand had commemorated the horrendous losses, German and French, at the battle of Verdun in 1916 with a symbolic display of friendship (though the photo of them holding hands looked somewhat odd). Cementing post-war German–American friendship and reconciliation seemed a similarly good idea. Less good, however, was the decision to hold the ceremony in a war cemetery near Bitburg where members of the Waffen-SS happened to lie buried. This, unsurprisingly, evoked big protests in the USA, and the President came under fire for his seeming readiness to honour SS men – perhaps even those responsible for the massacre of American soldiers during the Ardennes Offensive in December 1944. Kohl was taken aback. He did not help by claiming that cancellation of the ceremony would harm 'the feelings of our people'.[18] Accordingly, it went ahead, the public relations damage scarcely mended by an accompanying visit by Reagan to the site of the former concentration camp at Bergen-Belsen. The episode appeared to signify that West Germany was awkwardly trying to cast off the dark shadow of the Nazi past, an interpretation that gained credence during a major public dispute among German historians in 1986 over the place of the Holocaust in German history and national identity.

Once more, in October 1986, Kohl showed how maladroit he could be in foreign relations. During in an interview with the American magazine *Newsweek* he managed to insult the new Soviet leader, Mikhail Gorbachev, the man who, more than anyone before him, offered hope for greatly improved relations between the Soviet Union and the West. Astonishingly, he compared Gorbachev with the Nazi Propaganda Minister, Joseph Goebbels, 'also an expert in public relations'.[19] There was a predictably furious reaction in the Soviet Union. But the West, too, was less than impressed by Kohl's clumsiness. Kohl blamed the press. The able and diplomatically skilful Hans-Dietrich Genscher soon mended fences with Moscow. He recognized earlier than Kohl the potential of engaging positively with the new Soviet leader, particularly on the crucial issue of nuclear disarmament.

Relations with the Soviet Union improved greatly once Kohl agreed in October 1987 to remove Pershing missiles from German soil as part of a wider agreement to be rid of American and Soviet mid-range missiles worldwide. The initiative had come from Gorbachev and been backed by Reagan's administration. Kohl could hardly have opposed the agreed stance of both superpowers. He made known in Washington his own unease at the pressure to reverse his own defence policy – based on the stationing of the Pershing missiles in response to the Warsaw Pact's stationing of SS-20 missiles in eastern Europe. Still, it was an important step, and not easy to achieve. It faced opposition from within the Christian Union, and had to overcome resistance, too, from his own Defence Ministry.[20] But Kohl accepted the changed realities in altering West German defence policy. It helped greatly to establish a basis of trust in relations with Gorbachev.

Kohl's first visit to Moscow, in October 1988, with a delegation that included members of his Cabinet and leading representatives of big business, was a major step in this direction – sweetened by credits of 3 billion Marks to prop up the ailing Soviet economy.[21] Gorbachev later recalled the significance of the meeting with Kohl:

> Our spontaneous mutual trust was probably due to the fact that both he and I saw our 'political mandate' not only in establishing neighbourly relations between the Soviet and German people, but in achieving peace in all of Europe. He took this problem to heart, considering it a personal duty to ensure a safe future for his own family and children.[22]

Gorbachev's return visit to Bonn in June 1989 extended the good personal rapport with Kohl. This would become crucial during the collapse of the German Democratic Republic in 1989–90.

Only at that juncture could the prospect of a new Europe begin to take shape. Helmut Kohl would play a significant role in that process. Before then, however, for all his unquestionable belief in the 'European Project', meaning ultimately for him political union and a European federal state,[23] it is easy to overrate his achievements. He was an avid European, to be sure, driven by emotion as well as by reason. But the major shifts in the 'European Project' before the fall of the Wall came from others. In the crucial decision in 1986 to create the Single Market, offering a fundamental breakthrough in economic integration, the government of Margaret Thatcher made much of the running. And in giving the largely becalmed political framework of the European Communities new drive and impetus, the key figure was Jacques Delors. The part played in both by Kohl was secondary.

Had Kohl left office in spring 1989, he would have done so at a point when his political fortunes and popularity were in decline. For posterity, he would have been seen as 'an exemplary party boss, but an undistinguished Chancellor'.[24] Kohl's moderate reforms in domestic policy and, especially, his acceptance of the notable steps towards nuclear disarmament in Europe would, of course, have been acknowledged. His constant and steadfast support for closer European integration would also have been recognized. But praise would have been limited and muted. The accolades that were showered on him from all sides in his later years would have been unimaginable.

HISTORY-MAKER

The winds of change that Gorbachev sent gusting through eastern Europe were by October 1989 assailing the German Democratic Republic with great force. Gorbachev himself had been rapturously received on a visit to East Berlin at the beginning of the month and had plainly distanced himself from the East German leadership. Tens of thousands of citizens were by this time demonstrating for change to the system. The regime, strongly influenced by Moscow, backed down from any use of force and was plainly tottering. The crucial moment came, however, unexpectedly: on 9 November the regime allowed East German citizens to pass freely through the Berlin Wall into the West for the first time since 1961.

'Chancellor, right now the Wall is coming down', was how Kohl heard the news, passed on by one of his aides.[25] He was not even in Germany at the time. So little was he expecting such momentous events that he had gone on a state visit to Poland and was in Warsaw when the sensational news reached him. But he reacted swiftly. He hastened back and next day addressed a big crowd in front of West Berlin's town hall, standing alongside Genscher, Willy Brandt (who nearly two decades earlier had made the first moves towards an accommodation with the German Democratic Republic) and the mayor of West Berlin, Walter Momper. He counselled composure despite the euphoria.[26] Brandt, however, had already provided the most telling phrases: 'What belongs together is now growing together ... The parts of Europe are growing together.' It was an inspiring thought, not a far-sighted prophecy. No one knew how things would develop.[27]

Kohl, however, had his second set of preconditions. The first had shaped the first years of his Chancellorship after 1982. In November 1989, he inherited new and challenging circumstances, which he had done nothing to create but gave him the opportunity to make his own history. Already that month he started to do this. He faced obvious constraints. The fate of the two Germanies was not just a matter for the Germans alone. It was an international concern involving the former wartime Allies. The Four-Power guarantors of the post-war order still had a big say, though Britain and France far less than the two superpowers. Both Gorbachev and Reagan's successor as US President, George H. W. Bush, advised caution in exploiting the excited emotions to do anything that might destabilize the situation by any talk of reunification. Mitterrand and, especially, Mrs Thatcher were opposed to any change in the status quo. History made both of them fearful of the power and ambitions of a reunified Germany; a unified, substantially enlarged country would not only have preponderant weight in Europe but might revive long-dormant nationalism. For his part, the new East German leader, Hans Modrow, vehemently rejected any speculation about reunification – though majority opinion both in the GDR and in the Federal Republic was by late November favouring just that outcome. So Kohl had to tread carefully. Yet it was Kohl, earlier than anyone else, who saw the potential for epochal change in what was happening and took the initiative. He had no clear vision. He was guided by political instinct, not a plan of action. But what he did, improvised step by step, was to grasp the opportunity that had suddenly and unexpectedly presented itself. He scented the chance, felt the heady spirit of those weeks and converted it into still inchoate developments that were nevertheless starting rapidly to head only in one direction.

Kohl's first major intervention was his speech on 28 November 1989 in which he proposed a 'Ten-Point Plan' to overcome the division of Germany and Europe. He spoke of 'confederative structures between both states in Germany', but was careful to avoid awakening fears abroad or overheated expectations at home of early unification. The implication was that the 'confederation' would be a long-term relationship, not a short route to unification (though this, as it had explicitly been since the foundation of the Federal Republic, remained the ultimate goal). The chief role in the composition of the speech was played by Kohl's long-standing aide Horst Teltschik, who worked on it together with the usual speechwriters in the Chancellor's Office.[28] Teltschik, it seems, had gleaned that Kohl was already starting to think in terms of possible reunification. The former Defence Minister Rupert Scholz had privately encouraged Kohl in the same direction a week before the speech. Scholz advised, so he later said, a 'staged programme' towards unification, starting perhaps 'with confederative structures'.[29] The speech was the product of teamwork. But its key passages reflected Kohl's personal input. And, characteristic for Kohl's style of leadership, the Cabinet – even Foreign Minister Genscher – was kept in the dark. Only the American President was consulted in advance. That President Bush was not from the outset fundamentally opposed in principle to unification gave Kohl the encouragement he needed to proceed with his initiative.[30]

Reactions to the speech among European leaders were mainly negative. The Soviet Union was especially dismissive. Nevertheless, Kohl's speech marked an important shift. Privately, he spoke of the 'confederative structures' lasting for years – perhaps as long as twenty-five years. In reality, thoughts both in Germany – East and West – and abroad soon turned from the friendly co-existence of the two Germanies to the growing prospect of unification in the foreseeable future.[31]

A meeting in early December between Gorbachev and Bush still showed resistance to any moves towards early unification, and opposition came especially from Thatcher and Mitterrand, though also from a number of other West European leaders. Kohl's personal relations with Margaret Thatcher were in any event poor, though they were far warmer with François Mitterrand, whom he assuaged with assurances that any future united Germany would be embedded in closer European integration. Foreign leaders were, moreover, aware of the growing popular pressure for unification in both parts of Germany and recognized that they could scarcely deprive Germans of what they took as axiomatic in other cases: the right to self-determination, to shape their own destiny as a nation.

Kohl was also swept along by pressure from below. This was plainly apparent when he gave an emotional speech before a huge crowd in front of the ruins of the Frauenkirche in Dresden on 19 December 1989. He spoke of the development of 'confederative structures'. Then he added: 'Let me say this, too, here in this place so rich in tradition. My aim remains, if the historic hour permits it, the unity of our nation.'[32] That was what the crowd was wanting to hear. Choruses of 'Germany united fatherland' rang out. Kohl was deeply moved by his reception. He described it as his 'crucial experience' in the unification process.[33] He left Dresden ready now to believe that the 'historic hour' could not be long delayed.

Kohl's antennae were acutely sensitive to the driving force of popular opinion in both parts of Germany. His speeches both caught the mood and spurred on the increasingly and urgently expressed desires that the abundantly evident signs of collapse of the German Democratic Republic should lead to German unification in the near, not distant, future. Kohl's sense that this was indeed an approaching 'historic hour' which had to be embraced, not resisted, in turn conveyed the message to Bush and, above all, Gorbachev that the superpowers needed to take the decisive steps to channel the irresistible momentum into a framework for political action. Kohl was not alone in recognizing the strong tide coursing towards unification. The chorus of the East German demonstrators before the Wall fell had been 'we are the people'. By the end of the year this had changed to 'we are one people'. The East German leader, Hans Modrow, recognized that the trend was by now irresistible. In January 1990 he confirmed Gorbachev's new acceptance that 'German unification should be regarded as inevitable'.[34] In retrospect it looks inevitable from the outset. But for those who experienced the events at the time, either as ordinary citizens or as leading politicians, it only became obvious during the weeks that followed the fall of the Wall that events were starting to race towards unification. Kohl's part in those events had been important in driving on the momentum.

Gorbachev's change of stance was vital to what followed. He

accepted, at a meeting with Kohl in Moscow on 10 February, an American proposal that an international conference of the four former occupying powers and the two German states (a formula quickly known as 2+4) would delineate the route to unification. But the position of NATO remained a huge stumbling block. The USA, in its response to Kohl's Ten-Point Plan, had insisted that a reunified Germany should belong in its entirety to NATO. Gorbachev rejected such a notion outright, and still did so in February 1990. For the Soviet Union it was a matter of prestige. To accept the extension of NATO was tantamount to an open admission that the Soviet Union had lost the Cold War.[35] But Gorbachev's position, as President Bush recognized, was weakening almost visibly. The Americans were by now insisting on NATO being extended to the territory of the German Democratic Republic. Persuading Gorbachev to alter his adamant stance would not be easy, especially since the Soviet leader had earlier been given the firm impression that NATO would not be extended. Again, it was Kohl who took a significant initiative. He knew the D-Mark gave him a good hand in any 'negotiating poker'. The Soviet Union, its financial plight fully registered in the Chancellor's Office, had already in January sought aid for foodstuffs and been subsidized to the tune of 220 million Marks. When he met the President in the USA on 24–5 February, Kohl suggested that financial assistance for the Soviet Union could be a key factor: 'In the end it was a question of the price.'[36] The Soviets had to be pressed to name it.

The Soviet request for massive West German credits to cope with the increasingly disastrous financial position of the Soviet Union was made in early May. At the end of the month, Gorbachev yielded to the West's demands regarding NATO.[37] This was confirmed when Kohl visited Moscow in July. Interest-free credit to the tune of 15 billion Marks was agreed by Kohl and Gorbachev in September to cover the withdrawal of Soviet troops from GDR territory. The biggest hurdle to unification had been overcome. The other major international issue, the renunciation of any German claim on the former eastern provinces that had belonged to Poland since the war had, meanwhile, also been accepted by West Germany in March 1990. Finalizing the details took time. It was a difficult issue domestically, which Kohl astutely handled, though the complex diplomatic negotiations behind the scenes were mainly Genscher's work. The border between Germany and Poland along the Oder–Neisse Line was finally solemnly confirmed in June 1991 (and would be ratified in October that year).[38]

In the first months of 1990 it became ever more obvious that the German Democratic Republic was close to economic as well as political collapse. Kohl refused to prop up the tottering system with a huge injection of financial aid (though some emergency assistance for medical supplies was granted). Meanwhile, hundreds of thousands of East Germans were flocking to the wealthy West Germany, imposing a strain on the economy of both countries. On 6 February, Kohl decided to offer the GDR a currency union, swiftly gaining the backing of his Cabinet and parliamentary party for this crucial step towards political union.[39] Once Gorbachev had given the green light at his meeting with Kohl in Moscow the pressure to move rapidly was ratcheted up.

Elections in the GDR on 18 March were a triumph for Kohl. He had been rapturously received during the campaign by the tens of thousands of East Germans who flocked to his rallies – attracted quite especially by the thought of soon having the West German Mark in their pockets. The new East German government lost no time in agreeing to German unity as soon as possible, acceding to West Germany's stipulation that this should take place through incorporation of the five newly reconstituted Länder of the GDR – they had been abolished in 1952 and were re-established in July 1990 – into the existing Federal Republic under Article 23 of the West German constitution. The East German leadership coupled this with its prior readiness to enter into the currency union on the basis of an exchange rate of 1:1 D-Mark to East Mark. This was a critical issue, in which Kohl once more played a vital personal role.

The true exchange rate was 1:8 or 1:9. A conversion rate of 1:1 was, therefore, not only extraordinarily generous, but also potentially destabilizing. The near-bankrupt GDR economy would be completely uncompetitive at such a rate, meaning wholesale unemployment as factories were closed down, and the need for enormous financial support from West Germany. The Bundesbank and Kohl's Finance Minister, Theo Waigel, strongly advised, therefore, that the exchange rate should be 1:2. Kohl was initially persuaded by their arguments. But when this proposed exchange rate leaked out to the press, there was a furious reaction among East German voters, who before the election had been given the distinct impression that the rate would be the highly desired 1:1. Individuals looked, naturally enough, to the personal advantages of the better rate, unconcerned about (or just ignorant of) the wider economic implications. This rate was supported by all the GDR parties, by the West German SPD, the trade unions and social-policy experts. With local elections imminent in the GDR, Kohl retreated from his earlier position and backed the exchange rate of 1:1 for savings and pensions of up to 4,000 East Marks (6,000 for those over sixty years of age), and 1:2 only for larger savings and company debts. It paid off in the elections in the GDR. In West Germany, on the other hand, Kohl's popularity dropped as three-quarters of citizens viewed the GDR demands on economic union as excessive.[40]

Kohl later acknowledged that his government had underestimated the negative impact on the GDR economy.[41] The cost of unification was to prove exorbitant and weakened the German economy throughout the 1990s. But the effect on the economy of the former GDR was traumatic. As moribund industries collapsed, unemployment soared. East German citizens paid a high price for their new freedoms in lost jobs and worrying economic prospects. Those who did not have savings that allowed them to benefit from such a favourable exchange rate were especially badly hit. At the time, however, what counted was that the road to German unity was clear once the currency union came into effect on 1 July 1990. Legal and administrative complexities were ironed out by the end of August, thanks in good measure to the outstanding work of the Interior Minister, Wolfgang Schäuble. (Long seen as Kohl's 'crown prince', Schäuble would be severely injured, leaving him partially paralysed, through an assassination attempt by a deranged individual shortly after unification was completed.) What remained was for the GDR formally to leave the Warsaw Pact and for the four occupying powers to terminate their responsibilities. On 3 October 1990 Helmut Kohl, amid a vast celebratory crowd in Berlin, could enjoy his historic triumph as 'the Chancellor of Unity'. A year earlier that had been scarcely imaginable.

The astonishing events that had led in only eleven months from the opening of the Berlin Wall to German unification had become possible through the extraordinary transformation in the Soviet Union after 1985, driven by Gorbachev's reforms, and by the corresponding dramatic shift in its stance towards its satellite states in central and eastern Europe. From the fall of the Wall onwards, President Bush provided unstinting support for the steps that culminated in unification, and the American administration was particularly insistent on extending NATO to the whole of Germany. But there is still the part played by Helmut Kohl himself. He instinctively sensed the potential for fundamental change that had opened up. The 'Ten-Point Plan' in November 1989, the reaction to the heady atmosphere in Dresden the following month, the suggestion to Bush in February that a large cash injection – effectively a bribe – could overcome Soviet objections to the extension of NATO (and subsequent tricky negotiation of the deal by telephone), the electioneering triumph in the GDR in March 1990 and the decision for the 1:1 exchange rate introduced in July: these were all Kohl's personal work (though he had superb backing from his ministers and advisers). Kohl's personality also has to be taken into account in the way he built up a relationship of trust, even friendship, with both Bush and Gorbachev.

In the drama that ended with German unification, Gorbachev was the enabler, Bush the supporter, and Kohl the energizer and activator. Kohl himself, a solid and reassuring figure throughout the critical months, was riding the strong tide of popular feeling. At the latest from December 1989 it would have been impossible to stop the pressure for unification that had already built up in both parts of Germany. Conceivably, a different West German Chancellor would have acted similarly to Kohl. That can only be a matter of surmise. What *did* happen owed much to Helmut Kohl.

EUROPEAN INTEGRATION: THE LIMITS OF POWER

He had certainly never lacked self-confidence. But with the plaudits from all sides ringing in his ears, he now bestrode the political stage in Germany and beyond with the assurance that only uncontested great success can bring. All things seemed possible. Optimism was in the air. Kohl's own optimism was never greater. And Germany had acquired central importance in the new Europe.

Kohl's upbringing in the Rhineland-Palatinate, its geographical proximity to France – for so long Germany's arch-enemy – the boyhood experience of the horror of war and full recognition of what his country had done to destroy Europe, all played their part in moulding his passionate belief in European integration. Once the destroyer of Europe, the new Germany would in Kohl's eyes not miss the chance to lead the drive for European unity. For him, building the new Europe was a mission – all the more so, since domestic politics after unification quickly became less glamorous, less dramatic, more querulous and more laden with difficulties than could have been imagined in the euphoria of October 1990.

Jacques Delors, President of the European Commission, had breathed new life into the European Community already before the fall of the Berlin Wall. Delors wanted to use the Single Market (which eventually came into effect in 1993) as the stepping stone to political union. He thought this feasible within a decade or so. By the beginning of the 1990s, a unique and unforeseen opportunity had opened up to shape Europe's 'ever-closer union'. German unification, the collapse of the Soviet Union and the end of the Cold War gave dramatic impetus to a move towards European integration. Kohl was at its forefront.

By the time European Community leaders met at Maastricht in December 1991 to provide the blueprint for the newly constituted European Union, Kohl's vision for Europe had already taken shape. It was optimistic, and ambitious. Kohl was a firm believer in European political union and viewed the prospects for attaining it as favourable. Political union meant for him the creation of a European federal state, broadly modelled on the structure of the Federal Republic of Germany. 'I've never in my life been so motivated about a specific aim,' he told his party leaders in spring 1991. 'The first aim for me after German unity is to bring about the building of the United States of Europe.' He thought of it as essentially a west European project. He was open to extending membership at a later stage to east European states, but not for some considerable time. He envisaged the underlying structure of the European federal state as being in place by 1994. It was intended to be an irreversible transformation.[42]

Political union was meant to follow from currency union. Without political union, as Kohl told the Bundestag in 1991, currency union could not be sustained in the long run.[43] The currency union was to be constructed on German terms. This meant budgetary discipline, avoidance of national banks' responsibility to bail out states that had been imprudent in their spending and the creation of an independent European Central Bank to ensure oversight of monetary policy and price stability. The blueprint for the European Central Bank indeed came to be modelled on the Bundesbank.[44] But the way forward towards currency union – talked about on and off for years – was far from straightforward. Should it indeed precede political union? Or, as the President of the Bundesbank among others argued, follow it?[45] As for political union itself, Kohl was swiftly to learn that negotiating German unification was simple compared with this objective.

Attaining political union in Europe soon proved to be unrealizable. It remained no more than a utopia – or, in some eyes, a dystopia. It would have meant nation-states retaining some powers (as, say, Bavaria or Saxony did within the Federal Republic of Germany) but transferring much of their sovereignty and many of their crucial powers, including foreign and defence policy, to a central European government. Whether this would have been acceptable to the German Constitutional Court is questionable.[46] As it was, meetings with other European leaders, beginning with the key figure of François Mitterrand, whose full support was essential if the project were to take shape at all, made clear to Kohl that political union was no more than a pipe-dream. Expecting France, even less so Great Britain, to hand significant powers in foreign and defence policy, to look no further, to a European government was a non-starter. Significant objections to the practicalities of a political union which, almost certainly, would come to be dominated by Germany were likely, in fact, to come from most, if not all, member-states. So the aim of political union, while not officially abandoned, became in practice no more than a rhetorical device.[47] There was an obvious consequence. Currency union would neither precede nor follow political union; it would have to be a substitute for it.

On the European level, then, Kohl's powers had obvious limits when they ran up against the interests of other European states. Where he could work with, not against, these interests, his achievement in the Maastricht deliberations was far from negligible. The key player here, though, was Mitterrand. Both the French President and, even more so, the then British Prime Minister, Margaret Thatcher, had been extremely concerned about the implications of German unification for European peace and security. It was alarmist. But it was historically understandable. By the time of the Maastricht Conference, Mrs Thatcher was gone from power. Mitterrand was still there, however – and in the pivotal position. For the French President, whose country had been invaded three times from across the Rhine between 1870 and 1940, closely binding Germany into the new Europe was axiomatic. This had long been formative in the underlying French interest in currency union, and, from a different direction, it met Kohl's own keen pursuit of the objective. The agreement at Maastricht to introduce a common currency, at first without a name but soon to be called the euro, was the outcome of this meeting of Franco-German interests. Kohl was well satisfied that the structural arrangements for the new currency bore the German hallmark.

The Maastricht Treaty, signed in February 1992, certainly took the issue of European integration on to a new plane. But it was far less than Kohl had wanted. And the rejection of the currency union in Denmark and Britain (along with other exemptions from the stipulations of the Treaty), together with the cool reception of the Treaty also in a number of other countries, including France, showed how far Europe was from the political union that Kohl had envisaged.

THE WANING OF POWER

Helmut Kohl's power and influence were at their peak from 1989 to 1992, between the opening of the Berlin Wall and the signing of the Maastricht Treaty. Of course, as the triumphant 'Chancellor of Unity', his prestige was by now internationally sky-high. At home, his dominance within his party was unchallenged. Nevertheless, his popularity soon started to wane. Among the reasons were the high costs of unification on the German economy, and the decision to replace the iconic German Mark – the symbol of post-war prosperity and stability – with a common European currency.

Kohl's promise to the East Germans that unification would bring them 'blossoming landscapes' rang embarrassingly hollow in the early 1990s. The economic price of unification was, in the short term at least, extremely high for East Germans. Across Germany as a whole, in fact, the economy suffered throughout most of the 1990s. State indebtedness rose, unemployment increased, growth fell, exports declined, and high labour and welfare costs left the economy struggling to remain competitive. There was, of course, still pride and pleasure in unification, in spite of grumbling even in the most prosperous parts of the former West Germany at the cost. And there was widespread support for the aim of closer European integration. This theme, however, so close to Kohl's heart, was seldom dominant in German public opinion in the 1990s – apart from the emerging strong objection to their beloved D-Mark being offered as a sacrifice on the altar of European currency union. Beset, too, by discord and wrangling within his governing coalition with the FDP – especially after the FDP's leader and highly esteemed, long-serving Foreign Minister, Hans-Dietrich Genscher, resigned in 1992 – Kohl's popularity declined sharply, more in the West than the East. As the 1994 general election approached, only around a third of voters wanted him as Chancellor.[48] Yet the Christian Union, which had been languishing in the doldrums, went on to win the election.

Kohl's own contribution to what only months earlier had seemed an unlikely success cannot be underrated. He energized his party and, in a campaign that focused heavily upon his personal leadership, exuded confidence and optimism. He himself campaigned tirelessly, delivering more than a hundred speeches, many in the open air to crowds sometimes of 10,000 or more – though no longer cheering ecstatically as they had done four years earlier.[49] His high international standing and mastery – in contrast to his early years – of the medium of television were both advantages, not least in contrast to the colourless personality of the main opposition leader, the SPD's Rudolf Scharping. Kohl benefited, too, from factors beyond his personal control. One was that the SPD was divided and its leadership weak. It had a left wing that allowed Kohl to smear it with the cynically effect-ive device of associating it with Marxism. He accused the SPD of wanting to come to power together with the communists – meaning the Party of Democratic Socialism (PDS), the successor party to the former Communist Party in the GDR, whom (adapting a phrase of the first post-war SPD leader, Kurt Schumacher) he absurdly attacked as 'red-painted fascists' (*rot lackierte Faschisten*).[50] The second was that the economy had begun to pick up several months before the election, allowing Kohl to claim – not just to East German voters – that his policies had been right all along.

The economic uplift was short-lived. But revived optimism in the country came at the ideal time for Kohl. When the votes were counted, he remained Chancellor. The election had not, even so, been an unmiti-gated success. The vote for the parties of the Union had in fact dropped by 2.4 per cent, the coalition partners, the FDP, by just over 4 per cent, while the SPD and Greens had made slight gains. Still, the coali-tion ended up with a slight majority in the federal parliament. It was another victory for Kohl – though it would prove to be his last elect-oral triumph.

By the time of the next general election, in 1998, economic prob-lems were again a big worry. Kohl's government was patently running out of steam. Nevertheless, electioneering again revitalized him. He criss-crossed the country addressing huge rallies. He reck-oned that by the end of the campaign around half a million voters had attended his rallies.[51] His appeal to the party faithful was still undiminished. But he was no longer able to convince the waverers and the undecided. His personality could not compensate for a renewed economic downturn and gloom at the prospects. Faced with structural economic problems, Kohl's earlier electoral magic no longer worked. It could not combat the undefinable feeling that, after the CDU had governed for so long, it was time for a change. To add to this, his opponent for the Chancellorship by 1998, the much younger, vibrant, telegenic Gerhard Schröder, was formidable. He seemed to many to be the face of the future, capable – like Blair in Britain, whom he saw as an inspiration – of mastering the eco-nomic problems and leading Germany into the rapidly approaching next millennium. As the election campaign began, opinion polls indicated that twice as many preferred Schröder to Kohl as the next Chancellor.[52]

Kohl had been fortunate in 1994 to benefit from the recent (as it proved, short-lived) upturn in the economy. But Germany, the traditional economic powerhouse of Europe, was by the late 1990s uncompetitive, having to contend with high labour and welfare costs and the continuing financial burden of unification. Unemployment levels – officially over 4 million in 1996, in reality higher – were the most worrying manifestation of economic trouble, and a central theme of the election campaign. Kohl had no tangible major programme to offer. The state of national finances meant that balancing the budget through expenditure cuts, including politically risky reductions in welfare spending, was given priority. A turning point in Kohl's popularity in 1996 directly followed cuts in sickness pay. The forthcoming introduction of the euro added to his travails. Only 21 per cent of Germans favoured it; 52 per cent were opposed.[53] His popularity plummeted, most dramatically in the east. Where in election rallies he had once been cheered to the rafters, he was now jeered.

Kohl was blamed personally by many for the economic malaise and seen as lacking the energy and vision to overcome it. Ironically, helped by the huge sums that had poured into the East over the past eight years, former citizens of the GDR were now at just this time finally seeing their lives start to improve substantially. Construction sites pointed to impressive levels of investment. But, of course, major problems remained. Unemployment was much higher than in western Germany, the standard of living generally lower. Perceptions that eastern Germany was neglected by the wealthier west persisted. Kohl could do nothing to change this mentality, nor indeed to persuade a majority of voters in western Germany that he was able to revive the economy and guarantee higher standards of living.

The election proved a disaster for Kohl. The Christian Union won only 35 per cent of the vote. The SPD's 41 per cent (leading to a new coalition with the Greens) saw Schröder appointed Germany's next Chancellor. Kohl naturally carried the can. He was with some justification held personally responsible for the election defeat. He had become more resistant to advice, more over-confident in his own abilities, it was claimed. His insistence on wanting to prolong his time in office after sixteen years as Chancellor, and refusal to make way for a successor when his personal popularity stood much lower than that of Wolfgang Schäuble, long seen as his favoured successor, was seen as a serious mistake. Like many other leaders who had enjoyed a long time in power, he had been reluctant to give it up. But he had out-stayed his welcome. The stark fact was plain: the Kohl era was over.

His departure from office, after dominating the German political scene for so many years, was marked by an impressive and moving ceremony, watched on television by millions, outside the floodlit cathedral of Speyer, a magnificent building that symbolized the Palatinate's rich history, where centuries earlier Hohenstaufen emperors had been buried. It was the end of a career that had led from modest beginnings to unimaginable triumph.

LEGACY

Helmut Kohl played a major role in bringing fundamental and lasting change to Germany and Europe. That is quite some legacy. Of course, it was not just his own work. And, of course, he happened to be head of government when dramatic events that he had neither engineered nor foreseen gave him the opportunity to make a unique personal contribution to historic transformation. But that he did so establishes him as an important maker of history. Today's Germany and Europe are in no small measure his work.

The 'Berlin Republic', as united Germany's political system became labelled once the move, initiated by Kohl, from Bonn to the new federal capital, had taken place a year after he left office, is itself a lasting monument. He foresaw that a unified, economically strong Germany, the largest state with the biggest population, from its geographical location in the middle of the European continent would once again – though now with peaceable, internationalist aims – become the dominant force in Europe, and look to the East as well as to the West. Bonn, a small town on the Rhine which had served the modest polity of West Germany so well for decades, was no longer the most suitable capital for united Germany's central role in Europe.

In this wider, European context, Kohl's chief legacy is the euro, introduced on 1 January 1999. Alongside François Mitterrand, he was its main architect. With that, he had achieved one of his key objectives: to ensure that Germany's future was bound up with its place in a more integrated Europe. The foundations of Europe were so sound, he stated in a lengthy newspaper interview a year after leaving office, that they could not fundamentally be altered. How could he be so sure? 'The introduction of the euro, with all its consequences for the future of Europe', was his answer. 'With that, Europe has crossed the Rubicon ... It was crucial for me that we achieved the introduction of the euro – and I'm certain that would not have been possible without me as Chancellor of the Federal Republic of Germany.'[54] Was this an exaggeration? A unitary currency in the European Union – long in the minds of those who sought European integration – might well have come about at some point anyway. But Kohl was surely right to claim that, without his close rapport with Mitterrand, agreement to introduce the euro would almost certainly not have been reached at Maastricht. Whatever has happened since, that was a pivotal moment for Europe.

Helmut Kohl's last years after power had gone, down to his death in 2017, were clouded with tragedy – political and personal. His reputation suffered hugely, especially in Germany itself, when he became embroiled in a big donations scandal in 1999, refusing consistently to name those who had illegally financed his party. (Millions of D-Marks had been secretly paid by unknown donors to the CDU since 1991. It was not established that Kohl was a personal beneficiary. Even so, a criminal investigation was only halted in 2001 when Kohl agreed to pay a total of 300,000 Marks, half to the state, the other half to charity.) In 2000 the CDU, which he had led for a quarter of a century, revoked the honorary chairmanship it had granted him when he left office.[55] That some who had earlier belonged to his entourage and been essential props of his power-base were among those who approved this step amounted in his eyes to disloyalty which he was unable to forgive. So he broke with many of his one-time faithful retinue, including Wolfgang Schäuble and Angela Merkel. His published memoirs reflected his belief that his reputation had been unfairly tarnished and that he had not received full and proper recognition of his great historic achievements.[56] He had brought about a unified

Germany, but, he felt, the country was not sufficiently grateful for it. He deeply resented the fact, that while foreign leaders showered him with accolades, at home – even in his own party – he met widespread rejection.

There was also personal tragedy. His wife of forty-one years, Hannelore, took her own life in 2001. The funding scandal had deepened her already crippling depression, and she suffered increasingly from a painful and debilitating allergy to light, which the doctors were unable to cure.[57] At her funeral Helmut looked a broken man. Almost seven years later, in February 2008, he suffered a bad fall at his home which left him partially paralysed, confined to a wheelchair, with some brain damage, and with impaired speech. To general astonishment, during his hospital confinement he married again, to Maike Richter, who had worked in the Chancellor's Office and was thirty-four years his junior. She went on to build a protective wall around the former Chancellor so tight that it kept out practically everyone – not just inquisitive journalists, but almost all his one-time political circle, friends and even, to their great sorrow, his two sons.[58] Political life had totally consumed Helmut Kohl. In the end it devoured his own family.

Conclusion:
History-Makers – in Their Time

This book set out to explore how twelve European state and government leaders from different backgrounds and different political systems were able to acquire and exercise power, and to what extent that power transformed Europe in the twentieth century. If these individuals were, indeed, history-makers, it was in every instance because the leader was a product of a unique set of circumstances that made the specific acquisition and exercise of power possible. Outside the particular context, it is plausible to suggest (even if in the nature of things it is impossible to be sure) that they would have left no special mark on history. Their ability to exploit so successfully the conditions that they had done little or nothing to create made them stand out and able to preside over fundamental (sometimes highly destructive) change. So I wanted to assess the role played by personality in historical change by looking not just at the leader's personal actions, but also at the *impersonal, structural* conditions that made the impact of the individual possible.

Some of the leaders reviewed were dictators, others democrats. Did they have anything in common, other than the fact that they held power in their respective countries? Are dictators as unconstrained as they seem, and if so how do they attain that position? Are democrats as circumscribed in their power as constitutional arrangements imply? If not, when and how do personality and circumstances override theoretical restrictions on the exercise of power? The Introduction posed the nature of the problem, and I outlined there a number of propositions or assumptions about the interplay of structural conditions and individual power. This Conclusion seeks to test how far the above case-studies fit those generalized propositions.

As I pointed out in the Introduction, Karl Marx used 'class equilibrium' to conceptualize the preconditions that enabled Louis Bonaparte, someone he took to be a nonentity, to wield power in mid-nineteenth century France. By this he meant that, where neither the revolutionary nor the ruling class was strong enough to prevail, the space opened up for an 'outsider' wholly lacking in personal qualities to take over state power. However, 'class equilibrium' is of little help in the above case studies, with the possible exception of Spain in the 1930s.

There was no class equilibrium at the takeover of the communist leaders (Lenin, Stalin, Tito). Here, the ruling class had already been destroyed (even if it needed a ferocious civil war under Lenin to complete the destruction in Russia). Plainly, class equilibrium is irrelevant, too, in the case of Gorbachev. Officially, class distinctions did not exist in the 'dictatorship of the proletariat'. In reality, a stratum of apparatchiks whose service to the state and party gave them privileges and material advantages stood apart from the vast majority of the population, under Gorbachev as throughout the Soviet system. But it was not 'class equilibrium'.

Nor was this a precondition of power for Mussolini and Hitler. The political power of the working class had been drastically weakened already before their takeover. The newly installed dictators completed the destruction with savage repression. In Franco's case, the takeover came at the end of a horrific civil war that left the working class entirely at the mercy of the dictator and the victorious Spanish ruling class. The democratic leaders (Churchill, de Gaulle, Adenauer, Thatcher and Kohl) benefited in differing ways from the prevailing social and political power-structure, though this could not be described as a 'class equilibrium'. De Gaulle and Adenauer came to power, of course, after the existing political systems had been destroyed through war, though the underlying traditional social structures had only partly been destroyed along with them.

Having recently experienced how, out of the blue, the coronavirus pandemic could upturn societies across the globe, we need no special reminder of the importance of impersonal determinants of historical change (though its harmful impact could be significantly worsened by the role of individual leadership, such as that of Trump or the Brazilian President, Jair Bolsonaro). The twentieth century, too, in which the role of powerful personalities looms so large, was fundamentally shaped by crucial, sometimes hidden, patterns of change beneath the surface drama of major political events. Europe's population continued to grow, for instance, throughout the century despite declining birth rates and enormous human losses through war, disease, famine and genocide. The fall in death rates (a trend stretching back to the latter half of the nineteenth century), partly the result of astonishing medical improvements, was the chief reason. Industrialization and urbanization had major consequences for the livelihood of countless millions, but but though attempts could be made by political leaders either to promote them or to hold them back, the trends continued remorselessly. In the second half of the century, while urban growth continued, deindustrialization (bringing profound social and political change in its wake) occurred whatever the character of political leadership – though, as the case of Britain in the Thatcher era shows, this did affect the ways in which it was carried out.

The two world wars were the greatest motor of epochal change. The complexity, both personal and impersonal, of their causes and conduct is evident. If the First World War defies the attempt to lay the blame on any single individual, the origins of the Second seem clearer. Yet, however important his personal role was, Hitler was far from the sole cause even of the European war, which only became truly global with the entry of Japan and the USA into the conflict in December 1941. Nor was the outcome of either the First or Second World War attributable just to human agency. While the actions of the war leaders obviously paved the way for military success or failure, victory depended heavily upon forces beyond their individual control: economic might, geography, international relations, scale of armaments production and the ability to sustain huge armed forces for far longer than the enemy was able to do.

The two wars were not just immensely destructive. They stimulated technological innovation (including the jet engine, space technology and nuclear fission) and medical advances (like techniques of reconstructive surgery). They destroyed monarchies and empires, and gave rise both to communism and to extreme nationalism, but also mobilized democratic movements. The end of the Second World War unleashed unprecedented economic growth, promoted the onset of the welfare

394

state, stimulated new levels of prosperity and led to lasting peace in Europe. Other major secular trends – for instance, the declining influence of the Christian Churches, the demand for women's equality, emphasis on human rights, the impact of mass migration, the spread of computer technology and, increasingly, the effects of climate change – have been crucial to the history of Europe's twentieth century but were at best only partially affected by the role of individual political leaders.

Even so, without the impact of the leaders discussed in this book (and others) the lives of millions of European citizens in the twentieth century would have been drastically different. Leadership was not purely incidental to how history developed. It was a key component of that history. The impersonal forces beyond any individual's control made the impact of those leaders possible in the first place. A leader's personality could, however, then play a major role.

War was the most important enabler. Without the First World War the chances of Lenin (and his successor, Stalin), Mussolini and Hitler becoming leaders of their states would have been practically non-existent. Without the Second World War it is highly unlikely that Churchill, de Gaulle or Tito would have come to power. War and its legacy of devastation were the most obvious causes of extreme crisis that gave rise to the type of leader who could best represent the demand for an extreme solution to the crisis or offer hope of national salvation. War also produced the degree of chance that sometimes had extraordinary fateful consequences. How could Lenin have ever come to power in 1917 without the readiness of the German military to allow him passage into Russia?

In given circumstances, personality could evidently prove a decisive factor. The individuals who were the subjects of the preceding chapters were not interchangeable. A different personality would have produced a – sometimes drastically – different history. Perhaps this is obvious in the case of dictators. Hitler's leadership made the Holocaust possible. Without him as head of the German state the physical annihilation of Europe's Jews would probably not have happened. But the critical role of personality was true of democratic leaders, too. The appointment of Churchill – disliked by much of the political establishment – and not Halifax (the preferred choice of many) as British Prime Minister in May 1940 changed history, not just in

Britain. The narrow election of Adenauer as West Germany's Chancellor in 1949 had vital repercussions for Europe, as well as Germany itself, in the Cold War. Mrs Thatcher's impact on Britain, Europe and the world in the 1980s would not have been replicated by an alternative choice as Prime Minister. And it is barely imaginable that anyone other than Gorbachev could have instigated and pursued the policies that led to the collapse of the Soviet Union and the end of the Cold War. Helmut Kohl stands out from the other case studies in at least two respects. His ascent to the West German Chancellorship was not the product of a major crisis. Nor, until external circumstances affected his Chancellorship in 1989, was he a personality of more than national stature. Yet, as the above pages showed, in the extraordinary conditions that prevailed in Germany and in Europe following the fall of the Berlin Wall, Kohl did play a vital role internationally. Crucially, he was able, partly through his affable manner, to build a personal rapport and win the trust and liking of the superpower and European leaders (though not of Mrs Thatcher). They felt they could rely upon him, most of all his commitment to Germany's key part in a peaceful Europe. When it came down to it, personality was in Kohl's case, too, a crucial factor.

Were there any common components of the twelve history-making personalities considered in these pages? Few personal characteristics unite such disparate figures. Their social backgrounds differed greatly. So did their childhood experiences. The temptation to seek psychological explanations or roots in childhood and family history is best resisted. Leaving aside the fact that these individuals never lay on the psychoanalyst's couch to offer founded diagnoses and that hypotheses decades later can be no more than guesswork, the reduction of the profoundly complex developments that accompany and shape the actions of a leader to a supposedly defining single life-experience is grossly to short-circuit any worthwhile explanation of historical change.

Yet a number of similar traits of character are, perhaps, discernible. Each of the leaders examined above showed an unusual degree of single-mindedness, both before and after attaining power. Each had extraordinary determination, sufficient strength of character to surmount hardship and setbacks, a relentless will to succeed and a level of egocentrism that demanded extreme loyalty and subordinated everybody and everything to the attainment of desired goals. They were all 'driven' individuals. They felt – some of them said so – that they had a mission to fulfil 'destiny'. Few people have such feelings. Each, if in widely differing degrees, was instinctively authoritarian, ready and determined to command. This was often coupled with intimidating shows of intolerance and anger.

Dictatorial systems of course offered wide scope for despotic rule: none was as tyrannical as Stalin, but Hitler, Mussolini, Franco and Tito were also autocratic in the extreme. Democratic leaders had to restrain their authoritarian inclinations and operate more through persuasion, though de Gaulle (if he can be truly called democratic) behaved in an imperious fashion, Adenauer too could be autocratic, and Mrs Thatcher was often dismissive of opponents (and some of her close colleagues). Churchill was usually gracious, though under great stress he too could be unpleasantly high-handed with colleagues and subordinates. Even democratic leaders had to have a streak of ruthlessness. In dictators this was a qualification for the job. Leaders, democratic as well as dictatorial, also needed the ability to inspire and motivate those around them. They were effective in conveying a limited number of easily understood ideas through language that captured widely held attitudes, aspirations and prejudices. And it needs no underlining that each leader examined here had a pronounced taste for power and, once it was attained, was extremely reluctant to let go of it.

But in different contexts to those in which they played such an important part, these personal characteristics would have been ineffective. Lenin would probably have remained an exiled theorist rather than practitioner of revolution had not Russia reeled from the disastrous impact of the First World War. Hitler would not have been heard of without the calamitous impact of the First World War on Germany. Franco would have stayed a prominent military figure had he not been thrust into political leadership by the Spanish Civil War. Without the German invasion of France, de Gaulle would probably have continued to pursue a career as a high-ranking officer in the French army, as publicly unknown as countless others. Without the war, Churchill may well have stayed in what he regarded as the political wilderness. Mrs Thatcher and Kohl, on the other hand, rose through conventional channels of the party-political structures of western liberal democracies. Both could theoretically have become government leaders in different circumstances. However, the crisis of government and economy in Britain at the time enabled Mrs Thatcher to come to prominence when otherwise both her gender and her social class might have proved insuperable obstacles. Kohl, of all the leaders examined, was the most likely to have climbed the greasy pole to power anyway, through a normal electoral victory. But in the event, crisis played its part here, too. The prevalent sense that the existing long-standing coalition government was not capable of mastering the structural problems of the economy exposed by the oil crisis of 1979 was Kohl's pivot to political power. The type of leader was, in other words, also in the case of Mrs Thatcher and Kohl a product of unique conditions.

It is time now to consider the applicability of the seven general propositions about personal leadership outlined in the Introduction.

The scope for individual impact is greatest during or immediately following huge political upheaval when existing structures of rule break down or are destroyed.

This is largely synonymous with the conditions within which dictatorial power, with few constraints, can operate. Even then, there are some qualifications. The massive upheaval in Russia following the revolutionary destruction of the Tsarist regime provided the basis for Lenin's power. But Lenin, however strong his personal authority, was not free of constraint. In dealing with his subordinate leaders in the Bolshevik Party, he had to operate through persuasion and force of argument. Stalin's despotic power only gradually emerged from the maelstrom of revolutionary upheavals and their accompanying factional in-fighting after Lenin's death. His control of the party apparatus enabled him to dominate Bolshevik governmental structures – the Congress, the Central Committee, the Politburo – which were weaker than they appeared. Their erosion, accompanied by massively intensified terror, removed all constraints on his personalized power.

Mussolini's freedom of action was limited in the period of greatest upheaval in the years immediately following the First World War – the years in which he gained power. It became greatly extended only after he had surmounted the internal crisis of the regime in 1924–5. By the later 1930s, his scope for independent action, at any rate in foreign policy, was constrained (not that he acknowledged this) by his increasing dependence on Germany. Hitler had been a failure in the years of greatest turmoil following the war. His rise to power took place over a decade later. The long-drawn-out comprehensive crisis of state and society that had preceded his takeover of power had both weakened oppositional parties and enabled him to build a huge party wedded to the leader. Even then, had President Hindenburg not given in to the pressure from his close circle of advisers, Hitler could not have become Chancellor. Once in power, however, he removed internal constraints much more quickly than Mussolini had done. By eliminating the potential threat posed by his paramilitary wing in the summer of 1934 and moving swiftly to replace Hindenburg as head of state, Hitler established absolute power.

Democratic power benefits on the whole from stability and continuity, not upheaval and breakdown. And, crucially, it is constitutionally restricted. The power of leaders is circumscribed. Even where, as in the cases of de Gaulle and Adenauer, democracy did emerge out of enormous upheaval, power was constitutionally limited, whatever the authoritarian proclivities of the leader. De Gaulle, at France's liberation in 1944, was keen to stress the illegitimacy of the Vichy regime but the legal continuity of the French state. He soon found, to his chagrin, that the aura he had attained as wartime leader did not translate into freedom of political action in the reconstituted democracy. The Algerian crisis which prompted his recall to state leadership in 1958 gave him greater powers under the new constitution of the Fifth Republic, but although he largely liberated himself from parliamentary constraint he was still bound constitutionally and far from free to act in dictatorial fashion.

Adenauer's rise to the West German Chancellorship followed the total destruction of the German state in 1945. But the very premise of his acquisition of power was the return to government based on the rule of law. As lord mayor of Cologne before the Nazi takeover, he had been a skilled operator within the constraints on democratic power. He brought these skills to the Federal Chancellorship. His undoubted authoritarian tendencies were reined in by the need to operate collegially, in a democratic system. He attained his aims through powers of persuasion coupled with shrewd manipulation of party-political machinery. This was a case where huge upheaval and the destruction of an existing system of rule resulted in the enhancement, rather than the removal, of constraints on power.

Single-minded pursuit of easily definable goals and ideological inflexibility combined with tactical acumen enable a specific individual to stand out and gain a following.

With the exception of Helmut Kohl, this generalization relates to each of the individuals examined here, though above all to the dictators. Kohl certainly possessed tactical acumen, but until he was offered the opportunity to press for German unification in autumn 1989 he had not been an outstanding Chancellor. His advancement until then had been conventional enough. He had been single-minded in wanting to reach the top in his own party, and to become Federal Chancellor. His aims in power were, however, limited. His ambitions were those of a conventional party-political, conservative democratic leader. He neither had clearly definable goals, nor was he ideologically inflexible. Chance, in his case, came to his help, turning him into a major player on the world stage with the clear aim of German unification in view. The other democratic leaders more plainly embodied a single clear goal: victory in war and preservation of liberty (Churchill); France's liberation (de Gaulle); rebuilding democracy through bonds with the West (Adenauer); and renewing British 'greatness' through the freedom of the market to replace what were deemed to be the economic shackles of 'socialism' (Mrs Thatcher).

For fascist dictators, clear ideological goals became apparent over time once power had been won and consolidated. But they were not necessarily crucial to winning mass support. Mussolini was tactically adept, but ideologically opportunistic in winning support. His attainment of power rested more on ideological obfuscation than clarity. He successfully faced both ways – a revolutionary to paramilitary radicals, an upholder of order to the liberal-conservative elite. Hitler's personal obsessions with 'removal' of the Jews and attainment of 'living space' were not central to his rise to power. During the years of his astonishing electoral success between 1930 and 1933 his rhetoric focused far less on Jews than it had done a decade earlier when he had ended as a failure, while acquisition of 'living space' at some indefinite point of the future was irrelevant to the concerns of most Germans during a searing economic and political crisis. During that comprehensive crisis he repeatedly promised to sweep away the existing system of government and destroy Germany's internal enemies. He coupled his vitriol with vague notions of a future 'people's community' and the rebuilding of national pride and strength. More precise and clear ideological aims would have been a hindrance, not a help. The combination of utter loathing of a widely perceived bankrupt system of government, stoked-up fear of the revolutionary Left and the promise of national rebirth to create a completely new, strong and dynamic society was far more important than clearly defined goals to winning power for both Mussolini and Hitler. It shaped the climate in which the personality of the leader could play a decisive role.

In Spain the bitter and violent class conflict during the five years preceding the Civil War engendered many similar symptoms of national crisis. Franco had no mass base of support before the Civil War, when his personal sense of a nationalist crusade to crush the Left once and for all and to restore the glory of Catholic Spain did not stand out among those fighting on his side. The adulation he enjoyed after the war came from military success, not demagogic talent. And once power was won, there were no clear ideological goals beyond the constant fight against supposed enemies (internal and external), upholding nationalist ideals and sustaining his own power.

The communist leaders, Lenin, Stalin and Tito, all had publicly to show reverence for the doctrine laid down by Karl Marx and Friedrich Engels. Stalin and Tito had additionally to pay ritual obeisance to Lenin. But the ideological precepts of Marxism-Leninism were more important in forming and integrating the essential leadership cohort of the Bolshevik Party than in their mass appeal. Constructing a wide base of support came *after* not before the acquisition of power.

The exercise and scale of personal power are heavily conditioned by circumstances of the takeover of power and the earliest phase of its consolidation.

This proposition generally holds for dictators. Whether communist or fascist, the early consolidation of dictatorial power was accompanied by high levels of repression of opponents. Lenin demanded the expansion of terror against Soviet enemies during the civil war. As

Lenin's effective successor, Stalin's victory in the ideological battle over the development of the economy gave him the platform to build an impregnable base of personalized power, which he expanded through extreme terror directed at all real and imagined internal threats. Mussolini and Hitler could chalk up early successes, especially in their onslaught against the Left, that enhanced their own hold on power. Mussolini's personal dominance was only fully attained once the provincial party bosses had been 'tamed' in the mid-1920s (and even then the monarchy constituted an alternative focus of legitimacy). Hitler completed his route to outright personal power by crushing the potential challenge from his restless paramilitaries in the summer of 1934. Franco's takeover of power was effectively that of the victor in the Civil War. His supremacy was as a result unchallengeable. His use of terror against internal enemies (especially during the Civil War and in the years that immediately followed) was merciless. His personal power rested heavily, however, on his ability to manipulate the sectors of the ruling elite which saw their interests satisfied by his leadership. Much the same applied to Tito, whose wartime exploits enabled him to establish an incontestable base of power, which he could extend through corruption (especially, like all dictators, keeping party, military and security services happy), manipulative 'divide and rule' tactics towards subordinate leaders, and, of course, repression.

The proposition only applies with modification to the personal power of democratic leaders. These in general terms attain high office through a rules-based system which sees them elected as party and government leaders, and then obliged to function through collaboration not diktat. Mrs Thatcher and Kohl became government leaders through well-established political structures. In both cases the context of assuming and consolidating power in the state was not in itself fundamental to the later expansion of their personalized power. This derived largely from unforeseen events. The Falklands triumph was unquestionably a massive boost to Mrs Thatcher's personal standing and authority. The subsidence, then collapse, of the German Democratic Republic gave Kohl new personal authority – over seven years after he had become (a rather ordinary) Chancellor.

Emergencies provide a different pattern, however, even for democratic leaders. The crisis in Britain in April and May 1940 provided an unexpected opportunity for Churchill to take power. In wartime conditions, democratic constraints were limited. Even so, whatever his instinctive assertiveness, Churchill operated within a framework of collective government. De Gaulle and Adenauer had largely to start anew and to forge systems rather than inherit them. In these cases, the proposition can be said to hold. Adenauer had a strong party-base but was only narrowly elected Chancellor in 1949. He gradually extended his own initially precarious hold on power through successful policies (and the 'economic miracle'), dominating the new democracy in such personal fashion that it became dubbed a 'Chancellor democracy'. De Gaulle's authoritarian instincts were evident throughout. His triumph in the Second World War did not bring him the political power he expected. The conditions of his return to leadership in 1958 in the context of the chronic instability of the Fourth Republic and the crisis over Algeria allowed him to mould the nascent Fifth Republic as a vehicle for his own extended power – though within a democratic framework which would ultimately lead to his defeat in 1969.

The final case-study, that of Gorbachev, is in a sense anomalous. Gorbachev was no dictator, though he came to power through a dictatorial system. And as a committed product of Leninist structures of rule he was no democrat (though in a way he became one). His position as elected General Secretary of the Communist Party gave him enormous power from the outset. But his reforming agenda was heavily contested. He operated through forceful persuasion. His personal power was only gradually extended through the initial popularity of his reforms. But the effect of the reforms was gradually to undermine his authority to such an extent that it resulted in the collapse of his personal power and ultimately his essentially forced resignation. It could be said, therefore, that the conditions of his takeover and early consolidation of power removed constraints on Gorbachev, but that his very exercise of power subjected him over time to the restrictions that were to break that power.

In all systems, including democracies, the personality of a leader who is able to consolidate and extend power over a lengthy period of time has the potential to erode the limitations on the exercise of power.

Concentration of power enhances the potential impact of the individual – often with negative, sometimes catastrophic, consequences.

This seems self-evidently true of dictators. With the democratic leaders reviewed above it is less obvious.

The duration of Lenin's leadership was too short to judge the applicability in his case. He was, after all, in his last year crippled by a series of strokes and not powerful enough to prevent the succession falling to Stalin despite warning of his dangerous propensities – a warning that had become known to the party's top echelons. Had Lenin lived longer, and been in good health, it seems certain, however, that, given the aura he already possessed as the architect of the Bolshevik Revolution, 'democratic centralism' (as the doctrine was known in the Soviet Union) would have further strengthened his personal power. The enormity of the state-directed killing that took place under Stalin would probably not have occurred had Lenin ruled for longer, though his own record suggests that a high level of violence against any perceived internal enemies would have continued. Stalin, once he had vanquished his main rivals in the mid-1920s, relentlessly concentrated power in his own hands. Not only was this power unchecked; the entire system, with extreme lethal consequences, worked to put into practice the extraordinary paranoia of the leader.

The concentration of power in the hands of Mussolini and Hitler enabled the dictators personally to take the decisions that led to war and complete disaster for their countries. Their authority became so unchallengeable in the formative years of their dictatorships that those anxious about or critical of what they saw as highly dangerous strategies had no potential to halt them. The untouchable stature of the leader – at least before looming national catastrophe brought a new, despairing readiness by the fascist elite in Italy to topple Mussolini and by a small group of courageous army officers in Germany to attempt in vain to assassinate Hitler – arose partly because the dictatorships had large in-built bases of support or at least acquiescence. Institutional frameworks for collective decision-making were non-existent, and the scope to organize opposition almost totally eliminated. The dictators ensured, too, that the essential props of their rule – the party, the military and the security services – were kept contented. Concentration of power made Spain dependent on Franco's personal power and Yugoslavia on Tito's. The difference here was that the exercise of that dictatorial power, once it had been consolidated, was largely directed towards the maintenance of power as an end in itself, rather than the attainment of wider ideological goals that could involve their countries in war and destruction. Franco, admittedly, was only prevented from entering the Second World War through Spain's economic and military incapacity to do so.

Concentration of power is far less applicable to democratic leaders – even to those with aspirations to extensive personal exercise of power like de Gaulle. Adenauer, Mrs Thatcher, Kohl and (though to a far more limited extent) de Gaulle himself, whatever their directive tendencies, were hedged in by collective forms of leadership, institutional constraints and oppositional structures that in general led to more rational decision-making than is to be expected in highly personalized dictatorial systems. Churchill's tendency towards impetuous decision-making was more pronounced in military matters than in those of internal government. In both cases he accepted, if at times reluctantly, the counsel of his advisers.

Democratic leadership has to face many obstacles which those in charge often find irksome. It can be undermined from within so that it cannot sustain itself against an authoritarian challenge (as in Germany between 1930 and 1933). And it is certainly not immune from mistaken courses of action and harmful decisions. Chamberlain's appeasement policy, widely supported across the political spectrum and among the British people before autumn 1938, is a case in point. But constitutional constraints (and to some extent collective forms of decision-making) mean by their nature that democratic leadership is far less likely than dictatorship to produce decisions that have catastrophic consequences.

Gorbachev, here too, forms an exception to the norms both for dictatorial and democratic leadership. The concentration of power in the hands of the Soviet leader gave him, despite various forms of opposition, enormous potential to press ahead with his reforms. These turned out for many Soviet citizens to be economically damaging. They also weakened, and then ultimately destroyed, Soviet power, which to many people had been a source of great pride. On the other hand the reforms liberated millions within the Soviet Union and in its satellite states, subjugated for decades to Soviet domination.

War subjects even powerful political leaders to the constraints of military power.

Whatever the constraints of military power, war, if it results in territorial conquest, opens up vistas for the expansion of political power beyond the limits of what was possible in peacetime conditions, even for a dictatorship. The barbaric conquest of Ethiopia took Mussolini's power and prestige within Italy to new heights. Franco could build an unchallengeable basis of power through the merciless assault on his political enemies during the Spanish Civil War. Not least, the subjugation of Poland and then war in the Soviet Union presented Hitler with the conditions in which policies to annihilate Europe's Jewry could be devised and implemented. The so-called 'General Plan for the East' laid down the preparation for even much more extensive genocide, aimed at wiping out millions of Slavs to establish a German racial empire. But although war, as long as it appeared to lead towards victory and conquest, widened the scope for extreme inhumanity, even dictators were compelled to subject themselves to vagaries of military power beyond their control.

Only Adenauer, Kohl and Gorbachev of the cases examined above were never war leaders. Lenin liquidated as quickly as possible and at enormous initial cost to Russia participation in the First World War that he had inherited on taking power. Franco and Tito came to power through war, though subsequently, as heads of state, stayed out of external armed conflict. The remaining case-studies underline the relative autonomy of military power.

Hitler and Mussolini proved terrible military leaders whose interventions in strategic and even tactical decisions were disastrous once the Second World War settled into a lengthy conflict that exposed fundamental weaknesses in armaments, planning and economic resources. However strong their power was at home, they were constrained by the intrinsic limitations of their own countries in fighting a world war against far stronger military powers. Their own political power was increasingly and inexorably subordinated to the outcome of military campaigns that, once launched, they could no longer control. However hard they strived to implement Hitler's sometimes impossible demands, German generals could not prevent the military collapse that dragged down the political system with it. Mussolini's regime, militarily weaker from the start and humiliated by a mounting catalogue of disasters, was destroyed from within in 1943 as a consequence of its lack of military power.

Allied leaders were themselves constrained in their decision-making by military power. Churchill clashed repeatedly with his military leaders and, whatever his own wishes, mainly found himself acceding to their demands. He later in the war lamented his increased powerlessness in determining Allied strategy and his subordination to the imperatives of American military leadership. Stalin began the war in outrightly catastrophic fashion by ignoring warnings of the German invasion and subjecting the Red Army to huge and unnecessary defeats. He later often yielded operational power in deciding tactics to his military commanders, though he continued to intervene where he felt it was necessary and retained overall strategic control.

De Gaulle's power as leader of the Free French only became of major strategic importance during the Second World War once Vichy's control of the empire waned and the Allies had established supremacy. Military events largely beyond his control or direction allowed him to widen his own power-base in the second half of the war. Even then, to his great irritation, he was largely overlooked in the planning of the Normandy landings in 1944. There followed the lengthy hiatus when he was unable to translate military into political power. His return to lead France in the crisis of 1958 was on the expectation that he would bring about victory in Algeria. But he had no control over the military balance of power in the colony. French military forces soon proved unable within any tolerable framework to win the colonial war. De Gaulle's qualities as a political leader were shown by his recognition of this fact, despite the strong opposition of those, particularly in the army, who felt he had betrayed them.

Mrs Thatcher showed political boldness in launching the war to retake the Falkland Islands after the Argentinian invasion in 1982. She took the key decisions, supported by her War Cabinet, that followed during the campaign. The crucial figures, however, on whom the Prime Minister's own power rested during the short war, were not the politicians, but her military commanders. Once launched, military events developed their own momentum, only partially controllable from London. Mrs Thatcher's own intense nervousness throughout the conflict is itself testimony to the uncertainty of the outcome of military action and to the dependence of her political power on the power of the British armed forces. Victory was for her a triumph, and a turning-point in her own fortunes. Had the Falklands War resulted in defeat, she could not have survived politically.

The individual leader's power and room for manoeuvre are in good measure dependent upon the institutional basis and relative strength of support, primarily among the secondary conduits of power, but also among the wider public.

The above case-studies seem amply to demonstrate that, whether a dictator or a democratic head of government, an individual, however powerful, needs a subordinate apparatus of rule committed to the implementation of the leader's orders while posing little or no opposition. This may sometimes be called a 'power-cartel'. The term does not mean equality in status or decision-making but implies that the leader has only relative, not absolute, autonomy from the power-elite that supports the form of rule.

The rise to power, then the process of takeover, already sees a prospective dictator build a body of support drawn to the personality, ideological message and likelihood of success of the leader of a movement or faction. Max Weber called this 'the charismatic community'. Its members were usually followers of the leader from early times. Hermann Göring, Joseph Goebbels, Heinrich Himmler and Hans Frank remained key lieutenants of Hitler from the early 1920s until the final days. Lazar Kaganovich and Vyacheslav Molotov were subserviently loyal agents of Stalin from the 1920s until his death. The close allegiance to Tito of the other three members of the leadership 'quartet' after he established his dictatorship – Edvard Kardelj, Aleksandar Ranković and Milovan Djilas – dated back to the war years, though Tito later parted ways acrimoniously with the latter two. Suspected disloyalty, as in these cases, led to the ruthless breaking of whatever bonds had existed. Stalin was without parallel in his butchery of subordinates whom he imagined to be disloyal. Hitler certainly demonstrated his ruthlessness through the execution in 1934 of the Stormtroopers' leader, Ernst Röhm, one of his most important subordinates since the early years of the Nazi movement who was thought to be plotting against him, though purges were not actually a characteristic feature of his rule.

In dictatorships the 'power-cartel' invariably includes those who control the instruments of state security. If these become so powerful that they might constitute a threat to the dictator, then a strong leader acts to remove them. Stalin, his paranoia running riot, had two (actually loyal but increasingly distrusted) security heads executed. Hitler, in the very last days of his life, dismissed the leader of the SS, Heinrich Himmler, whose loyalty, however, before the end of the regime became imminent, had been an essential prop of the dictator's power.

No dictator can allow an acolyte to build up an alternative power-base that might undermine his own power. Any perceived sign of disloyalty, or perhaps just decline in usefulness, could have dire consequences. 'Divide and rule' was a useful strategy for an already strong dictator to ensure loyalty through the need to compete for the dictator's favour. Tito proved adept at this strategy. Stalin favoured outright fear, even against those in the highest echelons of his regime. Both Stalin and Hitler destroyed, or allowed to atrophy, the institutions of government that could have permitted any collective expression of opposition or criticism. Mussolini, in contrast, though dominating government and party structures, did not destroy them. The Fascist Grand Council, comprising prominent figures in the party who for two decades or more had been important agents of the dictatorship, sealed Mussolini's fate when it turned against him in 1943. Hitler never permitted any such collective body in the Nazi Party.

In each of the dictatorships under review, perceived achievements and successes welded the 'power-cartel' closer to the leader, deterred opposition and extended the basis of popular support that, in turn, bolstered the leader's security against any internal challenge from within the leadership cohort. Subordinate leaders, partly out of fear, but mainly to secure or expand their own power and advancement, bound themselves ever closer to the leader in demonstrating their own loyalty and dependability. This, however, had the effect of enhancing the leader's own standing and freedom from internal constraints on action. Exclusive control over the instruments and manufacture of propaganda enabled whatever genuine basis of popularity that existed to be elaborated into a personality cult that elevated the status of the leader far above that of any of his subordinates. In such ways, the leader who promised and brought success could over time expand his power and, accordingly, the room to bind his supporters to his own policy decisions, however little consultation had preceded them, and however costly and disastrous they might turn out to be.

Gorbachev, neither democrat nor dictator (though the creation of a dictatorial system), once again occupies a unique place in the above case-studies. He had no ready-built 'power-cartel' in place. He could not depend upon support from the top echelon of the Soviet leadership which he inherited and whose ingrained conservatism posed a significant obstacle to his reform programme. But he was able to use his power and patronage as head of the party to install relatively quickly a number of like-minded reformers in important positions. These provided a new, essential leadership corps which enabled him to push ahead with reforms, even though the obstacles remained great. When some members of this power-elite, earlier his strong supporters, broke with him in the later 1980s over the speed and character of the reforms, his own power was severely weakened. The popularity he had at first enjoyed collapsed as the economic and political crisis worsened severely in 1989–90.

Democratic structures of subsidiary power are, of course, fundamentally different. Success or failure for democratic leaders is usually measured by their ability to win elections, where levels of support can be regularly and routinely tested. Churchill's wartime leadership, when many of the normal rules of democracy were suspended, was an exception. But when democratic elections began again in 1945, Churchill, though a war hero, had to fight a campaign simply as a party leader – and lost.

Electoral success allowed the democratic leaders considered above to widen their scope to implement challenging policies. Adenauer won four consecutive election victories, Kohl also four, Mrs Thatcher three. Each leader nonetheless needed a loyalist entourage, drawn by the leader's personality and programme and underpinning the leader's primacy. De Gaulle in his later years as President of France could still draw on personal loyalties forged while he had been the exiled leader of the Free French. His parliamentary supporters even showed their loyalty in their name, labelling themselves 'Gaullists'. When he returned to office in 1951, Churchill also took with him into government devotees from wartime, and his unique stature naturally assured him of great personal loyalty. His support in his later years as Prime Minister was, however, less personal than conventionally party-political. That is, it rested, in the main, upon the internal machinery of his party and upon his ministerial colleagues, whose loyalty to the Prime Minister was tested by his evidently waning mental and physical abilities. Reluctant though he was to step down, when he could no longer function effectively as Prime Minister the well-established structures of government ensured that he could be replaced in normal fashion, without upheaval.

Command of the structures and machinery of their political party was the basis of the power of Adenauer and Kohl. Both, however, could also rely upon a solid inner phalanx of personal support, partly dating back to the years before they became leaders of government, which gave them an important sounding-board for arriving at important decisions. When they lost the support of the power-cartel their time was up. However reluctantly, they had to hand over power. Mrs Thatcher differed in that, although she had already in opposition attracted advisers who supported and encouraged her radical aims, she inherited no strong base of ministerial support. On the contrary, she had to contend with weighty opposition in her early years in government, only gradually (especially after the Falklands War) constructing a Cabinet of largely uncritical supporters – some by then even slavish devotees. Her own brand of 'charismatic community' was not, however, so solid that it could not turn against her when her policy decisions became an electoral liability. Her sense of betrayal at her departure from office in November 1990 was a sign that she had blurred the lines between personal loyalty and the political self-interest of her ministerial colleagues and her party.

Democratic government imposes the greatest limitation on the individual's freedom of action and scope to determine historical change.

This is the most straightforward of the propositions. Clearly, having to operate through forms of collective government, which can voice opposition and even obstruct implementation of policy, limits the freedom of action of the individual leader. Dictators face no such problems. Collective, democratic leadership is often cumbersome, awkward, slow to reach decisions and, of course, not always sound either in the decisions themselves or in the policy-implementation that follows from them. Nevertheless, well-thought-out, carefully arrived-at policy options have much greater chances of success than dictatorial fiats. The fewer the constraints on the leader, the more likely it is that rash, even catastrophic, decisions will be made.

The cases of democratic leadership outlined above nevertheless suggest that some at least of the outstanding democratic leaders of the twentieth century were temperamentally autocratic and that in certain circumstances their authoritarian tendencies were even advantageous. At points of great crisis, notably in war, slow and often ponderous processes of decision-making are usually inappropriate. Of the cases dealt with here, Churchill, de Gaulle and Mrs Thatcher had to take quick decisions which of their nature bypassed full democratic procedures. Even so, Churchill in the crucial decision of May 1940 about whether to fight on, and Mrs Thatcher in deciding on military action to take back the Falklands, did not operate in isolation as quasi-dictators. They consulted, though within a narrow circle, before reaching a decision. Adenauer, in his crucial rejection of the 'Stalin Note' in 1952, and Kohl, in taking the initiative in November 1989 that opened the door to early unification, also avoided any semblance of extensive democratic consultation. The decisions were too sensitive and needed such a speedy response that wide prior debate was deemed unsuitable, and perhaps harmful.

On returning to government in 1958, de Gaulle ensured that the new constitution gave him the right to take near-unlimited personal powers in a national emergency, and he ran his Cabinet anyway in such an imperious fashion that his personal fiat was what counted. Nevertheless, however autocratic his manner, France remained a constitutional state. Vibrant party-political debate continued. Though parliamentary parties had lost the more obstructive powers they had frequently wielded under the Fourth Republic, France was still a democracy. De Gaulle on a number of occasions successfully manipulated plebiscitary backing for his policies, which enabled him to outflank parliamentary opposition. When he realized, however, that his decisions no longer had popular backing, as he did in 1969, he peremptorily resigned from office. This, ultimately, is the test of democratic leaders: are they ready to go if defeated or can no longer rely upon their base of support? The democratic leaders assessed here were reluctant to give up power. But in the event each of them went – and peacefully.

By the time Helmut Kohl left office in 1998, the twentieth century was almost over. New leaders were entering the scene: Tony Blair in Britain, Gerhard Schröder followed by – the remarkable (and durable) – Angela Merkel in Germany, Nicolas Sarkozy and then François Hollande in France all came to be major players in important west European democracies. Personality remains without doubt a factor of central importance to the exercise of power – as Blair's rhetorical skills and dynamic persuasiveness, and Merkel's calm assuredness and pragmatism, have demonstrated.

Whatever the personality, however, even the most adept political operator struggles to surmount the enormous structural issues which confront them in today's world – problems quite different in character from those faced by their predecessors in the twentieth century. Attempting to deal with them within short-term electoral cycles that demand constant adjustment to fluctuating public opinion, itself strongly influenced by immediate news from across the globe as well as powerful social media, imposes formidable challenges on twenty-first-century democratic leaders. And the more inadequately democracy appears to function, the more the clamour for strong leadership grows. Parliamentary politics – mirroring society – are often mired not just in unbridgeable division, but in a climate of hostility, where opponents are turned into enemies. The temptations of authoritarianism lurk once democracies are in difficulties. These temptations have destroyed democracies in the past, as some of the case-studies in this book show. They could potentially do so again. And, as this book also shows, once in power, with the capacity to remove constitutional constraints, the actions of strong leaders have often turned out to be disastrous.

Western-style liberal democracy has certainly become more difficult to manage. Populism, which elevates the nation above all else, is a political force capable of eroding long-standing democratic values and is hard to combat. The emotional pull of identity politics, a deep well that populism can tap, is not readily susceptible to rational, dispassionate argument. Populist movements, partly driven by intensified inequalities in living standards (products in good measure of globalization and even more so of neo-liberal economics), feeding on the problems of mass migration and able to exploit the new potential for mobilization of social media platforms, have undermined traditional structures of democratic governance and attacked the legitimacy of the political elite. Huge protest movements – such as Extinction Rebellion, Gilets Jaunes, Me Too and Black Lives Matter – have proved hard to contain by conventional policing with democratic safeguards. The danger is that they might be not simply ineffective in attaining their professed goals, but even counterproductive in provoking a backlash that can both feed authoritarian tendencies and promote right-wing populism. In Hungary, Viktor Orbán has taken pride in what he has called 'illiberal democracy'; his country's slide towards authoritarianism has become a thorn in the side of the European Union. Poland, too, has used democracy to become more authoritarian. Democratically elected politicians, with much popular support behind them, are in these cases themselves destroying democracy.

The leaders of Europe's liberal democracies have also to contend with their growing relative weakness in dealing with powerful authoritarian leaders of some of the biggest countries of the world. The emergence in the twenty-first century of Vladimir Putin in Russia, Recep Tayyip Erdoğan in Turkey, Narendra Modi in India, and – most important of all – Xi Jinping in China has tipped the balance of power in international politics towards new forms of modern authoritarianism. Of these, Chinese authoritarianism seems most likely to create the greatest future geopolitical problems. Xi is certainly an extremely powerful individual. But the potential danger goes far beyond his personal power. To a far greater extent than the other authoritarian leaders mentioned (and others besides), Xi heads a well-established and so far highly successful *system* of rule which rests not upon the personality of a specific individual, but upon a unique blend of political, economic, ideological and military power. The system has the capacity to outlive Xi's personal impact. It appears to be more solidly based, more capable of reproducing itself and ultimately more powerful than was the Soviet Union, which for much of the twentieth century was seen as the greatest geopolitical danger.

Democracy is in some ways on the retreat. Donald Trump's four years as President of the USA showed alarmingly how personality could challenge (and even warp) the structures of the world's foremost democracy. The American constitution only just survived the battering it took from Trump, and its much-vaunted checks and balances proved to be weaker than had been presumed. The pseudo-monarchical executive powers of the President are, as Trump showed, so extensive that, in the wrong hands, they can endanger democracy itself. The damage Trump's narcissistic personality and autocratic style of leadership inflicted on the USA, and on democracy in other parts of the world, cannot yet be fully assessed. He came to power on the promise of upholding America's strength. But he has left the USA looking globally weaker as it contends with forces of authoritarianism, especially though not solely in China.

The character traits of twentieth-century authoritarian leaders and the structures that underpinned their rule, explored in this book, can perhaps at times be glimpsed in the rule of their twenty-first-century counterparts. How and to what extent over coming years these will determine global developments that will in turn shape Europe's future cannot of course be known. It can be surmised with some certainty that this future will be shaped not just by the actions of political leaders, but by long-term socio-economic and cultural eddies and currents alongside global concerns arising from climate change, and also by unforeseeable events that even the most powerful individual will be unable to control. Nevertheless, as in the twentieth century, political leaders personally will, within the context that makes their exercise of power possible, take decisions that will directly affect the lives of millions.

The individuals examined in the preceding case-studies were all makers of history. The role of individual leadership was plainly important as a factor in determining historical change. So were the traits of personality which forged their specific forms of leadership. That does not mean that the leaders dealt with above should be seen as 'great'. 'Greatness', I suggested in the Introduction, is a notion best discarded as applied to political leadership. Historical impact is another thing altogether. The maximum impact, certainly in the first half of the century, was arguably made by those held on moral grounds to have been most repugnant – Hitler, Stalin, Lenin. There is no doubt, however, that the actions of all the twelve leaders briefly explored in this book had a huge impact on their own societies, on Europe and, in some cases at least, on the world beyond. They left behind important, sometimes baleful, legacies. They were transformative leaders.

However powerful the individual had been, the legacy has faded over time – if in some cases a long time. (It might be argued that only a handful of religious leaders have left behind a timeless legacy.) Lenin's legacy lasted until the collapse of the Soviet Union in 1991. Stalin's involved the subjugation of most of eastern Europe for over four decades, even though the personality cult attached to him was denounced by Khrushchev as early as 1956. The longevity of impact was dependent in these cases on the ways in which the individual's leadership became embedded in a system of rule that developed strong foundations. When, in contrast, the legitimacy of the system was actually shallow and heavily dependent upon a single individual, as was the case in communist Yugoslavia – nominally resting on Marxist doctrine but in practice almost completely on the leader, Tito – its lifespan was short once the leader died. The highly repressive fascist dictatorships in Italy and Germany were inseparable from their leaders. So when the leader and his regime were demolished by military force, the only immediate legacy was destruction. The systems of Hitler, Mussolini and Franco died with them, the lingering minority taste of neo-fascism notwithstanding. The moral stain was, of course, a different matter. The moral opprobrium of Hitler has lasted to this day (and by no means only in Germany), though that of Mussolini – never so pronounced – has faded. Spain is still coming to terms nearly half a century later with the moral legacy of Franco's rule.

Leaders who come to power in democratic systems usually find their legacy short-lived – a natural by-product of the significant amendment or even reversal of policy when an oppositional party and leader take over. But the legacy could at least to some extent be curtailed in other ways, by the effect of long-term, powerful currents of historical change that the individual cannot control. Churchill and de Gaulle, both products of a colonial age, saw empire as central to the power and grandeur of their countries and fought to preserve it. Yet

Churchill lived long enough to see the unstoppable decline of the British empire. De Gaulle presided himself over the liquidation of the French empire. The anti-colonial movements that brought the fall of colonial empires had their own inspirational leaders. Yet the pressures that these articulated were not the creation of those leaders. They represented irrepressible forces that grew from the increasing rejection of colonial dependency. European leaders, whether, like Hitler and Mussolini, they sought brutally to impose imperialism or, like Churchill and de Gaulle, to preserve it, faced uncontrollable resistance from people unwilling, sometimes despite the most brutal repression, to accept the rule imposed on them by conquerors.

Each of the twelve leaders explored in this book made a unique (in some cases a disastrous) contribution to the making of Europe's twentieth century. But the leaders surveyed above were not just makers of the twentieth century. They were also made by it – that is, by specific conditions that enabled them to exercise their brand of power. The majority were products in one way or another of the dramatically destructive, transformative nature of the first half of the century.

In terms of their historical significance, the most crucial figures were arguably Lenin, Stalin and Hitler. Lenin masterminded the establishment of a completely novel political and economic system which totally transformed his own country and created the basis for a lasting ideological chasm throughout Europe. Stalin drove that system forwards with unimaginable brutality to turn the Soviet Union into an industrial and military behemoth capable of attaining victory in the Second World War and extending Soviet rule over half of Europe. That was largely the reaction to the unbelievably horrific war in eastern Europe and the western Soviet Union unleashed by Hitler's Germany. The main author of that war and the immense destruction – physical and human – that it wrought across most of the continent was Hitler. If unprecedented devastation is the overriding hallmark of that era, then Hitler's impact stands out quite especially.

The second half of the century was far more constructive, more prosperous – above all, more peaceful. But it was dominated by the Cold War and its potential for nuclear catastrophe. By the 1980s, as the effects of the Cold War took their toll on the moribund economy of the Soviet Union, the conditions materialized in which Mikhail

Gorbachev could play such a crucial personal role not just in Soviet but in European history. He destroyed the Soviet Union. But ending the Cold War and ushering in a new era on the continent (and globally), with its own enormous problems, certainly, though palpably different to what preceded it, was arguably the central, and most crucial, episode in Europe since the immediate aftermath of the Second World War. And in the complex process that resulted in the fall of the Iron Curtain and the reunification of the previously separate halves of the European continent, the actions of Mikhail Gorbachev were of paramount importance.

A greater contrast in personality and in the use of power than that between Hitler and Gorbachev is hard to imagine. Yet in their utterly different ways, Hitler in the first half of the century and Gorbachev in the second are the clearest manifestation of the importance of the individual in bringing about epochal historical change.

Notes

INTRODUCTION

1. Political scientists have, of course, often explored issues of political leadership, though usually to try to construct abstract models or leadership types. Valuable indications of this work, much of it excellent, can be found in R. A. W. Rhodes and Paul 't Hart, *The Oxford Handbook of Political Leadership*, Oxford, 2016, esp. 89, 150, 157, 210–11, 220, 230, 322–3, 343, 382–4 and chs. 22–8.

2. See, for example, E. H. Carr, *What Is History?*, London, 1st edn 1961, 2nd edn 1984, reprinted with an introduction by Richard J. Evans, London, 2018, ch. 2, 'Society and the Individual', and Evans's introduction, xvi–xvii.

3. Leo Tolstoy, *War and Peace*, trans. Louise and Aylmer Maude, Ware, 2001, xi, 541–4, 777–8, 889–92, 929–58.

4. Imanuel Geiss, 'Die Rolle der Persönlichkeit in der Geschichte: zwischen Überbewerten und Verdrängen', in Michael Bosch (ed.), *Persönlichkeit und Struktur in der Geschichte*, Düsseldorf, 1977, 23.

5. Volker R. Berghahn and Simone Lässig (eds.), *Biography between Structure and Agency*, New York and Oxford, 2008, 19.

6. Hans-Peter Schwarz, *Das Gesicht des Jahrhunderts. Monster, Retter und Mediokritäten*, Berlin, 1998, 18. Margaret MacMillan, *History's People. Personalities and the Past*, London, 2017, provides five thematic essays aimed at locating the role played by leading figures in the past within the wider context of impersonal economic, social and cultural structures and currents that shape historical change.

7. Jean-Baptiste Decherf, *Le Grand Homme et son pouvoir*, La Tour d'Aigues, 2017, 7–59, explores the roots and development of the image of the 'great man'.

8. Thomas Carlyle, *On Heroes, Hero-Worship, and the Heroic in History*, London, 1841, reprint, n.d., ii.

9. Carlyle, cxxvi.
10. His 'heroic' biography of Frederick the Great was said to have moved Hitler to tears as the final drama in the Berlin bunker approached in 1945. H. R. Trevor-Roper, *The Last Days of Hitler* (1947), London, 1973, 140.
11. Jacob Burckhardt, *Weltgeschichtliche Betrachtungen* (1st edn, Berlin-Stuttgart, 1905, cited here from the edn C. H. Beck, with a postscript by Jürgen Osterhammel), Munich, 2018, 217–19.
12. Burckhardt, 219.
13. Burckhardt, 238, 246.
14. Burckhardt, 258.
15. Burckhardt, 250–51.
16. Burckhardt, 222–3.
17. Lucy Riall, 'The Shallow End of History? The Substance and Future of Political Biography', *Journal of Interdisciplinary History*, 40/3 (2010), 375–97; Lucy Riall, *Garibaldi: Invention of a Hero*, New Haven and London, 2007, 390–97.
18. Riall, *Garibaldi*, 387.
19. Riall, *Garibaldi*, 397.
20. Joachim C. Fest, *Hitler*, London, 1974, 3–9; Joachim C. Fest, 'On Remembering Adolf Hitler', *Encounter*, 41 (October 1973), 19.
21. Geoffrey Best, *Churchill. A Study in Greatness*, London, 2001, 329–30, underlining that 'his title to greatness rests on achievements in the fields of war and politics', argues that 'he did what . . . the greatest of men can do: he changed the apparent course of history'. Geoffrey Wheatcroft, *Churchill's Shadow*, London, 2021, chs. 19–21, shows the extraordinary spread of the Churchill 'myth' long after his death.
22. Andrew Roberts, *Churchill. Walking with Destiny*, London, 2019, 786–9.
23. Max Weber, *Economy and Society*, ed. Günther Roth and Claus Wittich, Berkeley, Los Angeles and London, 1978, 215–6, 241–54, 1111–57. Arthur Schweitzer, *The Age of Charisma*, Chicago, 1984, applies Weber's concept to a variety of modern political leaders.
24. Frank Dikötter, *How to Be a Dictator. The Cult of Personality in the Twentieth Century*, London, 2019, provides a number of telling examples.
25. Karl Marx, *The Eighteenth Brumaire of Louis Bonaparte*, Moscow, 1954, 10. (I have slightly amended the translation.)
26. *The Eighteenth Brumaire*, Amazon reprint, n.d., 35–7.
27. Archie Brown, *The Myth of the Strong Leader*, London, 2014, 24, 61.
28. Heather Elizabeth Mitterer, 'The Role of Personality in Leader Effectiveness', 22 January 2014, https://sites.psu.edu/leadership/2014/01/22/the-role-of-personality-in-leader-effectiveness/, accessed November 2021.

29. Michael Mann, *The Sources of Social Power*, vol. 3: *Global Empires and Revolution, 1890–1945*, Cambridge, 2012, 5–13.
30. Weber, 53.
31. Mann, 13.
32. See Brown, 45.
33. Ruth Ben-Ghiat, *Strongmen*, New York, 2020, places Trump and other recent populist leaders in a genealogical line reaching back to the major dictators of the twentieth century.

CHAPTER 1: VLADIMIR ILYICH LENIN

1. Robert Service, *Lenin. A Biography*, London, 2000, 134–5, for the change of name.
2. Hans-Peter Schwarz, *Das Gesicht des Jahrhunderts*, Berlin, 1998, 231.
3. Geoffrey Hosking, *Russia and the Russians*, London, 2001, 362–85.
4. Michael Mann, *The Sources of Social Power*, vol. 3: *Global Empires and Revolution, 1890–1945*, Cambridge, 2012, 174–90, esp. 182–3, 188–9.
5. Service, *Lenin*, 232.
6. Dimitri Volkogonov, *Lenin. Life and Legacy*, London, 1995, 110, 156.
7. Service, *Lenin*, 204, 212, 247, 274.
8. Mann, 175.
9. Mann, 184.
10. Victor Sebestyen, *Lenin the Dictator. An Intimate Portrait*, London, 2017, 22–3.
11. Sebestyen, 156–7.
12. Service, *Lenin*, 200, 232.
13. Service, *Lenin*, 19, 22; Robert Payne, *Lenin*, New York, 1964, 14.
14. Service, *Lenin*, 197, lists fourteen major European cities.
15. Sebestyen, 30, 184–7.
16. Summaries in Payne, 147–54; Sebestyen, 138–41; Service, *Lenin*, 135–9.
17. Service, *Lenin*, 152–3.
18. Service, *Lenin*, 171, 176.
19. Hosking, *Russia*, 361.
20. Service, *Lenin*, 259.
21. Service, *Lenin*, 263–5; Martin McCauley (ed.), *The Russian Revolution and the Soviet State 1917–1921. Documents*, London, 1975, 54–5.
22. Lars T. Lih, '"All Power to the Soviets!" Biography of a Slogan', *International Relations*, 24 July 2017, https://socialistproject.ca/2017/07/b1454/, accessed November 2021.

23. Service, *Lenin*, 269.
24. Volkogonov, ch. 5, has pen-portraits of each of them.
25. Mann, 185–6.
26. Geoffrey Hosking, *A History of the Soviet Union*, London, 1985, 43.
27. Sebestyen, 337, for quotations.
28. Leonard Schapiro, *1917*, London, 1985, 131–2.
29. Isaac Deutscher, *The Prophet Armed. Trotsky, 1879–1921*, Oxford, 1970, 311–12.
30. Service, *Lenin*, 308–9.
31. Deutscher, 325; Robert Service, *Trotsky. A Biography*, London, 2009, 191.
32. Robert Gellately, *Lenin, Stalin and Hitler. The Age of Social Catastrophe*, London, 2007, 42–3.
33. Robert Service, *A History of Twentieth-Century Russia*, London, 1998, 73.
34. Schapiro, chs. 9–10; Service, *Lenin*, 314–19.
35. Sebestyen, 381; also Payne, 426.
36. Schapiro, 147–9; Service, *Russia*, 74–5.
37. Orlando Figes, *A People's Tragedy. The Russian Revolution 1891–1924*, London, 1996, 631, 642; Gellately, 46–8.
38. Figes, *People's*, 630–31.
39. Volkogonov, 313 (also 306, 311).
40. Figes, *People's*, 627–9.
41. Volkogonov, 148–9 (and ch. 5 for pen-portraits of Lenin's entourage).
42. Evan Mawdsley, *The Russian Civil War*, London, 2000, 7, for size of the army.
43. Service, *Lenin*, 336–40 (quotation 339); Mawdsley, 42–6.
44. Service, *Trotsky*, 216.
45. Service, *Lenin*, 403.
46. Figes, *People's*, 618, 622–3; Orlando Figes, *Revolutionary Russia 1891–1991*, London, 2014, 153.
47. Service, *Lenin*, 363; Gellately, 53.
48. Volkogonov, 233–4.
49. Volkogonov, 235–40.
50. Figes, *People's*, 640, 647, 649 (and 627–49 generally for the expansion of the terror).
51. Service, *Lenin*, 443 (and for further indications of Lenin's advocacy of terror, 395, 411–12, 431, 435, 444).
52. Figes, *Revolutionary Russia*, 159.
53. Service, *Lenin*, 408–9; Volkogonov, 388; Sebestyen, 460–61; Payne, 525; Service, *Trotsky*, 272–8.
54. Mawdsley, 349–61.

55. Service, *Lenin*, 412, 418–19.
56. Hosking, *Soviet Union*, 134–5.
57. Figes, *Revolutionary Russia*, 166–7, 190.
58. Service, *Lenin*, 422–33.
59. Figes, *Revolutionary Russia*, 189–94.
60. This paragraph is based on Service, *Lenin*, chs. 26–7.
61. Stephen Kotkin, *Stalin. Paradoxes of Power 1878–1928*, London, 2015, 498–501.
62. Archie Brown, *The Myth of the Strong Leader*, London, 2014, 217.
63. Service, *Lenin*, 475–81, for the last months and death.
64. Jan Plamper, *The Stalin Cult*, New Haven and London, 2012, 22.
65. Arthur Schweizer, *The Age of Charisma*, Chicago, 1984, 167.
66. Moshe Lewin, *The Making of the Soviet System*, London, 1985, 57–71.
67. Plamper, 24.
68. Figes, *Revolutionary Russia*, 181–2.
69. 'Russians Say Lenin Played Positive Role: Poll', https://www.rferl.org/a/russia-lenin-positive-role-levada-poll/28441045.html, accessed November 2021.
70. Alice Underwood, 'Why Lenin's Corpse Lives On in Putin's Russia', https://www.wilsoncenter.org/blog-post/why-lenins-corpse-lives-putins-russia, accessed November 2021.

CHAPTER 2: BENITO MUSSOLINI

1. Across the Atlantic, Mussolini enjoyed 'vast popularity' in the USA. John P. Diggins, *Mussolini and Fascism. The View from America*, Princeton, 1972, 23.
2. Winston S. Churchill, *The Second World War*, vol. 2: *Their Finest Hour*, London, 1949, 548.
3. Denis Mack Smith, *Mussolini*, London, 1983, xiv, 122; quotation in A. J. P. Taylor, *The Origins of the Second World War*, Harmondsworth, 1964, 85; R. J. B. Bosworth, *Mussolini*, London, 2002, 424.
4. R. J. B. Bosworth, *The Italian Dictatorship*, London, 1998, 76–81, surveys the persistence of the contemptuously dismissive views of Mussolini as a 'mountebank dictator' or 'sawdust Caesar' – in effect, a pretentious empty vessel.
5. Luisa Passerini, *Mussolini Immaginario*, Rome and Bari, 1991, 70–76, 99–101.
6. Hans Woller, *Mussolini. Der erste Faschist*, Munich, 2016, 57–8.
7. Woller, *Mussolini*, 59–60; Bosworth, *Mussolini*, 110; Mack Smith, 33.

8. Emilio Gentile, 'Paramilitary Violence in Italy: The Rationale of Fascism and the Origins of Totalitarianism', in Robert Gerwarth and John Horne (eds.), *War in Peace. Paramilitary Violence in Europe after the Great War*, Oxford, 2012, 89.

9. Adrian Lyttelton, *The Seizure of Power. Fascism in Italy 1919–1929*, London, 1987, 77; Robert O. Paxton, *The Anatomy of Fascism*, London, 2004, 117–18.

10. Dominique Kirchner Reill, *The Fiume Crisis*, Cambridge, Mass., 2020, 16–21.

11. Gentile, 'Paramilitary Violence', 89–92; Michael Mann, *Fascists*, Cambridge, 2004, 100–118; Wolfgang Schieder (ed.), *Faschismus als soziale Bewegung*, Hamburg, 1976, 75.

12. Roger Griffin, *The Nature of Fascism*, London, 1991, 26–7.

13. Michael R. Ebner, *Ordinary Violence in Mussolini's Italy*, New York, 2011, 25–34; Matteo Millan, 'The Institutionalisation of Squadrismo', *Contemporary European History*, 22/4 (2014), 556; Jens Petersen, 'Violence in Italian Fascism, 1919–25', in Wolfgang J. Mommsen and Gerhard Hirschfeld (eds.), *Social Protest, Violence and Terror in Nineteenth- and Twentieth-Century Europe*, London, 1982, 280–94, provides statistics of the extensive scale of the violence.

14. Lyttelton, *Seizure*, 44–6; Mack Smith, 52, for the discarding of the 1919 programme.

15. Paul Corner, *Fascism in Ferrara 1915–1925*, Oxford, 1975, 170–76.

16. Frank M. Snowden, *The Fascist Revolution in Tuscany, 1919–22*, Cambridge, 1989, 60–61, 102, 147.

17. Emilio Gentile, 'Fascism in Power: The Totalitarian Experiment', in Adrian Lyttelton (ed.), *Liberal and Fascist Italy*, Oxford, 2002, 144.

18. MacGregor Knox, *To the Threshold of Power, 1922/33*, Cambridge, 2007, 328; Woller, *Mussolini*, 72–4; Bosworth, *Mussolini*, 157–62; Pierre Milza, *Mussolini*, Paris, 1999, 282–9.

19. Knox, *Threshold*, 329.

20. Marco Tarchi, 'Italy: Early Crisis and Fascist Takeover', in Dirk Berg-Schlosser and Jeremy Mitchell (eds.), *Conditions of Democracy in Europe, 1919–1939: Systematic Case-Studies*, Basingstoke, 2000, 304–13.

21. Knox, *Threshold*, 268–81, 327.

22. Giulia Albanese, *The March on Rome: Violence and the Rise of Italian Fascism*, London, 2019, x, xiii, 74–7, 86–7.

23. Mack Smith, 62–3.

24. Albanese, 91–2.

25. Woller, *Mussolini*, 67.

26. Schieder, *Faschismus*, 80–83, for the growth of the party and its changing social character.

27. Adrian Lyttelton, 'Fascism in Italy: The Second Wave', in George L. Mosse (ed.), *International Fascism: New Thoughts and New Approaches*, London and Beverley Hills, 1979, 45, 48.

28. Bosworth, *Mussolini*, 199; Lyttelton, *Seizure*, 250.

29. Lyttleton, 'Fascism in Italy', 47–8.

30. Bosworth, *Mussolini*, 203; Lyttelton, *Seizure*, 265–6; Milza, 345–50.

31. Woller, *Mussolini*, 115–17.

32. Millan, 550; Lyttelton, *Seizure*, 269–307, deals extensively with the Farinacci Secretariat and the decline of the party. Milza, ch. 12, outlines the component parts of the power structure beneath Mussolini.

33. Ebner, 48–71.

34. Gentile, 'Fascism in Power', 169.

35. Amedeo Osti Guerrazzi, 'Das System Mussolini. Dic Regierungspraxis des Diktators 1922 bis 1943 im Spiegel seiner Audienzen', *Vierteljahrshefte für Zeitgeschichte*, 66/2 (2018), 217–25.

36. Woller, *Mussolini*, 118–19.

37. Emilio Gentile, *The Sacralization of Politics in Fascist Italy*, Cambridge, Mass., 1996, 136–9.

38. Stephen Gundle, Christopher Duggan and Giuliana Pieri (eds.), *The Cult of the Duce. Mussolini and the Italians*, Manchester, 2015, esp. 2–4, 27–40; Christopher Duggan, *Fascist Voices*, London, 2012, xi, 230, 241, 279; Piero Melograni, 'The Cult of the Duce in Mussolini's Italy', in Mosse, 73–90; Frank Dikötter, *How to Be a Dictator*, London, 2019, 14–19; Woller, *Mussolini*, 114–15; Milza, 555–62; Paul Corner, *The Fascist Party and Popular Opinion in Mussolini's Italy*, Oxford, 2012, 210–11, 280; Paul Corner (ed.), *Popular Opinion in Totalitarian Regimes*, Oxford, 2009, 122–46.

39. Corner, *Popular Opinion*, 138–41; John Gooch, *Mussolini's War*, London, 2020, 33.

40. Mack Smith, 220–21.

41. MacGregor Knox, *Mussolini Unleashed 1939–1941*, Cambridge, 1986, 9–10.

42. *Ciano's Diary 1937–1943*, London, 2002, 102 (18 June 1938), 110 (17 July 1938), 152–3 (4 November 1938), 208 (27 March 1939).

43. The term was initially used in Hans Mommsen, *Beamtentum im Dritten Reich*, Stuttgart, 1966, 98 n. 26.

44. MacGregor Knox, *Common Destiny. Dictatorship, Foreign Policy, and War in Fascist Italy and Nazi Germany*, Cambridge, 2000, 142–3.

45. Christian Goeschel, *Mussolini and Hitler*, New Haven and London, 2018, 45–52.
46. Goeschel, 89–90.
47. *Ciano's Diary*, 201 (15 March 1939).
48. Knox, *Common Destiny*, 137–44; Gooch, 15–17.
49. Gooch, 33.
50. Joe Maiolo, *Cry Havoc: The Arms Race and the Second World War 1931–1941*, London, 2010, 196–202; Gooch, 55–6; Knox, *Common Destiny*, 150–51.
51. Corner, *Popular Opinion*, 138–41; Christian Goeschel, 'Mussolini, Munich and the Italian People', in Julie Gottlieb, Daniel Hucker and Richard Toye (eds.), *The Munich Crisis. Politics and the People*, Manchester, 2021, 156–8, 161, 165–6.
52. Hans Woller, *Geschichte Italiens im 20. Jahrhundert*, Munich, 2010, 153–61; Woller, *Mussolini*, 164–71; Bosworth, *Mussolini*, 338–44.
53. Michele Sarfatti, *The Jews in Mussolini's Italy*, Maddison, Wisconsin, 2000, x, 42–3, 53–4.
54. *Ciano's Diary*, 264 (24 August 1939).
55. Knox, *Mussolini Unleashed*, 104–5.
56. Woller, *Mussolini*, 209.
57. Knox, *Mussolini Unleashed*, 18–30.
58. Woller, *Mussolini*, 200.
59. Gooch, 296, 350.
60. Filippo Focardi, 'Italy's Amnesia over War Guilt: The "Evil Germans" Alibi', *Mediterranean Quarterly*, 25/4 (2014), 8; Woller, *Mussolini*, 233–4.
61. Claudia Baldoli, 'Spring 1943: The Fiat Strikes and the Collapse of the Italian Home Front', *History Workshop Journal*, 72/1 (2011), 181–9; Gooch, 365.
62. Bosworth, *Mussolini*, 403–4.
63. Woller, *Mussolini*, 298–301; MacGregor Knox, 'Das faschistische Italien und die "Endlösung" 1942/43', *Vierteljahrshefte für Zeitgeschichte*, 55 (2007), 53–5, 77–9, 91–2; Meir Michaelis, *Mussolini and the Jews*, Oxford, 1978, 323, 348–50, 389–90, 408–14.
64. Claudio Pavone, *A Civil War. A History of the Italian Resistance*, London, 1991, 2014, ch. 5; Woller, *Geschichte Italiens*, 197–8; H. James Burgwyn, *Mussolini and the Salò Republic 1943–1945*, Cham, 2018, 335–6.
65. Hans Woller, *Die Abrechnung mit dem Faschismus in Italien 1943–1948*, Munich, 1996, 279.
66. Paul Ginsborg, *A History of Contemporary Italy. Society and Politics 1943–1988*, 92.

67. Woller, *Die Abrechnung*, 271–3; Filippo Focardi and Lutz Klinkhammer, 'The Question of Fascist Italy's War Crimes: The Construction of a Self-Acquitting Myth (1943–1948)', *Journal of Modern Italian Studies*, 9/3 (2004), 330–48.

68. Disputes about the level of support for the dictator arose especially following the publication of volume 4, *Mussolini il duce. Gli anni del consenso 1929–1936*, Turin, 1974. A strong critique of De Felice's method, approach and evaluation is provided by Wolfgang Schieder, *Faschistische Diktaturen*, Göttingen, 2008, 50–55.

69. Michael A. Ledeen, 'Renzo De Felice and the Controversy over Italian Fascism', *Journal of Contemporary History*, 11 (1976), 269–82; Renzo De Felice and Michael A. Ledeen, *Fascism: An Informal Introduction to Its Theory and Practice*, London, 1976, 2017.

70. Gundle et al., 252–4.

71. Ruth Ben-Ghiat, *Strongmen*, New York and London, 2020, 79–83 and 244–5, assesses the appeal of the 'strongmen' Silvio Berlusconi and Matteo Salvini.

72. Angelo Amante, 'Half of Italians Want "Strongman" in Power, Survey Shows', https://www.reuters.com/article/us-italy-politics-survey-IDUSKBN 1YA1X5, accessed November 2021.

73. Woller, *Mussolini*, 317–23; Bosworth, *Mussolini*, 413–19.

74. https://en.wikipedia.org/wiki/Benito_Mussolini, accessed November 2021.

CHAPTER 3: ADOLF HITLER

1. Jeremy Noakes and Geoffrey Pridham (eds.), *Nazism 1919–1945*, vol. 3, Exeter, 1988, 764–5 (also 740). Full references for this chapter can be found in my two-volume biography: Ian Kershaw, *Hitler, 1889–1936*, London, 1998, and *Hitler, 1936–45*, London, 2000. Other substantial biographies include: Alan Bullock, *Hitler. A Study in Tyranny*, 2nd edn, Harmondsworth, 1962; Joachim C. Fest, *Hitler*, London, 1974; and Volker Ullrich, *Hitler* (2 vols.), London, 2016, 2020; Peter Longerich, *Hitler: A Life*, London, 2019. Brendan Simms, *Hitler: Only the World Was Enough*, London, 2019, is practically alone in arguing that Hitler's central ideological preoccupation was Anglo-American capitalism.

2. The varied attitudes towards Hitler are summed up in Ian Kershaw, *The 'Hitler Myth': Image and Reality in the Third Reich*, Oxford, 1987, 264–6.

3. Hans Mommsen, 'Nationalsozialismus', in *Sowjetsystem und demokratische Gesellschaft*, vol. 4, Freiburg, 1971, column 702.

4. Claudia Schmölders, *Hitlers Gesicht*, Munich, 2000, 7–14.

5. Eberhard Jäckel and Axel Kuhn (eds.), *Hitler. Sämtliche Aufzeichnungen 1905–1924*, Stuttgart, 1980, 69.

6. Thomas Weber, *Hitler's First War*, Oxford, 2010, 250–55, 345–6.

7. Noakes and Pridham, vol. 1, Exeter, 1983, 13.

8. The authoritative edition is now that produced by the Institut für Zeitgeschichte in Munich: *Hitler. Mein Kampf. Eine kritische Edition*, ed. Christian Hartmann et al., Munich, 2016.

9. A point emphasized in the first systematic analysis of *Mein Kampf*, by Eberhard Jäckel, *Hitlers Weltanschauung. Entwurf einer Herrschaft*, Tübingen, 1969, 140–41; and most recently by Laurence Rees, *Hitler and Stalin*, London, 2020, 1–2.

10. Lothar Machtan, *The Hidden Hitler*, London, 2001, 88–93 (quotation 93).

11. Anton Joachimsthaler, *Hitlers Liste*, Munich, 2003, dispatches many unfounded stories and casts light, especially, on his relations with women.

12. Otto Gritschneder, *Der Hitler-Prozeß und sein Richter Georg Neithardt*, Munich, 2001, 51.

13. Gregor Strasser used feudal language – 'Duke and vassal' – in describing in 1927 the relationship of leader and followers as the essence of the Nazi Party. Noakes and Pridham, vol. 1, 54.

14. Kurt Sontheimer, *Antidemokratisches Denken in der Weimarer Republik*, Munich, 1962, 271.

15. Richard J. Evans, *The Coming of the Third Reich*, London, 2003, provides a perceptive and extensive guide to the multi-layered crisis.

16. Martin Broszat, *German National Socialism, 1919–1945*, Santa Barbara, 1966, 58–9.

17. Heinrich August Winkler, *Weimar 1918–1933. Die Geschichte der ersten deutschen Demokratie*, chs. 14–18, is an excellent guide to the complexities of the deepening, eventually terminal, political crisis.

18. Dietrich Orlow, *The History of the Nazi Party 1919–1933*, Newton Abbot, 1971, 294–6.

19. Benjamin Carter Hett, *Burning the Reichstag*, Oxford/New York, 2014, casts new doubt on the long-held view that a young Dutch former communist, Marinus van der Lubbe, was the sole perpetrator.

20. Leading constitutional lawyers underlined this interpretation: Noakes and Pridham, vol. 2, Exeter, 1984, 200, 476, 486.

21. Noakes and Pridham, vol. 2, 200.

22. Franz Neumann (ed.), *Behemoth: The Structure and Practice of National Socialism*, London, 1942, 75, was among the first to stress the importance of Hitler's charismatic power. Laurence Rees, *The Dark Charisma of Adolf Hitler*, London, 2012, assesses its impact.

23. Noakes and Pridham, vol. 2, 207.

24. Heike B. Görtemaker, *Hitlers Hofstaat*, Munich, 2019, explores the composition and character of the Berghof circle.

25. Leonidas E. Hill (ed.), *Die Weizsäcker-Papiere 1933–1950*, Frankfurt, 1974, 162.

26. Helmut Krausnick and Hans-Heinrich Wilhelm, *Die Truppe des Weltanschauungskrieges*, Stuttgart, 1981, 86.

27. Christopher R. Browning, *The Origins of the Final Solution*, Jerusalem, 2004, 241.

28. Gerald Fleming, *Hitler und die Endlösung*, Wiesbaden, 1982, 86.

29. Elke Fröhlich (ed.), *Die Tagebücher von Joseph Goebbels*, part 2, vol. 2, Munich, 1996, 498.

30. Noakes and Pridham, vol. 3, 1049.

31. Peter Longerich, *The Unwritten Order: Hitler's Role in the Final Solution*, London, 2001, 106.

32. E.g., Peter Witte et al., *Der Dienstkalender Heinrich Himmlers 1941/42*, Hamburg, 1999, 294, records Hitler's agreement on 18 December 1941 that Jews should be exterminated as partisans. Fleming, 62–8, 163–5, for Himmler's claim to have Hitler's authority for his actions.

33. Longerich, *The Unwritten Order*, 119.

34. Nicolaus von Below, *Als Hitlers Adjutant 1937–45*, Mainz, 1980, 398.

35. Ralf Dahrendorf, *Society and Democracy in Germany*, London, 1968, 402, 404.

36. Mary Fulbrook, *Reckonings*, Oxford, 2018, 245–58.

CHAPTER 4: JOSEPH STALIN

1. Nikita Khrushchev, *Khrushchev Remembers*, London, 1971, 587.

2. The following section depends mainly on Robert Service, *Stalin. A Biography*, London, 2004; Robert C. Tucker, *Stalin as Revolutionary 1879–1929*, London, 1974 (= Tucker 1); Simon Sebag Montefiore, *Stalin. The Court of the Red Tsar*, London, 2003; Edvard Radzinsky, *Stalin*, New York, 1996; and the more recent, exhaustively detailed study by Stephen Kotkin, *Stalin. Paradoxes of Power 1878–1928*, London, 2015 (= Kotkin 1).

3. Service, *Stalin*, 10–11, summarizes the issue.

4. Laurence Rees, *Hitler and Stalin. The Tyrants and the Second World War*, London, 2020, xxvi.

5. Khrushchev, 307.

6. Stephen Kotkin, *Stalin. Waiting for Hitler 1929–1941*, London, 2018 (= Kotkin 2), 234–5, 492–3.

7. Sebag Montefiore, 305–6.

8. Sebag Montefiore, 259–61.

9. Kotkin 1, 422.

10. Evan Mawdsley, *The Stalin Years. The Soviet Union, 1929–1953*, Manchester, 1998, 80.

11. See Service, *Stalin*, 165–6.

12. Adam B. Ulam, *Stalin. The Man and His Era*, Boston, 1989, 218–19; Tucker 1, 288–9.

13. Whether Lenin, who by 1923 was almost totally incapacitated by a series of strokes, actually wrote or dictated the document is doubtful. The hand of his wife, Krupskaya, seeking to muddy the waters of the succession by denigratory comments on other contenders as well as Stalin, has plausibly been seen at work. Kotkin 1, 498–501.

14. See Service, *Stalin*, 147: 'If he had died in September 1917, no one – surely – would have written his biography.' The terminal date might even be extended to 1924 and the revelation of Lenin's Testament.

15. See Moshe Lewin, *The Making of the Soviet System*, London, 1985, ch. 11, 'The Social Background of Stalinism'.

16. Robert Service, *A History of Twentieth-Century Russia*, London, 1998, 162.

17. A clear exposition of the rivalries in Tucker 1, 299–303.

18. Kotkin 1, 662–76; Alec Nove, *Stalinism and After*, London, 1981, 29–37.

19. Hans Mommsen, 'Cumulative Radicalisation and Progressive Self-Destruction as Structural Determinant of the Nazi Dictatorship', in Ian Kershaw and Moshe Lewin (eds.), *Stalinism and Nazism: Dictatorships in Comparison*, Cambridge, 1997, 75–87.

20. Moshe Lewin, 'Bureaucracy and the Stalinist State', in Kershaw and Lewin, 62–3, for a 15 per cent growth in officialdom between 1928 and 1939.

21. Kotkin 2, 162; Moshe Lewin, *The Soviet Century*, London, 2005, 84–9; Richard Overy, *The Dictators. Hitler's Germany, Stalin's Russia*, London, 2004, 65, 169.

22. The Stalin cult burst on the scene in 1929 in connection with the dictator's fifty-first birthday celebrations. It was then relatively dormant for three years, possibly to avoid connecting Stalin with the upheavals of collectivization, before returning even more expansively from mid-1933 onwards. Jan Plamper, *The Stalin Cult*, New Haven and London, 2012, 29, 36.

23. Robert C. Tucker, *Stalin in Power. The Revolution from Above, 1928–1941*, New York, 1990 (= Tucker 2), 444.
24. Kotkin 2, 497.
25. Kotkin 1, 739.
26. Kotkin 2, 131.
27. Archie Brown, *The Myth of the Strong Leader*, London, 2014, 256.
28. Service, *Russia*, 215.
29. Kotkin 2, 391–3, 479, 542, 586, 618–19, 740.
30. Lew Besymenski, *Stalin und Hitler. Das Pokerspiel der Diktatoren*, Berlin, 2004, 282–90.
31. Richard Overy, *Russia's War 1941–1945*, London, 1999, 117.
32. Overy, *Russia's War*, 287–8.
33. Laurence Rees, *War of the Century*, London, 1999, 323–3; Rees, *Hitler and Stalin*, 390–91; Service, *Stalin*, 512.
34. Rees, *War of the Century*, 152–3.
35. Jörg Baberowski, *Scorched Earth. Stalin's Reign of Terror*, New Haven and London, 2016, 362–71; Sean McMeekin, *Stalin's War*, London, 2021, 317.
36. Baberowski, 376–7.
37. Baberowski, 316–17.
38. Baberowski, 328–34, 382–4; McMeekin, 146–9.
39. Geoffrey Roberts, *Stalin's Wars*, New Haven and London, 2006, 22.
40. Roberts, 20–22.
41. Sebag Montefiore, 334; Dmitri Volkogonov, *Stalin. Triumph and Tragedy*, London, 1991, 413; Geoffrey Hosking, *A History of the Soviet Union*, London, 1985, 272; Radzinsky, 472.
42. Radzinsky, 472–3; Baberowski, 358.
43. Rees, *War of the Century*, 70–73; Ian Kershaw, *Fateful Choices. Ten Decisions that Changed the World 1940–1941*, London, 2008, 289–90.
44. Rees, *War of the Century*, 63–4, for his responsibility for the disastrous loss of Kiev, when 600,000 Red Army soldiers fell into German hands.
45. John Erickson, *The Road to Stalingrad*, London, 1975 (1998 edn), 335, 337–8; David M. Glanz and Jonathan House, *When Titans Clashed. How the Red Army Stopped Hitler*, Kansas, 1995, 105–6.
46. Erickson, 347, 349.
47. Marshal of the Soviet Union G. Zhukov, *Reminiscences and Reflections*, Moscow, 1985, vol. 2, 71–5, 86; Rees, *War of the Century*, 123–4; Roberts, 122–6; Rees, *Hitler and Stalin*, 196–202.
48. Zhukov, 79; Erickson, 370–71.
49. Zhukov, 87–100.

50. Roberts, 159–62; Glanz and, House, 129, 198–201, 259, 266; Rees, *Hitler and Stalin*, 369–70.
51. Laurence Rees, *World War Two behind Closed Doors*, London, 2008, 211, 240–42; McMeekin, 507–11, 600–602.
52. Radzinsky, 497.
53. Hans-Peter Schwarz, *Das Gesicht des Jahrhunderts*, Berlin, 1998, 260–61; Overy, *Russia's War*, 291.
54. *War Diaries 1939–1945. Field Marshal Lord Alanbrooke*, ed. Alex Danchev and Daniel Todman, London, 2001, 301 (14 August 1942).
55. Service, *Stalin*, 512; Sebag Montefiore, 436–7.
56. Service, *Stalin*, 583.
57. Service, *Stalin*, 561, 563–4.
58. Service, *Stalin*, 630.
59. Lewin, *Making*, 9. See also Lewin, *Soviet Century*, 10–11.
60. Brown, 255.
61. McMeekin, 652–5.
62. Service, *Stalin*, 635–6.
63. Roberts, 3.

CHAPTER 5: WINSTON CHURCHILL

1. David Reynolds, *In Command of History*, London, 2004, xxi: 'Churchill the historian has shaped our image of Churchill the Prime Minister. And that was his firm intention.'
2. Roy Jenkins, *Churchill*, London, 2001, 593.
3. Archie Brown, *The Myth of the Strong Leader*, London, 2014, 88; Jenkins, 775–7.
4. Andrew Roberts, *Churchill*, London, 2019, 904–6.
5. Roberts, *Churchill*, 113,
6. Thomas Jones, *A Diary with Letters 1931–1950*, Oxford, 1954, 204.
7. Roberts, *Churchill*, 210–11.
8. Roberts, *Churchill*, 294, 310, 314–16.
9. Hans-Peter Schwarz, *Das Gesicht des Jahrhunderts*, Berlin, 1998, 373.
10. Geoffrey Best, *Churchill. A Study in Greatness*, London, 2001, 138.
11. Roberts, *Churchill*, 183.
12. N. J. Crowson, *Facing Fascism. The Conservative Party and the European Dictators 1935–40*, London, 1997, 185.
13. Clive Ponting, *1940. Myth and Reality*, Chicago, 1993, 57.
14. Winston S. Churchill, *The Second World War*, vol. 1: *The Gathering Storm*, London, 1948, 601.

15. Andrew Roberts, *'The Holy Fox'. The Life of Lord Halifax*, London, 1997, 197.

16. Jenkins, 577–82; Roberts, *Churchill*, 494–500, for descriptions of the debate.

17. Ponting, 57.

18. Jenkins, 583–5; Roberts, *Churchill*, 507, 500–11; Ponting, 65–6; Roberts, *'Holy Fox'*, ch. 21.

19. Ponting, 103–11; John Lukacs, *Five Days in London. May 1940*, New Haven and London, 2001; Ian Kershaw, *Fateful Choices. Ten Decisions that Changed the World, 1940–1941*, London, 2008, ch. 1.

20. Ponting, 110–11.

21. Roberts, *'Holy Fox'*, 220.

22. The Foreign Office, without Churchill's approval, still considered the possibilities of approaches through Sweden towards a compromise peace settlement until mid-June. Ponting, 111–19.

23. Max Hastings, *Finest Years. Churchill as Warlord 1940–45*, London, 2009, 76–7, 93, for examples.

24. This paragraph is based largely on Richard Toye, *The Roar of the Lion. The Untold Story of Churchill's World War II Speeches*, Oxford, 2015, 227–32; also Roberts, *Churchill*, 535–6, 715–16.

25. Roberts, *Churchill*, 572, 747.

26. Toye, 206.

27. Lord Moran, *Winston Churchill. The Struggle for Survival 1940–1965*, London, 1966, 292.

28. Roberts, *Churchill*, 689–90; Hastings, 211–12.

29. *War Diaries 1939–1945. Field Marshal Lord Alanbrooke*, ed. Alex Danchev and Daniel Todman, London, 2001, xx–xxi.

30. Roberts, *Churchill*, 734.

31. Jenkins, 622–4; Roberts, *Churchill*, 573–4.

32. Jenkins, 777–8; Hastings, 246–7; Roberts, *Churchill*, 715. The most detailed assessment of the effectiveness of bombing is provided by Richard Overy, *The Bombing War. Europe 1939–1945*, London, 2013.

33. John Colville, *The Fringes of Power. Downing Street Diaries 1939–1955*, London, 1985, 183; *War Diaries*, 251.

34. Hastings, xx; Roberts, *Churchill*, 736.

35. Hastings, 43–4.

36. Hans-Peter Schwarz, *Das Gesicht des Jahrhunderts*, Berlin, 1998, 384.

37. Hastings, 124–30; Roberts, *Churchill*, 683.

38. Jenkins, 642; Hastings, 117; Colville, 315.

39. *War Diaries*, 282–6; Hastings, 312–14.

40. Hastings, 478–82.
41. Hastings, 493–6.
42. *War Diaries*, 458–9; Hastings, 409–21.
43. Colville, 574.
44. Roberts, *Churchill*, 812.
45. Laurence Rees, *Behind Closed Doors. Stalin, the Nazis and the West*, London, 2008, 155–63.
46. Roberts, *Churchill*, 884.
47. Hastings, 359–60.
48. Rees, 214.
49. Moran, 141.
50. Rees, 221, 239, 309, 315–17.
51. Diana Preston, *Eight Days at Yalta*, London, 2019, 117, 245; Hastings, 551.
52. Geoffrey Roberts, *Stalin's Wars*, New Haven and London, 2006, 220–21.
53. Best, 332.
54. Jenkins, 792; Brown, 89.
55. As is made clear in Paul Addison, *The Road to 1945: British Politics and the Second World War*, London, 1975.
56. Paul Addison, 'The Three Careers of Winston Churchill', *Transactions of the Royal Historical Society*, 2001, 183.
57. David Carlton, *Churchill and the Soviet Union*, Manchester, 2000, 131, 136, 141–3.
58. Hugo Young, *This Blessed Plot. Britain and Europe from Churchill to Blair*, London, 1998, 6, 10–18 (quote, 13).
59. Young, 19–22.
60. Jenkins, 818.
61. Roberts, *Churchill*, 948–9.
62. Roberts, *Churchill*, 963.
63. Addison, 'The Three Careers', 185.
64. Roberts, *Churchill*, 959. John Charmley, *Churchill. The End of Glory*, London, 1993, emphasizes the loss of empire as the contradiction of what Churchill had strived to preserve, but overplays his hand in seeing what was an inexorable process as resulting from a failure in his leadership.
65. Roberts, *Churchill*, 943–4.
66. Jenkins, 818.
67. 'Edward Heath, "a Euro-sceptic"? Churchill? Never', *Independent*, 26 September 1996, https://www.independent.co.uk/archive, accessed November 2021.

68. Roberts, *Churchill*, 960.
69. Young, 6.
70. Geoffrey Wheatcroft's critical assessment of Churchill's legacy in *Churchill's Shadow*, London, 2021, appeared after this chapter had been written.

CHAPTER 6: CHARLES DE GAULLE

1. Julian Jackson, *A Certain Idea of France. The Life of Charles de Gaulle*, London, 2019, 377 (speech of 1959); Jean Lacouture, *De Gaulle. The Rebel, 1890–1944*, London, 1990, 215 (= Lacouture 1).
2. Hans-Peter Schwarz, *Das Gesicht des Jahrhunderts*, Berlin, 1998, 208.
3. Schwarz, 216.
4. Jackson, 305.
5. Charles de Gaulle, *War Memoirs*, vol. 1: *The Call to Honour 1940–1942*, London, 1955 (= DG 1), 3.
6. Lacouture 1, 3; Jackson, 19.
7. Schwarz, 208.
8. Jackson, 329.
9. Jackson, 29.
10. Winston S. Churchill, *The Second World War*, vol.2: *Their Finest Hour*, London, 1949, 142.
11. John Colville, *Downing Street Diaries 1939–1955*, London, 1985, 159–60.
12. DG 1, 86; Lacouture 1, 203–12; Jackson, 119; Paul-Marie de La Gorce, *De Gaulle*, Paris, 1999, 252.
13. Schwarz, 204.
14. DG 1, 89; Lacouture 1, 223–6; Jackson, 3–6; Gorce, 254–5; Éric Roussel, *Charles de Gaulle*, Paris, 2002, 126–31.
15. Jackson, 140.
16. Rod Kedward, *La Vie en bleu*, London, 2006, 278.
17. DG 1, 256–9, 262; Lacouture 1, 309–19.
18. Jackson, 162.
19. Lacouture 1, 252–5; Roussel, 154–6.
20. Jackson, 186.
21. Kedward, 276.
22. Jackson, 133–4, 149.
23. Charles de Gaulle, *War Memoirs*, vol. 2: *Unity 1942–1944*, London, 1959 (= DG 2), 38–9; David Schoenbrun, *The Three Lives of Charles de Gaulle*, London, 1966, ch. 5 (97–140).

24. Jackson, 153.

25. DG 2, 15–17, 75–9, 101–2, 114–18, indicates the tensions.

26. Schoenbrun, 94–5.

27. Jackson, 158–9.

28. Joseph Bergin, *A History of France*, London, 2015, 230.

29. DG 1, 273–5; Jackson, 198–200; Lacouture 1, 378–80; Gorce, 353–9; Roussel, 267–9.

30. Lacouture 1, 445; Gorce, 457–8; Roussel, 362–3; Jackson, 271.

31. DG 2, 151–8.

32. DG 2, 226–7; Lacouture 1, 520–3; Jackson, 312–13; Gorce, 516–18; Roussel, 425–8.

33. Jackson, 315.

34. Lacouture 1, 529.

35. DG 2, 305–9; Roussel, 450; Lacouture 1, 575; Jackson, 328.

36. Jackson, 329; Lacouture 1, 577–8; DG 2, 311–14.

37. Charles de Gaulle, *War Memoirs*, vol. 3: *Salvation 1944–1946*, London, 1960 (= DG 3), 64–82; Jackson, 356; Roussel, 470–77; Gorce, 678–82; Jean Lacouture, *De Gaulle. The Ruler, 1945–1970*, London, 1991 (= Lacouture 2), 47–54. Stalin openly advertised the lethal character of his rule, boasting to de Gaulle of his brutality. Laurence Rees, *Behind Closed Doors*, London, 2008, 331.

38. Diana Preston, *Eight Days at Yalta*, London, 2019, 117.

39. DG 3, 233–6; Robert Gildea, *France since 1945*, Oxford, 2002, 37; Schoenbrun, 79, 83, de Gaulle's for long-standing views on leadership and personality.

40. DG 3, 278–9.

41. Max Weber, *Economy and Society*, ed. Günther Roth and Claus Wittich, Berkeley, Los Angeles and London, 1978, 1449–53. Arthur Schweitzer, *The Age of Charisma*, Chicago, 1984, 288–96, discusses de Gaulle as a charismatic leader, though only in the context of the war. See also Schoenbrun, 179. Jean-Baptiste Decherf, *Le Grand Homme et son pouvoir*, La Tour d'Aigues, 2017, 220–26, points to de Gaulle's neo-romantic belief that he was fulfilling destiny as France's national hero.

42. Gildea, 38.

43. Jackson, 389; Lacouture 2, 129–31 (text of speech, 130); Roussel, 534–5; Gorce, 749–50.

44. Kedward, 381.

45. Jackson, 395.

46. Gildea, 45.

47. Jackson, 429.

48. Jackson, 434–40; Lacouture 2, 154–5, 188–9; Gorce, 825–9.

49. Jackson, 464–5.

50. Gildea, 50–51; Kedward, 339; Bergin, 245.

51. Natalya Vince, *The Algerian War, the Algerian Revolution*, Cham, 2020, is a valuable guide through the thickets of historiographical interpretation.

52. Jackson, 549.

53. Jackson, 487–8, and Roussel, 603, both stress the intentional ambiguity. See also Lacouture 2, 186. Gorce, 923, has the text of de Gaulle's address.

54. Gildea, 32.

55. Jackson, 619.

56. Jackson, 641–2; Lacouture 2, 223–5; Gorce, 1034–8; Roussel, 622–3.

57. Jackson, 638–40.

58. Jackson, 639. The Council of Ministers had been no more than 'decorative' even under de Gaulle as Prime Minister, before becoming President. Serge Berstein and Pierre Milza, *Histoire de la France au xx. Siècle: III. 1958 à nos jours*, Paris, 2006, 12.

59. Jackson, 562–5; Berstein and Milza, 39–49.

60. Jackson, 669–71; Gildea, 58–9; Berstein and Milza, 62–3.

61. Kedward, 392–4.

62. Jackson, 758; Lacouture 2, 572–6; Gorce, 1317–19; Roussel, 906–7.

63. Jackson, 761; Lacouture 2, 581.

64. The title of the book by Eugen Weber, *The Hollow Years. France in the 1930s*, New York, 1996.

65. Jackson, 480–81.

66. Decherf, 14, 220–40.

67. Jackson, 781.

68. Jackson, xxix.

CHAPTER 7: KONRAD ADENAUER

1. Hans-Peter Schwarz, *Adenauer*, vol. 1: *Der Aufstieg*, Munich, 1994 (= Schwarz 1), 128.

2. Schwarz 1, 347.

3. Schwarz 1, 344–5.

4. Klaus-Jörg Ruhl, *Neubeginn und Restauration*, Munich, 1982, 124.

5. Klaus-Dietmar Henke, *Die amerikanische Besetzung Deutschlands*, Munich, 1996, 367–72; Schwarz 1, 429–34.

6. Schwarz 1, 467–73; Christopher Knowles, 'How It Really Was. Konrad Adenauer and His Dismissal as Mayor of Cologne by the British in

1945', blog, 30 March 2008, https://howitreallywas.typepad.com/how_it_really_was/2008/03/konrad-adenauer.html, accessed November 2021.

7. Schwarz 1, 473, 477–8, 500–503, 508–9.

8. Schwarz 1, 432, 436, 619.

9. Andrea Hoffend, 'Konrad Adenauer und das faschistische Italien', *Quellen und Forschungen aus italienischen Bibliotheken und Archiven*, 75 (1995), 481. I am grateful for this reference to Christian Göschel.

10. Schwarz 1, 293–5, 333.

11. Karl Dietrich Bracher, *The German Dilemma*, London, 1974, 152.

12. Schwarz 1, 522–7; Ulrich Herbert, *Geschichte Deutschlands im 20. Jahrhundert*, Munich, 2014, 586–7; Dennis L. Bark and David R. Gress, *A History of West Germany*, vol. 1: *From Shadow to Substance 1945–1963*, Oxford, 1989, 113–14.

13. Schwarz 1, 567, 619.

14. Bark and Gress, 236–44, 250–51.

15. Schwarz 1, 909–17; Bark and Gress, 298–300; Heinrich August Winkler, *Germany: The Long Road West, 1933–1990*, Oxford, 2000, 136–8; Klaus-Jörg Ruhl (ed.), '*Mein Gott. Was soll aus Deutschland werden?*' *Die Adenauer-Ära*, Munich, 1985, 130–31, 143–4; Herbert, 637–8.

16. Elisabeth Noelle and Erich Peter Neumann (eds.), *The Germans. Public Opinion Polls 1947–1966*, Allensbach and Bonn, 1967, 471.

17. See Schwarz 1, 920–24; Bark and Gress, 299–300; Wolfram F. Hanrieder, *Germany, America, Europe*, New Haven and London, 1989, 155–7; Herbert, 638; Winkler, 137–8; Arnulf Baring, *Im Anfang war Adenauer*, Munich, 1971, 246–54; Ruhl, 122–52; Rolf Steininger, *Eine Chance zur Wiedervereinigung? Die Stalin-Note vom 10. März 1952*, Bonn, 1985, 75, argues that there had been a chance.

18. Hanrieder, 154.

19. Schwarz 1, 926.

20. Herbert, 636, 639; Konrad Adenauer, *Erinnerungen*, 4 vols., Stuttgart, 1965–8, vol. 1, 570, 563; vol. 2, 298, 301–4.

21. Bark and Gress, 330–3; Winkler, 151–2.

22. Bark and Gress, 270; Winkler, 133.

23. Alan S. Milward, *The European Rescue of the Nation-State*, London, 1992, 136–7.

24. Bark and Gress, 381.

25. Hans-Peter Schwarz, *Adenauer*, vol. 2: *Der Staatsmann, 1952–1967*, Munich, 1994 (= Schwarz 2), 287–91 (quotation, 291).

26. Schwarz 2, 285.

27. Noelle and Neumann, 505.
28. Bark and Gress, 427; Winkler, 167–8.
29. Bark and Gress, 431–4; Hanrieder, 13–14.
30. Bark and Gress, 454–7.
31. Bark and Gress, 494.
32. Ruhl, 466–70 (for text of treaty); Bark and Gress, 516–17; Winkler, 198; Schwarz 2, 810–26.
33. Schwarz 2, 814–15.
34. Bark and Gress, 496.
35. Bark and Gress, 518; Winkler, 197–8.
36. Schwarz 2, 824–6.
37. Noelle and Neumann, 195, 200, 241, 243; A. J. Merritt and R. L. Merritt (eds.), *Public Opinion in Occupied Germany. The OMGUS Surveys, 1945–1949*, Urbana, 1970, 30–31.
38. Noelle and Neumann, 240–41.
39. Schwarz 1, 796.
40. Winkler, 184–5.
41. Winkler, 162.
42. Winkler, 167.
43. Winkler, 155–6.
44. Norbert Frei, *Adenauer's Germany and the Nazi Past: The Politics of Amnesty and Integration*, New York, 2002, 311.
45. Merritt and Merritt, 93–4, 121–3, 161; Mary Fulbrook, *Reckonings*, Oxford, 2018, 216–19.
46. Winkler, 155.
47. Herbert, 663–5.
48. Eckart Conze et al., *Das Amt und die Vergangenheit*, Munich, 2010, 493.
49. Fulbrook, 250–51.
50. Schwarz 1, 658.
51. Fulbrook, 242.
52. Reinhard-M. Strecker, *Hans Globke. Aktenauszüge. Dokumente*, Hamburg, 1961, assembled the anti-Jewish material on which Globke had collaborated. Globke was sentenced to death *in absentia* in a GDR show trial. Fulbrook, 242.
53. Noelle and Neumann, 296.
54. Pertti Ahonen, *After the Expulsion. West Germany and Eastern Europe 1945–1990*, Oxford, 2003, 104–5, 110–13; Winkler, 139.
55. Schwarz 2, 530.
56. Ruhl, 231–45, for the social reform proposals.

57. Winkler, 193–5; Herbert, 756–69.
58. Schwarz 2, 868, citing *Die Zeit*, 18 October 1963.
59. https://en.wikipedia.org/wiki/Unsere_Besten; and 'First German Chancellor wins TV Search for Greatest German', *Independent*, 1 December 2003, https://www.independent.co.uk/news/world/europe/first-german-chancellor-wins-tv-search-for-greatest-german–94160.html, accessed November 2021.
60. Schwarz 1, 902–3; Winkler, 149.
61. Hansard, Foreign Affairs, House of Commons Debate, 11 May 1953, vol. 515, columns 889–90, https://api.parliament.uk/historic-hansard/commons/1953/may/11/foreign-affairs, accessed November 2021, German trans. Ruhl, 164.

CHAPTER 8: FRANCISCO FRANCO

1. Hans-Peter Schwarz, *Das Gesicht des Jahrhunderts*, Berlin, 1998, 198.
2. For Franco's early life and career before the Civil War, see Paul Preston, *Franco. A Biography*, London, 1993, chs. 1–4, and Stanley G. Payne and Jesus Palacios, *Franco. A Personal and Political Biography*, Madison, Wisconsin, 2014, chs. 1–4 (= P&P).
3. Preston, *Franco*, 12.
4. Preston, *Franco*, 323; Enrique Moradiellos, *Franco. Anatomy of a Dictator*, London, 2018, 29.
5. Paul Preston, *A People Betrayed. A History of Corruption, Political Incompetence and Social Division in Modern Spain, 1874–2018*, London, 2020, 7, 19–24.
6. Mary Vincent, *Spain 1833–2002. People and State*, Oxford, 2007, 99.
7. Preston, *A People Betrayed*, 61, 81.
8. Vincent, 104–7; Frances Lannon, 'Iberia', in Robert Gerwarth (ed.), *Twisted Paths. Europe 1914–1945*, Oxford, 2008, 143–5.
9. Walther Bernecker, 'Spain: The Double Breakdown', in Dirk Berg-Schlosser and Jeremy Mitchell (eds.), *Conditions of Democracy in Europe, 1919–39*, Basingstoke, 2000, 405–6.
10. Preston, *A People Betrayed*, xii–xiii; Bernecker, 410–12.
11. Alejandro Quiroga and Miguel Ángel del Arco (eds.), *Right-Wing Spain in the Civil War Era*, London and New York, 2012, 52.
12. Preston, *A People Betrayed*, 228–9; Vincent, 120–22; Stanley G. Payne, *A History of Fascism 1914–45*, London, 1995, 254.
13. Preston, *A People Betrayed*, 237; Vincent, 122.

14. Michael Mann, *Fascists*, Cambridge, 2004, 329.
15. Vincent, 134.
16. Matthew Kerry, *Unite, Proletarian Brothers! Radicalism and Revolution in the Spanish Second Republic*, London, 2020, ch. 6 (153–80). I am grateful to Dr Kerry for information on the victims of the rising. Also, Preston, *Franco*, 104–7; Vincent, 133–4.
17. Moradiellos, 33.
18. Helen Graham, *The Spanish Republic at War 1936–1939*, Cambridge, 2002, 76.
19. Preston, *Franco*, 124, 129–30, 131–2; P&P, 114–15, 505.
20. Preston, *Franco*, 134–5.
21. P&P, 119–20.
22. P&P, 505.
23. Preston, *Franco*, xviii.
24. Preston, *Franco*, 164.
25. Preston, *Franco*, 182–5; P&P, 143–7.
26. Moradiellos, part 2 (57–147), outlines the derivation and exploitation of the Caudillo cult.
27. Preston, *Franco*, 187–9.
28. P&P, 168.
29. Paul Preston, *The Spanish Holocaust. Inquisition and Extermination in Twentieth-Century Spain*, London, 2012, 151–3, 191–2, 229–35, 665–71; Vincent, 139–40.
30. Paul Preston, *Comrades. Portraits from the Spanish Civil War*, London, 1999, 54; Preston, *Spanish Holocaust*, xi.
31. Zara Steiner, *The Triumph of the Dark. European International History 1933–1939*, Oxford, 2011, 192, 196–7, 220, 231.
32. Preston, *Spanish Holocaust*, xi; lower estimates in P&P, 198–9, 203; different figures again in Heinrich August Winkler, *Geschichte des Westens. Die Zeit der Weltkriege*, Munich, 2011, 817.
33. Preston, *Spanish Holocaust*, 505–6.
34. Michael Richards, *A Time of Silence. Civil War and the Culture of Repression in Franco's Spain, 1936–1945*, Cambridge, 1998, 47.
35. Preston, *Spanish Holocaust*, xi.
36. Preston, *Spanish Holocaust*, 119.
37. P&P, 193–5.
38. Stanley G. Payne, *Falange. A History of Spanish Fascism*, Stanford, 1961, 158–76; Sheelagh M. Ellwood, *Spanish Fascism in the Franco Era*, Basingstoke, 1987, 40–45; Moriadellos, 99–100, 127–9.
39. Preston, *Franco*, 344–5.

40. Preston, *A People Betrayed*, 358–9.
41. Stanley G. Payne, *The Franco Regime 1936–1975*, Madison, Wisconsin, 1987, 282, 333; Xavier Moreno Juliá, *The Blue Division. Spanish Blood in Russia, 1941–1945*, Eastbourne, 2015, 67, 70–71, 288, 297, 303–4; Xosé M. Núñez Seixas, 'Spain', in Jochen Böhler and Robert Gerwarth (eds.), *The Waffen-SS – A European History*, Oxford, 2017, 99–100.
42. Preston, *Franco*, 517–25; Payne, *Franco Regime*, 337.
43. Payne, *Franco Regime*, 397–8.
44. P&P, 299, 316.
45. Payne, *Franco Regime*, 397.
46. Payne, *Franco Regime*, 469–70.
47. Vincent, 167.
48. Payne, *Franco Regime*, 437–8, 470–71.
49. Moradiellos, 76–80, 188–9.
50. Sasha D. Pack, 'Tourism and Political Change in Franco's Spain', in Nigel Townson (ed.), *Spain Transformed. The Late Franco Dictatorship, 1959–75*, London, 2010, 55.
51. P&P, ch. 16 (391–413), ch. 18 (431–46), and 515–16, problematically portray Franco as Spain's 'definitive modernizer' and a 'development dictator'.
52. Payne, *Franco Regime*, 23, 234.
53. Preston, *Franco*, 337.
54. Preston, *Franco*, 783.
55. Payne, *Franco Regime*, 407–11.
56. P&P, 365–6.
57. Payne, *Franco Regime*, 400–401; J. P. Fusi, *Franco. A Biography*, London, 1985, 43.
58. Payne, *Franco Regime*, 399; Preston, *A People Betrayed*, chs. 12–15.
59. Moradiellos, 81–8.
60. Moradiellos, 197, describes Franco as a 'Bonapartist military dictator'.
61. Fusi, 45.
62. He was still railing against 'a conspiracy by leftist freemasons' in his last public address on 1 October 1975, just before his death. Fusi, 167.
63. Preston, *Franco*, 706–7; Preston, *A People Betrayed*, 406–7; Payne, *Franco Regime*, 405–7.
64. Preston, *Franco*, 752.
65. It surely goes too far to speak (P&P, 520) of a '"Spanish model" of democratization', for which Franco deserves some credit.
66. Moradiellos, 3, 7–8; Julián Casanova, 'Disremembering Francoism: What is at Stake in Spain's Memory Wars?', in Helen Graham (ed.), *Interrogating Francoism*, London, 2016, 206–7.

67. Preston, *A People Betrayed*, 547.
68. Townson, Introduction, 8.
69. Vincent, 240.
70. Preston, *A People Betrayed*, 549.
71. According to one assessment, Spain in 1975 was 'at approximately the same level of socio-economic development as it would have been had [Franco] never lived'. Edward Malefakis, 'The Franco Dictatorship: A Bifurcated Regime?', in Townson, 253.
72. Townson, Introduction, 12–13; Pablo Martín Aceña and Elena Martínez Ruiz, 'The Golden Age of Spanish Capitalism', in Townson, 45–6.
73. William J. Callahan, 'The Spanish Church: Change and Continuity', in Townson, 191.
74. Clearly shown by Casanova, in Graham, *Interrogating Francoism*, ch. 9.
75. Moradiellos, 5–6.
76. Preston, *A People Betrayed*, 539–43.
77. The title of the article by Ernst Nolte, 'Vergangenheit, die nicht vergehen will', *Frankfurter Allgemeine Zeitung*, 6 June 1986, which sparked the huge controversy in Germany known as the 'Historians' Dispute' (*Historikerstreit*).

CHAPTER 9: JOSIP BROZ TITO

1. It was not an uncommon first name in the part of Croatia that he came from, he pointed out. He took it 'because it occurred to me at the moment'. Vladimir Dedijer, *Tito Speaks. His Self Portrait and Struggle with Stalin*, London, 1953, 80–81.
2. Quotations from Milovan Djilas, *Tito. The Story from Inside*, New York, 1980, 4, 15, 33, 40, 46, 67, 116. See also: Marie-Janine Calic, *Tito. Der ewige Partisan*, Munich, 2020, 95; Jože Pirjevec, *Tito and His Comrades*, London, 2018, 391.
3. Pirjevec, 385.
4. Fitzroy Maclean, *Eastern Approaches*, London, 1949, 308, 311, 325–6.
5. Calic, *Tito*, 96–101. More improbable is the claim mentioned in Jasper Ridley, *Tito. A Biography*, London, 1994, 344, that she survived the purges and was still living in 1990 in the Soviet Union.
6. Dedijer, 35.
7. Dedijer, 90–91.
8. Calic, *Tito*, 101.
9. Pirjevec, 35–7.

10. Calic, *Tito*, 86–8, 96–101, 104; Pirjevec, 43–4.
11. Edvard Radzinsky, *Stalin*, New York, 1996, 412.
12. He had in practice held the position since 1937, following the execution of Gorkić. Ridley, 134–5.
13. Calic, *Tito*, 105; Pirjevec, 46.
14. Ridley, 245, for first meeting, in 1944.
15. Djilas, 26–9.
16. Calic, *Tito*, 106; Pirjevec, 48.
17. Their wartime importance to Tito was evident to Maclean (Maclean, 326–8).
18. Calic, *Tito*, 145.
19. Figures in Pirjevec, 75, 111; Calic, *Tito*, 119, 149, 166, 179.
20. Calic, *Tito*, 136.
21. Hans-Peter Schwarz, *Das Gesicht des Jahrhunderts*, Berlin, 1998, 584; Pirjevec, 132.
22. Djilas, 12–13.
23. Calic, *Tito*, 132 (and 134 for map of Tito's movements between 1941 and 1944).
24. Djilas, 13.
25. Pirjevec, 134–7; Misha Glenny, *The Balkans 1804–1999*, London, 1999, 532.
26. Maclean, 504–14, describes the impact of the Soviet troops.
27. Calic, *Tito*, 168, 182.
28. Archie Brown, *The Myth of the Strong Leader*, London, 2014, 221.
29. Richard West, *Tito and the Rise and Fall of Yugoslavia* (1996), London, 2009, 204–9; Pirjevec, 150–51; Calic, *Tito*, 206–7; Ridley, 260.
30. Calic, *Tito*, 195.
31. Calic, *Tito*, 198.
32. Geoffrey Swain, *Tito. A Biography*, London, 2011, 92, 187.
33. Robert Service, *Stalin. A Biography*, London, 2004, 631.
34. Marie-Janine Calic, *Geschichte Jugoslawiens im 20. Jahrhundert*, Munich, 2010, 191; Calic, *Tito*, 239, 243. Pirjevec, 199, gives a figure of 30,000 prisoners of Goli Otok 'and similar institutions', but without sources or details for the much higher figure.
35. Pirjevec, 152–3.
36. Calic, *Tito*, 203.
37. Examples in Pirjevec, 187, 190, 198.
38. Djilas, 21, 31, 92–116; Pirjevec, 144–9; Swain, 183.
39. Calic, *Tito*, 239–40.
40. Calic, *Jugoslawien*, 203.
41. Calic, *Jugoslawien*, 198–200; West, 244.

42. Pirjevec, 228–9; Calic, *Jugoslawien*, 192–3; Calic, *Tito*, 248–9; Djilas, 74–6.
43. Djilas, 161–2.
44. Glenny, 579, 581.
45. Pirjevec, 326–38; Calic, *Tito*, 323–6.
46. Glenny, 582.
47. Pirjevec, 338–9, 353–4.
48. Geoffrey Swain and Nigel Swain, *Eastern Europe since 1945*, London, 4th edn, 2009, 151.
49. Calic, *Tito*, 283.
50. Calic, *Jugoslawien*, 197; Ridley, 306–7.
51. Calic, *Tito*, 293.
52. Pirjevec, 275–7.
53. Calic, *Tito*, 310–11.
54. Pirjevec, 265–7.
55. Calic, *Tito*, 286–8.
56. Ridley, 358.
57. Calic, *Jugoslawien*, 202.
58. Pirjevec, 440–41.
59. Calic, *Jugoslawien*, 255–6.
60. Glenny, 583–5.
61. Barbara Jelavich, *History of the Balkans. Twentieth Century*, vol. 2, Cambridge, 1983, 196, 397.
62. Calic, *Jugoslawien*, 253–4; 257–8; Calic, *Tito*, 331–7; Swain and Swain, 181.
63. Pirjevec, 394; Glenny, 576.
64. Pirjevec, 345.
65. Calic, *Tito*, 375.
66. Glenny, 623.
67. Without Tito's leadership, Croatia especially might have followed a different path. Dejan Jović, 'Reassessing Socialist Yugoslavia, 1956–90. The Case of Croatia', in Dejan Jović and James Ker-Lindsey (eds.), *New Perspectives on Yugoslavia. Key Issues and Controversies*, Abingdon, 2011, 117–29, stresses the unique importance of Tito (an ethnic Croat on his father's side) in integrating Croatia into the post-war Yugoslavian state.
68. Calic, *Jugoslawien*, 286–7; Calic, *Tito*, 380.
69. Calic, *Tito*, 384–5; Mitja Velikonja, *Titostalgia – a Study of Nostalgia for Josip Broz*, Ljubljana, 2008, 129–34; Ridley, 420.

CHAPTER 10: MARGARET THATCHER

1. Hugo Young, *One of Us*, London, 1990, 383; John Campbell, *Margaret Thatcher*, vol. 2: *The Iron Lady*, London, 2003 (= Campbell 2), 303; Charles Moore, *Margaret Thatcher. The Authorized Biography*, vol. 1: *Not for Turning*, London, 2013 (= Moore 1), 745 note.

2. Young, 393–13.

3. John Campbell, *Margaret Thatcher*, vol. 1: *The Grocer's Daughter*, London, 2000 (= Campbell 1), 19.

4. Campbell 1, 2, 32, 446; Moore 1, 8–9.

5. Young, 98.

6. Campbell 1, 270–77; Moore 1, 259–63; Young, 82.

7. Steve Richards, *The Prime Ministers. Reflections on Leadership from Wilson to May*, London, 2019, 151–8.

8. Peter Hennessy, *The Prime Minister. The Office and Its Holders since 1945*, London, 2000, 408.

9. Campbell 1, 264.

10. Andrew Gamble, 'The Thatcher Myth', *British Politics*, 10/1 (2015), 9–10.

11. Campbell 1, 414.

12. Moore 1, 412–13.

13. Dominic Sandbrook, *Who Dares Wins. Britain, 1979–1982*, London, 2019, 9, 48, 50, 57.

14. Robert Tombs, *The English and Their History*, London, 2014, 759–61, and part 7 generally, convincingly illustrates the illusion of decline.

15. The term was invented by Geoffrey Howe, not Thatcher herself. Nigel Lawson, *The View from No. 11*, London, 1992, 100.

16. Campbell 2, ch. 11, uses the term to assess Mrs Thatcher's relations with her Cabinet.

17. Moore 1, 533.

18. Moore 1, 641.

19. Hennessy, 405–7, underlines their importance.

20. Young, 212–16; John Hoskyns, *Just in Time. Inside the Thatcher Revolution*, London, 2000, 275–85; Margaret Thatcher, *The Downing Street Years*, London, 1995, 132–9.

21. Lawson, 98–9, 246; Robert Skidelsky, *Britain since 1900*, London, 2014, 339.

22. Young, 203, 316, 318.

23. *The Economist*, 21 May, 4 June, cit. Young, 321.

24. George Eaton, 'How Public Spending Rose under Thatcher', *New Statesman*, 8 April, 2013, https://www.newstatesman.com/politics/2013/04/how-public-spending-rose-under-thatcher, accessed November 2021.

25. In practice, the 'Medium-Term Financial Strategy' of 1980 missed its target for reducing the growth in money supply each year, but economic depression of the government's own making (bringing a sharp increase in unemployment) brought the rate of inflation down sharply. Skidelsky, 341.

26. Young, 144.

27. Young, 193–5, 353.

28. Simon Rogers, 'How Britain Changed under Margaret Thatcher. In 15 Charts', *Guardian*, 8 April 2013, https://www.theguardian.com/politics/datablog/2013/apr/08/britain-changed-margaret-thatcher-charts, accessed November 2021.

29. Young, 241.

30. Hennessy, 412.

31. Young, 263; Thatcher, 177–9.

32. David Cannadine, *Margaret Thatcher. A Life and Legacy*, Oxford, 2017, 47.

33. Sandbrook, 761–4.

34. Campbell 2, 135.

35. Moore 1, 700–703; Thatcher, 205–8; Hennessy, 419.

36. Young, 275–6.

37. Young, 276; Moore 1, 712; Campbell 2, 145–6; Thatcher, 214.

38. Cannadine, 49; Sandbrook, 834, has her personal rating in early June at 53 per cent.

39. Sandbrook, 837–8.

40. Thatcher, 139–43; Lawson, 141, 144; Hoskyns, 274–5, 289–91; Young, 366.

41. Tombs, 817.

42. Richards, 178.

43. Charles Moore, *Margaret Thatcher. The Authorized Biography*, vol. 2: *Everything She Wants*, London, 2015, 146–7, for the estimated job losses in 1984–5.

44. Campbell 2, 361–2.

45. Moore 2, 151; Campbell 2, 359–60.

46. Campbell 2, 796; Hennessy, 428.

47. Campbell 2, 273–9; Moore 2, 117–35.

48. Thatcher, 463; Young, 303; Moore 2, 240.

49. Campbell 2, 292; Moore 2, 610.

50. Campbell 2, 605; Cannadine, 101–2.

51. Cannadine, 98.

52. Moore 2, 693; Cannadine, 95.

53. Lawson, 574.
54. Lawson, 561–2; Thatcher, 666–7; Hennessy, 428.
55. Lawson, chs. 71–7 (888–971).
56. Charles Moore, *Margaret Thatcher: The Authorized Biography*, vol. 3: *Herself Alone*, London, 2019 (= Moore 3), 561–6, 580–84, 587–92; Campbell 2, 701–6; Anthony Seldon, *Major. A Political Life*, London, 1998, 110–16.
57. Campbell 2, 744.
58. See Cannadine, 96; Campbell 2, 800; Peter Clarke, *Hope and Glory. Britain 1900–1990*, London, 1996, 400.
59. Moore 3, 853.
60. Moore 3, 645–6.
61. Moore 3, 853.

CHAPTER 11: MIKHAIL GORBACHEV

1. William Taubman, *Gorbachev. His Life and Times*, New York, 2017, 539.
2. Taubman, 5.
3. Taubman, 1–5.
4. Vladislav M. Zubok, 'Gorbachev and the End of the Cold War: Perspectives on History and Personality', *Cold War History*, 2/2 (2002), 61–100, offers a valuable analysis (75 for quotation). I am grateful to Christian Göschel for drawing this essay to my attention.
5. Taubman, 36.
6. Archie Brown, *The Gorbachev Factor*, Oxford, 1996, 29.
7. Taubman, 215–16; Brown, *Gorbachev Factor*, 92.
8. Taubman, 125.
9. John Miller, *Mikhail Gorbachev and the End of Soviet Power*, London, 1993, 61.
10. Stephen Kotkin, *Armageddon Averted: The Soviet Collapse, 1970–2000*, Oxford, 2001, 27, 173–4.
11. Archie Brown, *The Myth of the Strong Leader. Political Leadership in the Modern Age*, London, 2014, 166.
12. Brown, *Gorbachev Factor*, 90–91.
13. Mikhail Gorbachev, *Memoirs*, London, 1997, 277–9.
14. Miller, 62.
15. David Lane, 'The Roots of Political Reform: The Changing Social Structure of the USSR', in Catherine Merridale and Chris Ward (eds.), *Perestroika. The Historical Perspective*, London, 1991, 95–113.

16. Archie Brown, *Seven Years that Changed the World*, Oxford, 2008, 32.

17. Brown, *Myth*, 165.

18. Brown, *Myth*, 167–8.

19. Gorbachev, 638–9.

20. Taubman, 480.

21. Brown, *Myth*, 169–72.

22. Gorbachev, 224–9.

23. Margaret Thatcher, *The Downing Street Years*, London, 1995, 459–63.

24. Gorbachev, 280.

25. Gorbachev, 214, 280.

26. Gorbachev, 223.

27. Robert Service, *A History of Twentieth-Century Russia*, London, 1998, 441.

28. Gorbachev, 259–60.

29. Taubman, 207–10; Brown, *Seven Years*, 64, 202 n. 28.

30. Taubman, 198–8, 219–20; Brown, *Seven Years*, 50, 64.

31. Brown, *Gorbachev Factor*, 71; Miller, 54.

32. Brown, *Gorbachev Factor*, 131.

33. Brown, *Seven Years*, 13.

34. Gorbachev, 241–2.

35. Gorbachev, 248. Miller, 64–5, suggests that 1986 was the key year for Gorbachev's shift from reformer to radical challenger of the system. The change appears, however, to have been more gradual and cumulative than sudden.

36. Service, 486.

37. Brown, *Gorbachev Factor*, 155.

38. Taubman, 309; Brown, *Gorbachev Factor*, 166.

39. Service, 452; Brown, *Gorbachev Factor*, 147.

40. Brown, *Gorbachev Factor*, 145; Service, 460.

41. Brown, *Myth*, 166.

42. Brown, *Gorbachev Factor*, 178.

43. Service, 461.

44. Brown, *Seven Years*, 110–11.

45. Taubman, 371–2.

46. Taubman, 365–71.

47. Brown, *Gorbachev Factor*, 227.

48. Brown, *Gorbachev Factor*, 216.

49. Taubman, 300.

50. Taubman, 416.

51. Gorbachev, 592–7 (quotations, 596).

52. Taubman, 498.

53. Richard J. Crampton, *Eastern Europe in the Twentieth Century – and After*, London, 1997, 407.

54. Taubman, 480–81.

55. Gorbachev, 626; Ivan T. Berend, *Central and Eastern Europe 1944–1993*, Cambridge, 1996, 280.

56. Gorbachev, 625.

57. Brown, *Seven Years*, 263.

58. Zubok, 85–7.

59. Brown, *Gorbachev Factor*, 247–51; Zubok, 85–93.

60. Brown, *Gorbachev Factor*, 244.

61. Taubman, 493.

62. Taubman, 488.

63. Taubman, 552–3.

64. Taubman, 564.

65. Brown, *Gorbachev Factor*, 246–7.

66. Taubman, 569 and 767 n. 101.

67. Brown, *Gorbachev Factor*, 198–204, 289.

68. Taubman, 586.

69. Service, 522–5.

70. Taubman, 677, 685.

71. *The Sunday Times*, 23 May 2016, 13; *Guardian*, 21, 22, 24 March 2017; Taubman, 676–81, 684–6.

CHAPTER 12: HELMUT KOHL

1. Wikipedia entry for Helmut Kohl, https://en.wikipedia.org/wiki/Helmut_Kohl, accessed November 2021.

2. Helmut Kohl, *Erinnerungen 1982–1990*, Munich, 2005 (= Kohl 2), 270–73.

3. Gernot Sittner (ed.), *Helmut Kohl und der Mantel der Geschichte*, Munich, 2016, 26.

4. Helmut Kohl, *Erinnerungen 1930–1982*, Munich, 2004 (= Kohl 1), part 1 (15–108); Hans-Peter Schwarz, *Helmut Kohl. Eine politische Biographie*, Munich, 2014, part 1 (15–133).

5. Patrick Bahners, *Helmut Kohl. Der Charakter der Macht*, Munich, 2017, 21.

6. Kohl 1, 596–7, 60–69, 621.

7. Kohl 1, 629–44, 649.

8. Bahners, 120.

9. Sittner, 94.

10. Kohl 2, 52.

11. Kohl 2, 261–8.

12. Kohl 2, 27–30, 120–24.

13. Schwarz, 309–21, esp. 312–16; Bahners, 112, 122–5, 162, 281; Sittner, 82–95, 196–201.

14. Edgar Wolfrum, *Die Bundesrepublik Deutschland 1949–1990*, Stuttgart, 2005, 450.

15. Schwarz, 326.

16. Schwarz, 383.

17. Wolfrum, 455; Kohl 1, 43–4.

18. Ulrich Herbert, *Geschichte Deutschlands im 20. Jahrhundert*, Munich, 2014, 1018; Schwarz, 377–9; Bahners, 181.

19. Schwarz, 383.

20. Schwarz, 444–51, for the detail.

21. Schwarz, 460.

22. Mikhail Gorbachev, *Memoirs*, London, 1997, 565 (also 669–71).

23. Schwarz, 398.

24. Schwarz, 491.

25. Kohl 2, 965.

26. Kohl 2, 970–71.

27. Peter Merseburger, *Willy Brandt 1913–1992*, Munich, 2002, 837; Wolfrum, 537–8.

28. Kohl 2, 990–95.

29. Schwarz, 531–3.

30. Herbert, 1108; Kohl 2, 996.

31. Schwarz, 534–5.

32. Kohl 2, 1025.

33. Kohl 2, 1020; Bahners, 138.

34. Gorbachev, 682.

35. Wolfrum, 542.

36. Helmut Kohl, *Vom Mauerfall zur Wiedervereinigung. Meine Erinnerungen*, Munich, 2009, 218; Schwarz, 570–72; Herbert, 1123.

37. Herbert, 1125–6.

38. Heinrich August Winkler, *Geschichte des Westens. Vom Kalten Krieg zum Mauerfall*, Munich, 2014, 1064; Wolfrum, 544.

39. Kohl, *Vom Mauerfall*, 194–6.

40. Schwarz, 585–7.

41. Kohl, *Vom Mauerfall*, 271–2.

42. Schwarz, 692, 712–13.

43. Heinrich August Winkler, *Geschichte des Westens. Die Zeit der Gegenwart*, Munich, 2015, 19.
44. Schwarz, 691–3.
45. Kenneth Dyson and Kevin Featherstone, *The Road to Maastricht: Negotiating Economic and Monetary Union*, Oxford, 1999, 32.
46. The later judgement of the Federal Constitutional Court in connection with the Lisbon Treaty of 2007 pointed to the limits, under the Basic Law (constitution), of the delegation of sovereignty, effectively ruling out the possibility that the EU could become a state itself. Dieter Grimm, *Europa ja – aber welches? Zur Verfassung der europäischen Demokratie*, Munich, 2016, 233.
47. Bahners, 293.
48. Schwarz, 736.
49. Sittner, 114–15.
50. Timothy Garton Ash, *History of the Present. Essays, Sketches and Despatches from Europe in the 1990s*, London, 1999, 147.
51. Schwarz, 847. Also, for Kohl's campaign style, Sittner, 134–43.
52. Schwarz, 848.
53. Schwarz, 796 (also 831–2).
54. Sittner, 294.
55. Schwarz, 870–96, outlines the extent of the 'affair'. See also Bahners, 191–5, 224–5, 240–41, 246–9, and https://www.dw.com/en/the-scandal-that-rocked-the-government-of-helmut-kohl/a-5137950, accessed November 2021.
56. Sittner, 389.
57. Bahners, 253–7.
58. Bahners, 267–70, 275, 303; Sittner, 394–403, esp. 399–400.

Acknowledgements

The restrictions arising from the coronavirus pandemic made me especially grateful to Laurence Rees for encouragement, intellectual stimulus and invaluable comments on the draft chapters as they were written, and for his lasting friendship. I also owe a big debt of gratitude to Nick Stargardt and Christian Göschel, who subsequently read and helped to improve the completed typescript. My thanks for responding with expert advice to specific queries go additionally to Robert Service, Stephen Smith, Geoffrey Hosking, Paul Preston, Mary Vincent and Matthew Kerry. Simon Winder was, as always, an exemplary editor. The splendid Penguin team, notably Eva Hodgkin and Rebecca Lee, were most helpful, efficient and supportive. Scott Moyers at Penguin in New York offered not just encouragement but made a number of important suggestions. David Watson was a meticulous, sensitive and engaged copy-editor. Mark Wells compiled an excellent index. James Pullen at the Wylie Agency in London was as ever superb throughout. I offer my warmest thanks to all.

An inevitable side-effect of advancing age is losing close relatives and dear friends. Our daughter-in-law Becky's death, at the age of only 42, has caused our family immense sadness. Among our many German friends, Traude and Ulrich Spät always had a special place. So I was deeply saddened that Traude did not live to see the completion of a book in which she showed great interest from its beginnings.

My family have always been the foundation upon which everything rests. So as in previous books my immeasurable love and gratitude go to Betty, our sons David and Stephen, and our grandchildren Sophie, Joe, Ella, Olivia and Henry.

List of illustrations

p. x–xi. Lenin addresses a huge crowd in Petrograd. *Fine Art Images/ Heritage Images.*

p. xvi–xvii. Helmut Kohl, during his visit to Dresden on 19 December 1989. *Ulrich Baumgarten.*

pp.16–17. Lenin presides over a meeting of Sovnarkom (Council of People's Commissars) on 3 October 1922. *Hulton Deutsch / Corbis Historical.*

pp.48–9. Mussolini is greeted by admirers in October 1942. *Ullstein bild Dtl.*

pp.80–81. Hitler on his 55ᵗʰ birthday, 20 April 1944. *Ullstein bild Dtl.*

pp.112–13. Stalin leads the funeral procession of Mikhail Kalinin, the former Chairman of the Presidium of the Supreme Soviet in Moscow's Red Square on 5 June 1946. *Serge Plantureux / Corbis Historical.*

pp.142–3. Churchill on the deck of the battleship HMS "Prince of Wales" during the Atlantic Conference in August 1941. *Photo 12 / Universal Images Group.*

pp.172–3. De Gaulle in the midst of a large crowd during his first visit to Algiers in June 1958. *Daniele Darolle / Sygma.*

pp.202–3. Konrad Adenauer (right) is accompanied by the Mayor of West Berlin (and later Federal Chancellor) Willy Brandt and the American President, John F. Kennedy, 26 June 1963. *Bettmann.*

pp. 232–3. Franco is acclaimed as Generalísimo and Head of State on 1 October 1936 in Burgos. *Hulton Deutsch / Corbis Historical.*

pp.262–3. Tito and Soviet leader Nikita Khrushchev relax while cruising on the Adriatic during Khrushchev's 1963 visit to Yugoslavia. *Keystone / Hulton Archive.*

pp.294–5. Margaret Thatcher, with (from left to right) Nigel Lawson, Norman Tebbit and Paul Channon, on the eve of the 1987 General Election. *Keystone / Hulton Archive.*

pp.328–9. Mikhail Gorbachev meets Moscow citizens on 17 April 1985. *AFP via Getty Images.*

pp.360–61. Helmut Kohl waves to the crowd in Bonn on 23 June 1975. *Thomas Imo/Photothek via Getty Images.*

Index

Abyssinia (Ethiopia), 66–7, 69, 70, 76, 99–100, 406

Adenauer, Konrad: approach/attitude to the Nazi era, 224, 225–7, 229–30, 231; authoritarian tendencies, 208–9, 215–16, 229, 230, 231, 397, 399–400, 403, 412; authority ebbs away (early-1960s), 220, 227–8; background of, 205–8, 209; and Berlin crisis (1958–61), 223–4; binds FRG to the West, 205, 209–11, 213–22, 223, 224, 228–9, 231; clear/easily definable goals of, 209, 400; closeness to former Nazis, 226–7, 229–30, 231; constitutional constraints on, 208–9, 221–2, 399–400, 405, 412; domestic agenda, 210–11, 222–3, 229; economic policy, 211, 212, 222–3, 229; and electoral success, 212, 223, 225, 227, 410; emergence in post-war West Germany, 208–9, 211–12; falling popularity in early-1960s, 227; family of, 206, 207; as Federal Chancellor, 205, 212, 213–21, 222–8, 229–31;

Friendship Treaty with France (1963), 197, 200, 220, 229; 'General (German) Treaty, 213–14, 215–16; and 'Hallstein Doctrine,' 230–1; historical impact/legacy of, 205, 213, 216, 228–31; life during Nazi era, 207; name on Allied 'White List,' 208; as outstanding statesman, 14, 205, 209, 213, 216, 228, 231, 399–400; personality of, 206, 208–9, 229; political career in Cologne, 205, 206–7, 208–9, 399; political views, 206, 208–10, 212, 224; preconditions of power, 211–16; and reckoning over Nazism, 211, 230; and reconciliation with France, 197, 200, 210, 213, 214, 216–20, 222, 229; resignation (1963), 221–2, 227–8; and 'Spiegel Affair,' 227; and 'Stalin Notes' (1952), 213–15; tactical acumen, 209, 216, 231; and United States, 208, 209–10, 215, 219, 222, 228 *see also* subentries under historical change, leadership, power

457